THE LORD FOR THE BODY

McGILL-QUEEN'S STUDIES IN THE HISTORY OF RELIGION

Volumes in this series have been supported by the Jackman Foundation of Toronto.

SERIES TWO / In memory of George Rawlyk
Donald Harman Akenson, Editor

1 Marguerite Bourgeoys
and Montreal, 1640–1665
Patricia Simpson

2 Aspects of the Canadian
Evangelical Experience
Edited by G.A. Rawlyk

3 Infinity, Faith, and Time
Christian Humanism and
Renaissance Literature
John Spencer Hill

4 The Contribution of
Presbyterianism to the Maritime
Provinces of Canada
Edited by Charles H.H. Scobie
and G.A. Rawlyk

5 Labour, Love, and Prayer
Female Piety in Ulster Religious
Literature, 1850–1914
Andrea Ebel Brozyna

6 The Waning of the Green
Catholics, the Irish, and Identity
in Toronto, 1887–1922
Mark G. McGowan

7 Religion and Nationality
in Western Ukraine
The Greek Catholic Church
and the Ruthenian National
Movement in Galicia,
1867–1900
John-Paul Himka

8 Good Citizens
British Missionaries and Imperial
States, 1870–1918
James G. Greenlee and
Charles M. Johnston

9 The Theology of the Oral Torah
Revealing the Justice of God
Jacob Neusner

10 Gentle Eminence
A Life of Cardinal Flahiff
P. Wallace Platt

11 Culture, Religion,
and Demographic Behaviour
Catholics and Lutherans
in Alsace, 1750–1870
Kevin McQuillan

12 Between Damnation and Starvation
Priests and Merchants in
Newfoundland Politics, 1745–1855
John P. Greene

13 Martin Luther, German Saviour
German Evangelical Theological
Factions and the Interpretation
of Luther, 1917–1933
James M. Stayer

14 Modernity and the Dilemma of
North American Anglican Identities,
1880–1950
William H. Katerberg

15 The Methodist Church on the
Prairies, 1896–1914
George Emery

16 Christian Attitudes Towards
the State of Israel
Paul Charles Merkley

17 A Social History of the Cloister
Daily Life in the Teaching
Monasteries of the Old Regime
Elizabeth Rapley

18 Households of Faith
Family, Gender, and Community
in Canada, 1760–1969
Edited by Nancy Christie

19 Blood Ground
Colonialism, Missions, and
the Contest for Christianity in
the Cape Colony and Britain,
1799–1853
Elizabeth Elbourne

20 A History of Canadian Catholics
Gallicanism, Romanism,
and Canadianism
Terence J. Fay

21 The View from Rome
Archbishop Stagni's 1915
Reports on the Ontario
Bilingual Schools Question
Edited and translated by John Zucchi

22 The Founding Moment
Church, Society, and the
Construction of Trinity College
William Westfall

23 The Holocaust, Israel, and
Canadian Protestant Churches
Haim Genizi

24 Governing Charities
Church and State in Toronto's
Catholic Archdiocese, 1850–1950
Paula Maurutto

25 Anglicans and the Atlantic World
High Churchmen, Evangelicals,
and the Quebec Connection
Richard W. Vaudry

26 Evangelicals and
the Continental Divide
The Conservative Protestant
Subculture in Canada and
the United States
Sam Reimer

27 Christians in a Secular World
The Canadian Experience
Kurt Bowen

28 Anatomy of a Seance
A History of Spirit Communication
in Central Canada
Stan McMullin

29 With Skilful Hand
The Story of King David
David T. Barnard

30 Faithful Intellect
Samuel S. Nelles
and Victoria University
Neil Semple

31 W. Stanford Reid
An Evangelical Calvinist
in the Academy
A. Donald MacLeod

32 A Long Eclipse
The Liberal Protestant
Establishment and
the Canadian University,
1920–1970
Catherine Gidney

33 Forkhill Protestants and Forkhill
Catholics, 1787–1858
Kyla Madden

34 For Canada's Sake
Public Religion, Centennial
Celebrations, and the Re-making
of Canada in the 1960s
Gary R. Miedema

35 Revival in the City
The Impact of American Evangelists
in Canada, 1884–1914
Eric R. Crouse

36 The Lord for the Body
Religion, Medicine, and Protestant
Faith Healing in Canada,
1880–1930
James Opp

SERIES ONE
G.A. Rawlyk, Editor

1 Small Differences
Irish Catholics and Irish
Protestants, 1815–1922
An International Perspective
Donald Harman Akenson

2 Two Worlds
The Protestant Culture
of Nineteenth-Century Ontario
William Westfall

3 An Evangelical Mind
Nathanael Burwash and the
Methodist Tradition in Canada,
1839–1918
Marguerite Van Die

4 The Dévotes
Women and Church in
Seventeenth-Century France
Elizabeth Rapley

5 The Evangelical Century
   College and Creed in English
   Canada from the Great Revival
   to the Great Depression
   Michael Gauvreau

6 The German Peasants' War and
   Anabaptist Community of Goods
   James M. Stayer

7 A World Mission
   Canadian Protestantism and
   the Quest for a New International
   Order, 1918–1939
   Robert Wright

8 Serving the Present Age
   Revivalism, Progressivism, and
   the Methodist Tradition in Canada
   Phyllis D. Airhart

9 A Sensitive Independence
   Canadian Methodist Women
   Missionaries in Canada and
   the Orient, 1881–1925
   Rosemary R. Gagan

10 God's Peoples
   Covenant and Land in South Africa,
   Israel, and Ulster
   Donald Harman Akenson

11 Creed and Culture
   The Place of English-Speaking
   Catholics in Canadian Society,
   1750–1930
   Terrence Murphy
   and Gerald Stortz, editors

12 Piety and Nationalism
   Lay Voluntary Associations
   and the Creation of an Irish-
   Catholic Community in Toronto,
   1850–1895
   Brian P. Clarke

13 Amazing Grace
   Studies in Evangelicalism in Australia,
   Britain, Canada, and the United States
   George Rawlyk and Mark A. Noll,
   editors

14 Children of Peace
   W. John McIntyre

15 A Solitary Pillar
   Montreal's Anglican Church
   and the Quiet Revolution
   Joan Marshall

16 Padres in No Man's Land
   Canadian Chaplains
   and the Great War
   Duff Crerar

17 Christian Ethics and Political
   Economy in North America
   A Critical Analysis of U.S.
   and Canadian Approaches
   P. Travis Kroeker

18 Pilgrims in Lotus Land
   Conservative Protestantism in
   British Columbia, 1917–1981
   Robert K. Burkinshaw

19 Through Sunshine and Shadow
   The Woman's Christian Temperance
   Union, Evangelicalism, and Reform
   in Ontario, 1874–1930
   Sharon Cook

20 Church, College, and Clergy
   A History of Theological Education
   at Knox College, Toronto,
   1844–1994
   Brian J. Fraser

21 The Lord's Dominion
   The History of Canadian
   Methodism
   Neil Semple

22 A Full-Orbed Christianity
   The Protestant Churches
   and Social Welfare in Canada,
   1900–1940
   Nancy Christie and
   Michael Gauvreau

23 Evangelism and Apostasy
   The Evolution and Impact of
   Evangelicals in Modern Mexico
   Kurt Bowen

24 The Chignecto Covenanters
   A Regional History of Reformed
   Presbyterianism in New Brunswick
   and Nova Scotia, 1827–1905
   Eldon Hay

25 Methodists and Women's Education
   in Ontario, 1836–1925
   Johanne Selles

26 Puritanism and Historical
   Controversy
   William Lamont

The Lord for the Body

Religion, Medicine, and Protestant Faith Healing in Canada, 1880–1930

JAMES OPP

McGill–Queen's University Press
Montreal & Kingston · London · Ithaca

© McGill-Queen's University Press 2005
ISBN 0-7735-2905-5

Legal deposit third quarter 2005
Bibliothèque nationale du Québec

Printed in Canada on acid-free paper that is 100% ancient forest free
(100% post-consumer recycled), processed chlorine free.

This book was declared the Frank S. and Elizabeth D. Brewer Prize Essay of the
American Society of Church History, 2004.

This book has been published with the help of a grant from the
Canadian Federation for the Humanities and Social Sciences, through
the Aid to Scholarly Publications Programme, using funds provided
by the Social Sciences and Humanities Research Council of Canada.

McGill-Queen's University Press acknowledges the support of the Canada
Council for the Arts for our publishing program. We also acknowledge the
financial support of the Government of Canada through the Book Publishing
Industry Development Program (BPIDP) for our publishing activities.

Library and Archives Canada Cataloguing in Publication

Opp, James William, 1970–
    The Lord for the body: religion, medicine and Protestant faith
healing in Canada, 1880-1930/James Opp.

(McGill-Queen's studies in the history of religion; 37)
Includes bibliographical references and index.
ISBN 0-7735-2905-5

    1. Spiritual healing – Canada–History.   2. Protestantism – Canada –
19th century.   3. Protestantism – Canada – 20th century.   I. Title.   II. Series.
BL65.M4066 2005   234'.131'0882804   C2005–903757-1

The epigraph for chapter 4 is from *A Jest of God* by Margaret Laurence.
Used by permission, McLelland & Stewart Ltd.

The index for this book was made with support from the Faculty of Arts and Social
Sciences, Carleton University.

This book was typeset by Interscript in 10/12 Sabon.

Contents

List of Illustrations   viii

Preface   ix

Introduction   3

1 Bodily Knowledge   14

2 The Prayer of Faith   35

3 A Respectable Movement   64

4 Marching to Zion   91

5 Pentecostal Power   121

6 Revivals and Reactions   146

7 Exposing the Body   176

Conclusion   203

Notes   213

Bibliography   245

Index   267

Illustrations

2.1   In the grip of the drug monster   57

4.1   Zion smites sin   95

4.2   Zion's protest against the tyranny of unclean swine's flesh   98

6.1   Charles S. Price campaign, Edmonton, 1923   163

6.2   Charles S. Price campaign, Toronto, 1923   164

7.1   Case L, Price investigative report   188

7.2   Case Q, Price investigative report   188

7.3   Case O, Price investigative report   190

7.4   Case H, Price investigative report   191

7.5   Johnny Patterson, 1929   192

7.6   Sunshine, 1926   194

Preface

Explaining exactly what an historian "does" for a living can be an awkward exercise, especially when one's research interests include a subject such as faith healing. Inquirers who press me to expand on my topic often express puzzlement or bemusement that faith healing might be a subject worthy of a book-length study. Others are eager to embrace the project as their own and quickly recount personal stories of friends and relatives who found relief through various forms of pilgrimage, New Age healing, or simply extraordinary strength of will. As I quickly learned in these conversations, there is no shortage of opinion on the meaning and value of faith healing. Those expecting to find either a skeptical exposé of fakery or unshakeable evidence of divine truths will be disappointed. However, most readers will find that an historical approach to faith healing illuminates some of the complex themes evident in the overlapping spheres of religion, medicine, and the body.

This book began as little more than a vague idea that faith healing might serve as an interesting topic for a doctoral dissertation. Carleton University provided both financial support and institutional encouragement as I embarked on a long research journey as a graduate student. Revisions for publication were undertaken while I was associated with the Carleton Centre for Public History. It was there that I received invaluable encouragement, critiques, and advice from many people, including Bruce Curtis, Pamela Walker, Barry Wright, John Walsh, Joanna Dean, Norman Hillmer, Marilyn Barber and Del Muise. I am particularly grateful to A.B. McKillop and David Dean, two historians and colleagues who both immeasurably shaped my outlook as a scholar and a teacher. My research interests have brought me into contact with a remarkable community of scholars who are interested in aspects of religious history and the history of the body. I am indebted to David Marshall, Lynne Marks, Marguerite Van Die, Wendy Mitchinson,

Amanda Porterfield, Margaret Bendroth, Virginia Brereton, and Lori Beaman for taking time to discuss various aspects of this project. Cecil Robeck graciously shared material on Amelia and Lillian Yeomans. No colleague knows this work better than Janet Friskney, who helped me track down material in archives and persisted in sharpening my prose.

A wide variety of archivists and librarians provided unfettered access to the dispersed resources used to produce this book. Special mention goes to Callista Kelly at Carleton University Library, Inter-Library Loans and Bob Stewart at the British Columbia Conference Archives for the United Church of Canada. Glenn Gohr at the Flower Pentecostal Heritage Center, Springfield, Missouri, offered a warm welcome to a Canadian visitor and helped me locate numerous items long after my brief visit to the archive ended. I am also grateful to Lindsay Reynolds, a remarkable church historian who opened his home and his extensive historical research to me. The Archives of Ontario and the Archives of British Columbia both provided invaluable assistance in tracking down court records and trial transcripts.

My family has encouraged my academic pursuits from the beginning. My parents and my brother, Rob, deserve credit for their unflagging support over my long, and seemingly unending, life as a student. Those years were made joyous by the companionship of Pamela Williamson, who endured far too many sleepless nights and absent days. Words cannot express the debt I owe her for her tremendous patience and heart. It is fitting that this project came to a conclusion within months of the arrival of our son, Nevan. The wonderful experience of his birth and our own negotiation of medical structures and culture resonated strongly as I reviewed the final version of this manuscript.

Although the framework is very different, a portion of chapter 2 was originally published as "The Word and the Flesh: Religion, Medicine, and Protestant Faith Healing Narratives in North America, 1880–1910," *Social History / histoire sociale* 36 (May 2003): 205–224. Short sections spread across a number of chapters in the book were part of my initial musings on the history of faith healing, published as "Healing Hands, Healthy Bodies: Protestant Women and Faith Healing in Canada and the United States, 1880–1930" in *Women and Twentieth-Century Protestantism*, edited by Margaret Bendroth and Virginia Brereton (Urbana: University of Illinois Press, 2002).

Financial support for researching this work was received from the Social Sciences and Humanities Research Council, the Ontario Graduate Scholarship program, and the Faculty of Graduate Studies at Carleton University.

THE LORD FOR THE BODY

Introduction

The body's mischiefs, as Plato proves, proceed from the soul:
and if the mind be not first satisfied, the body can never be cured.
Robert Burton, *The Anatomy of Melancholy* (1621)

The epigraph above accompanies the title page to Robertson Davies' final novel, *The Cunning Man* (1994). In the opening pages of the book, the sudden death of Father Hobbes in front of the altar sets the scene for a symbolic exchange between the protagonist physician, Dr Jonathan Hullah, and his former friend Rev. Charlie Iredale, a high Anglican priest. When Hullah rushes to attend Father Hobbes, he is waved off by Iredale. The doctor muses, "We were members of two rival priesthoods, he the Man of God and I the Man of Science ... We were in a church, Holy Communion had begun, and the dying man was behind the altar rails, so I suppose I thought Charlie was on his own turf and must be respected accordingly." However, as *The Cunning Man* proceeds to demonstrate, the spheres of medicine and religion are not easily contained by such visible markers as an altar rail. There is a constant slippage in the borders that surround the body, soul, and mind, which overlay and subvert the binary nature of "rival priesthoods." Hullah concludes that "If I am lucky, I am able to say with Ambrose Paré, 'I dressed his wounds and God cured him.' Body and soul cannot be separated while life lasts."[1]

Faith healing is a practice where these two priesthoods converge, a space that is both corporeal and divine. The ambiguous position of faith healing as part of both worlds has traditionally kept it safely on the periphery of most historical narratives of medicine and religion. However, it is precisely because of its marginal position, bordering two key areas of social change in Canada, that faith healing offers such fertile ground for study. When viewed as a cultural practice, divine healing emerges as both a valid subject of historical inquiry and a window into the interaction between medicine and religion.

As an examination of Protestant faith healing in English-speaking Canada from 1880 to 1930, this book presents a unique perspective on the multiple ways in which medical and religious discourses competed in their constructions of the body. It explores the cultural practice of faith healing as both a devotional observance and a point of resistance to conventional medicine. In this work, faith healing is set within a matrix of religious and medical ideologies that were in turn enwrapped by constructions of gender, class, and social geography. While only a minority of Canadians were confident enough in their faith to actually take "the Lord for the Body," the act of participating in and testifying to faith healing spoke to a wide range of issues in the late-nineteenth and early-twentieth centuries as Canadians struggled to define the proper roles of religion and medicine in modern society.

FAITH HEALING AND HISTORY

While historians have occasionally offered accounts of various faith healers or faith healing movements, very few have attempted to present a "history" of faith healing itself. From the very emergence of faith healing within Victorian Protestantism, both proponents and critics framed the phenomena as a universal experience that ultimately transcended history. A.B. Simpson's *The Discovery of Divine Healing* (1903) traced the origins of praying for healing to Moses, to whom the promise of health was revealed even before the Ten Commandments had been given. Church fathers and historic Protestant figures, from Tertullian to Wesley, were routinely drawn into a continuous line of advocacy for divine healing.[2] Because divine healing was regarded as a "lost truth" that needed to be restored to the Church, any type of historical belief or expression of interest in God's curative agency was seized upon as evidence that healing was a constant, enduring element of true Christian practice and doctrine.

While many disagreed with the way Simpson and others drew upon past figures to support this position, the historical narratives of critics were constructed with a similar didactic intent. George Barton Cutten, president of Acadia University in Wolfville, Nova Scotia, was dismayed by the notion that people were being "led astray," ignorant of "the mental healing movements and vagaries of the past." To remedy the situation, he published *Three Thousand Years of Mental Healing* (1911) to demonstrate that there was "no originality" to the wave of healing movements that had recently emerged. Whereas advocates of faith healing stressed the continuity of a God who could heal as easily today as in apostolic times, Cutten's historical landscape deliberately predated the Christian era in order to present Christianity as just one of many different religions and superstitions that offered a theology of healing. "[M]ental cures are independent of any particular sect, religion, or philosophy," Cutten concluded. It was not "the creed," but rather "some force which resides in the mind of every one [that] accomplishes the cure, and the most that any religion or philosophy can do is to bring this force into action."[3]

Although the narrative structures of these histories collide in the struggle to present or deny the case for faith healing, they actually share common assumptions regarding their subject. Both proponents and critics thought that they knew what faith healing was and what it represented. Their histories were vehicles for presenting and demonstrating the operation of a phenomenon that transcended history. They started from different premises, but it was the continuity, the ahistoricity, of the experience compared across time that "proved" that faith healing was truly divine or simply a mental function. Thus, history acts as a distiller, extracting the true essence of the experience by offering the reader a perception of timeless continuity in the face of multiple contexts.

The idea that faith healing represents a phenomenon beyond history is an essentialism that continues to run deeply within historical treatments of the subject. Morton T. Kelsey's *Healing and Christianity* (1973) is unabashedly presentist and directed towards advancing the case for a spiritual healing based on Jungian psychology. Ronald Kydd's *Healing through the Centuries* (1998) develops a series of theological "models of understanding" by comparing different faith healing activities in the past. It is the continuity of different faith healers within the structure of these theological models that is important, connecting the nineteenth-century German J.C. Blumhardt to John Wimber and the late-twentieth-century Vineyard Ministries. Kydd is certainly more nuanced than most in his understanding of the historical differences between those he has grouped together, but the structure of his narrative reveals the underlying search for continuity.[4]

The desire to maintain an essentialist understanding of faith healing can also be seen in historians writing from an avowed secular perspective. Keith Thomas, in his classic work *Religion and the Decline of Magic* (1971), spends an entire chapter on magical healing during the sixteenth and seventeenth centuries. Uneasy with the "speculative psychology" that the historian is led to when examining "magical healers of an earlier age," Thomas nevertheless has no problem in relying upon the British Medical Association's 1956 declaration that the "real" explanation for divine healing could be found in one of six possible conditions: "(1) mistaken diagnosis; (2) mistaken prognosis; (3) alleviation of the illness; (4) remission; (5) spontaneous cure; (6) simultaneous use of other remedies." Although the social function of the healers is transformed over time, the actual experience of healing transcends history. As Thomas summarized,

"Magic cannot counter infection and is no substitute for hygiene, or X-rays and other modern aids to diagnosis. But it may have provided as effective a therapy for the diseases of the mind as anything available today."[5] While Thomas's work is framed within an anthropological functionalism, his understanding of faith healing is ultimately not very far removed from Cutten. Other historians have followed a similar line, assuming that where faith healing has been beneficial, it could only be so in cases where a mental therapeutics was required.[6]

How is it therefore possible to recover a history of faith healing without having some underlying understanding of what it "is," or what has "really" happened? Ultimately, the restoration of health is a bodily process, and as such, the first step in recovering a history of faith healing is to recognize that it is actually a history of the body that is being pursued. It is not enough to simply remain agnostic on the issue of whether any of the cures claimed under the rubric of faith healing are "real"; the biological reference points of the body itself need to be probed and exposed. Testimonials to healing through faith laid claim to more than the power of God – they were, at their core, epistemological statements anchored in a particular construction of the body.

The conceptualization of a history of the body is inextricably linked with the emergence of poststructural critiques of modernism, which attacked essentialist understandings of the body. Instead of assuming that scientific bodily categories are natural, the history of the body examines how various discourses imprinted themselves on the body in such a way as to be considered essential to its being. Michel Feher described this important conceptual shift by noting that the history of the body was much more than simply a question of representation, since "the history of [the body's] representations always refers to a real body considered to be 'without history' ... whereas the history of its modes of construction can, since it avoids the overly massive oppositions of science and ideology or of authenticity and alienation, turn the body into a thoroughly historicized and completely problematic issue."[7] This interest in the body's "modes of construction" owes a great deal to the work of Michel Foucault, who outlined the emergence of a medical "gaze" over the body in *Birth of a Clinic* (1973), examined the exercise of observational power upon the body in *Discipline and Punish* (1977), and then traced the construction of sexuality as an expression of the self in three volumes of *The History of Sexuality* (1978, 1985, 1986).[8] For Foucault, the body "is the inscribed surface of events (traced by language and dissolved by ideas), the locus of a dissociated Self (adopting the illusion of substantial unity), and a volume in disintegration."[9]

The attempt to liberate the body from the blinds of naturalized discourses has led to charges that Foucault and other "nihilists" have actually destroyed the body.[10] However, few would deny that by disengaging the body from its material ground, new questions have certainly been raised about whether a "thoroughly historicized" body can exist outside of its own historical constructions. Even while warning of the dangers of "floating off into the stratosphere of discourse analysis," medical historian Roy Porter admitted that "the 'body' cannot be treated by the historian as a biological given, but must be regarded as mediated through cultural sign systems."[11]

The adoption of a history of the body as an approach for the study of faith healing is therefore an explicit rejection of the essentialist categorization that has afflicted much of the scholarship on this subject. To use the scientific categories of modern medicine to "explain" faith healing as some form of mental function or psychosomaticization simply perpetuates the naturalization of medical discourse. It is only by exposing the medical gaze as a particular way of viewing the body that the competing bodily constructions of faith healing can be understood. To give faith healing a meaningful history requires an approach that allows the body itself to be historicized.

BODY AND EXPERIENCE

While the Foucauldian approach to the body has offered insights into the construction and regulation of the body, it has also received a great deal of criticism from those scholars who examine the body as a point of resistance to these processes. Foucault's conceptualization of a microphysics of power, as expressed through medicine and other sites of knowledge, produces a passive and docile body that implicitly accepts the naturalized order that has defined it.[12] Even medical historians who do not agree with Foucault's epistemology often adopt his determinism in the ultimate encroachment of professional medicine and its role in defining health and illness. And yet the very presence of groups devoted to the practice of faith healing suggests that these processes were not as complete or absolute as have been assumed. Divine healing implicitly and explicitly challenges the assumptions of the medicalized body, but the nature of this resistance has not been fully explored.

Approaching the history of faith healing as a history of the body is comparable in many ways to other bodily conditions that have been historicized, such as sickness, disease, pain, suffering, and health. Here, too, historians are faced with the ontological problem of relating these conditions to the historicized body in a meaningful way. One counterpoint to this loss of materiality has been the reassertion of a phenomenology of the self, a new focus upon subjective perception rather than an outside analysis of what is being perceived. Medical anthropologists

such as Arthur Kleinman and Byron Good have used phenomenology
as a means to position the body as an *a priori* material grounding
through which all experience is mediated. No matter how much the
body has been constructed, imprinted, or inscribed, the subjective self
has experienced a material physicality through the body before it encounters these surrounding discourses. Kleinman asserts that "*Experience* may, on theoretical grounds, be thought of as the intersubjective
medium of social transactions in local moral worlds. It is the outcome
of cultural categories and social structures interacting with the psycho-
physiological processes such that a mediating world is constituted." It
is an approach expressly designed to resist the "tendency toward dehu-
manizing professional deconstruction," while at the same time maintaining the socially constructed categories that surround the body.[13] As
an historical phenomenon, the cultural practice of divine healing also
needs to be understood as a subjective experience of the body.

The assertion that human experience is mediated prereflexively
through the material body sidesteps the ontological problem of histori-
cising the "real" body, but the moral and ethical issues surrounding the
history of faith healing remain. For those who pursued it, the bodily
process of healing proceeded from faith and an encounter with the divine. It is their narratives and testimonials that constitute the majority
of the material that the historian analyzes. Most participants perceive
their actions in religious terms, as a personal communion with God. If
divine healing is, as has been alluded to, a point of resistance to the
medicalized body, how can these texts be read to illuminate this process
without denying the primary subjectivity of the experience? Byron
Good has framed this same dilemma in relation to illness in asking,
"How can we recognize forms of self-deception and distortion, without devaluing local claims to knowledge? How can we write about illness in a manner that heightens our understanding of the realities of
lived experience and still speaks to the larger social and historical processes of which the actors are only dimly aware?"[14]

Rather than setting the personal religious experience of faith healing
against the larger historical and social processes, this study suggests
that it is only *through* the space of personal religious experience that
the points of resistance evident within the practice of divine healing
could emerge. As Robert Orsi notes, "Religious imaginings have generated compelling alternative visions to the authorized order ... religious
objects have an energy that subverts the powers possessed by the objec-
tifications of the social order."[15] This subversive energy can be observed in many places, including women's testimonials to faith healing,
where torturous experiences at the hands of doctors and narrations of
bodily strength undermined the medical constructions of, and control

over, women's bodies. It was the religious and gendered nature of this particular space that allowed such a public expression in opposition to medical authority. Drawing out points of resistance within these texts does not necessarily devalue the primary devotional grounding of the narrative, but to designate them as solely religious in nature risks denying their political import.

The potential for religion to counter aspects of medicalization exists on many different levels besides that of its social space. The entire epistemological structure of faith healing superseded the naturalized categories of medicine. By framing sickness, disease, and healing as cosmologically integrated with the categories of sin and grace, proponents of divine healing could reject the scientifically objective classifications of medical knowledge. Different faith healers at different times certainly adopted and appropriated various elements of the medical paradigm, but all of them (at least, those under consideration here) accepted the premise that the human body was naturally ordered in such a way as to receive the divine for the purpose of healing or restoring the body. To ground the history of divine healing within the body does not sever the subjective experience of faith from its devotional or transcendent intent. Indeed, it is only as a particular cultural practice of faith that the full potential for faith healing to engage and challenge medicine can be grasped.

LOCATING DIVINE HEALING IN CANADA

As a history of Protestant faith healing in Canada, the goal of this book is to analyse the cultural practice of divine healing within the context of a broader debate over the nature and meaning of the body. Simply locating faith healing within the religious landscape of Canadian history is a task difficult enough, given the dispersed and inconsistent nature of the available source material. In outlining the evolution and development of divine healing in Canada between 1880 and 1930, a wide range of reactions to the practice have been highlighted in various spheres. Public riots, newspaper editorials, medical critiques, mainline ministerial denunciations, and court actions all provide layers of context that not only situate the practice of faith healing, but also illuminate the contested sites within the popular culture that defined the proper roles of medicine and religion in relation to the body.

On any given Sunday, today as in the past, it is not unusual for prayers to be offered within Christian churches for the sick. While it could be suggested that this ritual in itself offers a form of faith healing, the starting point for this study is the emergence of a particular type of Protestant divine healing based on a theology of the atonement. This doctrine marked a departure from simply praying to God for relief by positing that Christ's crucifixion not only covered sin, but physical infirmities as well. Anyone with faith could achieve bodily wholeness, just as anyone with faith could be saved. This perspective was a key element in orienting believers towards a particular attitude and conceptualization of the body, and it is this form of faith healing in its various manifestations that is examined over a period of a half century.

Of course, many other types of divine healing took place in Canada at this time. The Catholic devotional revolution of the nineteenth century produced a renewed interest in sites of healing, and hundreds of thousands sought cures at Sainte Anne-de-Beaupré and the Oratoire Saint-Joseph. While Protestants and Catholics found themselves negotiating similar changes in medical culture, their respective forms of faith healing differed in both theology and cultural practice. Catholic faith healing never assumed that human bodies were deserving of perfect health, turning instead to the power of intercession. The material culture surrounding popular devotions and pilgrimages offered a distinctive social space in which healing was pursued. As one historian notes, the two "sacred universes of Protestants and Catholics differed as much as a whitewashed Puritan meeting house differed from the iconostasis of a Greek Orthodox cathedral."[16]

Encompassing all forms of faith healing in a single study would entail sacrificing the depth required to set this phenomenon within a consistent framework of social space and the wider context of competing ideologies of health. In order to broaden the scope of interaction between religion and medicine, this work traces the manifestation and cultural practice of divine healing drawn from atonement theology, focusing particularly on the social constructions of the body. In the late-Victorian and Edwardian periods, it was this position that informed most Protestant understandings of faith healing in Canada, and yet it is arguably the least understood.

Chapter 1 explores the relationship between the body and religion in the nineteenth century by interweaving the Victorian concern over the role of miracles and prayer with various aspects of medical pluralism. These currents were, in turn, drawn upon by the proponents of faith healing in order to integrate the phenomenon within the natural order, rather than offering "miraculous" cures. In this regard, the emergence of the divine healing movement was as much a way of understanding the body as it was an expression of God's power to heal.

In chapter 2, the informal networks that brought the theology and practice of faith healing to Canada are examined, particularly as defined through the spread of healing testimonials. These narratives reveal two important and inter-related aspects of late-Victorian faith

healing, namely the gendered nature of the activity and the private social space in which faith healing took place. Clearly, it was women's
bodies that were being healed, and it was largely women's networks
that carried the practice across the continent.

Chapter 3 follows with an examination of the institutional structures
erected to support faith healing in Canada. The activities of the Christian and Missionary Alliance are highlighted, but the role of the Salvation Army and its ambiguous relationship with divine healing is also
examined. Some of the medical and religious reactions to faith healing
are introduced, but it is argued that the association of a number of
highly respected and public men with divine healing buffered it from
harsh criticism.

The introduction of a more radical form of faith healing is explored
in chapter 4, which traces the influence of John Alexander Dowie, a
prominent Chicago faith healer at the turn of the century. Dowie's followers in Canada courted controversy, and their activities led to a series of legal actions concerning negligence and failing to provide the
necessities of life. The extensive court records from these cases provide
an intriguing perspective on how medical evidence aligned with the
crown in prosecuting faith healing as a threat to the public order.
Changes in the medical understanding of disease and public health
transformed faith healing from a moral and religious issue to a potentially criminal act, and the Dowieites, with their denunciations of medicine and medical practice, became the prime targets of the law.

Chapter 5 explores how the outbreak of pentecostalism at the beginning of the twentieth century reshaped Protestant faith healing. Although a traditional understanding of the theology of healing was
maintained, the experience of faith healing was expressed very differently through its close association with the pentecostal experience of
"speaking in tongues." A rhetoric of divine power and a renewed focus
upon healing as a particular end-time gift restructured divine healing
both for pentecostalism and for those traditional sites of faith healing
that remained outside its boundaries. The growing public nature of divine healing within the pentecostal tradition receives its fullest expression in the large urban evangelistic campaigns of the interwar period,
which are examined in chapter 6. On the platforms of packed arenas,
faith healing became a public spectacle, drawing crowds and criticism
from many quarters. Not everything has changed since the Victorian
period, however, as women still comprised the vast majority of healings. The nature and experience of faith healing, as well as the scientific
reaction to it, have been transformed since the divine healing movement first emerged in the 1880s, but the practice of faith healing remained deeply gendered.

The publicity generated by the urban healing campaigns produced a reaction in the form of local investigating committees, which attempted to place the cures claimed by faith healers within a scientific context. Chapter 7 outlines the composition, procedures, and resulting report of one such committee formed in Vancouver following the 1923 healing campaign of Charles S. Price. The committee exposed a medicalized body that resisted any claims to healing through faith alone, but proponents of divine healing responded with their own narratives of bodily restoration. The Price report illustrates how the extension of the medical gaze clashed with the understanding of the body held by the faith healers. These competing structures of knowledge are further examined through the life and thought of Dr Lilian Yeomans, a physician-turned-faith healer, who offers a unique perspective on how these "rival priesthoods" were negotiated. Faith healing offered more than an alternative representation of the body – it approached the body in a very different way than the prevailing medical discourse.

The terms "faith healing" and "divine healing" are used interchangeably in this work. For a short time the label "faith cure" was popular even among proponents, but despite continued usage in some library catalog subject headings, its employment is inappropriate for modern historians. Critics quickly linked "faith cure" with other forms of Victorian "cures" (the "Water Cure," the "Gold Cure," the "Mind Cure," etc.), and as the general acceptance of such treatments fell into disrepute, the reiteration of the term "faith cure" became a point of derision. The use of the term "divine healing movement" represents a more specific reference to an identifiable coalition of advocates for faith healing that existed from the 1870s to the 1900s. Although all of the groups under consideration engaged in "divine healing," and some may have laid claim to the heritage of this movement, there is no single "divine healing movement" that lasts until 1930. As this book demonstrates, the location of faith healing as a cultural practice itself shifts across different groups over time.

While this exploration primarily addresses Protestant divine healing in Canada, popular religious movements rarely define themselves by political borders. The intellectual debates surrounding faith and healing spanned the Anglo-American world, but the cultural focus and point of exchange for most Canadians was the United States. Evangelists from both countries freely crossed the border, but the nature of this activity was regional rather than transnational. Central and eastern parts of Canada relied heavily upon networks that extended to Buffalo, Boston, and New York. Proponents of faith healing in western Canada cultivated relations with California and Chicago, although certain elements of the latter also stretched into Ontario, as demonstrated in chapter 4. Rather than impose the structure of a strict national narrative, this study offers a more fluid perspective that traces many of these regional interconnections and areas of shared concern.

The historical task of "locating" a phenomenon such as faith healing requires much more than simply mapping its existence or outlining the history of its advocates. One objective of this work is to bridge the overarching intellectual history of faith healing as a theology with the cultural history of faith healing as a lived experience. This dynamic, in turn, is set against the broader social context of gender, class, medicine, and religion in Canadian society. The history of faith healing is particularly valuable as a window into the complex and multifaceted relationship between the "rival priesthoods." As the public debate over the question of divine healing evolved, English-Canadians provided a wide range of popular attitudes and opinions on the proper roles for religion and medicine in relation to questions of health, sickness, the power of the mind, and the position of the body. Therefore, the cultural practice of faith healing also needs to be positioned within the broader interplay of experience and explanation; as we shall see, the rationalizations of these cures proved to be as fluid as the practice itself.

The body remains central to this inquiry because it is the body that forms the intersection for all of these concerns, from the individual point of a subjective personal experience to the question of objective bodily constructions. Even the space surrounding the body transforms over time as the social geography of faith healing shifts from private contemplation in the bedroom to being "slain in the spirit" on the platform of a hockey arena before thousands. Although this work is arranged roughly in chronological order, it is in delineating these thematic layers and their interrelationships that the full meaning of taking the "Lord for the Body" is pursued.

There is an uncomfortable similarity in presenting the argument that faith healing became a public spectacle while at the same time maintaining the position of an historian who exposes an intensely personal religious experience to the public eye of academic analysis. In this narrative form, faith healing becomes a series of performances, a way of understanding religion acting through the body. It is well recognized, however, that in translating the lived experience of the past into historical forms, a great deal has been lost. The aesthetics of history demand a certain amount of spectacle, an exposure of that which is ultimately ineffable. Emphasizing the historical specificity of faith healing over its transcendent elements does not reduce its participants to having a deluded "false consciousness" or cast a cynical eye upon the depths of subjective experience of religion. "Body and soul cannot be separated while life lasts," and if this study has restored the question of the body to the history of faith healing, it is at the same time hoped that it has not lost its soul.

I

Bodily Knowledge

There is surely a piece of divinity in us, something that was before
the elements, and owes no homage unto the sun.
                              Sir Thomas Browne, *Religio Medici* (1643)

The body, at one time defined by the dominant religious discourses of
the age, is understood today primarily through the lens of scientific
medicine. In hindsight, the broad contours of the transformation from
a religious to a medical understanding of the body can appear as a
straightforward exercise of secularization, or more accurately, medicalization. Whether this process is regarded as the natural evolution of scientific progress, the exertion of social control in a capitalist society, or
the discursive extension of the Foucauldian gaze, the shifting relations
between religion and medicine produced new, competing constructions
of the body in the nineteenth century.[1]

Historical studies of the Victorian period typically have placed great
emphasis upon moral regulation, but religious understandings of the
body went much further than simply repressing corporeal vices. Many of
the alternative medical "sects" that flourished in the nineteenth century
relied upon metaphysical understandings of health and disease, explicitly
relating therapeutics to God's design or vitalistic forces. Such affiliations
did not appear incongruous in an age when the perfect harmony of spiritual and natural laws was widely presumed. By the end of the century,
however, these assumptions were being undermined by the ascendance of
scientific approaches which challenged the role of religion and propelled
medicine into new realms of knowledge and authority.

In order to comprehend the cultural practice of faith healing, it is important first to examine the complex, multi-layered intellectual context
that surrounded and shaped the emergence of the Anglo-American divine healing movement in the late-nineteenth century. For physicians,
theologians, and intellectual critics who commented on faith and healing, the point of convergence was the body. Previous studies have
traced the particular theological roots of Protestant faith healing, but

there has been little consideration of how this phenomenon was positioned in relation to medicine, health, and constructions of the body.[2] Accordingly, this study complements these theological trends with their physiological counterparts, particularly as expressed through sectarian medicine and health reform movements, in addition to outlining the broader debates between religion and science that vexed Victorian intellectuals. Faced with a revolutionary transformation in medical therapeutics, faith healing rejected the attempts of material science to disengage the body from its spiritual components, and dramatically reasserted a role for the divine in determining health.

THE PRAYER QUESTION

In 1871 Queen Victoria asked the clergy to pray for the health of her cholera-stricken son, Edward, the prince of Wales. The prince's eventual recovery warmed the hearts of those who had prayed, but it hardened the determination of scientific critics to discredit the validity of petitionary prayer. The most combative skeptic was John Tyndall, a self-taught British physicist with a passion for the emerging scientific materialism that challenged religious order as the guide for human conduct. To ascertain the true efficacy of prayer, Tyndall suggested that a scientific experiment could be conducted using two identical hospital wards with similar patients. One ward would be dedicated to prayer, while the other would serve as a control group; by comparing the mortality rates of the wards after a period of time, the "prayer gauge" would illustrate definitively whether prayer was effective in healing the body. Tyndall's proposition jolted Victorian sensibilities, and the issue was widely debated on both sides of the Atlantic.[3] The extensive discussion of prayer, materialism, and divine intervention prompted the Canadian Baptist to contend: "Either Tyndall is a blockhead or Christ is an imposter."[4]

The intense reaction to the prayer gauge debate was shaped by centuries of Protestant deliberations on the role of miracles in the modern world. In contrast to Roman Catholic "magic," Protestantism largely rejected the idea that miracles could occur in the post-biblical age. By the end of the eighteenth century, theologians led by William Paley (1743–1805) were suggesting that the modern evidence of God lay within the design of creation, working through a general providence of "happy shrimp" and "juicy peaches" instead of miraculous interventions.[5] The harmony of the universe's physical laws lay at the heart of Paley's natural theology and affirmed the reasonableness of Christianity in the age of Enlightenment. Protestants found Paley comforting in his assurance of God's existence, but disquieting in the distance that God appeared to maintain in relation to humanity. Scottish Common Sense philosophy provided a means to bridge this gap by arguing for an "empiricism of the mind." By dividing the mind into "faculties" that could analyze different types of data empirically, Common Sense philosophy suggested that the divine could be grasped inductively, both as a body of knowledge and a self-evident truth. The mind encompassed not only intellectual activity, but a moral sense of truth that extended beyond reason alone. God designed the mind in such a way that humans could behold not only the edifice, but also the divine architect himself.[6]

Forging a direct link between God and the human mind was particularly important for evangelicalism, which rose to pre-eminence in the nineteenth century. Characterized by a distinctive emphasis on the conversion experience, evangelicalism sought a more personal, inward relationship between humanity and Christ.[7] As Michael Gauvreau outlines, many evangelicals turned to Bishop Joseph Butler's *The Analogy of Religion, Natural and Revealed, to the Constitution and Course of Nature* (1736) as an antidote to the rationalistic theologies of the Enlightenment. Butler did not limit supernatural intervention to the biblical age, but suggested that, analogous to the laws of nature, "God's miraculous interpositions may have been all long, in like manner, by *general* laws of wisdom."[8] Natural laws could be superseded by the divine, but this was done rarely and only for the moral purpose of guiding humanity. Like the Common Sense philosophers, Butler believed the individual conscience was the arena that both defined the self and permitted humanity to rise above the status of mere machines: "our gross organized bodies, with which we perceive the objects of sense, and with which we act, are no part of ourselves." The self as a higher order existed independently of a corporeal shell. This separation of mind and body meant that one order of natural law was exercised over the body while a separate degree of revealed religion could be exercised upon the mind.[9]

The currents of Paley, Butler, and the Scottish Common Sense philosophers were prevalent in the nineteenth-century Anglo-American world. Geographic considerations did alter the lenses through which these works were viewed, but the basic understanding of the mind and body were generally consistent. Paley's theology alone was insufficient in addressing the evangelical concern for a direct experience of God, but the vision of a coherent universe of natural laws remained worthy of contemplation. Despite the rising challenge of Darwinian evolution, which threatened to replace providential guidance with the mechanism of natural selection, the natural theology of Paley continued to be asserted as an important avenue to behold the workings of God in the harmony and constancy of nature. In the face of scientific materialism, however, Protestants increasingly turned to the inherent superiority of the moral faculty and the intuitional grasp of the divine as the ultimate grounding for and evidence of the Christian faith.[10]

Within this context, the widespread debate over Tyndall's prayer gauge was far from an esoteric intellectual exercise; it raised fundamental concerns about the role of prayer in Protestant devotion. In particular, how could God answer petitions that involved external phenomena, such as weather or disease, without contravening the very uniformity of laws he had designed? Writing under the name "Fidelis," Agnes Maule Machar set out to answer this question, positioning herself against both Tyndall and some of the defences of Christianity that appeared to exclude the natural world from the sphere of prayer. Sparking an extended debate in the *Canadian Monthly and National Review,* Machar argued that the "Divine Prescience" would have foreseen every possible circumstance and event, "whether it be the action of a physical force or the craving of a human soul," and adjusted his creation accordingly so that what are only imperfectly perceived as natural forces could respond to the needs of his people. Miracles did not violate the harmonious natural order. When human knowledge has been exhausted, she posited, Christians "gladly trust to that unseen Will whose love and care they have already seen revealed in the provisions of nature." In this way, the believer was rewarded with "a peace and rest which those who are trusting simply to what we may call fortuitous results, cannot possibly know."[11] The conscious experience of the divine was more important than manifestations of the miraculous.

Countering Machar's assertions was the essayist and civil servant, William Dawson LeSueur, described by one historian as "the most wide-ranging Canadian-born intellectual of his generation."[12] Exhibiting a "critical spirit" of enquiry, LeSueur pointed out that Machar's division between spiritual manipulation and the normal operation of natural laws presented a separation of spheres, where "Nothing that is done in one really *affects* what takes place in the other; but it is arranged that *occasionally* what people pray for shall happen."[13] How could the efficacy of prayer be demonstrated if the intended result might or might not have happened without petitions for divine aid? This ambiguity extended to the specific question of the body and healing, which provided examples for both sides of the debate. Machar noted the recuperation of the Prince of Wales and argued that those who do not recover could still experience the blessings of God in the mind, such as the happiness produced from the "felt presence and support of the unseen Friend."[14] LeSueur rejoined that when people pray for the sick they are not hoping that God had foreseen every contingency beforehand; rather, they employ prayer so "*that the case may not be left to the action of the ordinary laws of nature.*" For LeSueur, there was a fundamental incompatibility between this assumption, inherent within petitionary prayers for healing, and the regular practice of medicine based on natural laws:

Prayer for the recovery of the sick is approved of; but how could it have any general efficacy without the science of medicine being completely overturned? It is suggested that God could "dart into the mind" of a physician the suggestion to use a certain remedy, and that thus the cure would appear to be a natural one. There is something a little grotesque in the idea of the Divine Being, while answering a prayer, taking such pains as it were, to cover up all trace of His special action ... Either the remedy suggested would be one adapted to all similar cases, or it would be one to which miraculous efficacy had been given for the special occasion. In the one case, a new rule of medical treatment would be established ... in the other, medical science would simply be confused ... In the one case, the Deity would really take the whole development of medical science into his own hands ... in the latter, there would be no such thing as medical science at all.[15]

Machar responded that LeSueur's separation of the spiritual and the physical did not take into account the true nature of the "actual material universe," where natural forces "are simply manifestations to us of the mind and will of God." She reminded readers that the "thoughtful mind must recoil with horror" at the idea that nature was controlled by chance or anarchy, rather than a Providential guide. Instead, Machar posited confidently that "any mother's heart" would find it "infinitely more consoling to be told that the issue of the disease was under the control of a wise and loving Father, who, though He acts in and through natural laws, has proclaimed Himself the Hearer and Answerer of Prayer." Even if a mother's child died, God would provide her with "the felt support of His strengthening love, and enable her to believe that he has guided the event wisely."[16] LeSueur did not doubt the value of such subjective experiences, but these alone were insufficient for the critical mind to determine if any temporal conditions had been altered in answer to prayer. If the operation of God is solely exercised through natural laws, why should prayers be offered for the efficacy of universal principles already known? There could be no point in "blessing the means" of medical science if both God and medical science confined their operation to the same standard of natural law.

While the debate in the *Canadian Monthly* moved into different areas of concern, the questions surrounding prayer, religion, and science would continue to surface. Writing in the *Presbyterian Review*, D.H. MacVicar of Montreal revisited the prayer debates in 1885, but his framework was noticeably different from that of LeSueur or Machar. For the Presbyterian divine, the act of prayer was "indelibly stamped" upon humanity, a disposition that was "innate and universal." And since, following the scientific language of the age, "Every organ is fitted into its appropriate environment," therefore "surely the faculties of the soul, the aspirations of our higher nature are not doomed to grasp at nothing." Prayer as an "intuitive exercise of the human soul" was fitted within the Darwinian body of adaptation, and the very presence of such intuitive faculties suggested that prayer served a tangible and meaningful function within human society and human bodies, even if that function was occasionally elusive to the minds of mere mortals.[17] The criteria of knowledge that had been demanded by Tyndall and LeSueur was based on the objective efficacy of prayer, but MacVicar sidestepped this issue by asking not how prayer worked, but why it existed within the human soul as a "universal" desire.

The ascendancy of the mind as the arbiter of experience and evidence for the reality of the divine met the needs of both evangelicals concerned with religious experience and other Victorians intent upon reconciling religion with science. However, this accommodation came at the cost of severing the mind from the body and physical matter, territory that was increasingly conceded to science alone. And yet, while the prayer question raged, the stirrings of a new movement promoting divine healing were being felt on both sides of the Atlantic and would emerge forcefully in the next decade. From the sole perspective of the prayer debates, it is difficult to ascertain how faith healing could have attained even the slightest inclusion within Protestant thought at the end of the nineteenth century. Nevertheless, by the end of the century, LeSueur's own sister and niece, both trained physicians, would turn away from science and medicine to embrace faith healing.[18] To understand the appeal of the divine healing movement, the theological apologetics and philosophical speculations separating the mind from the body need to be set against countervailing tendencies that were simultaneously redeeming the body and pulling it closer to the divine.

PERFECTIONISM AND THE GOSPEL OF HEALTH

In contrast to Butler's "gross organized bodies" as mere corporeal shells embodying the self, the popular Canadian revivalist, H.T. Crossley, offered audiences a different message: "Man is a trinity in unity, having three natures, the physical, the intellectual and the spiritual." In his address entitled "Points about Health," Crossley asked, "Shall we not have the worthy ambition to endeavor to make the most out of ourselves in every respect, and so be perfect men and women, and not weaklings or monstrosities?"[19] The call to be "perfect men and women" was one of the most powerful discourses of the nineteenth century. Unlike many of the philosophical and religious sentiments of the eighteenth century, which emphasized the purity of intellect above the base corporeality of the body, the nineteenth century offered a redemption of the body on many levels, including the moral, the intellectual, and the physiological. It was from this perfectionist strain that faith healing would build a foundation, and it was here that it would develop its most radical critiques of contemporary medicine.

The concept of Christian perfection was indebted to the legacy of John Wesley and the subsequent spread of Methodism in North America. Whereas Calvinism had traditionally emphasized the natural depravity of humanity and the sovereignty of God in human redemption, Methodism offered a more optimistic vision of the individual's personal role in achieving salvation. In the early-nineteenth century, Christian perfection became a state of "entire sanctification," a second blessing following conversion where the believer's heart is purified of sin and one's life is consecrated to God. While traditional Calvinists objected to the notion that a sinful humanity could ever achieve perfection, the idea of sanctification gained ground among evangelical revivalists of all stripes. Conversion was only the first step of a Christian's journey towards a true divinely-consecrated relationship with God. "New Calvinists" adopted a reformed version of perfectionism and, by the middle of the nineteenth century, Protestantism in America had been largely "Methodized."[20]

Perfectionism stressed the role of the individual in regenerating the moral self through one's service to God. Such consecrations could take a variety of forms. In antebellum America, for example, perfectionism was linked to various social reform movements, most notably the campaigns for abolition and temperance.[21] While some perfectionist strains reformed society, others turned inward to focus on spirituality and living a life of "holiness." In New York, Sarah Lankford and her sister, Phoebe Palmer, started to hold regular "Tuesday Meetings for the Promotion of Holiness." Palmer offered a "shorter way" to perfection by placing "all on the altar" and receiving an instantaneous spiritual baptism of the Holy Ghost.[22] Sanctification was a promise claimed through faith, and it removed the necessity of waiting for definite assurance or a witness of the spirit to demonstrate that one's heart was cleansed. In the revivals of the nineteenth century, the individual was increasingly endowed with the responsibility for his or her own spiritual life and Palmer's "altar theology" presented an appealing avenue to perfection.

The British colonies to the north were not isolated from these developments, especially in Upper Canada, or Canada West as it later became known, where the Methodist presence was strongest. The American Methodist evangelist, James Caughey, had been spreading the message of holiness in the Canadas since the 1830s, while Phoebe Palmer and her husband, Walter, toured extensively through British North America between 1853 and 1858. Their most famous campaign was in 1857, when an overnight stop in Hamilton turned into a three-week revival that spread far beyond the city. Phoebe Palmer estimated that at least two thousand people had been converted and hundreds more were sanctified in what has been marked as the beginning of a widespread holiness "awakening" in the middle of the century.[23] Palmer's books were reprinted by Wesleyan Methodist Book Room in Toronto and serialized in the church's magazine, the *Christian Guardian*. One historian suggests that "no branch of fragmented British Methodism retained the holiness legacy of Wesley to the extent of Canadian Methodism."[24]

Palmer's influence also stretched beyond Wesleyan circles, profoundly affecting the Presbyterian minister W.E. Boardman, who offered his own perspective on holiness in the widely-read *The Higher Christian Life* (1858). As such reformed versions of holiness gained ground in the second half of the century, Boardman co-founded a series of conventions at the English town of Keswick in 1875. Participants in the Keswick conventions rejected the Methodist emphasis upon achieving an instantaneous "second blessing" of entire purification from sin. Instead, Keswick holiness offered a form of perfectionism that was achieved gradually, not as a complete state but as a moment-by-moment condition of trust in victory over sin. Rather than a sinless state, the consecrated life required constant "infillings," "indwellings," or "enduements" of holy power to achieve the "higher life."[25]

While Keswick holiness resisted formal organization, some forms of Wesleyan holiness started to separate themselves from mainstream Methodism by the end of the century. Decrying the church as beholden to worldliness and formalism, splinter sects sought an increased emphasis on revivalism, entire sanctification, and a rigorous code of personal conduct. Fanning the flames, some groups modified the progression of conversion to sanctification by adding a "third blessing," namely a "fire baptism" of the holy spirit. Between 1893 and 1907, twenty-five separate holiness denominations were formed in Canada, although their numbers paled in comparison to the strength of the radical Wesleyan holiness movement in the American south and midwest.[26]

Even though mainline Protestantism refused to adopt the strict measures of holiness demanded by these breakaway groups, a widespread ethos of perfectionism infused American and Canadian evangelicalism in the nineteenth century. As a broad-based movement, holiness flowed across ecclesiastical and geographic borders, and while different theological nuances

shaped the many varieties of holiness in the nineteenth century, all sought
a form of sanctification that furthered the objective of spiritual perfection.
Within this milieu, it is not surprising that the language of sanctification
and the higher life could not be confined to the state of the soul alone, but
quickly extended to the body.

Crossley's "Pointers about Health" declared that "We should make it
part of our religion to look after our physical health."[27] For much of
the nineteenth century, the search for health spawned a wide variety of
therapeutic options, many of them informed by distinctly religious interests. As Robert C. Fuller notes, medical "sects" such as homeopathy,
hydropathy, and advocates of the health reform movement, all reflected
a "physiological counterpart to the period's theological perfectionism."[28] Living a sanctified life was a prescription that could be applied
to the body; moral categories were fused with dietary regimes and
treatments that sought to restore the body to its "natural" (and therefore, perfect) state. Theological perfectionism was notably influential
for American health reformers such as Sylvester Graham (1794–1851)
and Dr William Alcott (1798–1859), who both sought to discover
God's laws for bodily health.[29] Resolutions passed by the American
Physiological Society reflect the prevailing tone of health reform, maintaining that "the highest moral and religious interests of man require a
strict conformity in his dietetic and other voluntary habits to all the
physiological laws of his nature."[30]

The key to Christian physiology was the assumption that God had created a perfect body for humanity; therefore, understanding the laws governing the body involved both physical and spiritual faculties. Christians
had a moral duty to discover and observe these laws, whether in the
realms of religion, conduct, diet, sleep, or exercise. This gospel of health
was framed within the same context that perfectionist reformers sought
to improve society through abolition, temperance, or social welfare. Discovering God's design within the body was not simply a contemplative
act, it was an active part of the Christian's obligation to obey the laws of
the body and educate others about the gospel of health. If the exact prescriptions of Alcott or Graham were not always palatable to some, most
Victorians were very willing to assign a moral imperative to health. In
the words of Herbert Spencer, "the preservation of health is a *duty* ...
The fact is, that all breaches of the laws of health are *physical sins*."[31]

TRANSCENDENTAL MEDICINE

While the gospel of health searched for God's laws in the efficient operation of the body, other therapeutic trends harnessed the spiritual to similar ends. American historians who have traced the links between

medicine and religion in the nineteenth century typically follow a trajectory that aligns the early "vitalism" of the Swedish mystic Emanuel Swedenborg (1688–1771) and the Viennese physician Franz Anton Mesmer (1734–1815) to various mind cure philosophies, from theosophy to Norman Vincent Peale's positive thinking and twentieth-century New Age trends. In many ways, this perspective is an updated version of Perry Miller's original 1940 presentation of "From Edwards to Emerson," which connected the "inherent mysticism" of Puritanism with later forms of "transcendental idealism." Miller's emphasis on an American idealism progressively shorn of the creedal obstructions of theology has been mirrored by historians anxious to find lines of continuity in American religious thought.[32] The rise of a "therapeutic culture" in the twentieth century is constructed similarly as a progressive ideal that starts with a religious basis only to be stripped down to an essential core that is secularized by modern society. Fifty years after Perry Miller's "From Edwards to Emerson," T.J. Jackson Lears answers with "From Salvation to Self-Realization," but the path remains the same.[33]

In the realm of nineteenth-century healing, scholarly attention has focused particularly on Christian Science and various strands of the New Thought Movement, which asserted the primacy of the spiritual, the true reality of the divine mind, over the base world of matter. Achieving health required the adjustment and training of the mind to realize this positive reality, while at the same time denying the existence of all other physical forms. Since disease was considered a product of the material world, relieving bodily afflictions required the alignment of one's mental state with the spiritual reality generated by God.[34] In responding to the challenge of scientific medicine, mental cure philosophies rejected the body and turned to the mind for health and healing.

The mind-cure movements of the late-nineteenth century appear to fit the standard historical framework that traces the lineage between Mesmer and the present-day culture of self-help books. However, in plotting this course, historians have overlooked movements such as divine healing, whose theological orthodoxy prevented it from absorbing the pantheism and mystic transcendentalism that infused most varieties of mind cure. Evangelical Protestant faith healers confound the metanarrative of American religious history by remaining stubbornly orthodox in some areas, while refashioning other currents in a way that simply does not appear to suit the movement's ethos. Unable to fit into the model of "religious liberalism," one medical historian reduced the phenomenon of Protestant faith healing to "an offshoot of the stark literalism of fundamentalist religion."[35] A closer examination of the roots of the divine healing movement, however, suggests that it represented far more than an obscure offshoot.

The nineteenth-century fluidity of mind, spirit, and matter engendered a wide variety of sectarian medical philosophies. These elements were reconfigured in myriad ways to suit the particular designs of therapeutic philosophies, from homeopathy through hydropathy to chiropractic.[36] Of these, homeopathy served as a unique point of intersection between alternative medicine, holiness, and divine healing. Founded by Samuel Hahnemann (1755–1843), homeopathy was a therapy that, like many of the medical sects, sought to restore a balance between the body and the natural world. Hahnemann's main principles were encompassed within two laws, namely the law of similars and the law of infinitesimals. Homeopathy looked for substances in the natural world that would produce the same symptoms that the patient experienced, believing that "like is cured by like"; only remedies that exhibited the disease's characteristics in a healthy body could cure it. These substances, however, were given in infinitesimal amounts so that barely a trace of the curative agent was actually present in the drug. Hahnemann was able to employ such great dilutions because he believed that the power of the agent was activated through "dynamizations," a spiritual energy that could be unleashed in the process of preparing the drug through "excitations" such as shaking or rubbing.[37]

Introduced to the United States in 1825, homeopathy spread across the eastern seaboard and into Canada by 1832.[38] Hahnemann's system was appealing in part because it offered an assurance that the body, like the universe, was organized along coherent principles in harmony with the design of the divine creator. Homeopathy's laws were, like nature itself, fixed, universal, eternal, and heralded as medicine's answer to Newton's laws of physics. The operation of these laws were "eternal expressions of the divine will." Therapeutics could not be left in the hands of allopaths, destined to be "alone of all nature, destitute of law, given up to the dominion of chaos."[39]

If homeopathy prided itself on the harmonial nature of its laws, it also slipped into metaphysical understandings of health. In particular, Hahnemann was interested in the correspondence between the spiritual and material realms. A body's "vital forces" were ultimately numinous in nature, and therefore both health and disease were direct products of the spiritual forces animating the physical body. Infinitesimal doses were effective not because they produced profound chemical and physical changes, but because they were catalysts for activating the latent spiritual forces within. Homeopathists would later couch this process in more scientific terms as the century progressed, diffusing the spiritual side somewhat in suggesting that their cures worked because the preparatory process freed the "active principle."[40]

By the second half of the nineteenth century, homeopathic physicians in North America had started to question the assumptions of their founder, and long debates were held over the continued use of both laws. In 1860 a Canadian practitioner published an article in the *North American Journal of Homeopathy* calling for an end to "all that borders upon the transcendental and mysterious."[41] Some homeopaths began dispensing allopathic drugs in addition to their own, and for the next twenty years homeopathy was embroiled in a long series of internecine disputes over whether it should broaden its practice by adopting appropriate treatments from regular medicine, or if it should remain true to the principles established by Hahnemann. Despite these internal stresses, however, homeopathy in Canada grew from approximately a dozen practitioners at mid-century to over one hundred practitioners by 1888.[42] According to J.T.H. Connor, homeopathic physicians in Canada faced comparatively less hostility than their American counterparts. In particular, Ontario offered homeopathy full legal status and representation on the College of Physicians and Surgeons.[43]

The shared assumptions between Hahnemann's metaphysics and holiness might be symbolized by the union of Phoebe Palmer and her husband, Walter, a homeopathic physician. Holiness aligned and infused the self and the soul with God as a means to activate a life for service, while homeopathy activated one's inner spiritual forces to restore a body. Like the Christian physiology of the health reform movement, homeopathy complemented the prevailing religious tenor by presenting a body in harmony with the universe, based on the operation of natural laws that were both physical and spiritual in nature. In the second half of the nineteenth century, however, this relationship began breaking down. Not only was homeopathy openly aligning itself with regular medicine, but the very basis for the spiritual understanding of a body's vital forces was being undermined. As historian Martin Kaufman notes, "to prescribe homeopathically and to believe in its efficacy, the physician had to have an intense belief in a God who established natural laws. He also had to believe that there was an interrelationship between the spiritual and material aspects of life."[44] The debate over prayer had consequences beyond the theological; confining the operation of the divine to the intuitive mind undercut metaphysical understandings of healing. By the end of the century, the body was increasingly separated from spiritual forces and subjected to new forms of medical science.

THE SCIENCE OF MEDICINE

The popularity and appeal of sectarian medicine reflected more than medical pluralism's ability to offer patients a choice in therapeutic care. The model of health defined by the sectarian healers and advocates of health reform stood in direct opposition to the "heroic" model of allopathic medicine. In its focus on finding an immediate cure, regular medicine was accused of neglecting the question of prevention. Although the exact nature of disease varied between the sectarians, most agreed that when the laws of health were obeyed, the body could exist in a perfect state, free from disease. If the functioning parts of the body could be brought into harmony with its environment, the body would operate in a state of peak health and efficiency.[45]

Regular medicine itself was in the midst of what medical historian Charles Rosenberg has labeled a "therapeutic revolution." Early nineteenth-century interventionist practice was based on the ability to demonstrate its visible efficacy. Disease was regarded as an imbalance of natural forces that required "heroic" offsetting through drugs, purges, bleedings, or blisters. Rather than treating individual diseases with a particular cure, allopathic treatment was based on addressing common physiological effects. By the late-nineteenth century, however, regular medicine had started to develop more specific etiological theories of disease, reducing them to discrete entities with unique symptoms and treatments. Instead of a loss of natural balance, disease was a deviation from fixed norms that had a specific physiological cause. The transformation of nineteenth-century therapeutics was embodied in the semantic shift away from the "natural" body towards a universal set of "normal" conditions.[46]

What made this therapeutic approach revolutionary was the epistemological position of science as the objective basis of knowledge about the body and disease, rather than trusting the physician's own judgment. The earlier reliance on empirical, visible effectiveness in medical treatment was now subordinated to the ascent of medical science, which determined the universal norms that formed the basis of diagnosis and prescribed appropriate treatment for specific conditions. The new therapeutic model profoundly altered the relationship between doctors and patients. Illness was no longer readily apparent to the observer, patient and physician alike; however, comparing a set of specific symptoms to universal standards might determine a specific cause. The meaning of symptoms was transformed by the requirement for scientific accuracy, which diminished the role of the patient's verbal account of the affliction. Bodily samples were extracted and measured by instruments, resulting in chemical analysis or microscopic inspection. No longer dependent upon the description of conditions by the patient, the authority of the physician shifted dramatically as medical diagnosis became subjected to the criteria of experimental science.

The transformation of the physician-patient relationship had important repercussions for the professionalization of medicine at the end of the nineteenth century. The plurality of medical practice in the middle of the century was possible because the empiricist model allowed for a wide variety of hermeneutical understandings of disease. However, the ascendancy of science as the "objective" ground for medical therapeutics threatened the holistic approaches of the sectarians, which now appeared suspiciously metaphysical. As one physician remarked, "Modern science is indifferent to Hippocrates and Hahnemann. If their theories will not bear the bright light of the present, let them wander back into the darkness of the past to which they belong."[47] Homeopaths found that in order to maintain their status, they needed to reorient themselves away from the vitalism of their founder.[48] The professional identity of physicians was increasingly associated with the science of medicine, rather than the actual practice of medicine.

The revolution was not always peaceful. The investment of sound judgment in the form of "practical" knowledge was a well-established model for many "professional gentlemen" in the nineteenth century. In Canada, the development of a university medical curriculum based on science and laboratory experimentation was met with denunciations of "frogology." The *Lancet* worried that medical students were becoming "practical scientists [rather] than practical physicians."[49] As R.D. Gidney and W.P.J. Millar have noted, the cultural status of science itself was part of the displacement of the mid-century professional ideal of a liberal education, social respectability, and practical experience. However, unlike the clergy, who found their public authority undermined by the growing status and epistemology of science, doctors were able to don the mantle of science and remake themselves as professionals, even if they were sometimes uncomfortable about leaving behind the "gentleman profession."[50]

When Protestant faith healing emerged at the end of the nineteenth century, it drew upon the rhetoric of the earlier health reform movements but faced a very different historical context. The combination of professionalism and scientific authority wrought by the therapeutic revolution narrowed the definition of the body and gradually overwhelmed competing medical sects. Theological shifts separating the intuitive mind from the scientific body met the challenge of Darwinism, but also raised new questions about faith, prayer, and the role of God in the world. This dramatic transformation jolted the Victorian sensibilities of a generation of believers accustomed to a far more intimate relationship between body and spirit, the material and the numinous. For some the role of the divine would not be extricated easily from the corporeal realm.

THE DIVINE HEALING MOVEMENT

In North America the single most important promoter of what eventually emerged as the divine healing movement was Dr Charles Cullis

(1833–1892). Although he completed his training in conventional medicine at the University of Vermont, Cullis established a successful career
as a homeopath in Boston. The unexpected death of his wife sent Cullis
on a spiritual journey that led him to holiness and sanctification. Taking the call to consecration seriously, Cullis established a series of philanthropic enterprises that included four consumptives' homes, an out-
patient dispensary, an orphanage, a deaconess home, and a publishing
house, the Willard Tract Repository.[51]

In the late-1860s Cullis started to explore the links between faith and
healing. Despite the impact of the holiness movement, with its emphasis upon maintaining moral and physiological perfection, nineteenth-
century evangelicalism still commonly regarded disease and illness as a
means to bring the soul closer to God. As one patient of Cullis expressed, "How smooth the Lord can make a dying pillow!"[52] The assurance of spiritual salvation offered the sufferer peace of mind as the
soul transcended its mortal coil. Printing romantic deathbed narratives
provided good publicity for his philanthropic endeavours, but Cullis's
overlapping religious and medical interests led him to question the relationship between spiritual and physical salvation.

Instead of simply evangelizing to the incurable cases that reached him
and who often died "hearing about Jesus" in "perfect peace," Cullis
started to search for a more systematic method of promoting actual cures
through faith. Many scriptures suggested that faith alone could cure disease, particularly James 5: 14–15: "Is any sick among you? Let him call
for the elders of the church; and let them pray over him, anointing him
with oil in the name of the Lord: and the prayer of faith shall save the
sick, and the Lord shall raise him up." For Cullis the biblical prescription
seemed very clear: "I could not see why, with such explicit and unmis-
takable promises, I should limit the present exercise of God's power."[53]
In searching for cases of faith healing that would demonstrate that God's
presence extended into the realm of bodily healing, he discovered a biographical account of a Swiss faith healer, Dorothea Trudel (1813–1862).
Healed by her mother of smallpox as a child, Trudel laid hands upon
many when an epidemic broke out in the village of Männedorf. As word
of Trudel's ability to cure spread, Männedorf quickly became renowned
as a site of healing that lasted well beyond Trudel's death. Inspired by
this example, Cullis decided to adopt faith healing in his own practice.
In 1870 he asked a patient suffering from a brain tumor, Lucy Drake, if
she would "trust the Lord to remove this tumor and restore her to
health." Although Drake had "no particular faith about it," she agreed
to "trust the Lord," and after Cullis anointed her with oil and prayed,
she was able to stand and walk three miles. Eventually, all traces of the
tumor disappeared.[54]

Although hardly the first Protestant faith healer in North America, Cullis's ability to popularize the doctrine placed him at the forefront of the emerging movement. The Boston homeopath was already an important figure within the holiness movement, and his access to a well-established publishing infrastructure was invaluable. Through his wide personal associations, Cullis was also successful in introducing the doctrine to many key people within the holiness movement, including the president of the National Camp Meeting Association for the Promotion of Holiness, John Inskip, W.E. Boardman, R. Kelso Carter, the Baptist theologian A.J. Gordon, and many others.[55]

The emerging divine healing movement drew not only upon Trudel, but other European influences such as Johann Blumhardt and Otto Stockmayer. Stockmayer regularly attended the Keswick conventions and his *Sickness and the Gospel* (1878) quickly circulated through holiness circles in Britain and North America.[56] From these continental contacts, the Anglo-American divine healing movement developed a theology of healing based on the atonement of Christ. Blumhardt, Trudel, and Stockmayer all believed that faith healing was more than simply a miracle, or a suspension of natural law. Christ's crucifixion not only allowed for atonement from the weight of sin, but it also bore the afflictions of sickness and disease, which were ultimately the products of sin. Therefore anyone with faith could lay claim to the promise of healing, not as a call for miraculous recovery, but as a natural state of being, a mode of faith similar to sanctification, only applied to the entire body.

Atonement theology provided the basis for Protestant divine healing and marked the body as a site to engage the divine. Robert Bruce Mullin has argued that theologians of divine healing shared a fundamental commonality in promoting faith healing as a means to reject the position that miracles were limited to the biblical age. The modern miracles of healing were "a bulwark against skepticism and rationalism."[57] Although most proponents did object to the "cessationist" position, the question of the body remained the overriding concern, rather than apologetics for divine intervention. In many ways, atonement theology worked in the opposite direction, by distinguishing the act of healing as a specific promise that was separate from the other miracles performed by Jesus. For Boardman, "signs and wonders [are] occasional, not perpetual. The call for the use of bodily maladies and for healing through faith is as permanent as sin on the one hand, and as the economy of God in saving is on the other ... Signs and wonders are seldom repeated at all, and never more than once."[58] Faith healing might illustrate divine power, but it was not necessarily a call to tear down completely the walls between the biblical and post-biblical ages.

Proponents of faith healing were certainly aware that their doctrine had to be placed within the context of the prayer debates. Writing in 1884, R. Kelso Carter characterized the question of determining efficacy in prayer in terms remarkably similar to those of LeSueur. Carter noted that almost everyone could point to an occasion where "A dear one had come nigh unto death; physician's skill was exhausted, and no hope remained. But in their extremity they called upon God, and suddenly the symptoms changed, and the patient recovered." The problem, however, was that "such a case can never be cited as an illustration of the special power of God," since critics could simply point to the attending physician as the true agent of the cure.[59] What marked the divine healing movement apart from these typical cases of prayer for special intervention was the assumption that healing was not a case of special providence, but an open promise: "*God now heals bodily sickness, precisely as He now heals soul sickness ... through and by virtue of the perfect Atonement of Jesus Christ.*" Divine healing was itself a "natural law" made possible by the crucifixion. As Carter argued, "what law can be cited in the realm of physics, which is more universal and more inexorable, than that which declares that sin will surely cause anguish, anxiety, remorse and soul sickness? Is not this law just as truly 'natural' as that which governs bodily disease?"[60]

The Presbyterian theologian, B.B. Warfield, no friend of perfectionism or divine healing, recognized this blurring of lines between natural and supernatural and blasted the faith healers, accusing them of opening the door for skeptics to turn faith healing into a mesmerism that would destroy the unique miracles of Jesus.[61] However, for A.B. Simpson, a Canadian Presbyterian influenced by holiness and a proponent of faith healing, divine intervention in the body was simply a higher form of natural law; a "material scientist" might be "perfectly correct to say that a certain physical condition must certainly end in death, and yet a higher spiritual law may come in, a law of Divine life through which that physical condition shall be entirely changed, and that sinking body raised into vigor and health."[62] Like a chrysalis growing into a butterfly, the human body was designed to receive such blessings of a "higher law" from the spiritual realm.

The divine healing movement is often viewed as a prologue of "signs and wonders" that set the stage for the emergence of pentecostalism in the twentieth century.[63] However, this framework detracts from the primary concern of Protestant faith healing, namely the redemption of the body. Physical healing was a distinctive form of grace, analogous to the forgiveness of sin. While sympathetic to arguments for supernatural intervention, most faith healers stressed that theirs was not a "supernatural" healing, but a perfectly "natural" method for those who had the faith to seek it. Instead of separating the mind from the body as a means to preserve a realm of intuition where the divine could be perceived, the body and mind were synchronized; both became vessels for the experience of God, both could be cleansed of sin, and both could be restored to perfection. The body itself was the central focus of the divine healing movement, made "in the image of God" with the potential to "soar as high as you please in the atmosphere of perfect love and perfect peace and perfect health of soul and spirit and body."[64]

It is not difficult to see that sectarian medicine, with its emphasis upon defining a perfect state of health, offered a discourse readily appropriated by divine healing. The rhetoric of the "perfect body" was well established by the health reform movement, while the various currents of metaphysical healings offered, as Fuller suggests, "a particular lifestyle believed to be in objective correspondence with the invisible spiritual order of things."[65] When Cullis shifted from homeopathy to divine healing, the correspondence between the spiritual and physical order of things became embodied in the atonement: "I think we might claim, just as promised that while caring for this body – the clothing of the soul of man – it might be made well and kept in health, so that man can think better and feel better, clothed upon with Christ's righteousness, saved from his iniquities and his diseases."[66] Cullis's call for men to think, feel, and act "better" could have come straight from the pages of Alcott, Graham, or even H.T. Crossley. Where physical health had been seen as a moral imperative, however, divine healing suggested that health was more than simply discovering God's laws for the body; perfect health could only be achieved through the spiritual infilling of Christ. Faith healing not only redeemed the physical body: it transformed the body itself into a site for an encounter with the divine.

Until his death in 1892, Cullis remained a central figure within the divine healing movement. His Willard Tract Repository was the single most important publishing house for distributing works on faith healing. By the time Carter published *The Atonement for Sin and Sickness* with the press in 1884, an advertisement carried in the book listed seventeen titles on spiritual healing.[67] Cullis had also started to hold faith healing conventions in different venues across North America. Old Orchard, Maine became a favourite locale, and by the middle of the 1880s, Cullis's summer faith conventions had become "a recognized feature of the religious life of New England."[68]

Cullis started out in his healing ministry as practically a lone voice in North America in the 1870s, but by the beginning of the 1880s the divine healing movement had emerged as a significant religious force. Books, periodicals, publishing houses, and faith homes multiplied at a remarkable rate. The leadership of the movement was never formally organized, but key figures such as Boardman, Carter, Gordon, R.L. Stanton, and A.B. Simpson were widely recognized as authorities, and closely aligned to these theologians were women such as Carrie Judd, who had established her own faith healing home and publishing venture in Buffalo.

Not everyone agreed with the central position of healing in the atonement. A number of holiness proponents rejected the automatic nature of this position, arguing that healing only occurred when God willed it and under special conditions. The atonement doctrine was problematic precisely because its universality left the burden for healing upon the individual, and a lack of faith was implied for those who were not healed. It was a dramatic reversal when R. Kelso Carter published *"Faith Healing" Reviewed After Twenty Years* (1897). One of the foremost advocates of atonement theology, Carter had originally experienced divine healing through Cullis in 1879. However, continued physical sufferings took Carter in a different direction, earning a medical degree and practicing as a physician.[69] Reviewing his earlier position on faith healing, Carter claimed that while healing was included in the atonement, it was an error to assume that the full benefits of bodily restoration were automatically accessible by all. The laws of health and God's will were both modifying factors that could explain why the faithful might not always be healed automatically. Even though the act of atonement "purchased bodily deliverance for believers," it was important not to forget that "we live physically under the ordinary law of God for health, and must relegate the matter of special healing or affliction to the realm of the supreme will of our Lord."[70]

Carter went on to suggest that Cullis, Simpson, and Gordon had all generally occupied a similar "practical" position. This assertion, however, requires some qualification. By the 1890s, the traditional proponents of faith healing were being denounced by the flamboyant John Alexander Dowie, the controversial Australian evangelist based in Chicago. Figures such as Cullis, Boardman, and Simpson had always cultivated good relations with other denominations and rarely criticized the medical community, but Dowie's public disputes with ministers, doctors, and almost everyone else who did not agree with him created a serious image problem for the divine healing movement. It is within this context that some faith healers could refer the issue of afflictions that would not leave the body to the ultimate sovereignty of God, rather than follow the extreme position advocated by Dowie, who would lay any failure to recover upon the individual faith of the believer. If the leaders of the divine healing movement were moderating their position, this was no guarantee that such a move would be followed at the popular level, and publicly, the basic atonement position remained intact as the epistemological basis for the practice of faith healing. In 1892, when a "friend from Toronto" criticized Simpson's Christian and Missionary Alliance for advertising a position for a medical missionary, the organization's periodical quickly asserted that "we have never compromised at any time in our testimony on the subject of divine healing." Rather, it was for the multitudes "who are not able to trust the Lord" for their bodies that such a person was employed, and that "it would be simply inhuman to withhold from them any help that is not sinful." For Christians with the faith to trust God, divine healing was still the preferred method. And, in a subtle critique of Dowie, the editorial went on to suggest that "to take any more rigid ground would be to become extremely fanatical, and justly liable to the criticism and opposition of sober and sensible men and women. It is these extreme views which bring divine healing into disrepute with intelligent Christians."[71] In its early formation, the divine healing movement was far from a literalist or fundamentalist "offshoot." Rather, by reorienting the body within the familiar language of divine health, proponents appealed to "sober and sensible men and women" and "intelligent Christians."

Historian Bruce Haley has defined the Victorian concept of health as a state in which "the bodily systems and mental faculties interoperate harmoniously under the direct motive power of vital energy of the indirect motive power of the moral will, or both. Its signs are subjectively recognized, the production of useful, creative labor."[72] In this framework, nineteenth-century holiness and various forms of physiological perfectionism comfortably overlapped and occasionally merged. However, by the end of the century, both science and religion had moved away from their former reliance upon Paleyite natural law. The professional position of science, and the debates over prayer, had profound repercussions for a religious understanding of the body. Although the search for distinctive "laws of health" was still considered a moral duty, these laws were in themselves no longer proof of the divine. Instead of conceding the body as simply answerable to physical laws of medical science, faith healing redeemed it as a site for experiencing the divine.

The reconstruction of the body as being "naturally" infused with the divine drew upon a wide variety of contemporary discourses, including but not restricted to: holiness, perfectionism, health reform, and homeopathy. Some of these currents would continue to inform the practice of faith healing for decades, while others would disappear. Despite this shifting constellation of ideas and assumptions, the central axis driving the theory and practice of faith healing was the relationship between religion and the body.

The broad sweep of medicalization in western society is often characterized as a shift from "sin to sickness." According to Bryan Turner, this process was not necessarily an indication of religious decline, but rather it functioned as a transference of religious disciplines that reappeared in secular forms.[73] While the role of the physician as the moral guardian of health was certainly in ascendence, religion and the body in the nineteenth century continued to interact on multiple levels. Divine healing emerged at an important historical disjuncture between medical pluralism, which allowed religious and medical understandings of the body to inform and reinforce each other, and the therapeutic revolution, which transformed the role of medicine in society. Within the Victorian cultural world this became an entirely new ethos, not simply a transference of a former religious discipline.

In the face of this reconfiguration of medical authority, divine healing asserted its own claim to health, the divine, and the body. The philosophical trends that shaped the divine healing movement were complex, multi-faceted, and even contradictory. However, rather than viewing divine healing as an organic, self-contained idea, this chapter has explored how the body became a central point of convergence for a variety of currents of thought that affected its development. And yet the body serves not only to integrate public discourses, but also allows for the expression of local knowledge as well. Beneath the abstract, divine healing was also propelled by the popular practice and subjective experience of faith healing. In moving towards the personal body, new dimensions of divine healing, and its relation to medical culture, become apparent.

The Prayer of Faith

BEELER: Doctor says it's a natural cure. Says the new medical books explain it.
RHODA: Do you think, because they give it a name, that they explain it?
BEELER: ... You women don't want things explained!
You prefer hocus-pocus ... You women would live on it if we'd let you.
RHODA: Whether you let us or not, we do live on it, and so does the rest of the world.
BEELER: What the world lives on is facts ... With a few jokes thrown in for seasoning.

William Vaughn Moody, *The Faith Healer* (1909)

Carrie Judd's Buffalo-based periodical, *Triumphs of Faith,* was only in its second year of operation when the first accounts of faith healing from Canada were reported. From Stratford, Ontario, Mrs Le Messurier recalled how her son was stricken with epilepsy in 1879. Despite the best efforts of physicians, the epileptic attacks continued unabated. Turning to her pastor in the hope that he might provide encouragement or spiritual guidance, Mrs Le Messurier was disappointed to find that the minister could only offer vague suggestions for the care and protection of her son so that in time he "might recover." This advice was of little consolation to Le Messurier, who had an "inner feeling" that her son could be healed by prayer. Inspired by a verse of scripture given to her by a neighbour, the concerned mother secluded herself to plead for the life of her son: "While thus presenting his case before God, I felt a sweet assurance that my prayer was heard, and that my child was healed."[1]

Two years later a healing of a different sort took place in Hamilton. Mrs L.J. Mottashed was severely afflicted with a number of ailments, including a "complication of diseases" and "exhaustion of the nervous system." Her doctor was considered among the "most celebrated physicians in the city," and he found her condition very critical. Two women called on Mrs Mottashed to discuss the recent miraculous case of healing claimed by Carrie Judd, which had received extensive press coverage. The patient was sceptical of these reports, "feeling rather more the assurance of the blessing of God on the means used, than His blessing without them." However, an associate of Judd, "Miss C.," later attended her bedside and read aloud Carrie Judd's small book, *The Prayer of Faith*. Inspired by this account, Mrs Mottashed decided to seek healing through prayer, and Miss C. wrote to Judd on her behalf. Judd replied that a prayer group would pray for Mottashed at an appointed time, and that the patient herself must also pray at the same hour. When the appropriate day arrived, Mrs Mottashed was suffering both physically and mentally, possessed with "terrible temptations and doubts." However, a visit and prayer with her minister helped to calm her, and as she later contemplated the subject of divine healing, "Light commenced to break in upon me, and gradually I realized the power of Jesus ... One 'Who healeth all our diseases.' I then remembered that if I fully trusted in Jesus I was to *act faith* by getting up ... I felt an inward voice, 'rise up and walk' ... instead of resisting any longer, I was afraid of not obeying at once, so springing from the bed I called to a friend ... to give me her arm and with her I walked to the front door ... As soon as my feet touched the floor I felt no longer pain in my ankles or knees, and immediately my soul was filled with the love of Jesus!"[2]

The healing of Mrs Mottashed and that of Mrs Le Messurier's son were separated by a period of less than two years, but the differences between their accounts illustrate a fundamental shift in how faith and healing were conceptualized in Victorian Canada. Mrs Le Messurier's son had been healed in December 1879, and the mother noted that "at that time I had no knowledge of 'faith healing.'" Her search for a cure was carried out on an individual basis, pleading earnestly with God alone for the life of her son. In contrast, Mrs Mottashed was introduced to divine healing through the agency of a network of women, was read one of the most popular works on the subject, and participated in a prayer circle that crossed vast distances. These elements were all absent in the narrative of Mrs Le Messurier, and when she later became aware of the existence of the divine healing movement, the jubilant mother transposed the restoration of her son to the new interest in faith healing. In fact, her account actually belongs to the preceding era, before the theoretical and practical apparatus of divine healing had been effectively formulated within Canadian Protestantism. Both women sought and received an answer to prayer for their healing, but the "prayer of faith" held a new meaning for those who followed in the wake of Mrs Mottashed.

The testimony of Mottashed in 1881 signalled the arrival of the Protestant divine healing movement in Victorian Canada. Until the end of the decade, however, the practice of faith healing in Canada operated outside of any formal organizational or institutional framework. Those interested in faith healing, such as "Miss C.," would visit the sick at the bedside, but their local efforts were bound together by an informal network that shared books, tracts, and religious periodicals through the mail. Within this context, the healing narrative played an important role as a vehicle for propagating the message of divine healing across the continent. Healing narratives were an integral component of divine healing, as both a public outreach for encouraging the practice of faith healing and a private means in which the suffering could reconstruct their own perceptions of illness and healing. As an historical source, they offer a unique insight into how women and men negotiated the gender roles and social geography of health and medicine. The devotional elements of healing testimonials has tended to marginalize them in the eyes of historians, but their inherently religious nature endowed them with a subversive dynamic that critically engaged the surrounding culture.

NARRATIVE NETWORKS

The emergence and spread of the divine healing movement in North America was facilitated primarily by informal networks rather than by formal structures or organizations. These networks encompassed a wide variety of small-scale activities that relied upon intimate and personal contact through bedside visitations, sending tracts and books through the mail, and holding regular meetings of prayer groups. The amount of activity generated around faith healing led one self-described "invalid" to complain to the *Canadian Baptist* that he was tired of the several "sincere persons" who had written to urge acceptance of the "faith-cure" despite his disavowal of the practice. Feeling badgered by such well-wishers, the sufferer was angered that when he did not go along with his minister's wish to assign a time for special prayers for healing, the pastor "accused me of lack of faith."[3] For those who were more open to the message of faith healing, it was the availability of printed works on the subject that was often noted as a major influence in strengthening their conviction to trust in prayer. Particularly in rural Canada, where isolation compounded physical ailments, the arrival of a testimony or treatise of divine healing connected the sufferer to an extended community of believers who offered encouragement, support, and prayers.

The literature of faith healing generally fell into three categories: 1) theological books justifying the scriptural basis of divine healing; 2) devotional works or tracts that relied heavily upon recent accounts of healing; and 3) religious periodicals that offered some general news items but largely combined pieces of devotional inspiration with theological expositions. Although historical treatments of divine healing have concentrated on the theological treatises produced by men such as W.E. Boardman, A.J. Gordon, and R.L. Stanton, most sufferers who found relief in prayer credited the devotional tracts and books, composed largely of healing testimonials, as having inspired their decision to trust in faith healing. Healing narratives appeared in many places, often printed as letters to the editor or distributed as pamphlets and tracts. Since most individual testimonials were not long enough to warrant their own separate publication in book form, many were compiled together into volumes of healing narratives. Charles Cullis employed this technique to great effect in a succession of works: *Faith Cures* (1879), *More Faith Cures* (1881), and *Other Faith Cures* (1885). The remarkable popularity and availability of narratives inspired one editor, H.H. Spiher, to produce a robust volume entitled *The World's Physician, Christ the Lord, or, Five-Hundred Testimonials of Healing, Answer to Prayer through the Ages* (1895).

Perhaps the most popular account of faith healing in North America, and certainly the one cited most often in Canadian testimonials, was Carrie Judd's *The Prayer of Faith* (1880). *The Prayer of Faith* combined Judd's own account of healing with short expositions designed to encourage those seeking healing through prayer. Other healing testimonials of varying lengths were interspersed throughout the book. The form was generally similar to Cullis's *Faith Cures*, but Judd's work was written in a far more personal and intimate style; it employed a first-person narrative and a vocabulary rich in romantic imagery. Judd's mother was known locally as a poet, and Judd herself had published her own book of poems in 1878.[4]

The Prayer of Faith was very popular in Canada, and many others besides Mrs Mottashed gave it special notice in their later testimonials. Given the proximity of Buffalo to the Ontario border, it is not surprising that many narratives from this province mention Judd. But *The Prayer of Faith* reached other areas of Canada as well. Soon after its publication, proponents of faith healing in Montreal were sharing the book with those who might benefit from it, and in 1884 the book arrived in New Glasgow, Nova Scotia, where it encouraged at least one woman to hold on to the promise of healing despite the objections of her minister.[5]

Although Canadian advocates of faith healing lacked the publishing resources of their associates in the United States or Great Britain, they were nevertheless integrated within the transatlantic divine healing movement. Canadian testimonials were regularly carried in American periodicals, which had a wide circulation in Canada. Even *The Way of*

Faith, a holiness magazine based in Columbia, South Carolina, reprinted the occasional letter from Nova Scotia, and when evangelist
B.H. Irwin held a campaign in Winnipeg in 1896, he reported securing
thirty-seven new subscriptions for the serial.[6] In Montreal, publisher
F.E. Grafton took an interest in the subject and printed a compilation
of Canadian testimonials collected by a local minister, E.D. Mallory,
who was active in promoting divine healing. This work, *Touching the
Hem: A Record of Faith Healing* (1884), included an appendix of ex-
cerpts from Cullis, Boardman, and Gordon. In an advertisement at the
back of the book, Grafton offered many of the most popular works on
faith healing for sale, including Judd's *The Prayer of Faith*, and subscriptions to two monthly magazines: Judd's *Triumphs of Faith* and the
British periodical, *Thy Healer.*[7]

While Grafton's publishing connections and advertisements illustrate
one aspect of Canada's links to a transatlantic network of divine healing, the narratives collected by Mallory reveal a more striking facet of
the movement. With a title that drew upon the parable of the woman
who reached for the garment of Jesus as he passed by, *Touching the
Hem* reflected the gendered nature of Victorian faith healing. Of the
seven cases compiled by Mallory, all were first-person testimonials
written by women. Four letters from men were also printed, but these
were, without exception, written by clergy to support the claims of the
women rather than testimonials of their own.

This pattern of female voices dominating narratives of healing was
repeated throughout the divine healing movement. In the *Triumphs of
Faith*, more than eight of every ten testimonials were written by
women. A comparative sampling from the *Christian Alliance and Foreign Missionary Weekly* reveals a similar pattern.[8] The collections of
"faith cures" compiled by Cullis also point to the same conclusion:
women were, by far, the preeminent voice in narrating personal experiences of faith healing. Because historians have tended to focus on the
activities of theologians, the dramatic gendering of the divine healing
movement itself has never been explored. This aspect becomes visible
when the historical perspective is redirected towards popular devotional literature and the healing narratives themselves.

The focus on the theological aspects of divine healing has also tended
to obscure the active role of women in promoting the prayer of faith.
When the actual operation of the divine healing network is closely examined, the female presence is readily apparent. Illness was a private
affair at the end of the nineteenth century, falling within the parameters
of middle-class Victorian domesticity where women were the guardians
of both the physical and spiritual health of the family. The bedside of
the sick was a carefully controlled space in which doctors and ministers

were occasionally welcomed as visitors, but not without the watchful eye of a matron close by.[9]

The social space of Victorian illness allowed some women to take a more active role in encouraging healing. While they remained generally invisible to the public eye, healing narratives suggest that many women promoted faith healing by toiling at the bedside of the sick. In Toronto, Sarah Carline recalled that when she was suffering, "a lady called on me, and told me she believed God had sent her, and that if I would accept Jesus as the Divine Healer, he would restore me to health."[10] The healing activities of these women are a subtle presence in the background of many narratives, but very little is known about them because this ministry of healing was almost always informal and unofficial in nature. The personal experience and activities of Mary Gainforth of Trenton, Ontario, demonstrates how these networks operated. Introduced to the doctrine through an American holiness periodical, Gainforth recovered from an illness after being anointed with oil, but later lost her healing. After regaining her faith, she "immediately wrote Mrs. Best, of Peterboro [sic], and Miss Wood, of New York to unite with me in prayer for my healing. Dear Sister Best came to me ... friends in Peterboro [sic] had agreed to unite in prayer for me ... Mrs. Best came and prayed with me ... so we took the promise of God to cleanse me from all unrighteousness."[11] As a result of her recovery, people from the surrounding community started to come to Gainforth for anointing, an act which she was hesitant to perform at first. However, after attending a divine healing convention in Toronto, she returned emboldened and "felt that I could better help others." Anointing people thereafter became a regular feature of Gainforth's own ministry of healing.[12] Active, informal networks of women reinforced the lines of communication established by faith healing literature sent through the mail, and these networks continued to operate even after more formal structures dedicated to faith healing had been established.

The dominance of women in the practice of divine healing could potentially lead to strained relations within the family. The husbands of women who engaged in faith healing were often placed in an ambiguous position if they did not completely support the doctrine. While a number of male household heads expressed their encouragement, there are notable silences in many healing narratives about the role of the husband. Gainforth recounted how she felt God had called her to relocate to a house within the town of Trenton so that "I could be of more use for Him." However, her son was very sick and her husband had not consented to move. It was only after her husband relented in his decision that she was able to anoint her son on the forehead and he was instantly healed.[13]

While the practice of faith healing was deeply gendered, it was not an exclusively female activity. Men were also attracted to the divine healing movement, but in Canada men were often exposed to the movement in a very different way. Women were largely dependent upon the postal service and a close network of friends for information and support. Canadian men interested in faith healing often investigated the phenomenon at well-known centres in the United States. Rev. J.A. Ivison, of Strathroy, Ontario, was "a little skeptical" when he arrived at Judd's Faith Rest Cottage in Buffalo, but soon "all doubts vanished and my judgment became fully convinced of the glorious possibility of obtaining any blessing that we needed, spiritual or physical in answer to the prayer of faith."[14] Ivison found healing for his heart disease and rheumatism, and upon returning to Strathroy he was full of confidence that his wife too could be healed. The pattern of travelling to Boston, New York, or Buffalo to visit Cullis, Simpson, or Judd was repeated by many Canadian men interested in faith healing. W.J. Fenton, an Irish-born Presbyterian who had converted to the Plymouth Brethren, suffered from epileptic seizures until he left his home in Toronto to be anointed by Simpson in New York in 1886.[15] E.D. Mallory relocated to Boston in 1882 to serve as pastor of Cullis's Grove Hall Church and married the daughter of Cullis's second wife.[16] In contrast, when Mary Gainforth wanted to attend a convention in Toronto that featured A.B. Simpson, her husband declared that he could not afford to send her, and it was only through providential circumstances that she was able to go.[17]

Since the men who were actively engaged in the divine healing movement were usually members of the clergy, professional accreditation gave them a level of authority in dealing with the sick, particularly in relation to the sacramental nature of performing an anointing with oil, as outlined in James 5:14. Lacking official status, the women called to a ministry of healing nevertheless used their own position as guardians of domestic health to establish extended informal networks that were beyond the reach of any institutional control. Women wrote the vast majority of healing narratives, and were in turn far more likely to be inspired to seek divine healing through reading devotional literature and testimonials than men, who did not describe their experience of healing in terms of long periods of bedridden contemplation. Ministers and doctors were figures of male professional authority who operated on the fringes of the private, devotional space of women. When women turned to faith healing it was often the intimacy of contact with other women or the private contemplation of materials that had been sent to them that fostered a deeper desire to trust in the prayer of faith.

A CALL TO TESTIFY

Mrs Edwards of Woodstock, Ontario, received a healing for an inflammation of the lungs after corresponding with friends in New York State
who prayed for her at an appointed time. However, Edwards feared
that she "did not glorify God ... I only told a few Christian friends of
the blessing received in answer to prayer, and it was necessary for me to
have another trial of faith." Only after a second bout of illness was
Mrs Edwards able to realize her mistake, and writing to the *Triumphs
of Faith* became a way to fulfil the obligation to testify: "I make this
public statement of God's dealings with me ... that His name may be
glorified, and that other suffering ones may be led to look unto Him
Who 'Himself took our infirmities and bare our sicknesses.'"[18]

Testifying was a well-established practice within evangelicalism, but
the initial emphasis lay upon the conversion experience as a focal point
in marking the break between the former life of sin and the new life of
grace and salvation. During the nineteenth century, however, fears that
conversion had become too "easy" shifted the ground of testimonials towards the experience of sanctification. The call to testify became virtu-
ally an obligation upon consecrating oneself to God, particularly within
Phoebe Palmer's altar theology, which placed the responsibility to claim
the promise of holiness upon the individual. Public testimony was regarded as necessary evidence of a sanctified life and Palmer left little
room to manoeuvre on this point, claiming that "believing with the
heart, and confessing with the mouth, stand closely connected." Failure
to offer such a witness "proves that your faith is yet defective."[19]

With the close connections between holiness and the divine healing
movement, it is not surprising that bodily restoration became linked
with the will to testify. One faith healing evangelist echoed Palmer's
sentiments in declaring "If you, being healed, render not unto the Lord,
can you expect to stay healed? You must confess the blessing if you
wish to keep it."[20] Many who were initially healed, but then suffered
relapses, often blamed such setbacks on the failure to testify sufficiently
to their healing. One woman wrote to Carrie Judd that after her initial
healing she had been overcome by a deepening sense of despair. Confessing that she had testified "in easy places only," she declared "Today, on my knees, in my closet, I have promised my precious Saviour
that I would testify even in hard places, He giving me the power to do
so. I consecrated my heart and lips to His service, in this regard."[21] In
Toronto, Mrs Ellen Hatch described how, when she was afflicted with
so many ailments that she could not sleep, she "almost lived on narcotics." When she trusted in God, however, "I slept like a little child."
Unfortunately, she kept these prayers a secret and the insomnia

returned. It was only after she was willing to testify that her peaceful nights were restored.[22] Faith healing was not simply something in which one could believe, it had to be publicly professed both to maintain the state of health and to illustrate that the restored body was indeed working in "His service."

As a public declaration, the act of narrating sickness crossed a number of gendered boundaries. To openly discuss illness was to admit to bodily weakness, a social construction that did not align with masculine ideals of health and vitality. Historians of Victorian masculinity point to how the "inner experience of manhood – a sense of manly confidence radiating outward from the virtuous self," was transformed at the end of the nineteenth century into an external set of "physical characteristics" created by athletic endeavours.[23] Healing narratives, however, required the very exposition of "inner experience" that masculine anxieties were starting to shun as physical culture increasingly defined ideals of manhood. In her study of tuberculosis in America, Katherine Ott observes that the disease "emasculated men by taking away their ability to act ... A debilitated man could not carouse, sport, and labour; that is, he could not be manly."[24] Given these cultural constructions, it is not surprising that men were reluctant or unwilling to present themselves as "unmanly." The very structure and format of testimonials did not fit the new masculine emphasis on vigour, forcefulness, and decisiveness that men were expected to display in public.

Men interested in the divine healing movement often separated their personal experience of healing from general expositions on the nature of faith healing, conceptualising the phenomenon in abstract terms.[25] Because most of the men involved in the movement were either members of the clergy or lay evangelists, establishing the scriptural authority of divine healing was a central concern. As the pursuit of healing was tightly interwoven with men's professional identity, their writings reflect a wider engagement with theological issues justifying the prayer of faith. In contrast, women, who could not lay claim to the status or position of men, integrated their personal testimony with broad social concerns. It was women's personal experience in itself that granted them the authority, and the obligation, to witness publicly and carry forth the message of faith healing. This personal experience of the divine, an experience that required testimony to maintain it, provided women with a social space in which their voices could be heard.

In her analysis of evangelical conversion narratives, historian Virginia Brereton notes that testimonials hold both a primary devotional purpose as well as "submerged plots" that speak to a wider context: "There is an obvious, literal reading of the nineteenth-century narrative: whatever else it did besides, the narrative described an intense spiritual experience ...

But of course conversion took place in a wider social and cultural setting, and therefore its narration had great significance for women as social and cultural actors. Like other forms of nineteenth-century female writing, conversion narratives both affirmed women's role in a patriarchal society and subverted some of the assumptions of that society."[26] Narratives of faith healing operated in a similar fashion. Their primary focus was always devotional, encouraging one towards a deeper spiritual life where healing could be claimed. Underlying the literal reading of the text, however, were discourses that reveal how women negotiated alternative conceptions of the body and rescripted their experience of illness in relation to the social environment. As Brereton suggests, such narratives both affirmed and subverted the cultural constructions facing Victorian women.

What follows is a comparative examination of two of the most important healing testimonials published in the nineteenth century. The significance of Carrie Judd's *The Prayer of Faith* in carrying word of divine healing to Canada and abroad has already been noted. No Canadian woman could match Judd's stature within the divine healing movement, but in scale and influence, the most prominent Canadian testimonial was the healing of Maggie Scott. The two travelled very different paths, with Judd marrying a wealthy businessman, George Montgomery, and moving to the west coast where she was successively involved in the Salvation Army and pentecostalism while maintaining her "Home of Peace" in the temperance town of Beulah Heights, California.[27] Scott started out in the type of evangelistic work that Judd had pioneered, but later decided to pursue a missionary career. In 1890 she left for China under the auspices of the China Inland Mission, but returned within two years after falling ill and contracting tuberculosis, dying in 1893.[28] Although never as influential as Judd, in the early 1880s Scott's recovery and testimonial was the most famous example of faith healing in Canada, and her narrative was carried in religious periodicals as far away as California.[29]

Despite their divergent trajectories, the published accounts of the healing of Judd and Scott share a number of significant similarities. Although Judd was raised as an Episcopalian in an urban environment while Scott grew up in a rural Presbyterian household, their religious development was marked by a conversion at the young ages of eleven and thirteen respectively. Both traced their illness to a traumatic event that occurred in their youth. At the age of eighteen, Judd was on her way to classes at Buffalo Normal School when an unexpected fall on an icy sidewalk injured her spine. Scott was a fourteen-year-old girl walking the two miles of country roads between her school and "Mount Joy Farm" when back pain struck suddenly and left her immobilized.[30]

Both women traced their afflictions to a problem with "spinal nerves," which left them helpless and inflicted with a great burden. In Judd's case, the "hyperaesthesia" included an acute sensitivity to noise so that even the "tiniest jar or noise in the room, was something indescribably dreadful."[31] It was light that caused Scott the most difficulty, producing extreme pain in her head and acting on "every fibre, nerve and muscle of my body." Physicians could offer little assistance, but they duly diagnosed Scott's paralysis below the waist as "acute spinal disease," or "hyperaemia," and suggested that she would probably die at any moment.[32] Both women were secluded in their bedrooms, "utterly helpless," able to do little except occasional reading.

Judd and Scott were both quick to place their bodily travails within a religious context. Judd later recalled that "I had the idea that if I tried to be very patient during my affliction, this in itself would draw me nearer to the Lord."[33] Scott went even further in associating her growing physical ailments with a strengthening of religious conviction, revealing that "To me the prospect of death was a most delightful one. To be free from all pain; to be at home with Jesus." Her state of helplessness led to a deeper contemplation, a "perfect peace" that overcame physical distractions: "When my helpless body was racked with exquisite suffering, His 'everlasting arms' were indeed 'underneath' and around me, and while He held and kept me in His strong and tender embrace I did not doubt His love or wisdom in thus afflicting His child."[34] Drawing nearer to God and the desire to witness one so blessed were the reasons that Scott prayed that "every mental and spiritual faculty – might be preserved entire," despite the fact that she had been assured that if she lived, insanity would be the result of her suffering.[35]

The deathbed was widely regarded as a place of divine peace, and a large body of Victorian religious literature was devoted to the "good death." The narratives of Judd and Scott, each illustrating a young woman at peace with imminent mortality, also drew upon a more secular aesthetic that valued such deaths as "beautiful." The martyrdom of a young woman was a powerful Victorian metaphor in both novels and art, from the death of Jane Eyre's school friend, Helen, to the work of Pre-Raphaelite artists such as Dante Gabriel Rossetti, who immortalized his own lover, the poet Elizabeth Siddall, as she suffered through a prolonged fatal illness. As Edgar Allan Poe declared in an oft-quoted phrase, "the death, then, of a beautiful woman is, unquestionably, the most poetical topic in the world."[36] Healing testimonials, therefore, were framed within an aesthetic that could be simultaneously viewed through secular and religious lenses. The intended "beauty" or "good" in the midst of suffering constructed by Scott and Judd was faith and the divine presence of Christ. To outside observers, however, the image of feminine youth prostrated upon the sick bed could only compound the appeal of their narratives.[37]

If currents of Victorian romanticism were evident in the construction of illness, healing narratives both adopted and subverted the concept of a passive femininity that inspired through suffering. It was not the death, but the restoration of the body that was celebrated in women's testimonials; the idea that women's bodies *should* be strong was diametrically opposed to the romantic image of beautiful death. Scott was only partially satisfied that in suffering she was "doing His work on my bed, and that this was His will concerning me for the present – for a 'little while.'" When Judd informed her mother that she felt she still had a mission in life, her mother replied, "Your mission may be to lie here and suffer and be an example of patience to others, as you have been." Unconvinced, Judd replied, "No, Mother, I mean an *active mission.*" Patient suffering was not a virtue, but rather a preparation for a deeper religious experience, a "plowshare breaking up the hard ground, to make it ready for the work of the Holy Spirit."[38] Both Judd and Scott felt a distinct call to Christian service that was "active," something beyond the scope of ministering from the sick bed.

The catalyst for Judd's healing was a letter from an African-American faith healer, Sarah Mix. Mix introduced Judd to the practice of praying for the afflicted across distances at appointed times, advising her that "Whether the person is present or absent, if it is a 'prayer of faith' it is all the same, and God has promised to raise up the sick ones." However, certain steps were required in order to achieve healing: "You will first have to lay aside all medicine of every description. Use no remedies of any kind for anything. Lay aside trusting in the 'arm of flesh,' and lean wholly upon God and His promises … [the female prayer group] will make you a subject of prayer … I want you to pray for yourself, and pray believing and then *act faith*. It makes no difference how you feel, but get right out of bed and begin to walk by faith. Strength will come, disease will depart and you will be made whole." When Judd rose from her bed after praying at the appropriate time, she reported that there was "no excitement," but that her soul was filled with a "childlike peace and confidence."[39]

Because Judd had reproduced Mix's letter in *The Prayer of Faith*, Scott knew of this practice and promptly wrote to Mix, Judd, and Charles Cullis, requesting prayers and receiving replies from Cullis and Judd. At 3:00 pm on All Hallows' Eve, 1882, members of the Scott household retired to their rooms to pray for Maggie, only her mother remaining at her side. After spending almost an hour in prayer, Maggie felt a commanding presence and knew that "the Bridegroom cometh":

Lifting my heart to Him for more strength to make the effort to sit up, I made a slight effort to raise my head off the pillow, and at once I found myself raised slowly up to a sitting posture, by a power entirely outside of self. I felt no sensible impression upon me, nor any peculiar sensation whatever. The pain had not left me then, but I did not wait to think of that, I was too eager to go on to obey the entire command, to go out to meet the bridegroom! and again I looked up to Him to make me stand on my feet ... My first delightful feeling was that of having indeed met the Bridegroom, and of being held in His strong, loving embrace. I was standing! and about the pains. All were gone! they had been mysteriously removed while I was in the act of rising. I felt no weakness, I was perfectly healed, and the Lord Himself had done it![40]

The poetic death has been transformed from the prostration of the body to a submission of the will. The sexual overtones Scott employs were not uncommon in nineteenth-century evangelical devotion, but the spatial context of the bedroom recasts the site of death (literally, the deathbed) into a place of fulfilment (metaphorically marital). Subverting the multiple layers of romantic imagery is the restoration of the female body as whole.

Obviously, not all of the healing narratives follow this pattern exactly. Many of the women were not young, many were not suffering from diseases defined as a nervous condition, and a few narratives were written by men. However, there is a relationship between the popularity of these two cross-border testimonials and the aesthetic properties they share, which made them so inspiring to others. If not every narrative followed the exact same pattern, most exhibited at least some of these dominant elements, and all laid claim to the common ground of devotional inspiration.

Testimonials were written as a means to maintain divine health, a part of the "active mission" that consecrated bodies were called to. In this capacity they served as a dynamic force, rather than a static documentation of a singular experience. As an autobiographical form of writing, healing narratives defined the gendered self in multiple ways. John Barbour suggests that through autobiography, the writer "discerns the influences of various elements of her culture and affirms or challenges them. This normative assessment of the cultures forming the self reflects both moral and religious formation and self-transcendence."[41] For women who wrote testimonials, part of this self-transcendence was the projection of healthy bodies as a beacon to light the way for others to follow. This dynamic scripting of the active body also entailed a critical engagement with the world that surrounded them. The restoration of women's bodies as healthy and whole was a narrative strategy intended to inspire devotion, but it also intersected and countered the prevailing medical discourses of healing, health, and women's bodies.

DOCTORS, DRUGS, AND THE BODY

"Men don't want to be sick. Women want to be well," observed one commentator of Aimee Semple McPherson's healing campaign in Dayton, Ohio in 1920.[42] The statement encapsulated the gendered perceptions of the body that women faced in the nineteenth and early-twentieth centuries. Health was regarded as a normal state of being for men, but it had to be constantly sought by women. Victorian medicine was fascinated with the "oppositional" nature of women's bodies, defined by the universal norm of the male body. Sexual difference was the comprehensive key to understanding all aspects of women's health. A 1917 edition of *The 20th Century Family Physician* noted that "Woman's entire being, therefore, mental and moral, as well as physical, is fashioned and directed by her reproductive powers."[43] Popular medical books carried Victorian notions of the gendered body well into the twentieth century. *The People's Common Sense Medical Adviser* reaffirmed that it was woman's uterus and ovaries, "with which her system is in intimate sympathy," that rendered her "doubly susceptible to injurious influences and a resulting series of diseases," from which men were exempted. In short, "Physically and mentally, woman is man modified."[44] Women's bodies were effectively denied from achieving a perfect state of universal health, since sexual difference had rendered the female body incapable of achieving the efficient standard of wellness projected for the male body. As Wendy Mitchinson contends in her study of women and their physicians in Victorian Canada, "By focusing on the very part of the body that made women female, doctors deemed the poor health of women natural and something they could not escape."[45]

Critics of the divine healing movement were aware of its gendered nature and used the prevalence of female subjects and women's diseases as a way to explain and dismiss the phenomenon of faith healing. Dr Daniel Clark, superintendent of Toronto's Asylum for the Insane, noted that "the large number of invalids cured in this way are women, in whom nervous diseases, especially hysteria, do most abound. It is safe to say that at least 75 per cent of the whole are such weaklings. Women are more religious than men; they are more emotional, more sensitive and as a result are more impressionable, the imagination is more active, the sympathies are more intense, in fact the mind is more receptive in aught appertaining to occult agencies, for good or evil, acting upon these aptitudes and natural belongings."[46] As illustrated by Clark, faith healing intersected two central perceptions of gender and the body: women were "naturally" deemed to be both more inclined to religion and more susceptible to disease. However, what was perceived as women's weakness by Clark could also be inverted. These same gendered constructions of the body and religion were the basis for a claim to health through divine healing that explicitly and implicitly challenged the dominant medical paradigm. Because religious faith was constructed as a sacred, private, domestic space, women could lay claim to healing, and a wholeness of body, through the divine.

The key to subverting the scientific body was a redemption of the body as more than carnal and sinful, elevating it to the status of a valuable receptacle worthy of being filled with the divine. Not surprisingly, proponents of faith healing readily turned to the long-standing tradition of physiological perfectionism and health reform movements for the rhetoric and understanding of the body as naturally healthy and whole. In the hands of the faith healers, "health" was reframed and transformed from a materialistic understanding of the body operating at its peak efficiency, to a balanced bodily state, strengthened and sustained by a constant infusion of the divine. Faith healing was not understood as an instantaneous, miraculous cure, but rather as an acting-out of consecration, the body's diseases and decay being countered by the presence of the Holy Spirit. Henry Wilson, a Canadian Anglican divine who adopted faith healing, explained that: "Divine Healing is simply Divine Health; that is, God's health infused into us, physically as well as spiritually." It was this sense of "divine health" that proponents drew upon in redeeming the body as a "natural" receptacle for the higher spirit. For Carrie Judd Montgomery the "indwelling Health" abided within, "to spring up continually with rejuvenating power in every organ and nerve, in every tissue and fibre of this wonderful physical organism."[47]

Health as a consecrated state of spiritual indwelling appealed to women precisely because divine health was perfect, even for female bodies, which were automatically regarded as inherently flawed. Women could lay claim to a state of wholeness through divine healing that was denied to them by medical discourse constructed around universal male norms. It was precisely because their experience of healing was divine that women were allowed a voice in which to narrate their experience of illness. These voices have not been examined in relation to health and healing because they are deemed "religious" by historians and doctors alike, but it was the social space of religion that provided a meaningful platform for women to assert their own personal authority based on a divine experience. As patients, there were few places for women to articulate a serious critique of medical practice. As active servants of God, the restored bodies of women demanded testimonials to God's power. Narratives always subscribed to a devotional purpose, but their structure was flexible enough to allow an underlying commentary upon Victorian medical practice.

The didactic role of testimonials were never in doubt, as the dedication page of Judd's *Prayer of Faith* made clear by addressing the volume to "THE SUFFERING ONES Who are Toiling on with scarce Strength to Lift their Burdens" in order that it might bring "the Faith and Hope which will Inspire Them to Seek for Health of Body, and Greater strength of Soul, from Christ, the Great Physician." The narrative structure of the testimonials typically followed a formulaic pattern, adopting many of the conventions that were already well-established by the large body of conversion narratives that characterized evangelicalism. Opening with a few words of praise, scripture, or thanksgiving, the stories quickly move to recount the depth of suffering endured. Sometimes the symptoms were vague and indeterminate, while other testimonials went to great lengths to illustrate their exact condition, complete with doctors' technical diagnoses. At the nadir of despair or the height of a paroxysm, the believer finally submits to the will of God, but only after considerable soul-searching and spiritual awakening. Healing then restores the body, but even more joyful than the physical recovery is the consecrated state of the soul, which experiences an abundance of grace. Occasionally there are relapses, or periods of doubting, when an illness will return only to be conquered again. The narratives often closed with words of encouragement to others or a dedication to continue doing God's work in divine health.

There were many variations upon this theme, but in practically all of the divine healing testimonials the central dramatic tension was created by contrasting the unenlightened darkness of sin and affliction with the joy of sanctification and divine health. Within this conventional plot structure, however, women could insert a number of "submerged plots" that presented alternative narratives to the foremost devotional objective. Some of these plot lines mirrored those discussed by Brereton in her analysis of conversion narratives, such as the use of religious experience to justify exuberant behaviour or actions that women otherwise would have found socially questionable outside of the religious context.[48] What is particularly striking about the healing testimonials are the alternative storylines that engaged, and ultimately undermined, the position of medical therapeutics in nineteenth-century society. Discussions of medicine, the role of doctors, drugs, and the body were strategically located to subvert conventional medical assumptions. The religious nature of the faith healing narratives provided a legitimate space for women to reconstruct their own experience of illness, and to renegotiate their relationship to medicine and medical culture.

For the most part the leaders of the divine healing movement were careful not to criticize doctors and physicians directly. John Alexander Dowie was the controversial exception to this pattern, labelling "Physicians, Surgeons and Druggists" as "that banded trinity of poisoners and murderers."[49] Cullis, as a homeopathic physician, was far more charitable, claiming that doctors were still needed to treat the unconverted: "let the world have the doctors, and Christians the great Physician."[50] For W.E. Boardman, "the Lord has nothing against physicians, as such," which was demonstrated by the fact that even the apostle Luke was a physician as well as being a "beloved, honored evangelist and writer."[51] Of course, Boardman goes to great lengths to point out that Luke, "however highly he esteemed the healing art," obviously cherished divine healing more, since he was so willing to write accounts of it in the gospel. The evangelist Charles Ryder agreed with this line of reasoning, allowing that while "it may not be wicked" to see a physician, there was certainly "a better way." The distinction was made on the basis of faith: "If you haven't faith in God as a Divine Healer, it is your religious duty to get a physician, for your body is a very sacred thing. But if a man has given his body to the Lord Jesus it is the temple of the Holy Ghost, the meeting-house of God, and it seems to me that God wants His servants to have perfect confidence in Him and to be upheld by Him, and kept from bodily suffering by Him, so we need not depend upon medicine."[52]

The role of the physician enters into many of the healing narratives. For some the doctor is a "good Christian" who might point them towards divine healing as a last resort, or, at the least, pose no objections to patients who wish to take such a course. It was believed that the best doctors were those who combined physical diagnoses with a concern for the soul of the patient. Mrs Duncan was thankful for "the skill and patience of my physician, who had been enabled to give me temporary relief for the body and to minister spiritual consolation ... I *do* wish that no physician was allowed to give medicine who cannot also give spiritual counsel." Duncan was surprised when it was her physician that suggested that she turn to a faith healer for help.[53] Although it did not cure her serious "internal troubles," Libbie Osburn found her stay at a Christian "water cure" very refreshing, and her physician actively encouraged her to pray for healing while continuing her regular remedies.[54] At times, however, Christian doctors did not seem very enthralled with the prospect of divine healing. When Alice Bodaly from

Port Sarnia, Ontario, asked her doctor to pray for her, "He kindly but positively told me that for me there was no earthly help, and he didn't seem to believe in asking God for impossibilities."[55]

More often, the physician was used as a reference point in order to frame the severity of an illness. A critical diagnosis was all the more critical coming from a doctor "classed among the most celebrated physicians in the city."[56] Cases that could be referred to local medical boards were particularly dramatic. Perhaps conscious that critics were dismissing faith healing as little more than a variation of mental healing, Henrietta Houlgrave recounted in her testimony that a lung specialist from Stratford, Ontario, had "examined the mucus which I raised, and I myself saw through a microscope the living microbes, and then knew that ... [no] earthly thing could effect a cure."[57] Within these narratives, the doctor clearly serves as a professional authority employed to establish the veracity of an illness, perhaps a tacit acknowledgment that women's own testimonies on this issue might be regarded as untrustworthy. The American Methodist critic James Buckley was already questioning the validity of claims to faith healing on these grounds: "All honest and rational persons are competent to testify whether they feel sick ... but their testimony as to what disease they had, or whether they are entirely cured, is a different matter, and to have value must be scrutinized in every case by competent judges."[58] One woman reluctantly visited a physician in order to receive his diagnosis, admitting that she "had but one object in getting this information, to silence skeptics afterwards."[59]

The doctor as the good Christian and the professional expert were characterizations that were generally used to support the main plot of suffering, salvation, and recovery. However, alternative discourses recast the physician in less auspicious roles. Reflecting popular fears about how the development of obstetrics and gynecology gave physicians too much control over women's bodies, the most radical critique of doctors came from Dowie, who denounced them collectively as the "most immoral profession out of hell." Women were more than willing to give Dowie ammunition by testifying to mistreatment at the hands of their doctors: "when I lay upon that man's dissecting table ... he stole my virtue and defiled my body."[60] A long testimonial by Mary Schmitz complained bitterly about a doctor who hurt her spine, but instead of rectifying the situation properly, he "operated on a place he ought not to have touched." Another doctor "operated on my rectum, but I did not know that I ever had any disease there." Other difficulties and malpractice followed until she found herself on the operating table again, facing "about a dozen doctors, but I did not know any of them. When I came in they were all dressed like Butchers, with their white caps and aprons. They removed some important organs. In fact they left but little which was removable."[61]

Dowie's controversial battles with the medical profession encouraged this rhetoric. Schmitz's testimony was featured on the front page of Dowie's periodical, *Leaves of Healing*, with the glaring title "Mercilessly Butchered by Surgeons. Healed By God." More respectable publications would not relate accusations of sexual impropriety or welcome the analogy of physicians as butchers. Nevertheless, women's healing narratives reveal many subtle portrayals of doctors inflicting suffering upon the body, and women carefully constructed their experience with illness in a manner that undermined the authoritative claims of doctors.

A common narrative strategy was to question the authority of science and medicine by contrasting the wide variety of diagnoses that might be received by different physicians. Upon discovering a painful lump in her breast, S.A. Hanscombe testified that she approached "Dr. G." and "was laughed at for my fears," the doctor pronouncing it a swollen gland. After three months and the pain growing rapidly worse, she consulted "Dr. C.," a female physician who thought it was an enlarged gland, and possibly cancerous. "Dr. S." could not understand what it was, and after "much thought and many inquiries" she turned to "Dr. B.," who, although kind and sympathetic, could offer no relief. Two more physicians pronounced it as cancer and another female doctor offered to have the cancer removed by using a "plaster," but Hanscombe was afraid she would not live through the experience, and "Dr. R.'s" "Ointment" provided no relief.[62] Hanscombe's narrative compiles her numerous encounters with physicians in a manner that clearly undermines their professional status and claim to authority. Mrs Ella Welch similarly saw eight physicians, but a "confliction in remedies" caused blood poisoning, and then another physician "only added to my misery by applying a wash that drove the eruption inward, affecting the brain and nerves."[63] Ostensibly, these narrative elements were meant to reinforce the sense of suffering in the face of affliction before receiving divine healing, but they also illustrate an underlying sense of frustration, openly exposing the vagaries of diagnosis that one could receive at the hands of physicians.

At times the torments of the devil and the torments of the doctors appear to converge rather painfully. From New Glasgow, Nova Scotia, Elizabeth Rose recounted that in dealing with a back injury she "consulted one doctor after another, but medicine did me no good. Thirty-six Spanish-fly blisters were applied at different times, besides many other applications."[64] A recent immigrant to America, Matilda Scanlon suffered from internal pains. Her testimony recounted how a "dry cup" treatment to the back of her neck only brought about "a most dreadful headache." Her case was passed on to a Presbyterian hospital, "as doctors often do to get rid of troublesome and incurable cases, I suppose." After being blistered three times over portions of her body, she turned to a homeopathic physician. When his drugs failed, he tried leeching her from the temples. However, when the leeches dropped off, Scanlon continued to bleed for ten hours. After recovering for a brief period, her health again declined, leading to more leeching, a stay in a women's homeopathic hospital, and five more doctors.[65] Maimie Quinlan was hospitalized under the care of a "kind doctor" until he was replaced by a physician who "tried every kind of treatment," some of which "was almost torture ... and after all failed to cure me as I grew to be a living skeleton."[66]

Unlike the Dowieites, most women rarely criticized physicians openly, but through their narratives, physicians could appear as little more than torturers of the body. Socially, women had few avenues through which to challenge professional medical authority, but the alternative storylines embedded within the healing narratives reveal charges of malpractice, frustration with conflicting diagnoses and medical attitudes, and a general bewilderment over the variety of medical options still available in the nineteenth century.[67] Even for those who did not describe their sufferings in such detail, the binary structure of the narrative usually placed the physician on the side of darkness, sin, and the devil, in contrast to the light and salvation offered by God. The impotence of the physicians is underscored by their "helplessness," while the real power to heal rests with the Great Physician.

If attitudes towards physicians varied in type and intensity, a consistent theme running through a great majority of the healing narratives was a determination to abstain from all human remedies and drugs. In the divine healing movement, to turn away from the use of drugs was an important act that symbolized one's faith in God rather than in human efforts. Unlike the occasional allowances given to doctors, drugs and remedies were never regarded as beneficial, and even if some symptoms were alleviated, relief was only fleeting. The reliance upon "human means" was seen as an obstacle to faith and divine healing. As Miss "E.H.P." reasoned in her healing narrative, "I thought how in times past I had really limited the healing power and application of faith, in looking for merely temporary alleviation, and not radical cure."[68]

The rejection of medical remedies was a central feature in many of the healing testimonies, and as a narrative element it was often employed to symbolize and contrast the difference between the old life of sickness and the new life in divine healing. In Matilda Scanlon's case, the morning after she was healed she declared that "I put my pellets, bottle and all into the stove, and watched them burn up. I immediately got great strength from this act of faith."[69] At times, the denial of medicine was almost ritualistic and sacramental, as in the case of Mrs Merrell, who, after reading portions of *The Prayer of Faith*, went to her room and solemnly removed all "remedial appliances" and prayed, "Lord, I give these to Thee. I will never put them on my body again. I throw my entire self on Thy word." The ceremony continued as Merrell then walked into another room and, without warning to the rest of her family, dropped to her knees in prayer declaring "I have given Thee my medicines, because I believe on Thy word." Taking all of the medicines in the room, Merrell proceeded to pour them on the ground, "all the while asking help in the name of God."[70] There are clear echoes of Phoebe Palmer's altar theology in these accounts: to lay one's burdens at the foot of the cross, sometimes leaving tokens of a worldly life behind, was part of the process used to achieve the second blessing. Not all rejections of medicine were quite as formalized; the moment after she was healed, Mrs Masury sprang to her feet, "opened the window, and threw out every drop of medicine."[71]

Like physicians, drugs and remedies were narrative elements that both supported the main plot and provided an opportunity to express alternative discourses. Sin, vice, or a worldly life were expected to tempt the body, but as the use of drugs in medicine increased, so did concerns about the ability of drugs to control the body. Many women were clearly uneasy about this aspect of modern medical culture. Healing narratives often made explicit the connection between a continued state of illness and having taken drugs at an early age. Mary McKelvey suffered from asthma and had been "dosed and doctored" since she was a child, but the remedies to treat the condition only produced "serious organic diseases of the heart."[72] Mrs Senft had been under a physician's care since birth and "medicine was the first thing that passed my lips." She reportedly tried both homeopathic and allopathic treatments and underwent cycles of "drugging, dieting, reading 'Laws of Health' and studying books on hygiene" until her room resembled "an apothecary shop."[73]

If the refusal to take medicine was symbolic of the new life in divine healing, it also represented a reaction to the drastic increase in the use of drugs in the nineteenth century, both as remedies in the hands of physicians and as a marketable commodity that bypassed physicians altogether. By the turn of the century, newspapers were full of advertisements for all kinds of miracle cures. Dr Williams' Pink Pills for Pale People was touted as a tonic to make the blood richer, particularly in the wake of a winter of poor ventilation: "Nature must be assisted in throwing off the poison that has accumulated in the system."[74] Drugs were increasing in medical practice, not simply as curative agents, but also as painkillers and anaesthetics, which allowed interventionist medicine increased access to the body. Even many doctors viewed the arrival of anaesthetics with misgivings. Earlier in the nineteenth century, pain was regarded as necessary to the healing process, and the debate about the physiological role of pain as a possible curative agent lasted into the 1880s. For advocates of the nineteenth-century health reform movement who employed various styles of "natural healing," pain represented nature's warning that the laws of health were being transgressed.[75]

The development of anaesthesia raised concerns about the ability of the patient to maintain control over the body. Dowie reinforced such fears by pointing out that powerful drugs would allow lecherous doctors to take advantage of women. In support of his contention, Dowie would read anonymous testimonials from women, such as one who claimed that her physician "first tried to seduce me. Failing in that he drugged me, and I became his harlot."[76] The same desire to maintain control was also expressed by Emma Whittemore, well-known for her later founding of New York's Door of Hope Mission, who was "filled ... with repugnance" at the thought of a hypodermic needle, fearing the "risk of losing that sweet conscious sense of my Saviour's presence, for even a short while, by consenting to stupefying my brain just in order to dull the pain."[77] A similar sentiment was shared by Laura Howland, the wife of the former mayor of Toronto, who testified at an Alliance convention that when she had to have a tooth removed, she refused the chloroform and "declared her intention to depend on the strength of God." Even though the tooth broke three times during the operation, Howland claimed that "she did not feel it at all."[78] Drugs, particularly painkillers and anaesthetics, interfered with the natural ability of the body to achieve perfection through a divine indwelling of health.

Morphine was one of the few drugs to be directly named in the healing testimonials instead of being simply categorized as a vague "remedy." Conquering its addictive nature supported the main narrative of faith in divine healing, but the powerful control that morphine could exert over one's body was also cast in a light that disparaged the use of drugs in Victorian medicine. Mary Mack reported that a pain in her back had been diagnosed as an "inflammation of the kidneys," but after "all kinds of medicine" were used, her stomach could not keep anything down. Treatments of blisters and leeches followed, but she was "in such pain, and could take no medicine in my stomach, so the doctor began to inject morphine." By the time Mack had turned to the faith healing of Mix, "I had been in the habit of having morphine injected five or six times in twenty-four hours, and the doctor said it would kill me to leave it off, but in answer to the prayer of faith I was enabled to leave it off entirely."[79] Even physicians were not immune from falling victim to their

Fig. 2.1. Illustration by Charles Champe. *Leaves of Healing*, 6 March 1901, p. 742.
Flower Pentecostal Heritage Center

own drugs. In Winnipeg, the stress of her medical practice led Dr Lilian Yeomans into an addiction of morphine and chloral hydrate. When she was treated at a "nervous sanitorium," physicians continued to inject her with the drug after she fell unconscious.[80] Dowie's cartoonist, Charles Champe, highlighted morphine's tentacular grip in figure 2.1, a vivid illustration of the bondage of drugs.

Morphine was singled out in the narratives not only because of its dangerous properties, but also because it was readily identifiable as a "human remedy" that could be worse than the original disease. Few drugs exercised the type of control that morphine could have on the body, and fears about being "bound as with fetters" to drugs or in "constant bondage to the medicine" were commonly expressed.[81] The clear parallels between the "bondage" of medicine and the "bondage" of sin produced an alternative narrative, giving a voice to women's concerns regarding the entrenchment and reliance upon drugs in a therapeutic culture. While the male leadership of the divine healing movement generally refrained from attacking physicians, the healing testimonials of women offered a much deeper critique of medical practice.

THE SOCIAL GEOGRAPHY OF FAITH HEALING

Victorian faith healing was an activity pursued primarily within a domestic environment. As a moral space devoted to Christian nurture, the home acquired a sacred status in the nineteenth century. Set apart from the public world of politics and industry, the middle-class home embodied feminine virtues and served as a place of moral rejuvenation. As Colleen McDannell notes, the Protestant practice of "domestic religion" was increasingly reliant upon maternal leadership as the father's role in moral instruction diminished. Within the home, women served as the guardians of both spiritual and physical health.[82]

In healing narratives, men rarely discussed the time they may have spent bedridden with sickness, but women often went to great lengths in describing the thoughts and feelings they had while confined to the bedroom. The bedroom was where devotional works or testimonies were read, where intimate conversations took place, where letters to close female friends were composed, where physicians or ministers might call, where one might be anointed with oil, where prayers were offered, and where healing took place. The theme of private space, prevalent in the narratives of Scott and Judd, was also prominent in many other testimonials. Mrs Masury of Ridgeway, Ontario, had already visited Judd in Buffalo, but it was only in contemplation alone that she reached a spiritual state capable of asking for healing through prayer, which produced a "warm wave" that travelled from "my head to my feet," marking the physical restoration of the body.[83]

For middle-class Victorians, the house was commonly viewed as an extension of the body, and it is not surprising to find a close association between the concept of the sacred home and the practice of faith healing.[84] Early institutions established to promote faith healing emulated this domestic model in their design. When those seeking cures started to arrive at the Judd household, a parlour was set aside as a "Faith Sanctuary" that was furnished "not in any style of severe solemnity, but with reference to a home-like beauty and graceful simplicity, which would make us feel that this hallowed spot was indeed a part of our home, and that our Lord, in a special manner, had taken up His abode within our humble dwelling."[85] Faith homes reflected the proper relationship between God and the body through a material culture of domesticity. A warm, maternal haven that invited God to take his "abode" within was a spatialized representation of the soul's preparation to receive a divine indwelling.

Eventually Judd established a "Faith Rest Cottage," set aside entirely for this purpose, and other faith homes spread across North America and Britain. Nondenominational in orientation and largely run by "matrons," these homes offered women leadership roles in the divine healing movement, which were made possible by their explicitly domestic character. A faith home in Troy, New York, was described as a two-storey building that was eighty feet wide by sixty feet deep. The interior was remodelled to accommodate a chapel (seating close to 175 people), a book and tract room, parlour, dining room, kitchen, a separate "back kitchen," and a bedroom on the first floor. Storerooms and other bedrooms filled the second level.[86] Domestic elements surrounded the distinctively sacred space of the chapel in an effort to impress upon visitors that divine health was a lifestyle rather than an isolated occurrence outside of one's regular activities. The cultivation of a faith sufficient for the procurement of healing demanded a merging of the sacred and the domestic, the ideal environment for Victorian notions of spirituality to flourish.

Toronto's Bethany Home was founded by Rebecca Fletcher in 1890 to serve "Christians suffering in mind and body, who instead of going to some health resort or to a hospital would prefer a quiet home, where, surrounded by Christian influence and kind sympathetic friends, they could be directed to the Lord Jesus Christ Himself as the Healer of all their diseases."[87] The wife of lawyer James Fletcher, Rebecca was also the daughter of James Good, whose foundry had built the first steam locomotive in Canada. Suffering from a tumour, Rebecca Fletcher had approached her Methodist pastor about the possibility of employing a faith cure, but was informed that miracles had ceased with the apostolic age. Undaunted, she trusted in faith and was healed, but only became formally connected with the divine healing movement through attending the 1889 Alliance convention in Toronto.[88]

As the secretary of the Toronto Mission Union, Fletcher was disturbed to discover that visitors to the city who expressed any interest in divine healing were arriving at boarding houses and being pointed towards Christian Science, "a perfect counterfeit of Divine healing."[89] Together with Miss Griffiths and in close association with the Christian Alliance, a house on Maitland Street was rented and furnished, operating solely on the basis of free will offerings. In 1895 the home was moved to Gloucester Street. It was a model that had been well-established, and like "Bethshan" in London, England, "Berachah" in Nyack, and the "Faith Rest Home" in Buffalo, Bethany operated with a maternal management that trusted in God's will for maintaining its upkeep. The Toronto faith home's intended purpose, to offer a sacred, domestic alternative to the medical space of the hospital, was immediately realized upon receiving its first guest. A young Scottish woman, who had been in the hospital suffering from "ovaritis," was faced with the choices of "a fearful operation, or a life of suffering." After leaving the hospital, the woman met Fletcher and was persuaded to spend a week at Bethany, where her suffering was relieved.[90]

The faith homes were designed to reinforce the model of private devotion within the sacred home by surrounding the guest with those elements of domesticity conducive to promoting Victorian piety. This was in direct opposition to the institutionalized space of the hospital or sanitarium. Regular services were held Monday nights for "times of refreshing," and from its very beginnings, Bethany overtly contrasted the institutional and secular character of the public medical establishment with a space that was saturated with domesticity and religion. Merging the domestic with the religious was hardly new, but the assumption that bodily healing could best take place within this environment rather than under the scientific observation of medical professionals posed a clear challenge to the direction taken by modern scientific medicine.

Although faith homes promoted the ideal domestic space, the women who ran the homes were engaged in far more than domestic duties, since managing the homes required extensive public dealings. The control exercised by women over the faith homes did not go unnoticed by critics of the divine healing movement. J.M. Buckley charged that "Certain advocates of faith healing and faith homes have influenced women to leave their husbands and parents and reside in the homes, and have persuaded them to give thousands of dollars for their purposes." While the faith homes were established to support domestic piety, Buckley reversed the emphasis to claim that they in fact destroyed domestic life. In playing upon fears that women could use the faith homes as a space through which to escape the traditional bonds of domesticity, Buckley recalled a "heartrending letter" he had received from a "gentleman whose mother and sister are now residing in a faith institution of New York, refusing all intercourse with their friends, and neglecting obvious duties of life."[91]

Even when the message of divine healing was carried by touring conventions, the open services set apart for healing did not mean that healing itself was moving into the public arena. A clergyman from Montreal described the scene at Cullis's Old Orchard convention in 1881 and noted the careful anointing of each person: "the solemnity of the occasion was at times overwhelming. There was a wonderful sense of the presence and power of God."[92] At the first Christian Alliance convention in Hamilton in 1889, the *Spectator* reported that "Rows of benches were filled with women who desired to be consecrated with the seal, while the two reverend doctors and some local workers passed back and forth in their midst carrying small bottles of oil. Holding the upturned faces gently with one hand, they rubbed a few drops of the oil on the forehead, and with a brief, earnest prayer set each one apart as special servants of Jesus, trusting in Him to relieve them of every form of ailment from which they suffered. After the ceremony of consecration, each participant remained for a time with closed eyes rapt in silent communion with the Savior."[93]

While these scenes took place in a quasi-public space, the services were actually designed to reinforce the traditional notion of healing through a private communion with the divine. Immediate, miraculous recoveries were not demanded or expected; anointings, individual consecrations, and silent meditations were a means to open the heart of the faithful and mark the path to fulfillment, which was expected to take place within a more private setting.

Mrs A.F. Albright of Toronto was suffering from an inflamed knee that required an operation when her husband discovered that one of Simpson's divine healing conventions in New York had commenced. When Albright travelled to New York to attend, she trusted in faith by leaving her crutches in the church. Although she believed in her healing, she did not remove all of her bandages and a slip on the sidewalk re-injured the knee, leading husband and wife to pray at the bedside for true healing. Only then, when Albright turned in her bed without feeling pain, did she exclaim, "Glory to God! He has healed me." Discussing a later healing from rheumatism, Albright commented, "I will never forget that hour when my husband and I knelt in prayer confessing that we had not honored God in trusting Him fully as our Healer ... oh, how the burden rolled off my soul."[94] Instead of a miraculous spectacle, the meditative experience of the convention was expected to be carried back to the home, to find fulfillment in daily life rather than instant gratification.

It is not known how many found relief from this exercise in Hamilton, but Jennie Emory, the wife of a local physician, reported that she had been restored to health after a long affliction from a "wasting disease."[95] The Alliance conventions, and the smaller meetings that would continue after them, should be regarded as one of many buttresses supporting the apparatus of divine healing in Canada rather than a significant departure from it. Those who sought healing continued to be predominantly female, and testimonials to faith healing, written and oral, remained the most public aspect of the movement. Narrating God's work was public, but bodies and the process of healing through faith remained a private encounter. When Simpson was asked why he did not consider a request to have cases of faith healing fully explored by a medical investigative committee, he reportedly responded, "I should as soon expose the sanctity of my home life to the public eye, as the sacred work of God in human bodies ... to scientific criticism."[96] The analogy drawn between the "sanctity" of the home and the "sacredness" of the body was more than coincidental. Protestant divine healing in the nineteenth century was constructed within the interlocking boundaries of private space, religion, and domesticity. The development of faith healing as a public spectacle would not occur until the next century; for the moment, the infusion of the divine within the body remained rooted in a holiness ethos of self-searching, private contemplation.

To look to prayer for healing was not new in 1881, but the introduction of an apparatus of Protestant divine healing, a "faith cure" based on the assumption of healing through the atonement, and a cross-border network of prayer circles devoted to healing the body, was a remarkable development. Beyond the theological structures of the divine healing movement lay the popular practice of faith healing, a gendered activity shaped by Victorian concerns over health, domestic space, and the role of the divine within the body.

The divine healing movement cannot be understood without addressing the role of healing narratives, which served as an essential part of the healing process and an important medium through which the movement spread across the continent. These testimonials are also the single most important source for understanding the gendered nature of movement, exposing both who pursued the prayer of faith and how its practice was shared and spread. Women clearly formed the majority of those who sought healing and were willing to testify to the experience. Encountering the divine within the body offered women a social space and a personal authority in which to rescript their experience of healing. Although they follow a conventional structure, healing narratives also offer insights into women's reactions to the dominant medical culture of the late-nineteenth century.

The social geography of healing in the late-nineteenth century favoured the domestic space in which women exercised a considerable amount of power. Male critics not only suggested that family life could be disrupted by faith healing, but they also chastised the movement itself in gendered terms. In 1882 the *Christian Guardian* reprinted an article by Dr George H. Hepworth that characterized divine healing as the product of an "emotional nature when it is swayed by an inexplicable mysticism and becomes indifferent to such a low order of materials as facts and law."[97] Faith healing was represented as feminine irrationality, an immature belief that thoughtful Christians would reject.

Hepworth employed this gendered rhetoric as a tool of disparagement, but in some respects his argument cut closer to the truth than proponents of divine healing would have admitted. Although the movement itself eventually developed a more systematic theology (very little had been published at the time Hepworth wrote his comments in 1882), it was the practices, behaviours, and emotions that formed the basis of the movement rather than than abstract theology. The learned critic could not comprehend the "inexplicable mysticism" that seemed to be devoid of "facts and law." For the women who shared devotional materials, faith healing could not be expressed in such rational, scientific terms. As a personal expression of the body and the divine, faith healing was a cultural phenomenon that engaged and subverted medical understandings of the gendered body.

From the healing of Mrs Mottashed in 1881 to the establishment of Bethany Home in 1890, the divine healing movement in Canada was organized around informal networks of women, who interlinked their activities with centres of faith healing in the United States, notably Buffalo, Boston, and New York. Although narratives were produced from as far away as Nova Scotia, most of the early activity in Canada took place in southern and eastern Ontario as well as the city of Montreal in Quebec. Towards the end of the decade, formal structures promoting divine healing were established, and it is not surprising that the geographical areas that had already produced healing narratives and networks would become the focus of these institutionalizing efforts. As faith healing became more formally organized, a new cadre of male leaders would emerge, but the core activities of women remained notably significant to the movement.

3

A Respectable Movement

"I am asked if I believe in faith-cure ... [The Bible] abounds in the divine healing ... The sick shall be healed; women shall receive their dead raised to life again. Why not now? ..."

Perhaps Mrs. Frankland did not intend that declamation should be accepted at its face value; certain she did not expect it.

After a hymn, beautifully and touchingly sung, and a brief prayer, ladies put on their sealskin sacques, thrust their jeweled hands into their muffs, and went out to beckon their impatient coachmen, and to carry home with them the solemn impressions made by the discourse, which were in most cases too vague to produce other than a sentimental result.

Yet one may not scatter fire with safety unless he can be sure there are no dangerous combustibles within reach. The harm of credulity is that it is liable to set a great flame a-going whenever it reaches that which will burn.

Edward Eggleston, *The Faith Doctor* (1891)

The divine healing movement entered Canada as little more than a loose network of women who shared their personal experiences with each other – at bedsides, through letters in the mail, and in the pages of American religious periodicals that were distributed north of the border. American works on faith healing circulated widely in Canada, and interested Canadians routinely investigated the phenomenon by visiting various American cities.[1] Boston, New York, and Buffalo were the main centres of attraction as Canadians travelled south to visit Charles Cullis, A.B. Simpson, and Carrie Judd. By the end of the 1880s, however, new organizations were being established to foster sanctification and divine healing at home. In Canada, the primary vehicle for Protestant divine healing was the Christian Alliance, an interdenominational fellowship founded by A.B. Simpson in 1887 and based on a "fourfold" doctrine of Christ as "Saviour, Sanctifier, Healer, and Coming King." Among other contributions, the Canadian branch of the Alliance gave faith healing a formal, public face that confronted the scrutiny of religious and secular press. Armed with solid leadership from the most respectable classes, the Alliance found itself holding a privileged place within the religious landscape of a dominant Victorian evangelical culture.

While the Alliance found a welcome home in Canada, the practice of divine healing was exposed to a series of extended commentaries and critiques from a wide variety of sources. The wide range of religious and medical perceptions of what faith healing "really" represented reveals the fluid state of ideas surrounding the relationship between the body and the divine. These debates were clearly framed both within the intellectual context of the new science of psychology and a social context that gendered the practice of faith healing as feminine.

The Christian Alliance presented itself as an inter-denominational fellowship of respectable Christians, and yet in Canada the organization also formed a unique relationship with the Salvation Army, a movement usually associated with working-class religious exuberance. The Army was one of the few Protestant denominations to adopt an official position supporting faith healing in the late-nineteenth century. Both groups shared a heritage rooted in holiness theology, and for a short time the Canadian branches of the Salvation Army (the Dominion Corps) and the Alliance established common ground in the practice of faith healing. Personal and professional contacts between the two organizations comfortably overlapped, but the Army's initial support for faith healing turned to active hostility when internal divisions led to a secession of officers in Canada. The Alliance maintained its connections with many of those who left the Dominion Corps, but the Salvation Army itself moved towards a very different model of health that was incompatible with the Alliance's understanding of the body and the divine.

NATIONAL IDENTITY AND DIVINE HEALING

For some elements of the Canadian press, divine healing was regarded as a distinctly "American" phenomenon. When reporting on a Toronto faith healing convention in 1889, the *Empire* consistently referred to the "American expounders" of the doctrine, carefully noting that while "representatives from the United States" appeared on the platform, none of the Toronto clergy joined them, preferring instead to remain in the audience.[2] Such nationalistic constructions of divine healing as a movement of American propagandists delivering a foreign message would continue for many decades. What the newspaper failed to report was that divine healing entered Canada long before any of the "American expounders" had set foot on Canadian soil. Nor were all of the platform speakers exclusively American. Two of the star attractions were actually Canadian-born, and the organization they now represented was one that already boasted a significant element of Canadian leadership. By 1889 it was too late to push faith healing back across the border. Canadians would not only receive the message of divine healing, they would actively shape the movement at home and abroad.

Rev. John Salmon, one of the organizers of the 1889 convention, was arguably the most important figure in forging the organizational structure of the divine healing movement in Canada. Born in Glasgow, Scotland in 1831, Salmon was converted while serving as a sailor on an American packet ship. Deciding that his future lay in the ministry and encouraged by the support of a group of Methodists from Montreal, the former seaman attended Victoria College and earned his Bachelor of Arts degree in 1862. His appointment to Coaticook in the Eastern Townships of Canada East brought him into contact with Adventist teachings. However, instead of fortifying local Methodists against them, Salmon found himself adopting Adventist positions on premillennialism and baptism through immersion, and he started to express doubts about the immortality of the soul. A long spiritual journey took Salmon through Adventism, Congregationalism, a short period leading a Baptist congregation, and eventually back to a Congregational Church in Yorkville, Ontario.[3]

At some point in his spiritual searching, Salmon came across a volume that recounted "the work of an old German woman who had worked marvellous cures," which was likely Cullis's account of Dorothea Trudel. In 1881 Salmon went to London where he investigated stories of divine healing.[4] Inspired by his visit, Salmon turned to faith healing for relief from an inflamed eye. Reluctant to introduce the doctrine to his congregation, Salmon adopted a quiet approach of personal encouragement and visitation for those who might be interested.[5]

In 1885 Salmon was struck with kidney problems, but on this occasion his own prayers did little to relieve the suffering. After reading Judd's *Prayer of Faith*, Salmon decided to seek an anointing, but he could find no clergyman in Toronto willing to perform the duty. A.B. Simpson was in the middle of conducting his first travelling "Convention for Christian Life and Work and Divine Healing," which was scheduled to arrive in Buffalo in October. Despite the restrictions in place to contain an outbreak of smallpox, Salmon managed to talk his way across the international border without submitting to the required vaccination shot. After being anointed by Simpson, Salmon felt his pain leave his body and later testified to healing at the convention.[6]

Upon returning to Yorkville Congregational Church, Salmon faced opposition to his views on divine healing, and in order to avoid a public controversy, he held meetings on sanctification and healing in his own home.[7] As Salmon's informal gatherings were proceeding, a group of Toronto Quakers invited the Rhode Island evangelist, Dr Charles Ryder, to the city. Ryder was actively engaged in the divine healing movement, and he deftly turned the invitation from this small group into a major three-month campaign in the spring of 1886. The issue of faith healing was vaulted into the limelight, particularly when attention was drawn to Ryder's participation in assisting Ellen Hatch, the wife of a wealthy hardware merchant, find relief from various diseases, including back problems, fever, "nervous prostration," and eye ailments.[8]

Encouraged by these developments, Salmon became more outspoken about faith healing. In July 1886 he invited John Currie, the "Scotch Evangelist," to speak at Yorkville Congregational. Currie was a divine healing proponent who had lived in Montreal before moving to Brooklyn. The following September, Salmon was perturbed when an article that was hostile to faith healing appeared in the Congregational periodical, the *Canadian Independent*. The article was reprinted from the *Christian Standard*, and the Canadian editors had prefaced the selection by stating that they were not denying the power or ability of God to answer prayer, but rather they sought to combat the "fanaticism on this subject which is very prejudicial."[9] In response, Salmon requested that the editor reprint a selection from the recently-published report on W.E. Boardman's "International Conference of Divine Healing and True Holiness," an event that had been held in London, England the previous summer. One of the Australian delegates had been unable to attend the conference in person, but Boardman included his written submission as an appendix in the report. It was this appendix that Salmon sent to the *Canadian Independent*. The editors "cheerfully" published the "other side" of the faith healing debate, publicly acknowledging Salmon as the source.[10] When the article appeared, Salmon immediately faced division in his congregation over his public position on healing. After a protracted series of procedural wranglings that attracted widespread media attention, Salmon resigned from Yorkville and once again found himself without a denominational home. It would not be the last time that the Australian whose submission had precipitated the crisis would provoke public controversy in Canada; but at the time John Alexander Dowie remained largely unknown, and Salmon could not have foreseen that Dowie's arrival in America within a few years would significantly alter the course of the divine healing movement.[11]

In his search for a new denominational home, Salmon turned once again to A.B. Simpson, joining him at Old Orchard, Maine, for the founding convention of the new Christian Alliance. That the *Empire* would later label Simpson as "American" is somewhat understandable, considering that when Simpson attended Boardman's 1885 International Conference on divine healing, he was working in the United States and served as an American delegate, duly informing those present that his actual heritage was "half-English" and "half-Scotch."[12] Despite his disclaimer, Albert Benjamin Simpson was born in 1843 at Bayview, Prince Edward Island, and for the most part grew up in Chatham, Canada West. Graduating from Knox College in 1865, Simpson obtained his first pastoral charge at the prestigious Knox Presbyterian Church in Hamilton. He later moved south of the border to take up pastorates in Louisville, Kentucky, and New York.[13] In Kentucky, Simpson was drawn to holiness through a series of events, including reading Boardman's *The Higher Christian Life* (1858).[14] After moving to the east coast, Simpson came into contact with Cullis through the doctor's camp meetings at Old Orchard. Facing a number of bodily ailments and suffering from a nervous breakdown, Simpson claimed healing through prayer and slowly began to preach the doctrine. In 1881 Simpson left the Presbyterian Church and established his own independent tabernacle in New York.[15]

The travelling conventions on sanctification and healing that Simpson had launched in Buffalo in 1885 attracted a number of Canadians, both as audience members and featured speakers. At Old Orchard in 1887, Simpson officially organized this activity as the Christian Alliance, an interdenominational association dedicated to a basic fourfold gospel: Salvation, Sanctification, Divine Healing, and a Premillennial Second Coming. Of these, the Alliance emphasized the first three over the fourth, declaring that those who had reservations about premillennialism could still be accepted as full members if they professed the other tenets. The Canadian presence at this founding convention was keenly felt, as demonstrated by the names featured on the first executive. Simpson served as president, while Salmon, Alexander Innes MacKenzie from Hamilton, and John T. Dorland, Jr. from Wellington, were all founding vice-presidents. Canadian businessman W.J. Fenton and a Mrs Bryson of Montreal served on the General Committee. A parallel organization dedicated to missionary work, the Evangelical Missionary Alliance, was also established, with Fenton serving as a vice-president of that body as well.[16]

Another former Canadian who was to have an important influence over the Alliance was the formidable Anglican, Dr Henry B. Wilson. Born in Peterborough in 1841, Wilson attended Toronto's Trinity College on a Wellington Scholarship, achieving a Doctor of Divinity in 1883. As curate of the St. George's Cathedral in Kingston, Wilson became embroiled in controversy over his support for the Salvation Army, a stand that caused indignation among some pew holders and factions within the clergy.[17] In 1884 Wilson resigned his position and was attached to St. George's Episcopalian Church in New York, where he soon came into contact with Simpson's views on divine healing, which profoundly influenced him. Suffering from "chronic dyspepsia, catarrhal and throat troubles, [and] nervous depression," Wilson experienced a dramatic recovery and maintained until his death in 1908 that healing was encompassed within the atonement.[18]

When the Alliance conventions reached Canada in February 1889, Simpson and Wilson were two of the featured speakers, along with Judd, Ryder, and Rev. John Cookman of New York. Interest in the Alliance had been expressed from Montreal, Toronto, Winnipeg, and Halifax, but it was Hamilton's First Methodist Church that hosted the first Christian Alliance convention outside of the United States. The open conference was organized around expositions on the themes of sanctification, divine healing, and the second coming. Fenton, Maggie Scott, and Ellen Hatch offered their testimonies, and Simpson took time to answer questions about faith healing.

The Hamilton convention concluded with a business meeting to organize the Dominion Auxiliary Branch of the Christian Alliance. The Dominion Auxiliary was responsible for establishing local branches within Canada, each with its own president who would in turn serve as a vice-president for the national body. The Auxiliary was itself subject to the New York executive. Although four local branches were initially projected for Canada, only Toronto and Hamilton were able to organize themselves in 1889. Like its American parent, the Alliance was not intended to be an "ecclesiastical body," but rather it would serve as a "fraternal union of believers." Nevertheless, while the Alliance maintained that it had no intention of forming a new church, it did provide an institutional structure for the divine healing movement in Canada. Church historian Lindsay Reynolds reports that 1,300 people attended the Hamilton convention, and between 300 and 400 signed on to the Hamilton branch in its wake.[19]

John Salmon had wasted no time in promoting Alliance activity in Toronto even prior to the formation of the Dominion Auxiliary. Estranged from his former denominations, Salmon organized weekly meetings at Wolseley Hall on Gerrard Street, where he struggled to carry on an independent ministry that espoused Alliance principles without violating its interdenominational purpose. In May 1889 Salmon brought Simpson's convention tour to Toronto, an event that resulted in over 300 people joining the Alliance.[20] A smaller convention was held in Peterborough, which produced the third Canadian branch of the Alliance, while another in Brampton also yielded results.

The divine healing movement entered Canada as a loose coalition of like-minded believers who formed an extended community through personal contacts and American religious periodicals. By the end of the 1880s, however, divine healing was encompassed within a national organization, which was promoted by a regular series of conventions and tours and sustained by active, local branches. While some newspapers labeled the Alliance an "American" organization, Canadians were both influential in shaping the New York-based Christian Alliance and clearly in control of the formation of their own Dominion Auxiliary.

RESPECTABLE MEN

Despite the fears of Salmon's former colleagues at Yorkville Congregational about the potential fanaticism of divine healing, the new Dominion Auxiliary of the Christian Alliance could hardly be accused of catering to the "lower elements" of society. From its very beginnings, the Alliance, particularly its Toronto branch, drew its adherents from the respectable classes and boasted a public profile led by notable persons of high social status. It was Salmon's previous interdenominational work with the Toronto Mission Union that brought him into contact with a dedicated group of lay Christian leaders who would prove to be instrumental in the early formation of the Alliance in Canada. While never embraced whole-heartedly by all, faith healing was far from a socially marginal activity in English-speaking Victorian Canada.

The Toronto Mission Union itself was the creation of William Howland, the famous reforming mayor of Toronto from 1886 to 1887, who was subsequently elected the Dominion Alliance's first president at the Hamilton Convention in 1889.[21] The son of a father of Confederation, Howland was a strong nationalist whose religious convictions carried him into a wide range of social reform activities. Although born a Presbyterian, Howland converted to evangelical Anglicanism and was an active founder of what became Wycliffe College, the evangelical counterpart to the high Anglican Trinity College. Through Salmon and the Alliance, Howland became interested in divine healing and his wife, Laura, extended her own testimonial to faith healing at Alliance conventions.[22]

The connections between Howland, the Toronto Mission Union, and the prominent group of philanthropic businessmen active in the new Christian Alliance ran deep. When Howland stepped down from his mayoralty position, his chosen successor was Elias Rogers, a wealthy Quaker alderman who had been instrumental in bringing the Ryder divine healing campaign to Toronto. The public disclosure of his monopolistic business practices as a coal merchant cost him the election, but

Rogers remained close to the Alliance and even served on the Board of Managers in New York.[23] Another businessman who came to know divine healing through the Alliance was the Methodist philanthropist, William Gooderham. Although Gooderham had known Salmon for a number of years through the Toronto Mission Union, he did not become interested in divine healing until the 1889 Toronto Alliance Convention, which he attended "just to see if there was anything in it or not." Gooderham was anointed at one of the convention's services, and the following morning he "felt the divine power tingling all through his body," and "felt as vigorous as a boy."[24]

Howland, Gooderham, and Rogers were all publicly active evangelicals who were bound together through their involvement with the Christian Alliance and the Mission Union. These connections were reinforced through agencies such as the Toronto Willard Tract Depository. As an extension of Cullis's Willard Tract Repository, a publishing office was opened in Toronto some time before 1872. S.R. Briggs established and managed the Toronto Willard Tract Depository as a separate entity in 1873, and the company was publicly incorporated in 1882.[25] Howland, Gooderham, and Rogers all owned shares in the Depository, and all served as directors at some point, with Howland also acting as President. Under the management of Briggs, the Toronto Willard Tract Depository became Canada's premier evangelical publishing house and a centre for distributing works on faith healing. In 1886 the depository reported that its gross sales of bibles, books, pamphlets, tracts, bible study notes, and cards totalled over $60,000. Including the 350,000 items given out for free distribution, the publisher reported that it had issued 1,592,175 copies of material for the year, and had issued over six-and-a-half million since the depository had opened.[26]

The energetic trio of Howland, Gooderham, and Rogers were the most obvious public laymen who promoted the Alliance in Canada. Other prominent Toronto businessmen, including the Presbyterian biscuit magnate, William Christie, and Methodist Charles Wilson, owner of a ginger ale company, were also associated with the Alliance. The enhanced respectability of those who filled the ranks and leadership positions of the Alliance in Toronto was also evident in other locales. Manton Treadgold, the Mayor of Brampton, had been healed at an Alliance convention in that city in 1889, prompting comment from the *Christian Alliance* on the rapid spread of Alliance work in Canada "among the best classes of Christians."[27] When a convention was held in Montreal in 1891, the *Alliance* exalted that "The class of persons who attended the meetings in Montreal and came under the influence of the work was unusually intelligent and influential, and the work, we believe will reach a very wide and important class in that city." The paper went on to remark that "a good many" had already encountered divine healing through previous visits to New York and Old Orchard.[28]

Secular papers also noticed a class difference between advocates of divine healing and other forms of alternative healing. "We read much nowadays of the 'mind cure,' 'Christian Science' and the 'faith cure,'" commented the Toronto *Mail* in 1887, which despised forms of religious healing that had been "prostituted to serve the ends of unscrupulous men and women and are, therefore, to say the least, open to suspicion." The recent emergence of Protestant divine healing, however, was treated entirely differently: "Owing to the character of many of its advocates, the faith cure is entitled to more respect than the other so-called cures mentioned above, although it has yet scarcely begun to establish its claim to recognition as not merely a branch of the healing art but the only method of cure of bodily ailments sanctioned by God."[29] When another Toronto newspaper, the *Empire,* went looking for a ministerial reaction to the divine healing conventions, it discovered that very few clerics wanted to speak on the subject. It was apparent that public opinions were being held in check on social, rather than theological, grounds. Simpson's former principal at Knox College, Dr William Caven, was "reticent" about commenting because of the number of "respectable men" involved, and "he would not like to wound their feelings by harsh references." Rev. Le Roy Hooker of Metropolitan Methodist Church expressed similar sentiments, and although he would perhaps preach on the subject in the future, as far as the newspapers were concerned, "I would sooner not appear before the public in the matter at all. These are good people." Most of the Toronto clergy interviewed expressed reservations about divine healing, but none were willing to attack the Alliance openly with its elite group of "respectable men."[30]

Despite the generally positive publicity of the healings and the strong element of respectability associated with the leadership, defining the ecclesiastical nature of the Alliance in Canada was not always easy for the proponents of divine healing. Buoyed by the excitement that followed in the wake of Ellen Hatch's healing, Salmon began to search for larger quarters to accommodate the work of the Alliance. In 1889 he took out a lease on a church on Simcoe Street, renaming it Bethany Tabernacle. With the aid of the Salvation Army captain, R.J. Zimmerman, Salmon established a full program of church worship services, Sunday afternoon divine healing meetings, and week-night meetings.[31] However, to some within its ranks, this move raised fears that the Alliance was losing its interdenominational character. The opposition to Salmon was led by Plymouth Brethren businessman, W.J. Fenton, who decided to maintain regular meetings at Wolseley rather than move to Bethany.[32] While these issues brewed, the congregation at Bethany suffered the humiliation of being forced from its home when the church building was purchased by Christian Scientists in 1890, and it took three more years before a new building, Bethany Chapel, could take its place.[33]

By 1891 the dissension between Salmon and Fenton had caused a wider division in the Canadian Alliance, and Salmon declined to stand for re-election to the presidency of the Toronto Branch. Howland added the vacated position to his portfolio, which already included the presidency of the Dominion Auxiliary. A summer convention tour of Canada was intended to rally unity to the Alliance cause, but instead of patching up divisions, Simpson's arrival in Toronto in September 1891 only served to exacerbate them. Salmon had drawn up an official constitution for Bethany as an nondenominational church with a founding membership of close to ninety, and both Griffiths and Fletcher were listed as deaconesses. Zimmerman was to serve as the assistant pastor, since Salmon's activities kept him away from much of the necessary pastoral work, and the arrival of the convention presented an opportunity for Zimmerman to be ordained by Simpson, together with a "council of ministers and two Elders." For Fenton and a number of others at Wolseley Hall, the act of ordination, sanctioned by Simpson himself, was irreconcilable with the professed objective of the Alliance as an inter-denominational fellowship. The *Christian Alliance and Missionary Weekly* attempted to explain that this act "was not intended in any way to put the Alliance in any ecclesiastical posture, or for a moment suggest that it contemplates establishing new churches or denominations." Bethany was an "independent movement of brethren," and the objects of the Christian Alliance were declared to be "much wider than any single church, or denomination."[34] Despite such overtures, however, the paper noted with regret the absence of Fenton from the convention. Along with Rogers and many of the original Quakers involved in the Ryder campaign, Fenton left the Christian Alliance, and the Wolseley Hall meetings ended.

While the defections did little to bolster the divine healing movement in Toronto, the gradual loss of its most respectable figures crippled it even further. After jumping into the divine healing movement in the wake of the 1889 convention, the sixty-five-year-old Gooderham died just a few short months later. An even more serious blow was the passing of Howland in 1893. Only forty-nine years of age and still serving as the Dominion Auxiliary's president at the time of his death, Howland was clearly the most prominent lay figure associated with the Alliance in Canada. In the obituaries for Gooderham, the Toronto papers stressed his financial acumen, his philanthropic endeavours, and noted

his connections to the Christian Alliance, but they did not raise the issue of faith healing. For Howland, a similar respect was paid, but hints
of a deeper criticism towards prayer for faith were expressed in some
quarters. According to the *Empire*, Howland's illness was "grip,"
which "settled on the right lung" and developed into pneumonia. The
paper explained that, "Mr. Howland was a firm believer in the efficacy
of prayers, as was also his wife, and it was only last Wednesday that
Dr John B. Hall, the well-known homœopathist, was called in. He has
been in constant attendance ever since, but from the first he held out
very little hope for Mr. Howland's recovery, the disease having gained
such a headway."[35] That Howland turned to a homeopathist when he
finally consented to seeing a physician illustrates the common ground
that continued to be shared between divine healing and homeopathy.
The account of Howland's illness is worded very carefully, but there is
an implication that if medical aid had been sought earlier, perhaps Toronto's famous reforming mayor would not have died at such a young
age. The Toronto *News* was both more explicit in its criticism and
more confused about the situation when its headline asked, "Is 'Christian Science' Responsible for the Untimely End?" The *News* was critical about the delay in calling a regular physician, and the fact that
Howland and his wife did not call for medical assistance when he was
stricken with pneumonia was "sufficient to make the delay seem almost criminal in the eyes of those who regard Christian science [*sic*] as
a travesty on the name."[36] Despite their constant attempts to distance
themselves from Christian Science, proponents of divine healing might
have been grateful for the continued confusion in this case.

In the establishment of institutional structures to support faith healing in Canada, Salmon was able to draw upon the existing networks of
evangelical philanthropists in Toronto. Not all of the city's prominent
evangelicals were as enamoured with the Christian Alliance as Howland and Gooderham, but the presence of these figures working on behalf of the Alliance gave the small group an enviable social status that
protected them in part from critical attacks or dismissal as marginal fanatics. If, however, the Christian Alliance in Canada managed to escape
public censure for its position on healing, the practice of the "faith
cure" was subjected to a series of medical and religious discourses that
were far less hospitable.

FAITH CURE DELUSIONS

When the *Empire* commenced a search for comments regarding the proponents of faith healing, it soon discovered that the clergy were reluctant
to criticize the "respectable men" who led the Christian Alliance in
Canada. When it came to the abstract concept of prayer for healing, the

newspaper was more successful in extracting opinions. Rev. Dr Thomas had researched the topic and declared confidently that miracles had ended with the biblical age, and that the assumptions of the faith healers were not "consonant with a rational and comprehensive interpretation of the Word of God." Dr William Caven felt that the doctrine was "unortho-dox"; in the case of "nervous diseases" it possibly had an effect, for "the mind exercised a strong influence over the body," but it could not be sus-tained where "organic illness" was present. Rev. Dr Harper, a Methodist minister from Brampton, accepted that healing through prayer was possi-ble, but he did not regard it as a universal doctrine. Rev. D.J. Macdonnell noted that the question opened up "the entire philosophy of prayer," and while he felt that prayers to God for healing were beneficial, it was God who judged it best to grant such petitions; it would be "very wicked to refuse the highest medical aid which could possibly be obtained." Rev. C.M. Milligan agreed: "The wise man is he who uses the human means as if everything depended upon man, and then prays that these means may be blessed, as if everything depended upon God." Only when these avenues had been exhausted, should one cast oneself "solely upon God." The newspaper did find one minister, Rev. Hugh Johnston, who readily admitted his belief in divine healing. Johnston had been active in the di-vine healing movement in Montreal and was closely associated with Mal-lory and Cullis. However, Johnston disagreed with the Alliance's understanding of healing as "an article of a fourfold gospel," since "he had known it to lead to unhealthy effects."[37]

The responses of the clergy reveal a curious amalgam of contempo-rary theological and scientific currents that produced contradictory as-sumptions about the relationship between religion and the body. Most of the ministers relegated the age of miracles to the biblical epoch, yet none were willing to discount completely the ability of God to inter-vene in solitary cases. Even clergy could speak with the assumptions of medical discourse in distinguishing between functional and organic dis-ease, but if nervous diseases were affected by the mind through a mate-rial physiology, what was the role of religion or God in this process? The unresolved questions prompted by the Victorian prayer debate continued to haunt the public discussions surrounding faith and heal-ing in nineteenth-century English-speaking Canada.

However, the reaction to faith healing went beyond simply repeating the well-worn arguments of the prayer debate. The rhetoric employed by critics of the movement was far from neutral and dispassionate, and it remained marked with gendered connotations. As noted in the previ-ous chapter, this gendered language emerged very early in the reactions to faith healing, led by American critics such as G.H. Hepworth and James Buckley. Hepworth, in an 1882 article reprinted in the *Christian Guardian*, rhetorically questioned whether divine healing was based on "bad logic or a mild form of insanity," characterizing it as the product of an "emotional nature" swayed by an "inexplicable mysticism." Buckley was just as harsh in his assessment, accusing faith healing of producing "an effeminate type of character which shrinks from pain and concentrates attention upon self and its sensations ... It destroys the ascendancy of reason, and thus, like similar delusions, it is self-perpetuating; and its natural and, in some minds, irresistible tendency is to mental derangement."[38] Canadian critics were quick to follow suit. For the benefit of the reporter from the *Empire,* Rev. Dr Thomas practically lifted Buckley's words from the page in referring to the assumptions of divine healing as "pernicious, as it tends to produce an effeminate type of Christianity, which shrinks from pain and concentrates attention on self and personal sensations."[39] For these critics, only masculine reasoning based on "facts and law" offered a means to truth. The theory of divine healing, as far as Hepworth was concerned, was "the embodiment of a sickly sentimentalism rather than of sturdy scholarship."[40]

The gendering of faith healing as feminine superstition by critics was not only a reaction to the dominating female presence within the movement, it was part of a broader effort to redefine Protestantism as "muscular Christianity." This was an expression originally applied by critics of the British theologian and novelist Charles Kingsley (1819–1875), who articulated a vision of a healthy, socially committed, manly Christianity. It was thought that mysticism emasculated the believer by appealing to a feminine soul, and the recovery of an athletic and masculine Christianity was an important foundation for the development of the Social Gospel movement in the United States and Canada.[41] Expressions of muscular Christianity countered the anxiety raised over the prevalence of feminine domestic religion. Despite its own appeal to strength and health, faith healing was criticized for being too private, too devotional, and too mystical, all "feminine" qualities. Health was a godly object to pursue, but sports and physical culture were the method and means, not internal soul-searching. As the previous chapter demonstrated, women who narrated their healing experience linked quiet devotions and contemplations with a restoration of active mission and empowering strength, subverting romantic ideals of feminine passivity. Male critics reframed faith healing as beholden to these romantic ideals, offering a "sickly sentimentalism" and personal "sensations," rather than true, manly health.

Attacks upon divine healing in the press, secular and religious, did not go unanswered. The reprinting of Hepworth's article in the *Christian Guardian* hit a discordant note with a number of readers, including "J.A.I.," likely Rev. J.A. Ivison of Strathroy, who had attended Judd's Faith Rest Cottage in Buffalo. "I am aware that believers in 'faith cures' are liable to be branded as fanatics," complained Ivison in a letter to the editor. "It is not fanaticism to take a plainly pointed-out means for obtaining the blessing of health; it is the height of folly not to take it."[42] The *Christian Guardian* defended its actions, and although editor Rev. E.H. Dewart admitted that some of the language employed in the original article may not have been "in harmony with the gravity of the subject," he maintained that the piece was "in accord with Christian truth and sound reason." Dewart did not want to chill the ardour of devout believers, however, "we must not forget that people may be ardent and sincere Christians, and yet cherish views that are unsafe, and which cannot be generally adopted without serious harm."[43] Throughout the 1880s, the *Christian Guardian* continued to carry articles from other periodicals which were critical of faith healing.

There is a sense in Dewart's response, and in the words of the ministers interviewed by the *Empire*, that the clergy were more concerned with the practical effects and operation of faith healing than they were with constructing philosophical arguments to dispute the concept of divine healing. Underlying many of the comments is a fear that the doctrine was "unhealthy," a dangerous experience on both the spiritual and the physical level. As the original article from Hepworth stated, "Prayer as the accompaniment of human agencies, is the fulfilment of a pure and undefiled religion; but prayer alone, without the accompaniment of human agencies, is incredible fanaticism." It was the potential displacement of modern medicine that created the greatest anxiety for critics of divine healing. However uneasy ministers felt with the new materialistic science promoted by Tyndall and others, they were unwilling to jettison the mainstream medical apparatus of knowledge in order to accommodate the divine within the body.

Attitudes towards medicine figured prominently in the questions fielded by the Christian Alliance during their first conventions in Canada. At a session in Peterborough, one minister asked Salmon why patients should not simply put themselves "under the care of a Christian doctor who had asked God to guide him in his treatment of patients[?]" Salmon reiterated that "doctors were the gift of God in many instances," and that the Alliance had no quarrel with physicians or those who chose to use medicine. However, if "a doctor prescribed for a man and then that man asked God to direct the doctor's medicine so that it would have the desired effect ... here was an interference of God between the doctor and his patient, and he [Salmon] preferred to go directly to God."[44] The question was repeated on the next day of the convention when it was asked if it was mandated that members of the Alliance not call upon physicians. This time the answer came from one of the featured speakers, the "Tennessee Lady Orator," Mattie Gordon, who stated that she "never advised any one to consult a physician, and to ask such a question as this indicated that the person was not in a position to be a conscientious member of the Alliance. People may take their choice, but there is less glory to God." When it came to the use of drugs, Gordon reiterated that "Taking medicine was contrary to the fundamental principle of the Alliance, which [takes] Christ as its great healer and all-in-all."[45]

Why were most mainline Protestant clergy concerned that divine healing would potentially disrupt the role of the physician and medicine in society? In part, the rejection of medicine was closely linked to a rejection of progressivism. Modern medicine was widely regarded as one of the hallmarks of providential favour upon the superiority of Christian (Western) Civilization. If philosophers and scientists disputed the assumption that God's work could be perceived within nature and natural law, then surely the advancement of Christian nations in science, technology, living standards, morals, and military might, demonstrated the effect of religion. The power of progress could also be adapted to Darwinian evolution, whereby the success of Christianity offered evidence of its perfect representation of God's will and design for humanity. As one critic argued, the "whole drift of Christian history" lay in the progressive detachment of humanity from an immature reliance on miracles, pointing instead towards "the great, permanent demonstrations of God's power in the Church through the preached word, the sacraments, the power of personal character, the body of believers, the developments of Christian civilization." To turn away from medicine and modern medical therapeutics was akin to denying the divinely-sanctioned path of scientific progress for Christianity. Indeed, "the deliberate rejection of that human science and skill which it has been one of Christianity's noblest functions to develop, savors vastly more of presumption than of faith."[46]

Faith healing once again came into the spotlight in Toronto following the healing of Rose Kemp in the fall of 1889. A resident of Brighton, Ontario, Kemp had travelled to Toronto for treatment for an inflammation in her hip. In her account, she stated that she had followed the doctors' advice, doing only as much exercise as prescribed over the past seven years. When the suffering grew worse, her doctor advised her that the joint required blistering, and that it would be necessary to "burn to the bone in order to remove the matter that had formed there." Kemp had repeatedly prayed for God to bless the means of medical treatment, but when she was called upon by Sarah Carline, who testified to her healing by faith, Kemp "saw it was God's will that we be not diseased, for He sent His Son to die for our bodies." Inspired, Kemp prayed in faith, and was able to walk downstairs without pain, and, in time, the swelling disappeared.[47]

With the Alliance convention having concluded only a few months before, the Toronto *Empire* provided extensive coverage on Kemp's recovery. When the paper interviewed her physician, Dr Constantinides, the reporter received a noticeably different version of events. Admitting that Kemp had suffered an inflammation in her hip for more than seven years, the doctor claimed that he had prescribed rest, but "She did not remain in the hospital long enough to get well." When he urged her again to adopt "absolute rest" she became "restless[,] nervous and excitable and wanted home, with the result that her complaint, although a curable one, did not improve ... I advised her to go home for the summer, but I understand while there she went out walking, with the result that she got worse." Constantinides was far from pleased with the reports of Kemp's faith cure: "These people have prayed with her, made her believe she was well, and under their influence she got up and walked about – the very thing which I insisted that she should not do. She has been doing all along against my wishes what she is doing now. She has been going around all the time. I have made a life study, I might say, of the disease, and when a joint is diseased I always prescribe rest as half of the cure. Under the circumstances I think she temporarily feels well under the influence of these people and that there will soon be a relapse."[48] Constantinides unabashedly placed the blame for Kemp's suffering on the patient herself. At the same time he reinforced his own professional position by having made a "life study" of the disease and claiming that Kemp's condition was imminently curable, if only the physician's authority to prescribe had been respected.

The publicity garnered by the Kemp healing once again provided an occasion for the *Empire* to gather opinions on divine healing. Only this time the attention was drawn to the medical community. There was little reticence on the part of physicians to explain just what had happened in the Kemp case. Three physicians all expressed the opinion that faith could certainly play a role in the healing process, except that the object of faith was not restricted to the divine. It was "a matter of common observation," according to Dr Adam Wright, that "if a patient has confidence in her physician, whoever that may be, a frequently corresponding benefit will follow." Dr Thorburn, a professor of pharmacology and "one of Toronto's oldest physicians," reviewed Kemp's case and declared, "I could give you illustrations by the score of even more remarkable cases cured either by belief in Christianity or the doctor." Dr T.S. Covernton revealed, "The element of faith helps in the cure of any patient. Be it in the doctor or in the Almighty, the action is much the same on the human body. Faith in anybody acts upon the condition of the patient." What had been the unique restoration of the body through a divine indwelling for believers became a mental exercise of the patient, whose object of faith could just as easily be the physician.

The nature of this mental process of faith was linked to "hysteria" and the "nervous system" by Wright, and Covernton concurred: "I think cases of this kind have largely the nervous element in them. It is mental influence and not divine healing." Although Thorburn agreed that such cases are sometimes referred to as "hysterical joints," the pharmacologist went further than his counterparts by linking faith cure with the new work on hypnotism. "The manner in which Miss Kemp has got cured would in medical science come under the head of suggestive therapeutics," he claimed. "This study has also other phases; for example, the production of sleep by manipulation, mesmerism, and so on."[49] As Ann Taves notes in her wide-ranging study of psychology and religion, the 1880s and early 1890s were a period of flux, when the currents of the older psychological understandings of animal magnetism and mesmerism, employed by Buckley, mixed and overlapped with the scientific materialism of neurologists such as George M. Beard. Over the next two decades, the focus would shift towards a new interest in hypnosis and concepts of the subconscious, but for the moment most physicians and theologians drew upon a wide variety of sources in outlining psychological theories of religious experience.[50]

While agreeing with the clerical critics of divine healing that faith could sometimes influence the body, physicians were eager to divorce prayer from the transcendent and reduce its efficacy to that of a mental function. The mind could play a limited role in influencing the condition of the body, but the body itself remained firmly within the world of scientific law and order. Some of the Protestant clergy interviewed earlier would likely have objected that the potential for God to transgress these laws was omnipresent, but in practice they shared a vision of the body as naturally ordered within the material universe, not as a receptacle for the divine. To suggest otherwise opened the door to the murky world of "mysticism," "sentimentalism," and "emotionalism."

If the clergy were divided on where to situate faith healing in relation to natural law, medical practitioners were generally convinced that such phenomena were easily explained. The *Canada Lancet* noted that "The mind continually influences the various functions of the body ... Through this mental influence on the nervous system, physiological and pathological action is excited or depressed. Consequently, results are produced on the devotee, which, although strictly in accordance with physiological laws, are hailed as miraculous by many." That the faithful believed a miracle has happened did not change the fact that the process was grounded in "natural laws solely." The editorial called for those claiming to be healed to submit themselves to investigation by medical experts. However, even if no scientific cause could be determined, it would not prove that divine intervention had taken place.

"The fact that science has not yet arrived at the knowledge whereby these laws affecting the nervous system ... can be enunciated, is no evidence of the violation of these laws in any instance, but merely proof of our want of information concerning them."[51]

The most extended medical analysis of divine healing in Canada was produced by Dr Daniel Clark, superintendent of Toronto's Asylum for the Insane, who penned an article for *Knox College Monthly* on the "Faith Cure." Clark was more specific in his understanding of how the mind influenced the body, dividing cases of faith healing into four classes. In the first class were diseases of the "nervous and emotional" order, including hysterias and hypochondrias, which Clark confined to the realm of imaginary diseases that would undoubtedly benefit from belief in anything, be it "magnet, magic, stone, idol, orgies, saint or Deity." The second class consisted of those who were "intensely devotional" or "naturally superstitious" to such a degree that the mind was able to produce "great and healthy activity in one or more of the bodily organs, and by secretion, excretion, and stimulation, bring about normal action in diseased parts, not by miraculous interference but along physiological lines under natural law." The third class was comprised of those who simply lied or pretended to suffer from certain conditions, and the fourth class was designed as a temporary relief from pain through "unusual excitement." In illustrating this last case, Clark noted: "Many a tooth-ache takes its everlasting flight at the dentist's door on the way in."[52]

In his later text, *Mental Diseases* (1895), Clark refers to his work as being part of the branch of "psycho-physics," a term that illustrates Clark's perception of the mind as essentially an epiphenomenon of the brain. Other than the third class of healings, which was composed of false claims, the orderings of the phenomena outlined by Clark were all generally somatic. Divine healing was a psychological stimulus that either corrected a problem that was psychological to begin with, or triggered a measurable physiological response through the brain or nervous system. It was, however, a process that clearly lay outside the realm of supernatural intervention: "Faith, hope and mental excitement are powerful factors to determine our weal or woe in this world without any reference to the Christian religion."[53]

The bilateral "weal" and "woe" that such mental excitement could produce was a rhetorical position that explained the success of faith cures in terms of scientific materialism and natural law while at the same time warned people not to employ such strategies. Although benefits might be gained from such psychological stimuli, faith healing was actually an unstable and unhealthy practice to be guarded against. If religious beliefs held within them the power to heal through an unleashing of certain

mental functions, they were conversely perceived as dangerous and potentially damaging in their psychological effects. Clark worried that "In
such constitutions, the religious element produces, of necessity, great
physical as well as mental exaltation or perturbation."[54] Hepworth was
more forthcoming: "It plays on the imagination of the pious in a very
dangerous fashion, and is as abnormal and unhealthy in its effect as any
other kind of ecstasy."[55] Faith healing could be scientifically explained as
a somatic impulse, but the potential of religion to influence the mind and
body meant that "ecstasy" and "mental exaltation" were experiences to
be avoided in the pursuit of true health.

The dangers of religious enthusiasm were expressed repeatedly in
both religious and secular papers, although the perceived respectability
of the Christian Alliance in Canada shielded it from direct criticism.
The dynamic and understanding of faith healing was very different for
groups that lay outside of this middle-class standard. While a number
of radical holiness groups in the southern United States embraced divine healing in a form that challenged such respectability, in Canada it
was the Salvation Army that first embraced and then rejected the practice of faith healing.

SALVATION ARMY HEALING

Founded by Catherine and William Booth in 1878, the Salvation Army
merged the holiness call for consecrated lives of service with militaristic
trappings. With its distinctive uniforms, brass bands, and openness to
women – "Hallelujah Lasses" preaching as "officers" – the Army carried its campaign for righteousness into the streets. Calling sinners to re-
pentance in the "cathedral of the open air," the Army gained both
friends and foes for its aggressive evangelism and boisterous style.[56]
Sporadic bursts of Army activity had reached Canada in the early
1880s, but the work was not officially established until 1884, when the
London headquarters sent Commissioner Thomas B. Coombs to Toronto to formally organize the Dominion Corps.[57] The Army's reputation for "enthusiasm" drew a working-class audience, which appeared
somewhat removed from the respectable evangelicalism of the Christian
Alliance. A closer examination, however, reveals a series of complex interconnections, and for a time faith healing was one of the strongest
links between the two organizations.

Two key personnel were recruited from the ranks of the Salvation
Army to serve the Dominion Alliance from its inception: Captains
George E. Fisher and Reuben J. Zimmerman. Zimmerman, who continued to practice dentistry on the side in order to supplement his in-
come, experienced divine healing in early 1887, and he obtained leave
from the Army to work exclusively for the Alliance. Fisher had been

anointed and healed under the guidance of Salmon, and became an active member of the Toronto branch. Although he maintained closer connections to the Army than Zimmerman, Fisher aided in the organization of many Dominion Alliance conventions. Salmon's own relationship with the Army was both professional and personal. Because the Army was not authorized to perform marriages until 1891, Salmon, who still held valid credentials with the Congregational Union, was requested to perform these official duties. Salmon accepted, wearing the title of "Brigade Captain" for his work in conducting wedding ceremonies. In 1888 Salmon's eldest daughter, Charlotte Annie, joined the Army and, later that same year, Salmon married her to Army officer Colonel Reuben Bailey.[58]

With such intimate connections between the two movements, it is not surprising that the subject of faith healing would become an issue for the Salvation Army. One of Coombs's first initiatives was to establish a Canadian edition of the Army newspaper, the *War Cry*, in February 1885, and very quickly stories related to faith healing began to appear in the paper. Sergeant Eli Austin testified that consumption and epileptic fits had left four doctors unable to help him. Following the regular meeting, his corps held a "faith-healing meeting" and, while "the Captain and our brothers and sisters were praying the power of the Lord came down upon me; at the same time I felt all doubts and fears were removed, a thrill of joy filled my soul, and I realised The Supernatural Power of the Great Physician."[59] A few months later, Major Tucker reported that at their first faith healing meeting, "*Five came out for body healing and one for her soul.*"[60] Although the commissioner himself did not comment on divine healing in print, Coombs led meetings at the Toronto Temple where healing testimonials were encouraged and anointings were held, and he appears to have been supportive of the practice.[61] In 1888 Salmon and Fisher held a divine healing "convention" at the Army's camp meeting at Colonel Wells Hill. When the Alliance convention reached Toronto in 1889, the *War Cry* supported its divine healing focus, and there are reports of at least one officer visiting Cullis in Boston for healing. Faith healing was also reported in Army circles in Britain, but the Canadian Corps' close personal and professional connections to the Alliance added an extra dimension to the practice in the Dominion.[62]

It is difficult to judge the full extent of the practice of faith healing within the Salvation Army in Canada. Unlike Alliance and other holiness periodicals, first-person testimonials such as Sergeant Austin's were rare in the *War Cry*, although high-ranking officers occasionally received prominent coverage. In Britain and in Canada, Army leadership exercised tight editorial control over the content of the denominational newspaper, and occurrences of faith healing were usually either paraphrased or recorded in brief, often anonymously. In Stratford, Captain Payne was an enthusiastic reporter of healings, proud that in the Salvation Army, "the deaf hear, the lame walk, and the leprous sinners are cleansed."

The Salvation Army's conceptualization of divine healing in the 1880s was somewhat ambiguous. Occasionally, those who practiced faith healing within the Army veered towards an understanding of the atonement encompassing bodily affliction similar to that of the divine healing movement. "The Lord does answer prayer when it comes from the heart and goes hand in hand with that faith which takes Jesus at His word and steps out upon the promise right into the possession of the promised inheritance," wrote Payne. "It is for you, go right in and possess it."[63] Without actually admitting that the atonement included a redemption of the body, Payne skirts very close in his employment of the language of "possession," suggesting that healing is automatically available to all. Zimmerman, who had thoroughly adopted the Alliance perspective on the atonement, lectured on the topic of divine healing in Army barracks across Ontario, travelling as far west as Goderich in spreading the message.[64]

The Army hierarchy had a very different view of healing and the body. In an effort to impose a standardized discipline, the Canadian Headquarters published General Booth's *Orders and Regulations* in 1887. An extensive section on health stressed the value and economy of good hygiene and diet, suggesting that officers abstain as much as possible from consuming "flesh-meat." The most striking feature on health in the *Orders and Regulations* was an appendix entitled "Hints on Health by the Water Treatment," written by Catherine Booth. With respect to hydropathy, "there is no system of treatment so effectual in curing disease or in preventing serious consequences." A daily regimen of cold baths was strongly advised, and after waking up, the officer "should tie his nightshirt round his waist, kneel down and sponge his head and shoulders well ... then let him sit down in the water and sponge his shoulders and body, laving the water up in the sponge and letting it run down his back, then rise up and step in and sponge his legs. He can apply the water, much or little, as he feels he can bear it." Even the correct methods for drying off were outlined, with the best towel being a "thick, common, rough brown sheet" that should be used to "rub himself smartly, till he feels all in a glow."[65] In the treatment of fevers, wet sheet packs were prescribed while warm sitz-baths relieved cholera as well as bladder and urine problems. Vapour baths, mustard plasters, and hot foments all treated a variety of ailments.

For those advocates of divine healing who felt that medicines and remedies were an obstacle to faith, such treatments were incompatible.

Captain Payne reported that in one case, the son of "Mrs. S." was suffering from a problem with his spine. Army soldiers visited the boy at home and told Mrs S. of previous recoveries through prayer. The mother asked them to pray for her son and agreed to *"leave off using doctor's medicine* ... but still she did not do away with the use of everything, for she used simple remedies such as bathing his back in salt and water and rubbing on electric oil." However, when Mrs S. neglected her duties one day, she thought, "Well the Lord can heal him without the salt and water, and is *not the Salvation Army and other Christian people praying for this to take place?"* The son's recovery was presented by Payne as an obvious indication that "God did not heal so long as she used other remedies."[66]

The variety of perspectives on healing and faith in the Salvation Army was not made any clearer by the *Orders and Regulations*, which, in addition to its advocacy of hydropathy and advice on health, also adopted a qualified view of faith healing. According to the manual, "That God should heal the sick after this fashion is in perfect harmony with the views and experience of The Salvation Army from the beginning." Officers were expressly warned not to question the veracity of faith healing, even if they did not fully endorse it. However, Booth refused to accept that the atonement included the promise of bodily restoration and claimed that God was able to work through traditional medical means. This balancing act placed officers in a precarious position; on the one hand, they were entreated not to discourage faith healing in others, while at the same time they were admonished not to go so far as to "consider disease to be a sin" or deny that "God has been pleased to heal sickness and disease by the use of appropriate means."

The Army's official position appeared prudent and tolerant, allowing those who wished to turn to faith healing to do so, while permitting those who preferred traditional remedies to maintain them. "Where men are led by the Spirit of God to heal, or be healed, by faith, by all means let it be so ... But where they are not, let them use such means as commend themselves to their own judgment, and they must not be condemned for so doing."[67] However, with such close connections to elements of the divine healing movement, Canadians in the Salvation Army sometimes found these positions to be irreconcilable. As illustrated previously, an explicit denial of remedies and drugs was recommended as a means to strengthen faith and trust in God. Taking medicine was perceived as evidence of temptation, doubt, and possibly the devil. As seventeen-year-old Nellie Hardman of Listowel, Ontario, testified in the *War Cry*, "The devil told me I ought to take medicine to strengthen me ... I took it for about two weeks, then the Lord showed me I was doubting His power ... The devil often tempts me to take medicine, and sometimes my faith is tried very much, but I tell the Lord I have taken Him as my Healer, and His strength is sufficient."[68] The rejection of medicine was a powerful act of faith, and proponents of faith healing found it difficult to imagine that true healing could come through human intervention. The cultural practice of Victorian faith healing simply did not provide the kind of flexible balance Booth hoped to achieve.

In 1890, accounts of faith healing in the *War Cry* ended abruptly, which was no small measure of the impact of Commissioner Coombs's recall to London and his replacement by David Rees. Events in Britain, including Catherine Booth's own personal struggle with breast cancer, created new complications for those interested in divine healing.[69] In addition to the moral and theological questions surrounding healing, the growing consolidation of the Army produced divisions between Canadian-born officers and the British officers sent over to staff the Dominion headquarters. Herbert Booth's subsequent arrival as commissioner in 1892 did little to alleviate the tension. The resignation of P.W. Philpott, the only Canadian-born officer still assigned to the Dominion headquarters, was the catalyst for the withdrawal of a large number of officers. Several issues were at stake in this division, including disapproval of impositions of Army structure and discipline, disagreement with decisions to withdraw from unpromising fields, and dissatisfaction with the Army's move towards increased social service. Questions were raised over the distribution of funds, and many of the Canadian officers rallied a measure of nationalism, bristling at the increased control London was exercising in the Dominion.[70]

Although faith healing was never publicly mentioned as an issue in the secession, those who left the Army clearly aligned themselves closely with the Alliance, while the Alliance's own ties to the continuing Dominion Corps withered. In addition to Philpott, the most prominent Army "seceders" included Adjutant Alfred W. Roffe and Captain George Fisher. Zimmerman had already left the Army to devote himself to the work of the Alliance. Having lost their commissions with the Army, the seceders turned to the Christian and Missionary Alliance for ministerial sanction. Salmon and Zimmerman agreed to examine and ordain them as "Ministers of the Gospel," although mention of divine healing and premillennialism was avoided. The three former Salvationists founded the Christian Workers Missions, later known as the Associated Gospel Churches of Canada. This new organization did not officially adopt the fourfold position, but contact between the original seceders and the Alliance would continue to be strong, formally and informally. Fisher's sympathies for the Alliance and divine healing were well known, and from 1898 to 1900 he would serve as a regional superintendent in the Dominion Alliance. Philpott discovered that he had contracted tuberculosis only a few weeks after his ordination. At a Bethany healing service he was anointed and prayed for by Salmon, Zimmerman, and Howland. He recovered overnight.[71] Although his own denominational work in Hamilton remained outside of the Alliance, Philpott also served as an Alliance regional superintendent for both the Eastern and Western districts. Roffe was a regular participant at Alliance conventions, and in 1919 he was appointed District Superintendent for the Alliance in Canada, a position he held until 1925.[72]

The traditional links that had been forged between the Alliance and the Army were cut by the schism of 1892. In the midst of the Army's upheaval and consolidation, barely any mention of the practice of faith healing found its way to the pages of the *War Cry* in the 1890s. Articles on "Health" and various "Hygienic Hints" became the mainstay of the paper. In an article on "Religion of the Body," the British field secretary, Colonel Hay, recast the impetus of holiness within a framework that excluded the main premise of faith healing: "PRESENT YOUR BODIES to God – for the world, for its salvation. Never mind your infirmities; He knows how to make these effective in His service."[73] In 1892 Captain Dowell remarked that at every house he visited "there was someone sick" and concluded that "people don't do enough walking. We hear the dear sisters say, 'I wish I could do something for the Lord, but I am so sick,' and looking up the case I find it is their own fault to a great extent." He then continued to berate the fashionable fatigue of women as the result of sleeping too late, taking too many street cars, and having heavy suppers.[74] The curt dismissal of women's infirmities was in sharp contrast to a healing testimonial by Captain May Smith only a few years earlier. Following a physical attack that left her with a dislocated rib, Smith was healed through prayer at an Army "Rest Home" in St. John, New Brunswick. Initially, Smith thought of her healing as a miraculous act – "I had not thought to take God as the Healer of my whole body" – but upon arriving in Toronto she decided to put her entire self "into His hands" and reported that since then she had "enjoyed perfect health, and gained twenty-seven pounds." Smith reflected that "I ... see so many of our dear girls who love the fight, but through ill health are discouraged and the devil is whispering in their ears as he did in mine, 'You might as well give up and go home and make room for some one else who is able to work,' it makes me sad ... My prayer is that God will let the light stream in your soul as it did into mine, in reference to Divine healing. Lord make us real women of war!"[75] It was agreed that the body of the servant needed to be whole in order to carry out the Lord's work, but the perspectives of Dowell and Smith reveal gendered theological differences regarding the means by which "true" health is achieved. By the time Dowell's views were published, Captain May Smith had already left the Army, publicly siding with the seceders.

The Salvation Army's final break with faith healing came at the turn of the century, with the resignation of "La Maréchale," the Booths'

eldest daughter, Kate, and her husband, Arthur Booth-Clibborn. Their
ministry was largely centred in Europe, but Arthur's growing emphasis
on divine healing, premillennialism, and pacifism was not favoured by
the rest of the family at the International Headquarters in London. Although Kate's views on divine healing are not as clear, their children
were raised with "no remedies," and sickness was treated with "anointing and prayer."[76] Arthur claimed that he had believed in the atonement
position on healing for many years, but he was particularly inspired
when he heard John Alexander Dowie preach on the issue during his
1901 healing campaign in London. After an extended dispute over policy, the Booth-Clibborns finally left the Army in 1902, founding a European "Christian Mission of 'Friends of Zion'" for "friends and
members" of Dowie's Christian Catholic Church. Arthur's brother,
Percy, went to Chicago to join Dowie, and Arthur became a member of
the Christian Catholic Church. Noticeably, Kate did not join the church
and was never as outspoken about divine healing as her husband.[77]

The resignation of the Booth-Clibborns and Arthur's public association with the faith healing activities of Dowie were traumatic events in
Army ranks, and the estrangement from her family proved to be very
difficult for Kate, who was less than two months away from giving
birth. The General's response to the controversy was a "Memorandum"
on faith healing that denounced the "false, misleading, and ruinous"
views that had been spread on the question of faith healing: "Against
their acceptance I want to caution you – not only because they are un-
true, but because I know them to be dangerous, and productive of evil
to those who embrace them, and because *I cannot, therefore, permit
them to be taught amongst us*, either in our publications, in our meetings, or to our people in any other form, *by either Officers, Soldiers, or
anyone else*." The sixty-five page memorandum attacked the familiar
theological positions of divine healing on atonement and the tendency
to view sickness as sin, but special consideration was given to the role of
medicine in healing: "It is no part of the work of Salvationists to take
up cudgels for or against any particular species of physic or any particular school of Physicians." For Booth, God could intervene without reliance upon medical means if necessary, but he could just as easily restore
health through the hands of physicians. If humans needed food, water,
and sleep to sustain them, was not this simply one more "means" to
maintain health? It was in the "natural instincts of the Race" to alleviate suffering from whatever source and to use whatever means God had
providentially provided. There were occasions when a sufferer might
voluntarily desist from regular treatment to trust in God, but to do so
was to assume a "grave responsibility ... perilously near to the infliction
of a great wrong."[78]

If the divine healing movement drew upon the rhetoric and popularity of health reform in redeeming the body, why did the Salvation Army, which arguably stood the closest to alternative medicine in its adoption of hydropathy, reject both theological and fraternal associations with the faith healers? The personal circumstances of Catherine Booth and the family battles with the Booth-Clibborns certainly played a role, as did the antagonism of faith healers like Dowie, whose public controversies gave the divine healing movement a public reputation for fanaticism. As important, however, were differing approaches to the meanings of holiness and health. Barbara Robinson has noted that for the Army, the adoption of alternative therapeutic practices was rarely linked to the experience of sanctification, despite its own holiness roots. While the pursuit of health could empower one for service to God, "perfected body was not the physiological equivalent of a perfected soul."[79] In contrast, the divine healing movement drew strongly upon sanctification as key to the redemption of the body, a parallel made explicit by atonement theology.

What eventually made a reconciliation impossible, however, was the direction the Army took following the publication of General Booth's *In Darkest England and the Way Out* (1890). The saving of souls was interlinked with the alleviation of poverty and a broad program of social reform. Those suffering from hunger and cold were not likely to spend much time contemplating their spiritual state, so meeting the needs of the physical body became an evangelistic duty. It was clear that while salvation was still important, the health problems in the urban slums were to be met with practical means and treatment rather than trusting in prayer.[80] Where the divine healing movement viewed bodily restoration as an important end-result of one's sanctified state, the Army saw social reform, including public health and hospital work, as a vehicle for saving souls.

Faith healing in Victorian English-speaking Canada was primarily a private practice, a contemplative act that was set within a particular domestic social geography of health and healing. At the same time, Protestant divine healing maintained a public face, which also sought to define a broader social space for the practice of faith healing to continue. The Christian Alliance was clearly identified as the leading organization in Canada that strove to translate informal networks into a recognizable movement. Faith healing spilled into other groups at various times on a small scale, but the only denomination to come close to adopting it as official policy was the Salvation Army, which was itself closely aligned with the Dominion Auxiliary in Canada. Later the Salvation Army would retreat from both the Alliance and faith healing.

The organization of institutional structures to support faith healing also opened the door to a wide series of critical discourses surrounding the body. Newspapers were no longer simply commenting upon occasional, individual cases of faith healing. Now they could associate healings, practices, and beliefs with the conventions and branches of the Alliance. The influential presence of "respectable men" shielded the Alliance from direct charges of fanaticism, but the organization's public presence produced a wide variety of reactions on many different levels. Newspapers and mainstream religious periodicals generally reinforced the dominant discourse of the body by relegating faith healing to certain types of diseases or to the function of various mental impulses. Nevertheless, in the overlapping opinions of doctors, psychologists, and theologians, there was considerable fluidity in the ideas surrounding the exact relationship between religion and the body.

The comfortable position of the Christian Alliance Dominion Auxiliary at the end of the nineteenth century was shaken by the loss of a number of prominent figures within the movement. In the near future, however, it would face far more pressing dilemmas. The distancing of the Salvation Army from the practice of faith healing and the protracted dispute with the Booth-Clibborns signalled a growing polarization within the broader divine healing movement. Where the Alliance had once been able to bridge the enthusiasm of the Army with a respectable evangelicalism, the twentieth century would mark a breakdown of this middle ground as the Alliance struggled to maintain itself in the face of pentecostalism and a new conservative evangelicalism that rejected the extension of holiness to the body. In 1897 Simpson merged the Christian Alliance with the Missionary Alliance, but the reorganization also meant the dissolution of the well-established Dominion Auxiliary and its elected officers. Instead of representing a truly national organization, the Canadian field became simply an extension of New York, holding a status on par with the regional divisions of the Alliance in the United States. At times the newly merged Alliance appeared to be more intent on maintaining its own middle ground by concentrating efforts upon missionary activity rather than stressing the devotional aspects of the fourfold gospel.

Faith healing would emerge once again to resurrect the fortunes of the Alliance in Canada, but it would find itself occupying a very different role and place in the twentieth century. In the meantime, the public face of divine healing would shift from the moderate evangelicalism of the Alliance to the radicalism of John Alexander Dowie. The restraint of criticism in deference to the Alliance's respectable men would be replaced with scorn and vitriol, and Dowie's followers would be quick to respond in kind.

4

Marching to Zion

His slow feet walked him riverward, reading. Are you saved? All are washed in
the blood of the lamb. God wants blood victim. Birth, hymen, martyr, war,
foundation of a building, sacrifice, kidney, burntoffering, druid's altars. Elijah
is coming. Dr. John Alexander Dowie, restorer of the church in Zion, is
coming.
   Is coming! Is coming!! Is coming!!!
   All heartily welcome.

James Joyce, *Ulysses* (1922)

By the time Dr Lilian B. Yeomans, M.D., reached Chicago in 1898, she
had already attempted every remedy she could imagine to free herself
from addiction to morphine and chloral hydrate. For four years she
sought both conventional and unorthodox treatments. In her home town
of Winnipeg, the newly established Keeley Institute offered a "Gold
Cure" to treat drug addiction, but its effectiveness was no better than
that of the sanitarium for "nervous diseases," which she attended as
well. Yeomans even explored Christian Science, travelling to New York
to investigate the movement, but she returned to Canada disillusioned.[1]
   When she arrived at John Alexander Dowie's Zion Home in the care
of her sister Amy, a registered nurse, Lilian ate little and constantly
struggled with insomnia, diarrhea, and spells of vomiting. That the afflicted would turn to Zion Home was not surprising, but it was practically the last place one might find a trained physician seeking aid in
light of Dowie's notorious attacks on doctors, drugs, and the practice
of medicine. Dowie did have former physicians on his staff, but none
boasted the remarkable medical lineage of the Yeomans sisters. Their
father, Dr Augustus Yeomans, had served as a surgeon for the Union
Army during the American Civil War and had died while Lilian was attending medical school.[2] The following year, the widowed mother,
Amelia, joined Lilian by enrolling alongside her at the medical college
of the University of Michigan, Ann Arbor. The daughter-mother duo
graduated with their medical diplomas in 1882 and 1883, respectively,
and went into practice together in Winnipeg. Lilian concentrated on

medicine while her mother became an active social reformer, crusading for women's suffrage and temperance.[3] Amelia LeSueur Yeomans also happened to be the sister of William Dawson LeSueur, the critical essayist who had engaged in the Victorian prayer debate of the 1870s.

When Lilian Yeomans prayed to God in the expectation that he might guide her to an appropriate method of treatment, her plea was never "satisfactorily answered"; instead, "God seemed to say plainly, 'I am the Lord that healeth thee,' and so I came down to Zion." At Zion Home her narcotics were promptly removed and Dowie informed her that she would not be healed unless she lost all of her "confidence in drugs."[4] In the ensuing spiritual struggle, Lilian decided that she had to believe that she was cured of her addiction "in spite of all symptoms," and on 12 January 1898, the physician was both healed and baptized by Dowie.[5] While her status and background were unusual, the Yeomans' journey to Zion was not an isolated case. Canadians from many different parts of the country investigated the phenomenal reports of the famous Chicago faith healer, and Dowie reciprocated by sending evangelists into Canada.

Although small in number, the Canadians who marched to Zion sparked intense controversies that were usually large in scope and meaning. Unlike the quiet healing activities of the mainstream divine healing movement, which attracted only occasional public notice, the belligerence of the "Dowieites" engendered a hostile reaction faced by no other faith healing group. The mild criticism of ministers and newspapers gave way to a series of legal actions that shifted the ground of the faith healing controversy from the press to the courtroom. The sudden interest in laying criminal charges against faith healers reflected much more than a reaction to the pugnacity of Dowie and his followers. In an age of germ theory, divine healing was no longer a mere theological dispute. As new health regulations were implemented to contain contagious diseases, the practice of faith healing appeared to pose a danger to the public health in the eyes of medical authorities and government officials. In the early twentieth century, faith healing battled both the devil of disease and the encompassing apparatus of public health.

DISCOVERING DOWIE

When John Salmon had entreated the *Canadian Independent* to publish John Alexander Dowie's letter to the 1885 International Divine Healing Convention, the evangelist was largely unknown outside of Australia. By the mid-1890s, however, the faith healer had practically become a household name in North America. Born in Edinburgh in 1847, Dowie emigrated with his family to Australia when he was a teenager, although he returned to Scotland briefly for theological training. While serving as a Congregational minister in a church close to Sydney, Dowie was faced with an epidemic in 1876 that struck down many in his congregation. It was this experience that led him to the doctrine of divine healing and a heated exchange with an attending physician. In response to the doctor's suggestion that disease was simply part of God's cosmic plan, Dowie exclaimed: "How dare you, Dr. K—, call that God's way of bringing His children home from earth to Heaven? No, sir, *that is the Devil's work*, and it is time we called on Him who came to destroy the work of the Devil, to slay the deadly foul destroyer."[6] When Dowie's prayers raised the young woman from her sickness, he had found the sword that would slay the demon of disease.

Dowie resigned his pastorate to take on a variety of roles as an independent evangelist, social reform activist, and a parliamentary candidate. Unsuccessful in an electoral bid, his energies soon turned towards establishing a large tabernacle in Melbourne and founding the International Divine Healing Association. To give his organization broader international exposure, Dowie embarked on a missionary tour in 1888 that took him to the west coast of North America, and for two years the evangelist traveled from Mexico to British Columbia, establishing new branches of the association along the way. In August 1889, the evangelist reached Victoria, where he held his first Canadian divine healing mission. Dowie did not hide his uncompromising attitude towards medicine, but many of the clergy and prominent laymen appear to have either accepted or tolerated his position. On the closing night of the mission, seventeen people witnessed to having experienced healing through faith, and "many hundreds" accepted the doctrine of divine healing. While some minor events brought him some unflattering attention, for the most part the city press tended to ignore Dowie's campaign.[7]

In 1890 Dowie relocated his headquarters to Chicago, where his healing activities drew unprecedented attention from the public and the press alike. When the World's Fair reached the windy city in 1893, Dowie set up a wooden tabernacle across the street from Buffalo Bill Cody's Wild West Show. By the time Buffalo Bill was ready to leave town, Dowie's show was rivaling the Wild West Show, and even Cody's niece had crossed the street to be healed in the tabernacle. Few corners of the city were left unscathed by Dowie's bombastic tirades against other denominations, the clergy, secret societies, politicians, druggists, surgeons and physicians. The latter three were denounced as "THAT BANDED TRINITY OF POISONERS AND MURDERERS."[8]

Dowie's brazen style, and the numbers who flocked to him for healing, prompted the state of Illinois to prosecute him for practicing medicine without a licence. This challenge was unsuccessful, but the faith healer was soon engaged in another struggle with the Chicago Board of Health, which claimed that his healing homes constituted hospitals, and since no regular physicians were on hand, the close confinement of so many sick people with contagious diseases posed a public health risk. Dowie's own actions contributed to the constant sense of turmoil that surrounded him. In 1895 Dowie withdrew from his own International Divine Healing Association to found the Christian Catholic Church, taking the title of "General Overseer."[9]

The public controversy over Dowie's battles both solidified his support and distanced him from the broader divine healing movement. His harsh language and uncompromising hostility towards medicine were evident during the faith healer's time in Australia, but these traits were amplified during his American tenure. Despite his inclusion in Broadman's International Conference, Dowie's style was a far cry from that of Charles Cullis, A.B. Simpson, or Carrie Judd. Theologically, Dowie attacked the progressive understanding of salvation, holiness, and healing. Instead of divine healing serving as an extension of sanctification, a separate experience, Dowie regarded sanctification as being part and parcel of conversion and healing. Divine healing physically marked both the saving grace of God and the sanctified state of the believer, and Dowie resisted attempts to insert the word "holiness" into the name of the Divine Healing Association. Since disease was sin, the sanctified state would be attended by an absence of disease and the infilling of divine health.[10]

The strong association of all forms of disease and sickness with sin and the devil was present in Dowie's teachings from the very beginning of his healing ministry. The divine healing movement framed the "prayer of faith" as an internal spiritual struggle, a contemplative soul searching that was similar to discovering an inner conviction of sanctification. For Dowie, the battle against disease was a much wider cosmological reality. From his first encounter with the Australian epidemic, Dowie characterized what he faced in harsh terms: "Disease, the foul offspring of its father, Satan, and its mother, Sin, was defiling and destroying the earthly temples of God's children, and there was no deliverer."[11] Charles Champe illustrated this perception of sin and sickness in numerous cartoons published in the *Leaves of Healing*, which demonstrated the powerlessness of physicians and most "denominational ministers." As illustrated in figure 4.1, only the pure symbol of Zion sees the true "root" of afflictions. The divine healing movement had long embodied an underlying critique of medical culture and the new scientific discourses of the body, but Dowie's explicit attacks on the medical profession were unprecedented. In his view, physicians stood in the way of the faithful discovering the healing that had been

Fig. 4.1. Illustration by Charles Champe. *Leaves of Healing*, 2 February 1901, p. 456. Flower Pentecostal Heritage Center

promised them in the atonement, and therefore they were instruments of the devil. For those advocates of faith healing who had remained close to the respectability of the early divine healing movement, Dowie's language and vitriol were both inappropriate and damaging.

Nevertheless, it was the very respectable Dominion Auxiliary of the Christian Alliance that supported Dowie's first campaign to Toronto. Details on the six weeks Dowie spent in southern Ontario in November and December 1890 are sketchy, since the press in Toronto generally ignored the event.[12] However, one observer noted that "[Dowie's] accent is Scotch ... his style of speaking is very direct – too blunt for some super-sensitive ears. He calls tobacco smokers 'nasty stink-pots'[;] he speaks of Job's affliction as 'the vile stinking boils that came from the devil's dirty fingers.'"[13] By the end of the campaign a number of familiar faces shared the platform with Dowie, including John Salmon, and R.J. Zimmerman was elected president of the newly formed Toronto Divine Healing Association.[14] In the middle of his mission, Dowie took ten days to travel outside the city, focusing particularly on Peterborough where interest in faith healing had already been sparked by the Alliance. Here, as elsewhere, Dowie's personal style and "strong language" attracted as much attention as his healing message.

The mission in Peterborough faced controversy from the beginning, as Dowie criticized his audience for not being attentive enough and rebuked the "church people" who arrived late from their own evening services and then left before the address had concluded. When a local Methodist minister, G.H. Davis, stood up to challenge Dowie, the evangelist told him to sit down and the closing hymn was abruptly started. Davis complained to the local newspapers that Dowie demonstrated a "rudeness as though he had been living all his life in some part of Australia among the convicts and had not yet learned Christian courtesy."[15] In return, Dowie used the uncharitable Australian reference as a ploy to label his accuser as the discourteous one and demanded an apology, issuing his trademark "strong language" in the process. Frequent comment was made of Dowie's "strong invectives hurled with a loud voice and anything but refined language."[16] The denunciations of tobacco use, lazy Christians, and almost all of the ministers and denominations in the town, eventually resulted in the loss of the local Baptist Church for his meetings. Nevertheless, Dowie's harangues continued unabated, and to hisses, laughter, and cheers from the crowds he maintained his attacks. A number of cures were reported, the majority of them being from women.[17]

Despite the controversy in Peterborough, Dowie was successful in establishing a branch of his International Divine Healing Association (IDHA). Like the Alliance, these societies were designed to serve as an interdenominational fellowship. The organization was barely off the ground, however, when Dowie abruptly ended his relationship with the association in order to found his own Christian Catholic Church in 1896. The local branches quickly collapsed, if they had not already folded.[18] Dowie would eventually claim the title of Elijah the Restorer, changing the name of his work once again to the Christian Catholic Apostolic Church. By itself, the IDHA might have remained a minor footnote in the history of divine healing in Canada, but Dowie's growing prominence as a faith healer based in Chicago would continue to draw Canadians southward, and new gatherings of "Friends of Zion" would form. This time, however, the press and the public would not be slow to take notice.

PIGS AND DEVILS IN BRUCE COUNTY

For the quiet farming community of Brant Township, nestled in the middle of Bruce County, Ontario, the newspaper headline from the *Chesley Enterprise* was alarming in its bold type: "Religious Unrest in Bruce – Mormons and Zionites – Wholesale Slaughter of Swine – James Turner Sent up for Trial – Wilful destruction of Property; The

New Faith Conflicts with the Statutes." Something was disturbing the religious waters in the Chesley area, and in the opinion of the newspaper, "more religious disquietude seems to prevail in the county of Bruce than anywhere else in Ontario." The spread of Mormonism, tainted by its association with polygamy, was worrying for the newspaper, but this issue only amounted to a small part of the article. More pernicious, and closer to the good folk of Chesley, was a new "sect" that went by the name of "Zionites, Faith Healers, or Christian Catholic Church."[19]

How did the exploits of Dowie in Chicago become implicated in the religious turmoil facing Bruce County? The *Enterprise* was diligent in tracing the genesis of the sect's activities, locating the root of the problem in Miss Zinkan of Southampton. In 1895 Zinkan was engaged as an evangelist to assist Rev. Davey in his work at Chesley Methodist Church and a small Methodist outpost in the nearby hamlet of Vesta. Zinkan had read Dowie's magazine, *Leaves of Healing*, and was a firm believer in divine healing. According to the newspaper, Zinkan's first convert was Vesta's schoolteacher, James Turner. Turner and his family were soon engaged in a struggle with Rev. Davey over the issue of divine healing, and a number of Methodist families withdrew from the local Methodist churches over the issue. The Turners and others in the area began to visit Chicago; those who returned were more committed than ever to Dowie's Christian Catholic Church and eager to circulate copies of the *Leaves of Healing* throughout the community. The message of Zion spread beyond Methodist circles and the Turners' efforts bore fruit even in the family of a notable Presbyterian elder, William Fiddis, whose son and daughter both took up Dowie's teachings. When Fiddis demanded that his son, John, remove a book of Dowie's from the table, John and his sister, Ida, removed themselves from the household. Their advocacy of Dowie also led to a power struggle with the Presbyterian minister, and John and Ida later sparked a stormy withdrawal from the local Christian Endeavor group.[20]

As tensions grew in the community over the Dowieite disruptions, it required only a small pen of pigs to escalate an internal family dispute into a public religious controversy. Life at Zion demanded strict dietary measures against alcohol, tobacco, tea, coffee, shellfish, and pork. Dowie considered oysters and pigs as little more than "scavengers," and therefore both were deemed to be filthy animals unfit for human consumption. Those who dared partake of "swine's flesh" were "afflicted by scrofula, cancer, tuberculosis, skin diseases, trichinosis, cholera and many other diseases caused by filth in the blood."[21] Just as the cosmological categories of sin and sickness merged and intermingled, so too did the physical and moral states of the body; both were in danger of corruption from unclean foods. The very appetite for filthy flesh inflamed devilish

ZION'S PROTEST AGAINST THE TYRANNY OF UNCLEAN SWINE'S FLESH.

Fig. 4.2. Illustration by Charles Champe. *Leaves of Healing*, 17 August 1901, p. 523. Flower Pentecostal Heritage Center

passions, while the actual consumption of pork and oysters spread disease. As portrayed graphically by Champe in figure 4.2, cancer patients and harlots were equally bound as servants to swine.

John and Ida Fiddis left their family for a household more favourably disposed towards Dowie, but John also left behind his hog operation. According to one report, the Fiddis farm had an extensive pen, complete with new buildings and a solid breeding stock that made the business profitable.[22] After adopting Dowie's attitude towards pork, John sold four of his pigs. However, since these were still being consumed by humans, thereby infecting them with disease and unhealthy passions, John was troubled by a guilty conscience, and he resolved to dispose of the remaining eleven pigs in a more permanent fashion. John Fiddis and James Turner returned to the farm and drove the pigs into the bush, killing and burying them. Two days later, Turner boarded a train for Chicago in order to enroll in Dowie's Zion College. Outraged at what had happened, William Fiddis swore out an arrest warrant for

Turner on a charge of stealing. The prospective student was arrested in London and forcibly returned to Walkerton, where he was eventually released on $400 bail. The Crown prosecutor decided to add to the charges the willful destruction of property, and the case was committed to trial.[23]

The arrest of James Turner not only sparked the interest of Bruce County in the activities of the Dowieites, it drew the notice of Dowie in Chicago, who exploited the event in the *Leaves of Healing*. Turner wrote Dowie letters detailing his brief imprisonment, and Dowie promptly shipped him a box of 1,000 pamphlets entitled "Zion's Protest Against Swine's Flesh as a Disease-Producer." The situation offered Dowie a favourable result, no matter what the outcome: if Turner went to jail, he would be a perfect martyr for Zion's cause, and if he were set free, it would illustrate the triumph of Zion over her enemies.[24] For the readers of the *Leaves of Healing*, the Turner case illustrated that "He who ceases to eat swine's flesh meets with jibes and sneers, but he who destroys the Devil's beloved hogs is thrown into jail, branded as a thief, maligned by the Devil's newspapers, and bitterly denounced by the Devil's own so-called Christians in the Denominations."[25] The judicial battle did not last long, since the proceedings quickly became embroiled over the actual ownership of the pigs and whether they were the property of the father or son. The charges were thrown out, and Zionites celebrated by distributing the anti-swine pamphlets across the county.[26]

William Fiddis prosecuted Turner instead of his own son for reasons that went beyond blood and kinship. The Turner family was widely regarded as the main source of the religious turmoil facing Bruce County. Davey's successor at Chesley Methodist Church, Rev. C.J. Dobson, expressly warned some who were considering divine healing to stay away from the troublesome Turners.[27] Geography also played a large role in who was targeted in halting the spread of Dowie's teachings. While the *Enterprise* declared that religious turmoil was everywhere, faith healing was a peculiarly localized phenomenon in Bruce County, and to many observers, Zion had clearly captured "some of the most prominent and respectable residents on the 12th concession [of Brant township]."[28] Running along the north end of Brant township, the 12th concession lay near a few small hamlets and villages, but the closest large town was Chesley. Although Turner taught at Vesta, a short distance away, his family was largely settled along the 12th concession, and it was there that Dowie's influence was felt most strongly.

One of the original crown deed holders on the concession was an established Methodist family with Irish roots, the Leggetts. According to her later testimony, Sara Leggett was a "rugged" sixteen-year-old until an accident injured her left side. Doctors explained that the numbness in her side was produced by either a damaged spleen or heart problems. Overwork and mental anguish over the death of a sister added to Sara's problems, and in 1894 she found her side partially paralyzed. Dr Gimby of Chesley prescribed salt baths, port wine, and medicine that, according to Sara, "nearly killed me, being too strong for my heart." Sara's sister, Lydia, had eye difficulties that had forced her to give up her teaching career. Medicine also did little to help Lydia, as her physical strength was "completely shattered by the use of medicine and electricity administered by doctors." In December 1897, the newly arrived Methodist minister, C.J. Dobson, remarked to Sara that perhaps she should think about the possibility of looking to God for healing. Whether or not Dobson was aware of the difficulties his predecessor had encountered regarding divine healing, it was a suggestion Dobson would soon come to regret.

Sara and Lydia had read accounts of healing and were interested in pursuing the prayer of faith for themselves. Dobson prayed with Sara at her request, but she experienced no immediate results. Lydia's eyes worsened, but after much soul-searching and quitting her medicine, she was eventually healed. Sara's condition, however, grew more serious with the discovery of a tumor near the abdomen, and Gimby doubted if she would live more than a few months. After experiencing disappointment with a prayer request sent to A.B. Simpson, Sara started to read copies of the *Leaves of Healing* that had been left behind after a visit from Mrs Turner. When Sara asked her minister for his opinion of Dowie, Dobson warned her to be wary of both Dowie and the Turners and revealed that he had attended the faith healer's earlier meetings in Toronto, which he characterized as a failure.

Despite this negative assessment, Sara persevered in her desire to seek divine healing even after the pain increased. When the family finally decided to send for the doctor, Sara demanded that Dobson also be sent for, claiming she would not take any medicine unless she consulted her minister first. Dobson quickly supported the doctor, contending that it would be presumptuous not to use available means and assuring her that her mind "was just a little disturbed" by the suffering. Sara and Lydia were vexed by Dobson's attitude, but Sara agreed reluctantly to the minister's advice. Neither body nor soul were assuaged, however. Both physician and minister attempted to reconcile Sara to her impending death, but Sara was determined that faith would heal her. At one point she insisted that Dobson should anoint her, which he assented to do despite Lydia's misgivings about their minister not having "the prayer of faith."

The Turners continued to encourage the Leggetts to pursue faith healing by sending over copies of the *Leaves of Healing*. After reading a number of back issues and having exhausted other possibilities, Sara and Lydia resolved to go to Chicago for themselves. In July 1898 the Leggett sisters set out on their journey, singing "We're Marching to Zion." When they reached Zion Home, Dowie laid hands upon Sara, and she was able to walk, believing she was perfectly healed, although it took some time before all symptoms disappeared.[29]

The healing experience of the Leggetts and the arrest of James Turner over the pig slaughter brought together the families on the 12th concession who were active members of the Christian Catholic Church. Meeting as a "Gathering of the Friends of Zion," or simply the "Malcolm Gathering," they started to hold open evangelistic meetings in Chesley in May 1899. In reporting on the activities of the "Brant Zionites," the *Enterprise* found that Sara Leggett's control over the meeting and her address represented "excellent order" and offered nothing that would "give offence." The paper's opinion of John Fiddis was far less salutary: "John may not have intended to say what he did and probably has no idea what he did say, he simply opened his mouth and there came forth disconnected sentences abusing ministers, doctors and druggists, all of whom were set down in his (the learned John Fiddies' [sic]) opinion as servants of Satan." The article was clearly written by William McDonald, editor of the *Enterprise* and a staunch member of Chesley Methodist Church.[30] Ridiculing Fiddis's speech as "the kind of twaddle [that] may win over some silly people who are longing for a new religion, not more religion," McDonald assessed the *Leaves of Healing* and concluded that "there is neither love nor Christianity in Dowieism." One suspects that the editor's layout of the newspaper was deliberate; the end of the piece on Dowie was placed squarely next to a series of advertisements for patent drugs, the local druggist, and the butcher shop promoting a special on pork.[31]

The editor of the *Enterprise* was not the only one interested in what was happening with the Malcolm Gathering. In Victoria, British Columbia, Eugene Brooks was reading a copy of the *Leaves of Healing* with Sara Leggett's picture and testimonial on the front cover. Struck by both her photograph and her healing narrative, Brooks wrote to the Gathering to offer his evangelistic services. Although it took almost a year for the arrangements to be finalized, the two corresponded amicably, and Brooks entertained thoughts of marriage.[32]

Eugene Brooks was a Virginian who had been healed of constipation and numerous digestive difficulties at Zion in 1896. In his capacity as an evangelist for the Christian Catholic Church, Brooks had been sent to the west coast of Canada in May 1899 to take over a field that had been "pioneered" by Rev. George Armour Fair only a year previously. A colleague commented that the fledgling Vancouver congregation consisted largely of mechanics, clerks, and day laborers.[33] In Victoria, Brooks started with a small following of seventeen and quickly doubled its numbers. He had intended to leave for Ontario sooner, but he found himself fighting off attacks from Fair, who had turned against Dowie and now sought the support of his former congregations.

When the crisis had passed, Brooks finally boarded a train for Bruce County, still contemplating nuptial ties. The night he arrived at the Leggett household he proposed to Sara. After a short spiritual struggle, Sara agreed to marry Brooks in Chicago within a week.[34] While the wedding plans were being arranged, Brooks and the Malcolm faithful launched an evangelistic campaign at Chesley Town Hall. Unfortunately for Brooks, the timing of his meetings was less than ideal. Not only had Chesley welcomed the extraordinarily popular Canadian evangelistic team of H.T. Crossley and J.E. Hunter less than two months before, but his thick southern accent did little to endear him to an audience that was caught up in the nationalistic imperialism of the ongoing Boer War. The meetings were tumultuous, and according to the *Enterprise*, Brooks claimed that "the biggest rowdy" was one of the Crossley-Hunter converts. Any chance of a sympathetic hearing was quashed when Brooks reportedly criticized the Boer War, calling it "the devil's protracted meeting" and declaring that contingents of Canadians were "fighting the battles of the devil."[35] After his comments became known, some of the town's "boys" loaded their pockets with eggs and potatoes in preparation for the next night's meeting. The result was "pandemonium," as Brooks challenged the "dirty devils" to come at him: "I have been in cattle pens before and understand how to handle cattle." As eggs flew through the air, the lights were put out and only with great difficulty was Brooks able to continue speaking. A similar "riot" took place on the final night of Brooks's meetings, with Brooks again "shelled by decayed hen fruit" and forced to take shelter "behind the ladies."[36]

Brooks's own account of events in the *Leaves of Healing* painted a somewhat different picture. The evangelist claimed that nightly he had stood in the face of two to three hundred "bowling, infuriated devils." In addition to eggs, potatoes, snowballs, and frozen clods of earth, the crowd "hissed, they yelled, they cursed, and they would have murdered us if they dared." The riotous acts continued outside as the mob chased Brooks's sleigh, "yelling like the demons they were." For Brooks, the blame rested clearly on the shoulders of McDonald, a "big gun" in the church and a "first-class Methodist editorial hyena," who was the head of the "roughs in town."[37] It was suggested that part of McDonald's animosity towards Brooks stemmed from his courtship of Sara Leggett; that a local girl could be lost to a coarse Yankee was anathema in loyal Chesley.[38]

In the 1880s and 1890s, the "respectable" faith healing inspired by Charles Cullis, A.B. Simpson, and Carrie Judd had produced only muted criticism. However, by the turn of the century Dowie and his followers sparked violence, riots, and invective in their battle against the devil. Despite sharing the basic atonement position on faith healing, the march to Zion marked a strict separation of the faithful from the profane world of medicine, unhealthy appetites, and established denominations. Implicit critiques had been long embedded in women's testimonials, but Dowie provided a forum for explicit attacks that divided families, churches, and communities. However, the refusal to compromise in the pursuit of faith healing carried its own dangers, and when deaths were linked to the activities of the Zionites, Brooks faced a different form of judgment.

IN THE KING'S COURT

Eugene Brooks and Sara Leggett were married by Dowie in Chicago on 22 February 1900. Two days later, Eugene was ordained as an Elder, and Sara was commissioned as an evangelist. The Brookses returned to Victoria in May, but it was not long before they were vaulted into the public spotlight once again. The Zionites would find themselves in Canadian courts, but this time the issues at stake were far more serious than legal disputes over the ownership of pigs.

The Maltby family had recently joined the Christian Catholic Church in Victoria, although Mrs Jessie Maltby, a former member of the Salvation Army, had been a believer in divine healing for the past four years.[39] When five-year-old Claude Maltby fell ill, Elder Brooks prayed for him without success. After the boy's death on 21 November 1900, the family applied for a death permit but was refused, as no doctor had attended the child. Instead, a sanitary inspector quarantined their home for fear of diphtheria, posted a red card on their door, and stationed a guard outside of the house. The Maltby family and a boarder, Amanda Hatt, were removed to an isolation hospital for fumigation. The next day an inquest into the death commenced, and suddenly Elder Brooks was again making news.

The coroner's inquest disclosed that Claude Maltby had taken ill five days before his death. Brooks was present several times during the child's illness, and both the Maltbys and Brooks testified that they believed that the child was suffering from "membranous croup," not diphtheria. The provincial health officer, Dr C.J. Fagan, testified that a post-mortem examination had revealed the presence of diphtheria bacilli in the throat. Claude's father, Willie Maltby, and Brooks both claimed that they had seen diphtheria before, but that Claude's affliction did not resemble the infection. Prior to adopting divine healing, Maltby testified that he had "buried four children under the care of doctors" and that one of these had died of diphtheria.[40]

While the inquest was being held, a medical inspection of the Maltby household revealed that the entire Maltby household was suffering from diphtheria, including the boarder. Whether they had contracted the disease from Claude or from their exposure in the isolation hospital was a question that was not pursued. The eldest daughter was in a critical state when the family was returned to the hospital, but the Maltbys tried to refuse medical treatment. The children caused a commotion when they were separated from their parents, but Dr R.L. Fraser, the Medical Health Officer for Victoria, threatened to send for the police if the Maltbys would not submit to treatment and allow their children to be removed.[41] While in isolation from each other, young Ivan Maltby attempted to smuggle a note to his parents, but the illegal communication was intercepted by a nurse:

Dear Mamma & Papa

I am getting about as sick as I can from medicine ... When I came here I was as well as could be. Now I have a sick stomach. My head is near aching. After the injection last night, baby cried herself to sleep ... We are continually dosed with iron and swabbed with acid. We have to eat whether we want to or not. Brandy is mixed with everything we eat ... These nurses and doctors can do [sic] be like devils ... It is just horrible here[.] Once nurse was swabbing my mouth I got mad and told her the way we connected "Doc., Drugs and Devils" and she says "what and where do nurses come in" so I told her that they were Devils ... Your strong boy is poisoned to the bone ... The medicines are killing me. I have [been] praying most of the time ... We had egg-nogg [sic] just now with Brandy.

In addition to the alcohol-laced eggnog, Ivan particularly disliked the conduct of the nurses, who "talk of nothing but their work, [their] training[;] it is just sickening."[42] After ten days, Willie and Jessie Maltby were released, and their children were gradually returned. The eldest daughter received an operation and recovered. While their home was under quarantine, the Maltbys could only communicate with others by opening a window and speaking outside to visitors on the sidewalk. Conversations were monitored by the guard at the gate.

The presence of an infectious contagion like diphtheria meant that the Maltby case was seen not only as an individual death, but as an issue of public health. By the end of the nineteenth century, germ theory defined the etiological understanding of disease. Rather than simply treating the localized disease within an individual body, medicine had started to regulate the social environment which bred and spread microbes. Urban concerns with unsanitary conditions and public health were not new, but germs were now mapped through the scientific methods of bacteriology, and new controls and legal responsibilities upon the body were introduced under the direction of physicians and specialists.[43] The Maltbys felt the full force of these controls once the sanitary inspector entered their home, imposing a quarantine and guarding their gate. It was in the name of public health that a city health officer could threaten the use of the police in order to enforce treatment on the Maltby children. Earlier testimonials rejoiced at the empowerment gained by rejecting drugs and remedies, but the new apparatus of public health subjected the Maltby children to injections, swabbings, and dosings, despite their opposition.

The Maltby inquest reflected more than an investigation into an individual death; the overriding concern was the issue of public health and the dangers of infectious disease. It was revealed that, since Brooks's arrival in Victoria, Claude was the second child to have died while Brooks prayed. Willie and Jessie Maltby both testified that they were unaware that there were cases of diphtheria in their neighbourhood, despite the fact that they both admitted knowing that a home had been quarantined two houses down the block.[44] The sanitary officer, who had quarantined the house only a week before Claude's death, later testified that he had warned Mrs Maltby that it was illegal to dump human waste in her garden, informed her of the diphtheria, and cautioned her to be careful with her children.[45] Brooks was closely questioned about his practice of praying for children, and what steps he took when attending cases of infectious disease. The Elder replied that he took precautions to fumigate his clothing not because he was afraid of disease, but "because of those who do not believe." However, since he assumed that Claude Maltby was suffering from membranous croup, he took no steps to fumigate himself after visiting the Maltby home. Despite the municipal regulations, Brooks did not regard it as his responsibility to inform the authorities about the existence of infectious disease.[46]

When faith healing was debated in journals, newspapers, and religious publications, the issues were largely framed within a context of personal belief, faith, scriptural exegesis, and the role of medicine in society. The deaths of Gooderham and Howland in the previous century had produced little comment. Now, however, faith healing was being observed through a legal lens that potentially recast it as not just morally objectionable, but also criminally liable. An inquest was not a court of law, but it nevertheless constituted a legal exercise that could lead to judicial proceedings. It was a particular legal space that was increasingly controlled by physicians and relied heavily upon medical evidence in its findings. Theological issues meant little here, but the question of whether the practice endangered the public good was suddenly front and centre.

Although the Malby inquest was presided over by the coroner, Dr E.C. Hart, it also had jurors who not only rendered a decision, but also were able to direct questions to witnesses. It quickly became clear that the jurors were not simply interested in what the Maltbys and Brooks *had* done to aid Claude Maltby's suffering; they also wanted to know what they *would* do in the future. Willie Maltby was asked if he would call a physician as a last resort if he knew a child was about to die. The father replied, "I would ask that if I knew the child was going to die, what would be the use of calling a doctor?" The juror persisted, "If you thought a doctor could save the child, would you call one?" Maltby remained steadfast in his answer, "I do not believe a physician could have saved the child under any circumstances. I know the mortality is greater with than without doctors." When Jessie Maltby was asked the same question, her response was "No: what good could a doctor do?" When asked how she could account for her son's death, Jessie Maltby contended, "There was sin in the heart. If my husband and myself had been without sin, the child would have recovered."[47]

The jurors took only a half hour to reach their conclusions. The coroner noted that Mrs Maltby could not be indicted because her husband, as head of the household, was legally responsible for any omission in the care of his family. Brooks could be held liable for influencing the household head in neglecting the care of the child. When the jurors declared Willie Maltby and Eugene Brooks responsible for the death of Claude Maltby, their decision was only partly aimed at the circumstances of the individual case. The practice of faith healing as advocated by Brooks was regarded as a threat to the public, and a public stand was required to stem his influence.

Arrest warrants were awaiting Maltby and Brooks as the inquest concluded and the two were summarily committed for trial. The province had already determined that the practice of faith healing was dangerous to the public, and the seriousness of the affair was evident when the British Columbia Attorney General's Office took over the prosecution of the case. Section 210 of Canada's recently adopted Criminal Code regarded the head of the family as criminally responsible for the "legal duty to provide necessaries for any child under the age of sixteen years." In May 1901, Maltby and Brooks were indicted on eleven counts, including manslaughter, criminal neglect, failing to provide the necessities of life, and conspiracy to cause death.[48]

Lawyers George Powell and J.S. Yates were retained to represent Maltby and Brooks, but the Christian Catholic Church's own lawyer in Chicago also examined the evidence and sent a brief to Victoria on the case.[49] The trial was by judge alone, with the deputy attorney general, H.A. McLean, prosecuting for the crown. From the beginning, the crown's case focused heavily on the medical evidence of five doctors and one health inspector. The latter, James Wilson, had quarantined the Maltby home following Claude's death. The physicians included Dr Ernest Hall, the doctor who had refused to issue a death certificate to the Maltbys; Dr Owen Jones, who performed the post-mortem examination; Dr E.C. Hart, the coroner who had presided at the inquest; Dr C.J. Fagan, the provincial bacteriologist; and Dr R.L. Fraser, the city's medical health officer in charge of the isolation hospital. McLean's strategy was to demonstrate that Claude Maltby would have been easily saved by medical intervention if a physician had been called. In his cross-examinations, however, Powell effectively shifted the focus from the defendants' religion to the medical ambiguities surrounding diphtheria, croup, and medical treatment. Very quickly, the courtroom became immersed in issues of diagnostics and therapeutics rather than scrutinizing the practice of divine healing. At times it was unclear if it was the doctors or the defendants who were on trial.

Dr Hall explained to the court that diphtheria was a bacterial infection with two potentially lethal effects: it could produce a poison concentrated enough to paralyze parts of the body and even stop the heart; it also created a false membrane in the throat that, particularly in the case of children, might completely close off the windpipe and lead to suffocation. Antitoxins could counteract the highly contagious disease, but if the membrane in the throat had progressed too far, a tracheotomy could be used to bypass the obstruction. These techniques for dealing with diphtheria were relatively new. Hall estimated they had been adopted by physicians only in the past five or six years, but their employment had made the infectious bacteria a very controllable disease. If the antibodies were given early enough in the course of the disease, a 90 per cent recovery rate could be expected.

In its cross-examination, the defence pressed Hall on the efficacy of the antitoxins in the later stages of the disease; the physician insisted he would administer them as long the patient was alive. However, Powell produced hospital statistics illustrating that the injections were of little use unless the antitoxins were administered in the first forty-eight hours, suggesting instead that the mortality rate was closer to 60-70 per cent. Hall was forced to admit that he could not be certain that the child would have been saved if medical assistance had been provided the morning Claude Maltby died; the physician did not even know for certain if the child had died from suffocation or from the toxicity of the infection, a point that would become very important for the defence.

At the inquest, both Brooks and the Maltbys claimed that they did not regard Claude's illness as very serious. Up until the morning of his death, his symptoms appeared to resemble "membranous croup." Hall's testimony suggested that the early stages of the illness were gradual; only in the last twelve to six hours did the false membrane start to grow across the throat. Because of its vague symptoms, diphtheria was difficult to diagnose in its early stages, and Powell was able to bring out the fact that Hall, Fagan, and Fraser had disagreed about the presence of the infection in at least two other cases. The situation was further complicated by the ambiguity of the term "croup." Hall noted that the public's understanding of what was "croup" could mean different things, and that most people did not regard it as a dangerous condition. The doctor admitted that the Maltbys' statements to him about what had happened to Claude up until just before his death gave them no justification to think that anything other than "croup" was affecting the child. Dr Hart dismissed Brooks and Maltby's use of the term membranous croup, claiming that it represented the same thing as diphtheria, but he also acknowledged a difference between the professional standards and public perception: "Popularly, any disease of the lungs, throat, larynx, or windpipe, causing obstruction or difficulty in breathing, is known as croup."[50] With all of the doctors, Powell continued to raise afflictions that had similar symptoms to diphtheria, particularly "spasmodic croup" and "acute catarrhal laryngitis."

Powell managed to shift the ground further when he asked Hall what would have happened if a homeopath had been sought instead of a conventional physician:

A: Judging from the homeopathic treatment as I understand it, I think it would have had the same result that he had from prayer.
Q: Homeopathy is a standing system of medicine, is it not – recognized by the State?
A: Yes, recognized by the State.
Q: Government allows them to practice here?
A: Yes, unfortunately.[51]

On his redirect, McLean pointed out that homeopaths would also have employed a tracheotomy to prevent suffocation, but Powell's point was clear; at least one legal and licensed system of medicine would not have administered antitoxins, and even if a tracheotomy had been performed, there was a strong chance that the child may have died from the poisonous byproduct of the disease in any case.

And exactly what did Claude Maltby die from? In his post-mortem examination, Dr Jones suggested that the colour of the lungs and state of the heart indicated a possible oxygen deficiency, produced by strangulation or suffocation. A membrane covered the back of the pharynx and the vocal chords. Jones had no doubt that the diphtheria had suffocated the child by obstructing his breathing. For McLean, Jones was a doubly valuable witness for he had been the physician to attend to the diphtheria in the house down the street from the Maltbys, and he had even performed an emergency tracheotomy on one child who survived despite only taking antitoxins at the latest stages.

The problem with the crown's scenario was that if Claude Maltby had died from strangulation, he would have struggled violently at the end. Hall and Jones both testified that this was likely the way the child had died, and initially this fact bolstered McLean's attempts to illustrate that a suffocating child was clearly in need of medical attention. However, all of the available witnesses – Brooks and Willie Maltby in their depositions for the inquest and Jessie Maltby and Amanda Hatt at the trial – suggested that Claude had been pale and died quite peacefully. Their consistency on this point allowed Powell to call his own medical expert, Dr John Davie. Davie contradicted the inferences Jones had drawn from his post-mortem examination, claiming that none of the evidence demonstrated positively that Claude Maltby had died from suffocation. Under cross-examination, the physician maintained that it was impossible to die from suffocation with a white face, and when McLean tried to press the issue, Davie accused the crown attorney of asking "stupid questions." Powell's point was made; he had thrown open the possibility that Claude had died because of the toxic effects of diphtheria, leaving reasonable room for doubt about whether a doctor could save him at the last moment. And since diphtheria was difficult for even doctors to pinpoint accurately in its earliest stages, the Maltbys were hardly culpable in not believing anything was seriously wrong with their child.

After the closing arguments were completed, Justice Martin declared the defendants not guilty. The ambiguous nature of the medical evidence and the consistency of the testimony suggesting that Maltby and Brooks did not regard the illness as serious forced him to give them the benefit of the doubt. Martin hastened to add that his decision was the product of "legal doubts, not the doubt of weak-minded men, but of a judge in the full realization of his responsibility." However, the defendants did not escape the judge's own opinion of their actions. Even though Jessie Maltby was not on trial, Martin felt compelled to comment that he had been "shocked" at her statements. Willie Maltby was chastised to "search in his conscience" and to amend his conduct "to insure [*sic*] the due performance of his duties as a father." Brooks was dealt with the most severely. The judge characterized his behaviour as "morally vile in the extreme – like that of a man who would stand by and see another perish without raising a hand to save him."[52]

The crown had failed, but not because Brooks was no longer a threat to the community – the judge clearly agreed with the crown's intimation that the faith healer was dangerous, despite the acquittal. It failed because of inconsistencies in the presentation of medical evidence, which left doubts about whether the symptoms in question should have led the defendants to call for medical assistance. For the moment, Brooks escaped imprisonment, but it would not be long before he would face the Court of King's Bench again. However, the crown and the medical authorities had learned their lesson and would not make the same mistakes twice.

CONVICTIONS

Only a few months after Brooks had finished his courtroom battles in the Maltby case, he was asked to attend to another family fighting an illness. John and Alice Rogers lived not far from the Maltbys and had been members of the congregation for about eighteen months. When their eldest son took sick with a sore throat, Brooks prayed for the boy who recovered after coughing up a piece of membrane two inches long. Unfortunately, Alice and her three-year-old daughter, Nellie, both contracted the same illness. Brooks recommended that the family quarantine themselves, not by formally notifying the authorities but simply by restricting access to the household. Nellie appeared to recover but suffered a relapse a few days later. Worried that their prayers were not giving them victory over the disease, Brooks telegraphed Dowie and asked for the prayers of Zion to help the Rogers children. After returning to the house, Brooks stayed with the child through the night; however, on the morning of 4 September 1901 Nellie Rogers died.[53]

Coroner Hart arrived for the body, removing it to the morgue, and returned with a Provincial Police Superintendent at his side. Hart examined the rest of the family and declared them all to have diphtheria in various stages, including the seven-month-old infant, Cecil. Later in the day, Hart returned with Dr Fraser, but upon examining the infant's throat, Fraser declared that Cecil was not suffering from diphtheria. Zionite suspicions of the morality of doctors were not put at ease by Fraser's suggestion that members of the family should be stimulated with whiskey. Additionally, Fraser's term as City Health Officer ended that evening at midnight, and although he apparently informed his successor of the child's condition, he did not return to the Rogers household, despite a promise to do so. Fraser later admitted that one of the reasons he did not check again on the child was that his "previous experience with this sect was not very attractive, and I was not any too anxious to have anything more to do with the case than I could avoid."[54]

An inquest into the death of Nellie Rogers was held the following day. With the experience of the Maltby trial behind them, Eugene Brooks and John Rogers both objected to answering questions and were guarded in their replies, knowing that they might be used against them at trial. Brooks felt guilty about withholding information, however, and he later provided a statement that filled in more details of his activities over the previous two weeks.[55] For Rogers sorrow would only be doubled when he returned to his home on Sayward Avenue; while in attendance at the inquest, his infant son, Cecil, had also died.

Rogers and Brooks were each charged with eight counts in the deaths of both children, including manslaughter and failing to provide the necessaries of life.[56] However, this trial took a very different course than the Maltby case. Unlike their previous court experience, Brooks and Rogers were tried separately, which allowed the crown to call each defendant as a witness at the other's trial. John Rogers was arraigned on 25 September and Justice Walkem was immediately concerned that Rogers had no legal counsel to represent him. To this point, neither Brooks nor Rogers had engaged lawyers, in part because Brooks was confident, after his previous acquittal, that they could not charge him again. However, the magistrate handling the preliminary proceedings in Police Court decided that the Maltby decision was based more on the uncertainty of the facts in the case rather than a silence on the part of the law, and he duly committed them. Rogers, who had worked both as a labourer and as a clerk for the fur department at the Hudson's Bay Company, may not have been able to afford counsel, or there might not have been enough time to consult with Dowie about a course of action. Brooks later claimed that Powell was out of town and unavailable, but there was some question as to the validity of this excuse.[57] Facing a familiar foe, Deputy Attorney General McLean, Rogers found himself struggling not only against the prosecutor, but also against a decidedly hostile Justice Walkem. Unfamiliar with proper procedure and unable to challenge the medical evidence that the crown submitted, Rogers was at a great disadvantage.

With the experience of the Maltby case fresh in their minds, McLean and the physicians altered their strategy. Where previously the medical opinion had determined that Claude Maltby would certainly have struggled during his death, Dr Frank Hall, who performed the autopsy on Nellie Rogers, now declared that it was entirely possible for the child to suffocate quietly and gradually. McLean had a free hand to present his medical evidence succinctly and without the drawn-out debates regarding the nature of diphtheria, croup, or problems of diagnosis. Fagan boldly predicted that if antitoxins were used, in McLean's words, "at anything like a reasonable time," one could expect a 94 or 95 per cent success rate. Rogers could not produce statistics to counter such statements, but he did question Fagan about the incorrect diagnosis of his son. Fagan argued that Cecil, who did not have a diphtheritic membrane, had died from the toxic effects of diphtheria, while Nellie had died of suffocation; a doctor who examined them would have immediately recognized Nellie's condition, but he might not have realized what was wrong with the infant.[58] McLean likely understood that this point was the weakest part of his case, and it is notable that he did not call Fraser to the stand, probably out of a concern that the former health officer's mistaken diagnosis might justify the inaction of Rogers.

Since Rogers was without counsel, the judge was expected to assist the accused in understanding points of law and the crown's case against him. Walkem, however, exhibited considerable hostility towards the defendant from the very beginning. When he took the stand in his own defence, Rogers tried to call attention to the fact that during the trial the physicians were making the case that Nellie had died of suffocation. However, previously at the inquest, Drs Hall and Fraser had suggested that it was the toxic effects of diphtheria that was the most likely cause of death. This was a serious discrepancy, and, judging from the Maltby precedent, it was one that could have been used to demonstrate a great deal of uncertainty. However, Walkem appeared annoyed by the suggestion and cut off Rogers abruptly, "You can make that remark by and by; it is a matter of comment. You don't know anything about medicine do you?"[59] Lacking defence counsel, Rogers found it difficult to navigate the legal proceedings effectively. As a result, the authority of medical science remained largely unchallenged.

Although the two trials were separate, it is apparent that McLean was already maneuvering to make the case against Brooks even while Rogers was still before the court. In particular, the crown's cross-examination of Alice Rogers was aimed more at implicating Brooks than it was in determining the culpability of her husband.

Q. What is it that has induced you — what induced you to form this belief [that it is wrong to employ doctors and use medicines in sickness]?
A. Hearing Mr Brooks.
Q. Hearing Mr Brooks?
A. And reading the Leaves of Healing.
Q. Hearing Mr Brooks preach?
A. Yes

Q. Before you heard Mr Brooks preach you had never formed those opinions?
A. We had never had a doctor; we had used drugs a little.
Q. But up to that time you did not consider it wrong to use drugs, did not consider it sinful until you heard him preach?
A. No we didn't know it was wrong.[60]

If the crown could directly tie Brooks to the beliefs held by the Rogers, the evangelist would be guilty of counseling neglect. Individual actions were one thing, but Brooks's influence in the community represented a threat to the public order.

At the conclusion of the Rogers's trial, Justice Walkem had not the "slightest doubt" as to where responsibility for the deaths lay. Addressing both parents, the judge lamented that they had "despised the practice of two thousand years and discarded skill and discoveries for the teachings of Brooks. They had prayed to God but discarded the discoveries of men of genius whom God had created." Walkem was sympathetic to the suffering that the Rogers family had endured through the death of two children, but, he exclaimed, "that is not exactly the point. Others will not be permitted to do as you do and sacrifice human life ... It is against common morality to teach as Brooks does." After all, the "community was struggling hard against these diseases, and it was a terrible thing that they should be allowed to set up centres of disease which imperilled the community."[61] John Rogers was convicted of manslaughter, but given a suspended sentence, which reflected the divided mind of the judge who needed to establish the legal authority for the public good. However, Walkem did not want to punish the father who had already suffered tremendous personal loss.

Brooks went to court two months later, with Justice Drake presiding over a one-day trial. As expected, McLean entered Brooks's testimony from the Rogers case as evidence, and the familiar panel of medical experts paraded through the witness box. With Rogers already convicted, Brooks was in a much more difficult position; unlike the Maltby case, Brooks could not claim that he was unaware of the potential hazard of the condition, since he had specifically mentioned diptheria in his telegram to Dowie. As in the preliminary hearings, Brooks represented himself instead of retaining counsel. In contrast to Rogers's experience, however, Brooks was more skillful in attacking the medical evidence, quoting from medical books to suggest that the recovery rate of diptheria after treatment was closer to 33 per cent, not the 95 per cent that the physicians had claimed. The transcripts of Brooks's trial have not been located, but newspaper reports suggest that the proceedings developed into "a discussion of doctors and their methods of treatment between the witness and the accused, who tried to show that doctors continually differed in their opinions as to the nature and treatment of diseases."[62]

Drake wasted no time in rendering his decision. According to the judge, Brooks "had a perfect right to his own opinions, but he had no right to influence his followers to commit criminal acts. He was more guilty than his deluded follower Rogers." The Elder was found guilty on six of eight charges, those relating to counselling Rogers to neglect the necessaries of life, and not guilty on the two counts that were directly related to manslaughter. Brooks was sentenced to three months in jail without hard labour.[63] Legally, manslaughter was the more serious charge, and yet the respective sentencing of Brooks and Rogers, who had been found guilty of manslaughter but only given a suspended sentence, reflected Drake's opinion that the Elder was "more guilty." Like the crown, Drake placed the case in a broader perspective, and the sentence spoke to a desire to stop those who were most responsible for spreading a faith healing perspective that denied the role and validity of medicine. The judgment was appealed, but the original decision was upheld by the appeals court, which was composed of three judges, two of whom, Justices Martin and Walkem, were very familiar with the issue of faith healing and the law.[64]

Doubts regarding the medical facts had led to Brooks's earlier acquittal, but lacking proper counsel, Brooks and Rogers found themselves unable to exploit obvious deficiencies in the crown's case. Despite repeated attempts to express their religious convictions, the court had little patience for theological arguments. When Brooks declared, "I must obey God if I have to suffer for it," Justice Walkem's response was, "Oh, you have got to use a little common sense in these things."[65] It was not Rogers's or Brooks's personal conduct as a potential conduits for infectious diseases that worried the court as much as the evangelist's ability to corrupt the "common sense" of others. The newly established apparatus of sanitary regulations demanded an understanding of contagious diseases as materially grounded in the spread of microbial germs and bacilli. Physicians were now endowed with the professional authority to monitor and guard the health of the community. Brooks's cosmological understanding of illness and outright hostility towards the medical profession threatened the very foundations of public health.

PRISON LABOURS

Eugene Brooks's jail time was deferred temporarily in order to allow him to care for his wife, who had gone through a difficult pregnancy and a still-born birth. Early in 1902, Sara had recovered enough both physically and mentally that she took over the services while her husband served his time. Sara also appears to have taken on the role of faith healer, responding to calls for prayer even in cases of broken bones and diptheria.[66] When Eugene completed his sentence, the pair decided to follow the growing exodus to Zion City, Illinois, Dowie's newly founded theocratic community, to await their next call. Around forty members of the Victoria branch of the Christian Catholic Church had already made the move. The Brooks's sojourn at Zion was short, and they returned to Canadian soil in the fall of 1902. Before long, the Elder found himself again in trouble with the law and facing court action.[67]

In Toronto a small gathering of Zionites had been active since 1899, but it was not until 1901 that Zion Tabernacle was established on the corner of Queen and Victoria Streets. When the Brookses arrived, they took charge of the Tabernacle work and travelled widely in southern Ontario to spread the message of divine healing. Their return to the Chesley area again provoked riots and eggings, and, according to Elder Brooks, conflict over the rental of halls occurred in a number of places where "the prejudice against Zion" was "insanely bitter."[68] It was in the midst of planning a tour through western Ontario that Brooks received a letter from Marshall Harman, a farmer from Victoria Corners, Brock Township in the County of Ontario, a few miles outside of Uxbridge. Harman was interested in hearing Brooks and in applying for membership in the Christian Catholic Church. Brooks had no idea where Victoria Corners was, and was heading in the opposite direction, but he sent the requested forms and outlined what members of the Church believed.[69] The campaign westward went ahead as planned, but when the Brookses returned to Toronto, the Elder would find himself embroiled in yet another legal conflict.

Two very different versions of what transpired within the Harman household emerged at the later trials, but a brief summary of the events is helpful. On 7 June 1904 Annie Harman gave birth to the couple's first and only child after a difficult delivery without medical attendance. For some time Annie was "dropsical" and very swollen in her legs and feet. Marshall wrote to Brooks in July and explained that his wife was still ailing and had not yet "gotten the victory."[70] At the end of the month, Brooks travelled to meet the Harmans at their request, praying for the health of Annie and laying hands upon her. On 2 August Annie died of nephritis, which was vaguely defined as an inflammation of the kidneys. A post-mortem examination determined that medicine may have prevented her death, and Marshall Harman was arrested for failing to provide the necessaries of life.[71]

The Maltbys and the Rogers could draw upon the support of a small, but close community of believers in turning to faith healing. In Victoria Corners the Harmans appear to have been practically alone in their belief, and this isolation in combination with family stresses made the pursuit of faith healing a complicated and emotional issue. Annie's mother, Jane Thompson, felt that her daughter should have had a doctor investigate the "dropsical swellings" in her legs. Marshall Harman was adamant about trusting in faith for healing and rejected these overtures until Jane felt that she "was not welcome to the home of [Annie's] husband." Knowing that her daughter was of "a very quiet even temper and not aggressive," Jane feared that "she would rather submit to her husband than have any difficulty," and she was sure that Annie "was under the husband's control."[72] Annie's cousin, Catharine Thompson, confirmed this opinion of Annie as "submissive to her husband's wishes" and unwilling to oppose him. Catharine also testified that Annie spoke as if she expected to have a doctor, expressed doubts about faith healing, and did not believe it was necessarily a sin to take some medicine. Catharine and a neighbour, Mary Thom, attended the birth, but their repeated requests for a physician were rebuffed. According to Catharine, when she could finally reach the head of the child, Marshall "jumped over the foot of the bed and endeavored to see for himself and took his hand and tried to remove it himself." Catharine "told him to get out of this and go for a Dr." Marshall finally left the house, giving in to demands to contact a physician, but the child was born before either the husband or doctor arrived. Eventually, a physician examined the child and mother but made no significant diagnosis or prescription.

A key issue during the trial was the nature of the relationship between husband and wife. In the previous cases where children had died of diptheria, the legal responsibility clearly fell to the husband as head of the household, but in the Harman case the attitude of the wife and the expression of her own will became a central point of contention. Her brother, Hewitt Thompson, confirmed the family's characterization of Annie, declaring that his sister "would not resist anyone," and that "in their domestic relations Harman's will was law." Thom recounted that when she approached Harman about a physician during Annie's confinement, he claimed that Annie "was his wife and he would do as he liked [and] that he was capable of running his own house."[73]

Marshall Harman's version of events contrasted sharply with that of the Thompson family and Mary Thom. He agreed that Annie was a "peaceful" and "obedient" wife who never quarreled, and she understood that he was the "provider" and the "head of the house." However, this did not make him the final "boss" of the home, and she often said that she "had as much right in the house" as her husband. Marshall maintained that he never would have denied his wife medical attention if she had requested it. He also pointed out that faith healing was not new in their household; Annie had apparently thrown out all of their medicines and started to practice it five or six years previously. She twice had been healed of other ailments through prayer. Marshall made clear that it was at her request that he had asked Brooks to come and pray for her on the Saturday before she died.

While Annie's family clearly blamed him for the tragedy, Marshall in turn suggested that the real cause of death was her weakening faith, which resulted from the repeated badgering for medical treatment by the very people who were supposed to help her. Harman insisted that he was not a domineering husband, but rather a protector of his wife's desire not to rely upon medicine. When he made it known to the women that he would only call in a physician at Annie's request, they were not dissuaded and instead tried to convince Annie of the right course to take: "they turned on her and coaxed her for more than an hour ... It grieved me very much. Their actions were nothing but inhuman. At last she says he can do as he liked and then I went for a doctor ... I knew from the grip on her hand she didn't want me to leave her." In the tense moments before the birth, Marshall claimed that the women who attended Annie refused to "do anything," even when she begged them, as part of their pressure tactics. He denied ever trying to help deliver the child in any capacity except for holding his wife's hand. Marshall was characterized as cruel and uncaring for leaving Annie alone at times, but he did not feel that he could trust those in the surrounding community to stay with his wife on account of their hostility towards their beliefs. Leaving his wife alone on the day he had to return Brooks to the train station in Uxbridge was "one of the hardest things I had to do."[74]

These competing versions of events played out within a gendered judicial context that shaped perceptions of Marshall Harman's conduct. As Carolyn Strange vividly illustrates, Canadian courts at the turn of the century often viewed domestic relations through the lens of "chivalric justice," scripting gendered expectations of behavior.[75] The characterization of Marshall as brutish and bullying cast him as deficient in his gentlemanly duty to protect the defenceless. The portrayal of Annie Harman as completely submissive to her husband's will, both reinforced her femininity and highlighted her husband's moral and legal responsibility as the patriarchal head of household. To counter these assertions, Marshall defined himself as the protector of his wife's religious beliefs, but this approach required a careful negotiation of gendered roles, situating Annie as assertive of her religious beliefs without supplanting his own position as "provider."

Harman was found guilty of failing to provide the necessaries of life and sentenced to a year in jail with hard labour, a decision that was upheld on appeal. After a number of delays, Brooks's trial was finally completed in January 1906.[76] Although only some of the actual transcripts are available, Harman's conviction and Brooks's own criminal record undoubtedly hurt his case. Brooks's lawyer attempted to focus attention on the fact that the Harmans had rejected medicine long before meeting the evangelist, and that Annie Harman had previously turned to faith healing for an "ulcerated stomach."[77] Despite the limited contact between Brooks and the Harmans, the Elder was convicted and sentenced to six months of hard labour for counselling to neglect the necessaries of life. However, technical issues over the proper handling of witness depositions landed the case in appeals court, where the conviction was overturned and a new trial ordered. Since Brooks had spent a number of months in Toronto's Central Prison already, the court strongly suggested that the crown consider a *nolle prosequi*, refraining from further prosecutions, and it appears that this advice was followed since Brooks was released from jail three months early.[78]

Unlike the trials in British Columbia, which focused upon the deaths of children from contagious disease, the Harman case involved an adult woman faced with complications from pregnancy. The public health concerns that had dominated the discussions surrounding the Maltby and Rogers families were practically absent. Instead, the pivotal issue at stake was the nature of domestic relations and whether or not Annie Harman truly wished to rely on faith healing alone. While women generally tended to favour the pursuit of divine health more than men, Annie's tragic death precludes any definite assessment of her wishes. The Harmans could not rely on a close community of faith to help them, and the women who surrounded Annie, both family and friends, were adamantly opposed to faith healing. In the courtroom, however, gendered expectations of Marshall Harman's conduct were central to his conviction.

The common thread in all three cases was the perception of Brooks as a threat. Even though the Elder resided in Toronto and had visited the Harmans only once, he was still held liable for the beliefs instilled in the husband. Long before the trial, many in Victoria Corners had already assessed the evangelist as partly responsible; when Brooks attended the inquest, he reported being struck and having his hat trampled after leaving the proceedings late at night.[79] In both British Columbia and Ontario, preaching the concept of faith healing and advocating a strict refusal of medical aid was viewed as dangerous and insidious.

When Maggie Scott of Martintown was healed through prayer in 1882, the community rejoiced and newspapers celebrated the event. When public figures died, very little criticism was ever directed against the "respectable men" of the divine healing movement. When Eugene Brooks brought the message of Zion to Chesley less than twenty years later, riots erupted. And when followers of Dowie in Canada died, a faith healer was taken to court and, on at least two occasions, jailed.

No small part of this shift in the public reaction to faith healing can be attributed to the language employed by Dowie and his followers. Their denunciation of the grand institutions of church and medicine was not the respectable image projected by the early divine healing movement. In their uncompromising attacks, doctors were transformed from a second best alternative to health into devils. The personal style, rough language, and American accent of Elder Brooks undoubtedly contributed to his difficulties in Canada.

However, other circumstances had also altered the public perception of the practice of faith healing in modern society. The development of a germ theory of disease and public health reforms created a new historical context whereby those who denied the validity of medicine and disease were regarded as threats to the public order. Because Dowieites regularly refused to report the existence of contagious diseases, their beliefs could lead to actions that would spread contagions to the rest of the community. The medical treatment forced upon the Maltby family, both within and outside of their home, indicated the growing willingness of the state to intervene and regulate the private health of citizens, forcibly seizing and operating on the bodies of children when deemed necessary.

Through its control of such regulatory agencies as death certificates and inquests, medical authorities could bring the faith healers to the attention of the crown, but it was the provincial government that ultimately decided whether or not to pursue legal action. The criminal code obliged the head of the house to conform with the legal responsibility of providing the necessaries of life, and the state, medical authorities, and many judges obviously understood necessaries as including conventional medical treatment. The rejection of medicine and the medical regulation of public health thereby became a criminal act. Isolated cases were not as dangerous as those who threatened to spread such pernicious doctrines within the community, which remained at risk even when contagious diseases were not a factor.

This perception of faith healing influenced the role taken by government officials in pursuing legal actions against religious healing. In the 1880s, at least two Christian Scientist practitioners were charged and unsuccessfully convicted with practicing medicine without a licence. Provincial regulations were designed to protect the professional status of physicians above all, and these prosecutions meant little to orthodox Protestant faith healers who did not see themselves as medical practitioners, nor did they charge for their services. In the 1890s, however, Canadian authorities shifted their focus to manslaughter, but they failed to secure a conviction until the trials of Rogers and Brooks in

1901. A similar case that same year proceeded in Toronto, where a follower of Christian Science, James Henry Lewis, was found guilty of failing to provide the necessaries of life for his son, who also died of diptheria.[80] Although Christian Scientists spent more time in court, no practitioners or "demonstrators" were ever convicted in Canada; in fact, Eugene Brooks appears to have been the only faith healer to serve a jail term for practicing and advocating a form of religious healing. The remarkable story of the Brookses' activities demonstrates that certain forms of faith healing had not only become less respectable in style and status, but also that they were increasingly seen as a danger to the public health of the nation.

In 1906 the theocratic dream of Zion City imploded when financial stresses and discontentment with Dowie prompted a revolt among the city's managers and overseers, led by Dowie's own hand-picked deputy, Wilbur Glenn Voliva. Dowie's health was already in decline by this point, and after losing legal title to the city in a drawn-out battle, he died in 1907. However, Zion City, like the rest of North America, was quickly hit by a transformative religious event that was ultimately more far-reaching than the passing of the venerable Dowie. Waves of pentecostal "latter rain" were starting to fall, and many of Dowie's followers would turn towards this new spiritual experience. The practice of divine healing carried on in the wake of Dowie, but pentecostalism would reshape the nature and meaning of healing through prayer and faith.

5

Pentecostal Power

Calla is holding herself very still. I can feel the tension of her arm through our
two coats. If she speaks, I will never be able to face her again. I can feel along
my nerves and arteries the squirming and squeamishness of that shame, and
having to walk out of the Tabernacle with her afterwards, through a gauntlet
of eyes.

Silence. I can't stay. I can't stand it. I really can't. Beside me, the man moans
gently, moans and stirs, and moans –

That voice!

Chattering, crying, ululating, the forbidden transformed cryptically to
nonsense, dragged from the crypt, stolen and shouted, the shuddering of it, the
fear, the breaking, the release, the grieving –

Not Calla's voice, Mine. Oh my God. Mine. The voice of Rachel.

Margaret Laurence, *A Jest of God* (1966)

Clara Hammerton was a recent English immigrant living in Ottawa
who had grown dissatisfied with her Anglican upbringing. In 1910 she
became aware of a group known as the Apostolic Faith Movement and
started to attend their meetings at Queen's Hall on the corner of Bank
and Somerset Streets. After three months of spiritual struggle, Hammerton found salvation, sanctification, and healing. However, she also
discovered something else: "After five days tarrying, the Lord graciously baptized me with the Holy Ghost and spake through me in
other tongues as the Spirit gave utterance." Although the terminology
of a spirit baptism, or Holy Ghost baptism, was not new, Hammerton's
experience was marked by "speaking in tongues." Unheard of in Canada just five years before, the new phenomenon of glossolalia reshaped
the religious landscape in a way that profoundly influenced the experience of divine healing.[1]

Along with tongues, Hammerton also found healing. However, the
language she employed in her narrative was notably different from earlier Victorian testimonials: "I have also proven His mighty healing
power, He having raised me up off a bed of affliction without earthly
physicians. Praise be to Jesus!"[2] Pentecostalism introduced a new form

of bodily expression that now complemented the traditional understanding of divine healing. As a result, descriptions of faith healing started to resemble the pentecostal experience of speaking in tongues; healing now became more immediate, more dramatic, and closely associated with a vocabulary of "power." Hammerton's narrative is also notable for what is missing, namely the elements of domestic religion, which had been so prominent in women's healing testimonials in the nineteenth century; the "bed of affliction" was no longer a literal space, although it remained a metaphorical one.

This narrative shift took place at a time when the relationship between healing and private domestic space was increasingly strained. The growing authority of modern hospitals transformed the social geography of health and healing, and the practice of faith healing subsequently shed many of its domestic attributes. In contrast, the pentecostal experience was itself communal in nature, marking one's entrance into a restored primitive church that expectantly awaited the second coming, rather than a private experience that was later testified to in public. Within this framework, faith healing increasingly adopted the characteristics of tongues and was set within a sacred space where a tangible divine power could take hold. While many historians point to divine healing as a precursor to pentecostalism, in Canada pentecostalism also redefined the social expression of healing to reflect the new bodily experience of speaking in tongues.[3]

Pentecostalism served as the point of convergence for many of the different strands of faith healing that had already developed within Canadian Protestantism. From such Alliance stalwarts as John Salmon and George Fisher to the Dowieite Brookses, the fall of the pentecostal "latter rain" embraced a wide cross section of faith healing advocates. Even an organization like the Christian and Missionary Alliance, which was not sympathetic to the new concept of tongues as a baptism of the holy spirit, was transformed by its encounter with it. For both those who accepted and rejected the baptism of tongues, pentecostalism stood at the centre of a restructuring of Protestant faith healing in the first decades of the twentieth century.

PENTECOST FALLS

Situated on Toronto's Queen Street, the East End Mission was opened by Ellen and James Hebden in May 1906. Recent emigrants from England, the Hebdens had intended their three-storey building to serve as a faith healing home. It was in the midst of praying for power to heal the sick that Ellen Hebden felt a divine presence take control of her hands, which were suddenly "clasped ... tightly together, and then moved ... with such rapidity that it seemed as if they were severed from my arms." Her hands were then raised to each of her cheeks and "pressed very hard." When Ellen inquired as to the meaning of this gesture, "a very quiet yet distinct voice said 'Tongues.'" Possessed by the spirit, Ellen introduced the pentecostal baptism to the mission, singing in another language and delivering messages that God spoke through her. A month later James also received his baptism, and within five months between seventy and eighty others had marked their experience through tongues.[4]

When news of what was happening at the small mission spread, a train of evangelists, missionaries, and seekers made their way to Toronto. The East End Mission became a crossroads for those interested in pursuing the pentecostal baptism, and according one estimate, there were fourteen pentecostal congregations in Canada by 1910, most of them having some connection to the Hebdens.[5] Canadian pentecostals were quickly integrated within the continental and transatlantic revival of pentecostal gifts that would profoundly reshape Protestantism in the twentieth century.

The modern manifestation of glossolalia is often traced to Agnes Ozman, a student of Charles F. Parham's Bethel Bible College in Topeka, Kansas. Both Parham and Ozman were well acquainted with the wide variety of holiness-inspired faith healing centres, including A.B. Simpson's bible institute at Nyack, New York, and John Alexander Dowie's Zion healing home in Chicago. Parham, already known for his faith healing activities in the Topeka area, was particularly influenced by the eccentric holiness preacher Frank W. Sandford, who presided over a large institutional complex known as Shiloh in Durham, Maine. Like Parham, Sandford was a proponent of divine healing and premillennialism, but he also believed that the imminent arrival of the Second Coming would be marked by a new gift that would allow Christians to evangelize the world.

Inspired by Sandford's conceptualization of apostolic gifts that would emerge as the end-time approached, Parham declared that neither sanctification, divine healing, nor the variety of ecstatic "fire baptisms" claimed by some holiness groups represented the fullness of God's power. When he opened Bethel College in October 1900, he impressed upon his students that the true baptism of the holy spirit had not yet arrived, but that they would be privileged to receive it if they were to be saved in the rapture of the last days. In December, Ozman spoke a few words in another language, and then on 1 January 1901 she underwent an experience that resulted in speaking and writing for three days in Chinese. In the days following this incident, the rest of the school was drawn into a revival of these pentecostal gifts, and the link between speaking in tongues and a definable "Baptism of the Holy Ghost" was forged.[6] Parham's expectations were fulfilled, and glosso-lalia became the "initial evidence" that a full spiritual baptism had been received.

While it was the Azusa Street mission in Los Angeles that emerged as the leading centre for this new experience, Parham set his sights on Zion City. In 1906 Dowie's position had been usurped by Wilbur Glenn Voliva, and the unsettled state of affairs led Parham to delay his plans for visiting Azusa in order to introduce the pentecostal experi-ence to the theocratic municipality. As Parham's support rose, Voliva responded by threatening dismissal from the Christian Catholic Apos-tolic Church for any who dared to attend his meetings. Such restric-tions did little to prevent a pentecostal outpouring of tongues, and many of the Zion faithful became associated with the new movement. The new adherents included Sara Brooks's sister, Lydia, and her hus-band, George Mitchell, who kept the Brookses informed about the fall of latter rain at Zion.[7]

When Parham set out on a tour of the northeast in 1907, he made contact with the Toronto branch of the Christian Catholic Apostolic Church, and Eugene Brooks invited him to address a wider audience at Wolesley Hall. A number of pentecostal missions in Toronto, including the Hebdens', united for the occasion, and Parham's campaign was well-attended, although there was no great spiritual outbreak. After three weeks, Parham suggested to Brooks that Harry Robinson and his wife, Martha Wing Robinson, who both had strong Canadian connec-tions, be called from Zion City to take over the new work.[8] The Robin-sons were willing, but neither had yet received the baptism of tongues; and the Wolseley Hall meetings could not compete with the success of the East End Mission. According to Brooks, as the last month's rent on the building started to loom, the audiences diminished to only two men, "One of these slept while the other nodded, and they didn't have a penny between them."[9] Parham's ambitions were left unrealized, both in Toronto and Zion City, as internal factions within the Apos-tolic Faith Movement moved against him and allegations of sexual im-morality surfaced.[10]

Such divisions would continue to plague the amorphous movement as the latter rain of glossolalia brought new questions to old doctrines. For those like Parham, who had a strong holiness background, sanctifi-cation continued to serve as a distinct "second blessing," while the baptism of the holy ghost marked a third work of grace, identifying the believer as fully "sealed" with God. Maintaining the second work of grace was not as appealing to those with reformed leanings, and doubts were expressed over the intermediate stage of sanctification. William Durham was inspired to seek the baptism after visiting Los Angeles in 1907, but upon returning to Chicago he departed from the Azusa mission's holiness emphasis. Unlike those who insisted that sanctification preceded baptism just as salvation had preceded sanctification, Durham denied the "second blessing" of sanctification altogether, claiming that the initial point of conversion marked the "Finished Work" of salvation. No holiness "cleansing" was required before receiving the spiritual baptism of tongues.[11] Although he only remained at his North Avenue Mission until 1911, Durham's work in Chicago was particularly influential for Canadian pentecostalism in Winnipeg and in western Ontario, and the majority of Canadian pentecostals would eventually adopt the "Finished Work" doctrine.[12]

In the early years of the movement, however, these theological positions remained fluid, and Canadians quickly established contact with a wide variety of notable figures. In 1909, A.G. Ward, a former worker for the Christian Alliance, organized a Pentecostal Camp Meeting outside of Stouffville, Ontario. The featured speakers offered a panoply of pentecostal leadership. Vicar A.A. Boddy from Sunderland, England, was the most prominent pentecostal minister in Britain. William and Lydia Piper, from the Stone Church in Chicago, were former Dowieites who had established a sizeable following across town from Durham. Also present was Joseph H. King, general overseer for the Fire-Baptized Holiness Church, who had first heard of the pentecostal baptism of tongues while conducting a campaign in Ontario.[13]

Canadians did not simply wait for American evangelists to bring them the message of pentecost, but rather they were eager to investigate it for themselves. On 11 December 1906, R.E. McAlister arrived at Azusa Street, received the baptism of the spirit, and quickly brought the news to Vancouver. A former evangelist for Ralph Horner's Holiness Movement Church, McAlister had grown up near Cobden, Ontario, and was later influential in establishing pockets of pentecostalism in the Ottawa Valley.[14] When McAlister returned to California, he emerged as a central figure in the "Oneness" controversy that split pentecostalism between those who maintained a traditional understanding of God as a triune of three-in-one and those who came to view Jesus as the full revelation of the Godhead in this dispensational age.[15] McAlister was one of the original founders of the Pentecostal Assemblies of the World, which adopted this "Oneness" or "Jesus Only" position. However, the drift towards a modified unitarianism was resisted by others, most notably the fledgling Assemblies of God, which reasserted a traditional trinitarianism in its 1916 "Statement of Fundamental Truths."[16]

California was the destination for another prominent Canadian evangelist, Andrew Harvey Argue. Born in 1868 at Fitzroy Harbor, a small town west of Ottawa, Argue was converted by the Salvation Army while living in North Dakota. With his wife, Eva, and his growing family, Andrew moved back across the border to establish a successful real estate business in Winnipeg. Of all of the young cities in western Canada, Winnipeg had some of the strongest connections to various strands of the holiness movement, and Argue integrated himself into these informal networks.[17] At an Alliance convention that featured A.B. Simpson, Argue received prayer for "chronic internal trouble."[18] Upon hearing the reports of glossolalia in 1907, Argue travelled to Durham's North Avenue Mission to investigate. After twenty-one days of "tarrying," Argue received the baptism and returned to Winnipeg to spread the pentecostal message, giving up his business interests to pursue a full-time evangelistic career.

The Argue home became the centre for pentecostal work in Winnipeg and, by extension, much of the prairies. Tarrying meetings were held in his house until the attendance grew large enough to rent a building on Alexander Avenue in Winnipeg's north end. Opposition to the new group was also growing, with firecrackers, stones, and eggs being thrown through the windows.[19] While the Argue family returned to California to serve in evangelistic campaigns along the west coast, the split over the "Jesus Only" issue brought the Argues back to Winnipeg to calm the faithful. The congregation continued to grow, moving into the former Wesley Church (now renamed Calvary Temple), and by 1920 the former real-estate agent could devote himself again to full-time evangelistic work.[20]

The doctrinal disputes and amorphous nature of the pentecostal movement led to calls for a more formal association between the loose network of local missions. In Canada all moves in this direction were hampered by the antagonistic position taken by the East End Mission, which remained Canada's pre-eminent site for pentecostalism. Like many others in the movement, the Hebdens were steadfast in their aversion to any sort of organization or creed. They described their work as "one in Spirit with all the body of Christ all over the earth, with the Holy Ghost as leader and teacher, and the Word of God as the only creed, Jesus being ... the Head over all things to the Church."[21] The erection of any sort of "man-made" structure threatened the "free leading of the Spirit," and the Hebdens vehemently opposed the early attempts to establish the Pentecostal Missionary Union in Canada, which, without the support of the Hebdens, quickly dissipated in 1909.[22] However, the fires of revival could not sustain the movement without a more formal organization.

A decade later, discussions among Canadian pentecostals finally led to the granting of a federal charter for the Pentecostal Assemblies of Canada (PAOC). Despite the initial appearance of unity, doctrinal controversies continued to split the ranks. Many Canadian pentecostals agreed with the American Assemblies of God that a traditional understanding of the trinity should be maintained, and even McAlister had shifted his views on this issue. However, a significant body led by Winnipeg's Frank Small continued their adherence to the "Oneness" theology. The "Jesus Only" issue resulted in Small's rejection of the PAOC and the founding of the Apostolic Church of Pentecost in Canada. Despite this division and other complications over the organizational structure of districts, the PAOC emerged in 1922 as Canada's largest pentecostal organization.[23] After a tumultuous beginning, pentecostalism established itself as a permanent fixture within Canadian Protestantism, but its presence also reshaped traditional sites for divine healing.

ENCOUNTERS AND REACTIONS

When the question of tongues first arose, the Christian and Missionary Alliance quickly took notice of the reports from Azusa. A.B. Simpson was initially favourable to the idea that the outpouring of the pentecostal spirit may indeed mark the nearness of the end times. Classes at the missionary institute at Nyack were suspended for two weeks in the fall of 1906 when a pentecostal revival swept through the student body. The leadership of the Alliance did not want to suppress the spiritual movement, but a fear of "fanaticism" tempered their enthusiasm. When restraint was urged, the Alliance lost members who claimed they were obstructing the work of the Holy Ghost. On the other hand, where tongues was permitted, those who were opposed to the new experience might also threaten to leave. It was not a phenomenon the organization could ignore, however. Congregations in Ohio were particularly touched by the new movement, and Simpson dispatched Henry B. Wilson to investigate. Wilson's report did not approve of the pentecostal movement, but it cautiously admitted that the experience of tongues may be genuine.[24]

Pentecostal waves continued to sweep through Alliance conventions, with one of the most dramatic outpourings taking place in Beulah Park, Ohio. It was here in 1907 that the patriarch of Alliance work in Canada, the seventy-five-year-old John Salmon, received his baptism of the spirit. During the summer convention, Salmon engaged in a long night of prayer and eventually found himself shaking in the straw that covered the ground, "uttering a few words in a tongue to me unknown."[25] According to one later recollection, Salmon's "anointing" was unusual in that it was "accompanied by an exquisite aroma, as though litteral [sic] perfume had been poured upon him, so much so it could be smelled off the straw on which he lay, for days after, and his wife could smell it off the pastor for some time after."[26]

For the Alliance, the problem with pentecostalism was not the actual experience of speaking in tongues, which Simpson cautiously regarded as genuine. The real issue was whether or not tongues was the only "initial evidence" of a spirit baptism. The Alliance, along with other holiness groups at the end of the century, had adopted the language of the "baptism of the spirit" and "pentecostal power" well before the Azusa outbreak.[27] However, Simpson rejected the way Parham and other pentecostals defined this experience. The baptism of the spirit was "not merely a baptism of power; power is merely incidental to it. It is the baptism with the Holy Ghost and His coming brings holiness, happiness, healing and all the fullness of God."[28] This was a reiteration of the fourfold gospel that could be enhanced by such a baptism, but unlike many pentecostals, Simpson refused to add the refrain "Jesus as Baptizer" to the fourfold roles of saviour, sanctifier, healer, and coming Lord.

The Christian and Missionary Alliance also faced a serious problem with the loss of congregations and buildings to the new movement. As an interdenominational fellowship, local trustees held the deeds to most Alliance buildings and properties. In Canada, W.J. Fenton's fear of denominationalism and Salmon's congregational background had ensured that this local control was maintained. After seeing property pass into the hands of pentecostals, Simpson and the board of managers started to pressure local churches to sign over their deeds to the Alliance itself. Although it still maintained that it was a fellowship rather than a church, the Alliance was in practice already operating as a separate denomination, and dealing with pentecostalism only further entrenched this trend.[29]

The original emphasis on divine healing within the Christian Alliance was also eroding. In 1896 missionary activity and fundraising were combined with the traditional Alliance conventions that focused on sanctification and healing. As Lindsay Reynolds notes, all of the previous Canadian conventions had climaxed with a service for healing, but for the conventions after 1896, missionary appeals received the keynote position.[30] The focus on missions challenged the position of divine healing within the Alliance in multiple ways, not the least of which was coming to terms with the use of medicine within mission work. The alarmingly high death rate of young men and women sent into the overseas mission field raised new questions about whether quinine should be employed in malarial countries. After all, how could missionaries, whose lives were obviously consecrated to God's work, fail in achieving health through faith? R. Kelso Carter, after his reversal from proponent to critic of the atonement theory of healing, was quick to point to the problem of missions, arguing that no issue vexed the Alliance more than "the failure of the holiest missionaries to withstand the African fever purely by faith." After a large number passed away, its missionaries "were finally driven to see that natural law, given and made by God, operates today just as it ever did. Most of the missionaries have used quinine and other remedies freely, and all have been and are instructed to observe most carefully the rules of the climate for rest and food and clothing."[31]

Perhaps no one embodied the struggle of maintaining the Alliance position on divine healing in the face of missionary demands as much as Rowland V. Bingham, the eventual founder of the Sudan Interior Mission. A Salvation Army captain until the 1892 secession, Bingham served as a pastoral assistant for Salmon at Bethany Chapel, and he became an ardent disciple of the redoubtable Alliance leader. After a year, however, Bingham decided to answer a call to missionary work in Africa. Howland and Salmon laid hands on him before his departure, but Bingham's desire to maintain health through faith alone was tested by the ravages of malaria that struck him and killed his companions. The missionary held steadfast to his belief in faith healing until a second trip in 1899 also ended in a malarial fever. While he continued to hold Salmon in high esteem, Bingham became a determined opponent of divine healing based on the atonement, criticizing the Alliance for assuming that "prayer excludes means ... when natural forces in many cases readily meet the need of the suffering one, and glorify God just as much."[32]

The whole-hearted adoption of divine healing through the atonement by the pentecostal movement further contributed to the Alliance's own distance from this doctrine. While the Azusa fires raged, Alliance periodicals witnessed a severe decline in articles and testimonies related to healing. As a result, the public perception of the Alliance shifted accordingly. During a 1907 convention in Winnipeg, newspapers reported that the Alliance's "chief interest is in missionary work. They also engage in evangelistic work to some extent. However, this is only a minor part."[33] Healing never entirely disappeared, and the fourfold gospel of the Alliance never revoked the understanding of Jesus as healer. However, the doctrine had clearly lost considerable ground. The outbreak of pentecostalism particularly hurt the Alliance in western Canada. A number of conventions were held to raise interest in the organization in Winnipeg, but by 1910 the Canadian district reported that no meetings dedicated to Alliance work were continuing despite Simpson's visit only two years previously.[34] Pentecostalism claimed both a significant portion of the membership and many of the leaders of the Alliance in Manitoba.[35]

The Alliance was not the only group to be affected by the appearance of pentecostalism. Small holiness denominations like the Holiness Movement Church and the Gospel Workers' Church, both of which had rejected the atonement healing position, lost ministers and members. F.D. Goff, editor of the *Holiness Worker*, was particularly critical of the assumed link between tongues and the baptism of the spirit, warning that "Satan is capable of powerful manifestations and wants nothing better than to get us relying on them for evidences that we are right with God."[36]

Although the outbreak of tongues produced acrimony in some quarters, in other places peaceful relations were maintained, and some even found common ground. Pentecostal and Alliance networks overlapped in Toronto, largely because of the presence of the venerable John Salmon. Although he received a pentecostal baptism of the spirit in 1907, Salmon remained within the Alliance fold while in Canada. At the same time, it is clear that he never felt restrained in working with pentecostals or pentecostal missions. When the Hebdens opened a larger rest home for those tarrying in expectation of the baptism, Salmon was visibly present at the dedication ceremony.[37] In 1908 Frank Bartleman, a leading figure of the Azusa revival, arrived in Toronto. The evangelist spoke at three pentecostal missions and also made a point of visiting Salmon's Christian and Missionary Alliance meeting.[38] That same year, Salmon attended a pentecostal convention in Winnipeg and was later prominent at the 1909 Stouffville camp meeting.[39] The patriarch of Alliance work in Canada even continued his fellowship with Alliance defectors, such as the former Salvation Army captain, George Fisher, who had formed his own "full gospel" pentecostal mission.[40] Another mission on Concord Avenue was led by George A. Murray and his wife, both former Alliance missionaries. When Murray died unexpectedly at the age of fifty, Fisher, Salmon, and Ellen Hebden conducted the funeral service.[41]

Despite these intimate cross-connections, there was still a perceivable gap between the established Alliance and the new pentecostalism. Martha Robinson attended some Alliance meetings in Toronto during the first week of July 1907, and her impressions are revealing: "They are seeking pentecostal baptism, but they are so afraid the Holy Ghost may not be just as moderate and modern and polite as He ought to be; they are scared, and so He does not manifest Himself to any degree."[42] The Alliance had lost its most visible, public men, such as Howland and Gooderham, but in Toronto it still maintained elements of that Victorian respectability that had characterized its past.

The issue of respectability was not only based on the expectations of class, but was also rooted in how the mainstream elements of the divine healing movement understood the nature of religious experience. Carrie Judd Montgomery adopted pentecostalism, but the account of her struggle in accepting the baptism of the spirit illustrates the social distance between traditional Victorian holiness and the new expression of pentecostal power. Until reports from Azusa Street reached her, Montgomery had always assumed that the baptism of the spirit was a consciousness of "the Holy Spirit's work in revealing Jesus in and to me," which empowered one to testify and opened "the Word of God." When news of the dramatic manifestations reached her, Montgomery related: "At first I was perplexed. I knew my experience ... was real and lasting in its effects. How could I cast it away?" She resolved to watch the new movement carefully and observed that there "was much that did not appeal to me ... Many of the manifestations did not seem at all like the word of the calm, majestic Spirit of God. In many meetings there was much confusion." Through a number of friends, however, Montgomery became aware of her own "thirsting" and realized that "I had tiny streams, but not rivers [of living water]." Perhaps still wary, Montgomery sought a "fulness" that would resemble "quiet, sweet manifestations, which would reveal His majesty and dignity, and not such as might seem like excitement of the flesh." When the baptism came in 1908, the experience was overpowering: "In a few moments I uttered a few scattered words in an unknown tongue and then burst into a language that came pouring out in great fluency and clearness. The words seemed to come from an irresistible volume of power within, which seemed to possess my whole being, spirit, soul and body. For nearly two hours I spoke and sang in unknown tongues ... rivers of living water flowed through me and divine ecstasy filled my soul. I felt that I drank and used up the life and power as fast as it was poured in."[43]

Montgomery's concern with the "quiet" and "majestic" experience of God contrasts with the pentecostal "confusion." A number of historians have searched for the roots of pentecostalism within the broad network of holiness and higher life advocates, particularly within the divine healing movement, which established an environment described by Donald Dayton as constituting "a sort of pre-Pentecostal tinderbox awaiting the spark that would set it off."[44] However, to view the divine healing movement as little more than a precursor to pentecostalism obscures the important cultural differences between them. Martha Robinson was not the only one to notice the "moderate" and "polite" characteristics of the Alliance in Toronto. In 1901 the *Globe* newspaper described Alliance divine healing meetings as "marked by orderliness and earnestness," with only "the ejaculations common to such gatherings" such as "Amen" and "Hallelujah" rising above the voices of the speakers.[45]

Canada's geography accentuated the perception of a gap between the moderate character of the Victorian divine healing movement and pentecostalism. As noted earlier, holiness and divine healing links to the northern United States were strong, particularly through New York, Boston, Buffalo, and Chicago. Conversely, Canadians maintained relatively little contact with the radical Wesleyan holiness groups of the American south and midwest. According to Vinson Synan, the scenes from Azusa were "nothing new" to those familiar with the "Fire-Baptized Way" of these regions.[46] The Canadian preference for Durham's "Finished Work" doctrine rather than the "second work" emphasis, popular among holiness pentecostals in the south, points to the continuation of this general pattern.

Some of Dowie's former followers in Canada were also unsure of what to make of the new pentecostal movement. The first few years after the decline of the Robinsons' and Brookses' ministries at Wolseley Hall were financially difficult for both families. Of the four principals, only Sara Brooks had received the baptism of the spirit, and without denominational or congregational support, daily needs became a matter of prayerful struggle. Martha Robinson recorded in her journal that one day "we had just two car tickets and two cents. We finished bread and tomatoes [for breakfast] ... and took the last slice of bread to East End for lunch."[47] The Brookses' furniture was seized when they could not pay their rent.[48] Both couples moved continuously, boarding with each other or with friends and relatives.

The turning point came in November 1907, when Martha Robinson was praying in the kitchen of the Hebden Mission. During her vigil, she went through an unusual bodily experience that not only healed her infirmities, but also marked a new stage in her life. Robinson explained that "I felt my God had moved in and, as it were, had eliminated me. My mind did not seem to work at all – my spirit [seemed] off in heaven. It seemed that Christ was just borrowing, as it were, my body. Christ was living in me, and yet *I* did not seem to live at all."[49] Robinson was heavily influenced by the quietism of the seventeenth-century Madame Guyon, and this mystic aspect would later distinguish the work of the small group. Following her experience, Robinson manifested gifts of prophecy and divine "wisdom."

Although Eugene Brooks initially opposed her new gifts, the two couples reunited in Toronto in 1909. Meetings were held in a home, unadvertised, and all four of them seemed to encounter the same type of bodily possession of the spirit that Martha had experienced two years earlier. Martha, however, maintained a prominent position within the group through her ability to "discern" the will of the Lord. In December 1909 the gathering felt called to establish a faith home in Toronto. A

house was rented, and the two couples moved in together. From this beginning, contact was made with Sara's relatives in Zion City, where another faith home was founded. The Brookses and the Robinsons both
made trips between the two cities, and eventually the Toronto work was
discontinued in 1911 to concentrate solely on the now-multiple homes
in Zion. The homes were a "work of faith," taking no collections and
charging visitors nothing. They had no official publication and did not
advertise themselves. They became spiritual centres where services,
prayer meetings, and bible study were regularly scheduled, and those
who felt called to ministry or service would stay at the faith homes for
training. Although the homes were identified with pentecostalism and
would influence many of its leaders, the mystical inwardness was
stressed more than the exercise of tongues.[50]

The Zion faith homes were noticeably different from the late-
nineteenth-century healing homes, where the domestic space was emphasized and sacralized to serve as the ideal environment in which to
encourage divine healing. Pentecostals often turned to faith homes as
alternatives to bible institutes that provided support and training. They
were retreats for refreshing and providing guidance for workers, rather
than environments specifically instituted to promote bodily healing.[51]
This transformation in the role of the faith homes was not unique to
pentecostalism. In addition to Toronto's Bethany Home, the Alliance
had at one time maintained homes in New York, Philadelphia, Atlanta,
Pittsburgh, Cleveland, Chicago, Los Angeles, Santa Barbara, and Oakland. Simpson's grand Berachah could accommodate more than a hundred guests. In the twentieth century, however, the healing focus of the
homes started to diminish. Instead, they became rest homes for Christian workers, places for retreat, or were operated as Christian hotels.
By 1920 all of the Alliance homes were closed. The official reason offered was that the widespread proclamation of divine healing had made
localized special homes unnecessary.[52] More importantly, the Victorian
concept of domestic religion had lost much of its lustre, and the connection between healing and religion in the private space of the bedroom was no longer widely assumed or accepted.

A variety of factors accounted for this restructuring of the relationship
between religion and healing. The growing dominance of the hospital as
the proper site for treating illness was eclipsing the notion of the private
bedroom as a feminine space where health was nurtured by matronly
care. Once the domain of the urban poor, the status of hospitals rose
quickly in the twentieth century as the development of professional staff,
scientific laboratories, and antiseptic operating rooms made them the
pre-eminent institutions for the acute-care treatment of all classes. These
technical resources were both symbolic and substantive in elevating the

prestige of the hospital, and the institution's twin pillars of scientism and professionalism extended both outward and inward. The development of modern hospitals offered medicine a physical structure in the city land-scape that suggested medical progress and a guardianship of health. Within their walls, the patient was surrounded not with remnants of do-mesticity, but rather with a wide range of diagnostic tools, options for treatment, and a strictly regimented life where the body and bodily func-tions were scrupulously observed and measured.[53] As the hospital bed became the site for middle-class patients to receive acute care, Victorian illness narratives, which favoured the romantic and domestic, gradually lost their appeal. However, fostered by the impetus of pentecostalism, di-vine healing would refashion a new sacred space for itself.

A PENTECOST OF HEALING

William Durham embarked on a Canadian campaign in 1910 that took him to Berlin (now Kitchener), London, and Toronto. Two of his assis-tants on this tour knew southwestern Ontario very well. Growing up near the town of Ingersoll, Aimee Kennedy had discovered the baptism of the spirit through Robert Semple, an Irish-American evangelist who maintained close connections to the Hebden Mission in Toronto. Aimee and Robert were soon married and after moving to Chicago, both were ordained by Durham. The early months of 1910 held great promise for all three pentecostal workers, who were determined to spark a revival in southwestern Ontario. Aimee would face new challenges after the tragic death of Robert six months later and her turbulent second marriage to Harold McPherson the following year. However, in 1910 Aimee Semple was known more for her local connections than the international notori-ety she would later gain as a faith healer.[54]

Durham's account of the pentecostal meetings held in London offer a sense of what the introduction of the pentecostal experience was like for a Canadian community. The faithful and the curious gathered in the home of William Wortman, a Methodist class leader and the owner of a local manufacturing plant. The meetings began on 13 January and continued "night and day" for twenty days: "No pen can describe these meetings. Sometimes they were quiet and the people listened at-tentively to the Word of God; again the glory and power of God would rest upon us in such a measure that we could not proceed with any reg-ular order of service, but would simply yield to God and allow Him to work in His own way." Surprised at the calmness that pervaded "a people so unaccustomed to seeing real manifestations of power," the evangelist reported that "People would fall and lie as dead under the power. Others would be shaken mightily, and some would be praying, some singing in the Spirit, some speaking in tongues, yet all seemed to be praising God in perfect harmony." Durham was noticeably impressed that the meetings brought together "all classes," including "business men, capable teachers in the schools, rich and poor, learned and unlearned alike." Over the twenty days, thirty-two people received the spirit baptism, and the number grew to fifty-eight in the days after his departure.[55]

Not everyone accepted pentecostal outbursts with the calmness Durham reported in London. Aimee Semple McPherson returned to southwestern Ontario for a series of camp meetings in the summer of 1915 and was subsequently invited to the town of Mount Forest by Elizabeth Sharpe. When a "young man" started shaking and shouting, Sharpe recounted that "The church people who had gathered for the meeting became alarmed and terrified, and left, telling men on the streets that I was hypnotizing this young man." A doctor pulled the youth off his chair and applied ice to his chest "to keep the fire from burning." Still shouting to the glory of God, his father eventually arrived and "dragged him home." The raucous meetings eventually led an exasperated police magistrate to fine Sharpe one dollar for disturbing the peace.[56]

The manifestation of tongues operated within a different social space than the mainstream evangelical perception of sanctification or "higher life" that had informed Victorian divine healing. The public face of the "second blessing" was the willingness to testify to the experience, since the inward change might not otherwise be perceived. Tongues, however, was a bodily expression of religion that was both immediate and often displayed publicly, an open demonstration that the baptism had been received. Although testimonials remained a significant element in pentecostal culture, the full impact of tongues was felt when others could see and hear the spirit fill the vessel.[57] Glossolalia was an individual communion with God, but its expression became increasingly public in nature. As historian Grant Wacker observes, "The experience may have been personal, but rarely private."[58]

This remapping of social space can be seen in the experience of Herbert Randall, a missionary recently returned from Egypt, who had heard of the latter rain falling in Toronto. Lodging with the Hebdens at East End Mission, he recounted his baptism of 1907:

About midday I felt that God was dealing with me as never before, and the power of God was working in every part of my body, and at times came near my jaws and mouth. But it was reserved for the public service at night for the full benefit. I then went forward to the altar, and after kneeling some little time ... the power then began to operate as in the afternoon, but to a greater degree. I felt it coming into my jaws, my mouth began to move in a strange way, queer sounds began to proceed, and finally I was speaking in a strange language, and waxing bolder and bolder in it.[59]

For Randall, the "full benefit" of his baptism could not be expressed until the "public service." Only within this environment could the believer receive the "greater degree" of power. When pentecostalism first arrived in Winnipeg, Eva Argue recalled "We always felt that if we missed a meeting we would miss seeing someone come through with whom we had been tarrying. We wanted to be there to rejoice with them."[60]

Public displays of corporeal religious experiences were certainly not new; the "enthusiasm" of early Methodists and the Salvation Army was marked by shaking, shouting, dancing, and prostrations of those struck by the power of the spirit. Some Wesleyan holiness groups continued these traditions in the twentieth century.[61] However, the cultural practice of faith healing, especially within the "respectable" milieu of the Christian Alliance, refrained from associating healing with these behaviours. Mainstream holiness and the contemplative search for inward cleansing provided a better model for the bodily pursuit of divine health. While there were exceptions to this pattern, particularly in the United States where mass "trances" and ecstatic faith healings accompanied the revivals of Maria Woodworth-Etter, such scenes were absent north of the border.[62]

For those who embraced the "latter rain," the emergence of tongues restructured the social space that surrounded divine healing. The long episodes of "tarrying," prayer meetings, and after-meetings that followed regular services were intimate practices that reinforced the faithful as a sacred community; these gatherings became the embodiment of a restored apostolic church. Baptism in the spirit marked a corporate identity, and the gifts that were now available to the community were best expressed when members gathered together in praise and worship. Sacredness was personified by the faithful "saints," the gathered church, rather than embedded within the individual home or the bedroom. Faith healing found itself entwined with glossolalia within this communal space, and as a result it became increasingly separated from notions of domesticity.

This change of context and environment occurred despite the fact that the pentecostal position on divine healing was grounded firmly in atonement theology. "We believe healing to be in the atonement," McAlister reiterated emphatically in bold type. "Bodily healing is not only a supernatural outward evidence of the divine origin of salvation, but is a normal product of salvation itself."[63] The Hebdens similarly maintained a traditional position of the atonement as having "all remedies for soul or body sickness."[64] One of the more extended examinations of divine healing was provided by George Fisher, who made no attempt to distinguish between his understanding of healing while he was a member of the Alliance and that of his new pentecostal outlook. In 1910 he outlined a threefold understanding of sickness that would not have been out of place in the pages of Alliance periodicals a quarter of a century earlier. Fisher suggested that some sickness was simply a result of personal foolishness that leads to "a violation of the laws of nature." However, a second form of sickness was that which came as "a direct onslaught of the devil," who continually sought to destroy the faithful in "spirit, soul and body." The third type was "a sickness that is permitted of God; the devil is the agent, but it is permitted of God for tuition when we will not learn a lesson any other way."[65]

Despite such assurances of theological continuity, Fisher may have realized that a shift was occurring in the bodily expression of divine healing. Concerned that too many people seeking healing through faith wanted to "have some feeling like as if we had been touched by an electric battery," Fisher warned that if you "feel an electric shock go through you, you will think you are healed because you feel it. There is not faith in that at all ... Faith works in the dark, and if you feel it and believe it because you feel it, your faith isn't any good."[66] The former Salvation Army Captain was appealing to the Victorian holiness understanding of the "prayer of faith," which relied on an inward stillness, a grounding of faith in complete submission to God's will, rather than depending on outward signs or the physical elements of a subjective religious experience, such as an "electric shock."

Fisher, however, was the product of another time; the defining point of identity for pentecostals was precisely the type of experience that he warned against. In the previous century, the divine healing movement had framed healing as a bodily extension of the process of sanctification or higher life. It is not surprising that pentecostals, particularly the "Finished Work" adherents who had rejected the second blessing of sanctification as a distinct work of grace, would restructure faith healing in light of the baptism of the spirit. Traditionally, divine healing was not considered a miracle, since it operated through the atonement as a process akin to grace, open to all if faith was sufficient. Rather than transgressing natural laws, the human body was naturally ordered to receive the divine. Pentecostal accounts of faith healing, however, stressed the miraculous aspect of a divine restoration of the body as evidence of God's continuing power over natural law.

The growing interest in healing as a form of miraculous power can be seen in the case of Mabel Sipes of Ingersoll, who was sent to Durham's London meetings by her mother in the hope that she could be healed of consumption. After receiving the baptism of the spirit, Sipes asked Durham to pray that God would heal her. In the midst of others who were lying prostrate or speaking in tongues, the evangelist "noticed Miss Sipes kneeling near me with face bowed nearly to the floor. I felt the time had come to lay hands on her and felt the assurance in my heart that God would heal her. I reached over to lay my hands on her, thinking to lay them on her back as near the lungs as possible. My left hand reached her first, and the instant it touched her she fell as dead and was for at least an hour mightily under the power of God. When she arose she declared that she was healed."[67] The healing of Sipes is not only public and instantaneous, but it is actually merged with being "slain" in the spirit, falling "as dead" for an hour. It is the power of God to heal that is emphasized, rather than the internal struggle to lay claim to divine health.

The narrative of Sipes's recovery reveals another shift in the experience of faith healing that occurred. Durham's account emphasizes that he "felt the assurance" that God would heal her, and it was the actual touch of his hand that delivered the power of God to the body. The evangelist has taken on a more exalted role as the vehicle for divine manifestations. Pentecostals appended divine healing within the atonement to the concept of apostolic "gifts" of the spirit. As A.A. Boddy explained, these "latter days" produced "Elders, both men and women, to whom the Lord has given these gifts of healing, channels of the quickening Spirit."[68] Proponents of divine healing in the nineteenth century strenuously emphasized that only God, not the messenger, could heal. Pentecostals agreed with this position, but modified it by suggesting that certain people were endowed with the "gift" of healing and could serve a particular role as a "channel" of God's power. The language of gifts suited the style and context of the pentecostal experience, which stressed the fall of the "latter rain," and the outpouring of God's power amidst the faithful.[69]

Both the adoption of tongues and the apostolic gift of healing reveal an underlying hermeneutic of history that set pentecostalism apart from the divine healing movement. As many modern studies have emphasized, pentecostalism was based on a strong restorationist impulse with eschatological overtones.[70] Since the time of the second coming was drawing near, the restoration of the primitive church of apostolic times was connected to the outbreak of tongues. Premillennial dispensationalism became a framework for understanding these historical developments, dividing the past into a series of "dispensations," marked by different covenants and relationships between God and humanity.[71] Time itself was bifurcated by the two distinct peoples of God, "Israel" and the "Church." Dispensationalists calculated that the fulfilment of

"Israel's" true historical time was only seven years away from completion when God suspended time (the "Great Parenthesis") in order to deal with the historical development of Christianity. When the Rapture arrives and withdraws the faithful Church from the world, apocalyptic time is continued and seven years of tribulations ensue before the second coming of Christ. The dispensational basis of pentecostalism explained why tongues had disappeared so long ago but was reappearing in the twentieth century.[72] However, this perspective was very different from that of the early divine healing movement, whose proponents had traced a continuity in the presence of divine healing within the atonement that had been variously exercised at different times by the church. Like the grace of salvation and sanctification, divine healing was available to all throughout history, and if these had not been exercised in the past it was because the church had lost its original teaching. Simpson's fourfold gospel included the provision for premillennialism, but he was not a dispensationalist.

In 1917 the Winnipeg evangelist A.H. Argue published an article in Montgomery's *Triumphs of Faith* that examined all of the traditional territory of divine healing. Argue stressed that "the great atonement not only covers all our sin, but also our sickness," and distinguished between miracles and healing. He reiterated that the laying on of hands did not "necessarily mean an instantaneous healing," since "when a disease is smitten at the root, and the trouble begins to dry up, there may be symptoms of the old trouble for a few days." None of Argue's exposition was unfamiliar in the pages of the periodical that had preached divine healing for almost forty years. At the end of the article, however, Argue's tone changes: "It is evident that the times of the Gentiles is about fulfilled, for truly we see the shadow of the awful tribulation over us and the coming of the Lord is at hand." The evidence for this assertion could be found all around: "Surely the Lord expects that His word shall be so fulfilled in His people that they may be cleansed from all sin, baptized with the Holy Ghost as recorded at the beginning of this dispensation ... and that the gifts of the Spirit, wisdom, knowledge, faith, gifts of healing, working of miracles, prophesy, discerning of spirits, diverse kinds of tongues, and interpretation of tongues, be in our midst."[73] Argue's dispensationalism is readily apparent, as is the link between historical time and the appearance of the "gifts" of tongues and healing.

Four years later Argue would take the subject of healing even further. At the 1921 meeting of the General Council of the Assemblies of God, the Winnipeg evangelist preached to his ministerial brethren on the importance of maintaining the "essential things" of the Gospel rather than "side issues." The essential truths identified by Argue included the exaltation of Christ as "the One who heals the sick, as the One who baptizes with the Holy Ghost as at Pentecost, as the One who is coming again very soon." The evangelist's advice to the gathering on the best method to pursue healing was particularly instructive: "one of the greatest secrets in the healing of the sick, is to get those who come for physical healing to seek to be filled with the Holy Ghost, and when they receive the Baptism of the Spirit there is almost invariably such a mighty inflow of divine life that their sicknesses vanish."[74] Like Durham's account of Sipes's healing, Argue merges the baptism of the spirit with divine healing. It is no longer the "prayer of faith," but a "tarrying" for the baptism that shocks the body with such a "mighty inflow" that bodily ailments are also conquered. It is the power of a God who possesses the body to move the mouth of the believer that also cleanses the body of disease.

DIVINE POWER

After the initial excitement over Azusa had died down, few Canadian newspapers noticed the small group of believers who spoke in tongues, particularly during the war years when the nation's attention was elsewhere. In 1919, however, a Toronto *Star* reporter visited Trinity Pentecostal Assembly, which met in a former YMCA building on the corner of Yonge and McGill. The correspondent immediately noticed a dichotomy in the congregation between the "pale, pinch-faced invalids … sick folk lured by what they have heard of miracles of 'divine healing,'" and the "big, stalwart, men; buxom, smiling women, and clear-eyed, strong-limbed children, many of whom claim to have been raised from beds of pain through the laying on of hands."

Before the regular service, a prayer meeting was held in the basement where worshippers were "pouring out ejaculations, coherent and otherwise." In the auditorium, people were busy discussing the "latest story of divine healing." A song service opened the regular proceedings, with choir and congregation singing the verses in unison rather than harmony, and everyone kept time with their feet. The hymns themselves were described as "off the beaten track." A session of prayer followed, and people were "swept with an extraordinary storm of emotion" as appeals were given, most of them having to do with absent persons dealing with some form of sickness. It was a "strange and incongruous scene," commented the reporter, to one "accustomed to more decorous devotions." There were more prayers and stranger scenes to come: "Three handkerchiefs were laid on a table on the platform, and three men laid their hands on them. There was another burst of vehement prayer from all sides. By the laying on of hands those handkerchiefs became charged with divine power, and when they are slipped beneath the pillow of the sufferers to whom they belong the patients will be cured or at least relieved of their maladies." The sermon was long, but it was delivered quietly and "without demonstration" from the audience. In the address, Mr F.M. Moffatt declared that since the regular churches know "nothing experimentally of the baptism of the Holy Ghost," they were unable to "receive and exercise the gifts of healing." At the end of his exposition, Moffatt added a few words about the impending fall of civilization that could be witnessed in "the spread of Bolshevism." He also suggested that the manifestation of the Anti-Christ was imminent, but the faithful would be caught up in the rapture to escape the terrible days of tribulation. An after-meeting was held and many made their way to the basement where "[s]eekers after health of body or soul, or both, waited behind and eagerly sought counsel of those qualified to advise." Having already spent over two hours with the congregation, the intrepid reporter did not venture to attend the after-meeting. In all, the experience was akin to "having visited another planet," but if the Pentecostal Assembly was "the strangest" sect he had visited, it was at the same time "the happiest."[75]

The *Star* report raises a number of intriguing characteristics about the religious culture of pentecostalism. Despite the fact that speaking in tongues was the defining feature of the movement, divine healing dominated most aspects of worship at Trinity. The understanding and expression of healing was obviously removed from the careful scriptural expositions and quiet services for anointing that were commonly found in the Alliance conventions. The style of worship, including such elements as music, exaltations, and prayers, comprised "another world" that would have been unacceptable to the respectable Methodists, Anglicans, and Presbyterians who supported the Alliance in the 1880s. It was this distance from tradition that pentecostals took pride in, since mainline denominations had lost the "joy and power," which produced only a "deadening formality" and "Sad Christians." The rhetoric of spiritual gifts linked the experience of healing with the baptism of the spirit and designated the faithful congregation as representing a true restoration of the apostolic church. Divine healing, tongues, and the imminence of the end of time were woven together into a worldview that infused both the body and political events with an overarching cosmological significance.

Although rarely acknowledged in theological works on faith healing, the use of handkerchiefs was a familiar practice for both pentecostals and earlier proponents of divine healing. What was new about the pentecostal practice was the increasing emphasis on divine "power" that became embedded within the fabric when they were prayed over, had hands laid upon them, or were anointed with oil. In the nineteenth century, handkerchiefs had been used as a means of encouragement. Like healing testimonies, they provided support and reminded believers that the prayers of the faithful were supporting them. For many pentecostals, handkerchiefs meant much more.

At Trinity Pentecostal Assembly, the *Star* noted that "vehement prayer" broke out on all sides when the handkerchiefs were being prayed over and hands laid upon them. In a sense, the presence and power of the spirit that was engendered by the public gathering of the faithful were transferred to the handkerchiefs. For the believer it was not the knowledge that individuals were praying that mattered; rather it was the fact that the handkerchiefs were blessed in the presence of the moving spirit of God. To those who waited for the after-meeting, their bodies would serve as vessels of God, both for tongues and for healing. Bodies were situated within a quasi-public sacred space where the spirit could be present, marking the boundaries of the apostolic church. For those whose bodies could not be physically brought within this space, handkerchiefs served as a way to incorporate the bodies of others within this spiritually charged environment. Ideally, the circle was completed when those who were restored could rejoin the community and testify to their healing. During one pentecostal campaign in Montreal it was reported that "Scores of handkerchiefs were sent in to be prayed over and anointed," while the efficacy of the practice was demonstrated when "sick ones testified to the Lord's healing touch from these."[76]

The use of handkerchiefs was a cultural practice that was fostered from below, rather than encouraged by the leadership of the movement. Dr F.E. Yoakum, a former physician who ran the Pisgah faith healing centre outside of Los Angeles, operated one of the most far-reaching handkerchief prayer networks in North America. He regularly received prayer requests from as far away as Britain and conducted healing campaigns in Canada in 1911 and 1913. This activity was forced upon Yoakum by a "chain of circumstances" when a mother sent him a handkerchief in the mail, accompanied by the request to pray for her nine year-old son who had resided within an insane asylum for five years. She included the scriptural reference Acts 19:11–12: "And God did extraordinary miracles by the hands of Paul, so that handkerchiefs or aprons were carried away from his body to the sick; and diseases left them and the evil spirits came out of them." Yoakum placed the handkerchief on a bible opened to that verse and "with fear and trembling" laid his hands upon the fabric, which was returned and credited with curing the boy. A second request also came unsolicited, and the results were even more startling. A faithful sister secretly placed a consecrated handkerchief under the pillow of her alcoholic brother, and he began to seek sobriety.[77] Under the conventional understanding of faith healing, such an event would be inconceivable, since the divine restoration of the body proceeded from the progressive experience of salvation and sanctification, not through the expression of spiritual power embedded in a material object.

Yoakum's protest that this ministry was forced upon him rather than sought after is a pattern that appears to be supported by other evidence. Despite the multitude of articles on healing and the gifts of the spirit, detailed expositions that discuss the use of handkerchiefs are extremely rare in pentecostal periodicals. And yet their popular appeal was very strong among Canadian pentecostals. In 1920 Elizabeth Sharpe held a series of meetings in the vicinity of Huntsville in the Muskoka district of Ontario. She reported that she "never before prayed for so many sick and anointed so many handkerchiefs to be sent to sick friends."[78] Requests for handkerchiefs came from the sick or friends of the sick; however, their use was far from regularized or even particularly encouraged.

For people who sought healing, however, the use of handkerchiefs was a significant element of the material culture of religion, and they were invested with great significance and power. Marie Griffith points out that as items "associated with wiping away tears or sweat or mundanely blowing one's nose, the handkerchief's cleansing function was easily extended into the realm of divine healing."[79] An artifact of everyday life was drawn within a sacred space, and its normal operation in the removal of bodily excretions was transformed and inverted to serve as a carrier of divine power. One man wrote to Argue to request "prayer for the healing of a rupture." Prayer was offered, and a "handkerchief sent in the name of the Lord" was dispatched. Even before it had arrived, the recipient realized that healing was starting to take place, and when the handkerchief reached him, "his whole body was filled with the power of God."[80]

The conceptualization of tangible divine power manifested within the physical world was also linked to the presence of Satan and evil spirits. From Palmerston, Ontario, Mrs Alfred Elsey described her experience in terms that reflect the intimate reality of a cosmological struggle between good and evil: "The enemy of my soul which possessed me sought to deceive me by false manifestations every time I presented myself as a seeker, until it became very evident that I was possessed of an evil spirit." Elsey suffered from, among other things, a poisoning of gas fumes that would instantly throw her into "spasms" the moment she encountered a raw gasoline odour. During these episodes, she was paralyzed, and "when the power of God came in contact with my body, demon power in my flesh would immediately exert itself, seizing my vocal organs, locking my jaws to prevent me from praising God. This was my experience many times, both in the meetings and in private." Although she received some healing for heart troubles, a full restoration was only possible after the evil spirits had been exorcised: "Though the demons fought fearfully when in contact with anyone who had authority over them, completely controlling both my mind and body at times, yet God continually increased my faith for full deliverance so that when at last the victory came and the demons were cast out, my whole being burst forth in unutterable joy."[81] The body became the battleground for forces of light and darkness, each possessing the body and controlling its functions towards either praising or turning away from God. The transference of divine power was the currency exercised by personal agents of good and evil, and the reality of this struggle was visibly demonstrated by the state of health offered by the body.

Despite these manifestations, there were significant elements within the pentecostal movement that attempted to maintain a more traditional understanding of divine healing. Perhaps no one exemplified the familiar connections between faith healing and "divine health" as much as Dr Lilian B. Yeomans, the former physician healed by Dowie. Having moved to Calgary to work as a stenographer at a postal inspector's office, Yeomans discovered pentecostalism in 1907 when a friend from Winnipeg arrived bringing news of the baptism of the spirit.[82] Starting in 1912 when she first began to publish articles on divine healing for Montgomery's *Triumphs of Faith*, Yeomans became a noted authority on divine healing in pentecostal circles, producing numerous books on the subject. Although healings marked by the "power" of God were prominent, Yeomans insisted on reconnecting divine healing with the familiar rhetoric of health: "Not divine healing alone, but divine health – superb, all-round physical well-being, one hundred per cent physical efficiency, every organ functioning properly." For Yeomans the body in divine health was simply the achievement of all parts of the body working "in perfect harmony and unison toward the end for which the organism was created."[83] This was a fulfilment of the natural order, rather than miraculous contravention of natural laws. The religious culture and social space of pentecostalism distanced it from the earlier understanding of divine healing, but many of the original themes and concerns surrounding the nature of the body continued to be expressed and reformulated.

Pentecostals maintained the basic doctrine of healing through the atonement, but this experience took place within the broader context of a "full" gospel, marked by pentecostal gifts. Earlier understandings of healing placed it as a bodily extension of the process of sanctification, or the ultimate sign that a life was fully consecrated to God. Now, however, the baptism of the holy ghost displaced healing as the ultimate achievement of faith, and faith healing had to be accommodated alongside the bodily manifestation of tongues. Faith healing was restructured to resemble, and even merge, with the baptism of the spirit. The instantaneous and powerful "possessions" of the spirit became themselves characteristics of divine healing. Armed with a hermeneutic of history that associated the reappearance of apostolic gifts with the end times, divine healing was caught between notions of "natural" and "supernatural," between healing as a continuous extension of the atonement and as the new product of a restored apostolic age.

The use of handkerchiefs underlines how pentecostalism shifted the bodily understanding of divine healing. Handkerchiefs usually had hands laid upon them by those whose bodies were infused with pentecostal power. In turn, the consecrated objects were laid upon or near the ailing body, who could then receive the power of the divine. In the Alliance tradition, and even for Dowie, cleansing the soul was the key to healing, and the sacramental externals, such as anointing and laying on of hands, were intended to encourage the deeper faith rather than actually transfer a tangible physical element of "power." For pentecostals, the recovery of apostolic gifts created an economy of divine power that could be exchanged, held, and embedded within material objects. As Grant Wacker has noted, "Despite strenuous insistence by pentecostal writers that the Holy Spirit is a person and not an impersonal power, in the daily devotional life of the people the Spirit often emerged as just that: impersonal power."[84] It is not the body in isolation that is restored to its natural state, but the body as part of the community of the apostolic church that is divinely infused.

Pentecostalism reconfigured Protestant faith healing in Canada, both through its own activities and its encounters with others. Despite the efforts of Salmon to bridge the Alliance with the new movement, pentecostalism had clearly emerged as the most appealing avenue for those who would seek healing through faith. It was successful in part because it had managed to adapt a new social space for healing that was viable in the twentieth century as the traditional notions of domestic religion declined and the faith homes steadily closed. In the decade that followed World War I, faith healing would shift yet again, emerging as a public spectacle in urban arenas across the country.

6

Revivals and Reactions

It was not her eloquence but her healing of the sick which raised Sharon to such eminence that she promised to become the most renowned evangelist in America. People were tired of eloquence; and the whole evangelist business was limited, since even the most ardent were not likely to be saved more than three or four times. But they could be healed constantly, and of the same disease ...

She alienated many evangelical pastors by divine healing, but she won all the readers of books about will-power, and her daily miracles were reported in the newspapers. And, or so it was reported, some of her patients remained cured.

Sinclair Lewis, *Elmer Gantry* (1927)

Weeks of planning were suddenly jeopardized when the auditorium booked for the revival campaign burned down. The pentecostal workers in Lethbridge, Alberta, managed to secure the local curling rink in its place, and for two weeks in June 1920 the newspapers covered the nightly meetings held by the "famous lady evangelist," Aimee Semple McPherson, and queried "Can a Mere Woman Preach the Gospel?" While the fact that the evangelist was a woman was a curiosity, it was her healing activities that drew the most notice. The *Lethbridge Herald* described the scene as testimonials were given to the power of God to heal the body:

The people are leaning forward in their seats. Every face is turned expectantly toward the pulpit. The ushers have placed most of the sick in the front rows. Judging from the list of addresses, about half of them are from points outside of Lethbridge. A large crowd of spectators are in attendance. Two local ministers and a doctor or two are observed sitting excitedly in the suburbs of the tabernacle. 'Tis time now for the "miracle woman" to appear. Thrills intensify as the renowned revivalist steps to the front of the platform.

The evangelist gave her address, declaring that the chief business of the Lord's ministry was forgiving sin and healing the sick. She assured the audience that "None were in such darkness but that He could bring them to light. None so sorrowful and afflicted that He could not bring them to happiness and health." As her discussion came to a close, the altar call was given and forward came the penitent and afflicted. The choir sang "The Physician Now is Near" as the altar filled with the "sick and the sobbing" and "sacred tears" fell to the floor. As a woman on crutches approached, the evangelist "reverently prays for her thus: 'Oh, Lord Jesus, we believe that thou are just the same today. We know that thou art able to make this dear woman whole from this very hour.' At this juncture the woman, slowly at first, made a step forward without her crutch, then leaving her crutch behind, walked briskly up and down the aisles – up the steps of the platform, praising the Lord."[1] Before crowds of up to 2,000 people, the evangelist talked about faith, the baptism of the spirit, and the second coming of Christ. The healing services were the most spectacular aspect of the campaign, however, and sentimental remembrances of the atmosphere of music, expectations, and dramatic healings filled reports on the revival's success.

Aimee Semple McPherson was just hitting her stride when she campaigned in Winnipeg, Lethbridge, and Montreal in 1920. She would be the first of a wave of evangelists to tour the nation with the message of divine healing incorporated within the context of an "old-fashioned" revival. Despite her later prominence in the United States, McPherson's Canadian campaigns were surpassed by those of later American evangelists, such as Charles S. Price and F.F. Bosworth. Tens of thousands of Canadians attended a variety of healing campaigns that filled arenas across the country in the 1920s, drawing support from both small sects and mainline denominations. After disappearing from the notice of most major newspapers for twenty years, divine healing suddenly re-emerged in the nation's consciousness through front-page headlines.

There was nothing "old-fashioned" about the social geography of evangelical faith healing in the decade that followed World War I. From the close community of believers that drew upon healing as divine power, the professional evangelists transformed healing into a full public spectacle. One was made whole "this very hour" in the arena, not through long, private contemplations. The marketing of consumer culture that shaped the emergence of urban evangelism also restructured the nature of faith healing, which was now presented to a mass audiences. No longer an end in itself, faith healing became a tool to convert souls and change lives.

The publicity created by the large urban campaigns of the 1920s attracted more than the notice of the nation's press. As the public exposure of divine healing increased, the scrutiny of its critics was correspondingly brought to bear. However, direct action against the faith healers was largely confined to letters to the editor in local newspapers, denunciations from the pulpit, and editorials within the religious press rather than egg riots or legal charges. Popular ideas about what divine healing "really was" reflected the psychological trends of the age, focussing on the power of the unconscious and suggestibility. Critics also noted the physical space of healing, claiming that the charged atmosphere of the revival produced hypnotic effects. By the end of the decade, even proponents of divine healing were starting to question its association with professional evangelism, fearing that the methods required to draw crowds had compromised the spiritual purpose of the campaigns.

PROFESSIONAL EVANGELISM

When McPherson first arrived in southern Alberta, the *Lethbridge Herald* was quick to label her the "Woman Billy Sunday," but the visiting evangelist was less than thrilled with the comparison to the famous American preacher. As the campaign continued, the newspaper corrected itself, commenting that McPherson "resents the name given her of the woman Billy Sunday. She does not endeavor to pull off any stunts but tries to win converts to the Lord by preaching the gospel in a woman's fashion."[2] The distinction between true revivalism and "stunts" could be a fine one, however, and it certainly did not prevent McPherson from leaping off the platform to lead a procession around the interior of the curling rink, waving a tambourine while the orchestra played "Revive Us Again." When the song and the marching ended, people shouted down the walls of unbelief, imitating the fallen walls of Jericho. After all, it was "Just as Right to Shout for Christ in Church as to Shout at a Ball Game."[3]

McPherson's reference to a ball game hinted at the large shadow of influence cast by Sunday, the former baseball player, over the style of professional evangelism in the Jazz Age. Employing a full-time organizational team for planning his revivals, Sunday maximized his own personal exposure and image through large-scale newspaper advertisements, picture postcards, and other campaign souvenirs. The gospel message required marketing, and Sunday was masterful in playing to the press and aligning himself with powerful business interests. It was not any one particular aspect of Sunday that vaulted him above other evangelists of the time as much as it was his ability to present a convincing package of efficiency and information that could save souls. Not only did he use his own image to draw an audience, but within his meetings the skilful coordination of musical elements, sermons, exhortations, and altar calls became a well-established pattern emulated by dozens of hopeful imitators. Sunday's musical director, the trombone-wielding Homer Rodeheaver, joked with the crowds and produced gala musical numbers. None of this was entirely new; Laurence Moore has traced similar elements characterizing the "marketplace of culture" within evangelism through the nineteenth and early-twentieth centuries. From the perspective of 1920, however, Sunday was the reference point against which all other evangelists were compared.[4]

Billy Sunday, however, was no faith healer, and few popular evangelists before World War I had dwelt on the issue. As pentecostals started to hit the sawdust trail, the issue became more prominent, but it was McPherson who would take faith healing to a new level within professional evangelism; and it was her model that would prove to be particularly influential in Canada. Key differences existed between Sunday and McPherson: Sunday's emphasis on business and masculinity did not suit McPherson's more feminine style (or "woman's fashion"), and her organization was less structured, relying heavily upon the local networks of pentecostals for support. However, the structural elements of modern revivalism were clearly evident in the careful positioning of music, messages, testimonies, and exhortations. In arenas across the country the spectacle of faith healing took centre stage, and the crowds who flocked to see the faith healers often found themselves to be part of the performance.

McPherson's 1920 campaign in Montreal illustrates the public demonstration of faith healing and how the surrounding elements of professional evangelism supported it. Despite the fact that her own retinue was still small at this time, the revival was far from spontaneous. Pentecostals in Montreal had done "weeks of patient, steady preparation," and insured the placement of a "fully organized staff, every saint ready to fit in his or her respective place." The results were indeed remarkable:

What a sight, the lame, halt, and blind, seeking deliverance … The piano and stringed instruments played softly, "My faith looks up to Thee," as the prayer of faith was ascending and God did the rest … Quietly and sweetly the music floated over the air, suddenly all eyes were turned on a young girl who ascended the platform with crutches in great difficulty. Mrs. McPherson relieved her of them laying them down on a near by chair, asking her in the meantime of her faith in the ONE who was to heal her. Prayer was offered, she arose to her feet and to the amazement of the crowded house she walked across the platform with Mrs. McPherson's aid but no crutches, suddenly she started out alone, and there was no longer silence but great exclamations of joy and praises to God arose all over the congregation. Shortly she ran like a child of ten, throwing herself in the outstretched arms of Mrs. McPherson. The people could no longer keep their seats but stood to their feet and in one volume there arose the sound of many hands clapping together for joy at what God had wrought among them.[5]

In this account, healing emerges as a performance, carried by floating music and successfully achieved to the joyful clapping of the audience.[6] The musical numbers, McPherson's dramatic pacing, and previous weeks of organizational work, were all necessary preparations required to produce a modern revival.

The scene was very different at St. James Cathedral in Toronto. In 1920 James Moore Hickson, a lay Anglican spiritual healer, was in the midst of a world tour to promote faith healing. The Toronto *Star* described organ music playing softly during the sacramental procession: "One by one, those that were able knelt at the altar, and on their heads the famous healer laid his hands. Then they filed out with renewed hope and confidence writ plainly on their faces."[7] Hundreds sought healing, but the process of praying and laying on hands was carried out with no instantaneous, ecstatic cures or exclamations from the audience. Anglican interest in spiritual healing was widespread in the early twentieth century, and various societies, associations, and guilds emerged to promote it.[8] However, all of them rejected atonement theology, and all generally rejected the showmanship and performance aspects of professional evangelists such as McPherson.

Pentecostals, on the other hand, embraced the combination of divine healing and modern evangelistic methods. During her Canadian tour, McPherson was hosted in Winnipeg by the Argue family, who were also in the process of transforming themselves into professional evangelists. A.H. Argue had already worked as a full-time evangelist in the United States before the family returned to Manitoba in 1917, but in the 1920s, his sons and daughters were starting to play larger roles in his campaigns. The trend towards sensationalist advertising and professional promotion is evident in the billing of A. Watson Argue as the "Athlete Evangelist" or the "Canadian Boy Evangelist." Publicity photos illustrated his vigorous pursuits. One picture showed the energetic preacher in his swimming outfit, while another captured the traditional pose of the modern evangelist, one hand pointed towards the sky and the other grasping a trombone.[9] Watson would promote the campaigns by going into high schools and performing gymnastic stunts. Zelma and Beulah Argue both took up the trombone to hit the sawdust trail of itinerant evangelism, and A. Wilbur Argue became musically adept at both cornet and piano. In 1921 the "Argue Evangelistic Party" was joined by the "World's Youngest Preacher," Earl Williams, who started contributing to their campaigns at the tender age of six.[10] McPherson was well-known for her folksy style, and her catch-phrase slogans, such as "less pie, more piety," were crowd-pleasing headline material.[11] The Argues had their own "Argueisms," such as "When the outlook isn't bright, try the uplook," and "The Bible is many centuries old, but still it does not hobble on crutches."[12]

The published recollections of the Argues do not mention the 1920 McPherson campaign in Winnipeg, but there appears to have been a great spurt of family evangelistic activity in the wake of the revival. Soon after the McPherson meetings ended in early March, the Argues headed east for campaigns in Montreal, Kitchener, Arnprior, Ottawa, and Owen Sound. In the nation's capital, R.E. McAlister was impressed with the healing aspects of the campaign, particularly when Mrs R.M.T. Stephens, the wife of a commander in the Canadian Navy, was healed from an inflammation of the bladder and kidneys.[13] During November and December, the Argues joined McPherson in Montreal, with Andrew, Zelma, and Watson taking the lead in the afternoon healing meetings.[14] Throughout the 1920s various combinations of Argues campaigned across both Canada and the United States. They never reached the status of McPherson, but few could and they were still able to make a name for themselves as a talented evangelistic family with faith healing playing a prominent role in their revivals.

Pentecostals were not the only ones to employ divine healing within the new framework of professional evangelism. In 1921, the recently appointed minister of Parkdale Tabernacle Church, Oswald J. Smith, requested that the Canadian district of the Christian and Missionary Alliance consider bringing the evangelistic team of the Bosworth Brothers to Toronto. A delegation was sent to investigate a Bosworth campaign in Detroit, and despite some concerns about Bosworth's understanding of the baptism of the spirit and the insistence on healing as part of the atonement, all agreed that the Bosworths were effective in saving souls.[15]

The uncertainty that accompanied the decision to invite the Bosworths reflected a broader insecurity over healing within Alliance circles. A.B. Simpson died in 1919 and was replaced by the popular evangelist Paul Rader, who was successful at raising funds for missionary activities but did not seem to place as much emphasis on sanctification and divine healing as his predecessor. In Canada, leadership fell to District Superintendent A.W. Roffe, who effectively continued the Alliance tradition of missionary conventions. However, membership within the organization itself had stalled. Roffe expressed his frustration with the Canadian situation to the New York board of managers, who did not understand Canadian geography or the problem of adjusting to the new policies that downplayed the traditional interdenominational work in favour of planting churches. As Roffe explained, in Canada the Alliance found itself answering elementary questions from inquirers that reflected a confused state: "Is it a new denomination? Is it part of the Tongues movement? Has it anything to do with Christian Science? Is it an American organization?"[16] Threatened by pentecostalism and not wanting to betray its traditional mainline support by aggressively planting new churches, the Christian Alliance in Canada was having difficulty defining itself as something more than a missionary organization.

It was in the midst of this unsettled state of affairs that Smith, a former Presbyterian, merged his independent tabernacle work with that of the struggling Parkdale Tabernacle under the auspices of the Christian Alliance. Smith's theology veered towards a strong focus on Keswick holiness and an eschatology based on dispensationalism, but it was pastoral needs rather than fine points of doctrine that Roffe was interested in, particularly given the Alliance's own theological flux at the time.[17] Smith was a strong advocate of professional evangelistic techniques, and it only seemed natural to bring the Bosworth brothers across the border to light revival fires in Toronto. Their appearance would practically transform the organization's fortunes in Canada.

The Bosworths held a five-week campaign in Toronto from mid-April to the end of May. For the first week, Parkdale Tabernacle was used, but with crowds overflowing the 900-seat sanctuary, the meetings shifted to the prestigious 3,400-seat Massey Hall for the rest of the campaign. The Nebraskan-born Fred Francis Bosworth was a former bandleader in Dowie's Zion City, and he had been drawn towards pentecostalism by Parham's activities. Even after his attentions shifted to Dallas, Texas, he remained periodically in touch with Martha Robinson and the gatherings at the Zion Faith Homes.

Bosworth had started as a prominent leader within the pentecostal movement, but he began to have doubts about the "initial evidence" perspective, viewing it as too restrictive to limit the baptism of the spirit to the expression of tongues. Bosworth was convinced that one could receive the baptism without necessarily experiencing glossolalia, and his stand on the issue led to his resignation from the Assemblies of God in 1918. While pastoring a large Christian Alliance assembly in Dallas, "F.F." simultaneously launched an evangelistic career with his trombone-playing younger brother, "B.B.," who became the song leader.[18] Their recent campaigns in American cities had been marked by well-publicized healings, and their revival in Toronto was no different.

The Bosworth campaign opened with song and prayer, and comment was made of the uniqueness of evangelistic meetings where "the speaker plays the cornet and the leader of the singing the trombone." Testimonials to healing were given, and then F.F. delivered the main address. Dressed in a fashionable "sack suit," the *Star* suggested that "he might have been a master salesman explaining his art to a class of eager students." Prayer for the sick followed the sermon, and Bosworth made it clear that people were welcome to leave, even pronouncing a benediction, but "so charged was the very atmosphere, so it seemed, that scarcely a person went out." An extensive team of workers had been assembled by the Alliance in Toronto to help the Bosworths with the campaign. While the evangelist laid hands on those seeking healing, other attendants carried small bottles of oil, and after a prayer a few drops were "rubbed gently" on the scalps of those on the platform. Some people felt no change, but were spiritually uplifted; others claimed to be healed immediately after prayer was given, to the crowd's applause.[19] Bosworth warned that cures may not be instantaneous, but he reiterated that "It is God's will to heal every afflicted person in Toronto of their afflictions."[20] The *Star* reported that the Alliance was trying to maintain a "complete 'follow-up' system" in order to trace every person who had sought spiritual or physical blessings, insuring that those who had claimed healing maintained their healthy state, but what was done with this accounting was not revealed.[21]

After five weeks, one newspaper placed the number of those who had sought healing at 7,000. The success of the campaign was "in no small measure" attributed to "the singing of Mr. B.B. Bosworth and his choir, which has done much to create a spiritual atmosphere favorable for the preacher."[22] Smith continued the revival by parading a steady stream of evangelists through Massey Hall until Eaton's was able to manufacture a tent large enough to accommodate 1,800 people. The interest that Smith had drawn from the Bosworth campaign led to the construction of a new tabernacle on Christie Street, and with a capacity of 2,500 people it quickly became the centre of Alliance activity in Canada.[23]

Despite the popularity of the faith-healing brothers, the Alliance was still divided on the issue of healing, and its President, Paul Rader, warned that the main objective was to save souls through missionary work, not to become a "healing cult."[24] After Rader resigned in January 1924, the Bosworths were able to return to Canada for a seven-week campaign in Ottawa. As before, the success of the meetings forced their relocation, first to Horticultural Hall, which could accommodate 3,000 people, and then to the newly completed auditorium that they packed with up to 8,000 spectators. The Bosworth meetings typically ended with three types of invitations, one for the converted, one for those seeking the "baptism of the spirit," and one for those seeking healing. These three separate groups were then divided and workers spread amongst them for counselling and guidance. It was, however, the healings that attracted the attention of the audience and press alike. Even some of the city's physicians supported the campaign. Dr Leonard Derby informed the Ottawa *Citizen* that "he knew of six cases of deafness that had been cured, some cases of weak eyes, and varicose veins had also been cured." Dr R.M. Cairns and Dr C.T. Bowles sat on the platform with the Bosworths, the latter testifying to his own improvement in eyesight after being anointed.[25]

Also supporting the evangelists by their presence on the platform were Baptist, Methodist, holiness, and pentecostal ministers. Through a show of hands, however, the audience revealed a somewhat different composition. About three quarters of those in attendance were Methodists, Presbyterians, and Anglicans, each with about 2,000 people. More surprising was the sizeable presence of 800 Catholics, including one nun whose healing of back pains was widely publicized.[26] When the reports of this healing hit the press, the Roman Catholic hierarchy reacted swiftly, claiming that the eighty-six-year-old woman had left her convent almost thirty years ago and was not a nun, despite her continued wearing of her own habit. Canon Fitzgerald at St Patrick's warned his congregation that it was a "grievous sin" for Catholics to attend the meetings. Presumably, it was not the idea of faith healing as much as the Protestant character of the campaign that was objectionable, considering the continued popularity of Catholic healing shrines in the 1920s.[27] In contrast to such proper sites of religious devotion, however, the faithful across the city were reassured that no miracles were happening at the Bosworth meetings, since the cures "were the result of religious Coueism or the power of suggestion." A Presbyterian minister, Rev. Dr Wyllie, arrived at a similar conclusion, publicly questioning the value of the Bosworth meetings and suggesting that no real healings had taken place.[28] However, by the end of the campaign, Presbyterians formed the largest contingent of those who identified themselves by denomination.[29]

When the Bosworths completed their campaign, 6,000 people filled Union Station and sang gospel songs as the evangelists were carried on shoulders to their train. It was reported that 12,000 had been converted, roughly half of this number had sought healing, and over 1,500 testimonials of healing by those who had been anointed were received.[30] As in Toronto, the campaign led to the erection of a tent to maintain the interest in Alliance work and construction of a tabernacle was commenced. The success of the Bosworths in Ottawa led one frustrated critic to comment in a letter to the *Citizen*: "So if any young man is undecided as to the choice of a profession, let him take up faith healing. With a fair amount of assurance and an insensibility to ridicule and contempt, he cannot fail. No matter how absurd his pretension. No respectable paper will dare say a word against him, and medical men so far from opposing him will actually give their aid. As for the general public – well there is one born every moment, two or three in

Ottawa."[31] While divine healing encountered little criticism in the nation's capital, such was not the case elsewhere in the country, where faith healers endured a much more sustained attack.

CHARLES S. PRICE

The faith healer who had the greatest impact on Canada during the interwar period was Charles S. Price. Born in England in 1887, Price had received his law degree from Oxford, but a restless spirit sent him journeying to Canada. The young lawyer could not find employment on the prairies and was forced to take up railway labour to make ends meet. After travelling south to Spokane, Price was converted at a Free Methodist mission. Gradually, however, his theology drifted towards liberal modernism, downplaying revelation and transcendence in favour of divine immanence and historical approaches to scripture. As a pastor for a Congregational Church in California, Price encountered Aimee Semple McPherson on the campaign trail in San Diego, where the Canadian evangelist sparked a revival that would establish her as an American cultural icon. Her message shattered Price's own modernist theology as well as his hostility towards pentecostalism. After receiving the baptism of the spirit, Price joined the McPherson team for a short time in 1922 before deciding to undertake full time evangelism on his own.[32]

One of the first locations that Price turned to in his new career was Albany, Oregon, where his message of healing particularly touched the local Presbyterian minister, Rev. T.J. McCrossan. Through McCrossan family connections, Price's activities came to the attention of Dr W.J. Sipprell, minister of Victoria's Metropolitan Methodist Church, who set out to investigate the reports of healing. Catching up with the Price campaign in Roseburg, Oregon, Sipprell liked what he saw and recommended the evangelist to the Victoria Ministerial Association, which quickly extended an invitation.[33]

In the nineteenth century, A.B. Simpson was able to draw upon the support of mainstream Protestant evangelicalism. When Price entered British Columbia, the middle ground of evangelicalism was split increasingly by the controversies of fundamentalism and modernism. Denouncing modernists for their use of biblical "higher criticism" and their perceived accommodation to secular thought and culture, fundamentalism reasserted a literalist interpretation of the bible, emphasized the transcendence of God, and championed the premillennial return of Christ. While this was ultimately more divisive in the United States than Canada, the liberalizing tendencies of the "social gospel" worried many conservative evangelicals. Such liberalism appeared to shift concern away from individual conversion in favour of social reform. These fissures were evident during the earlier campaign of French Oliver to British Columbia in 1917, when the decision of the Vancouver ministerial association not to sponsor the American fundamentalist bitterly split the Protestant community.[34]

Despite his pentecostal theology and anti-modernist views, Price was able to find a broad base of support in Victoria. At this time, however, the evangelist still referred to himself as a Congregationalist pastor, and the issue of tongues remained very subdued. Unlike Vancouver, Victoria had not experienced theological acrimony during the Oliver campaign, and in contrast to Oliver, Price was considerably more genial in tone, although he remained firmly opposed to theological liberalism. When the evangelist reached Victoria in April 1923, crowds overflowed the main auditorium of Metropolitan Methodist Church, and the meetings were moved to Willows Arena, where a lucky 8,000 people managed to squeeze inside while up to 4,000 people were turned away. If the estimates on attendance are correct, then between ten and twenty-five per cent of the population of the greater Victoria area were attracted to this relatively obscure faith healer. The magnitude of the crowds required special arrangements for extra street cars.[35]

Price's evangelistic team was composed of five people and included his wife, his secretary, an organist, and Edith Carvell, a soprano soloist, who also assisted in his healing activities. Salvation Army bands and mass choirs occupied the seats behind the centre platform. In his campaigns Price developed a method whereby the opening meetings emphasized evangelism and explained the doctrine of divine healing without performing any healings. It was only after he felt that the message of consecration and personal trust in God had been accepted by the audience that he moved to actual anointing services, and even then the suffering were asked to attend morning preparatory meetings where workers would discuss both their ailments and their personal spirituality. These preparatory meetings also served an administrative function, with Price's team keeping careful track of names, addresses, illnesses, and later, noting whether they were healed and the permanence of the healing. Those deemed good candidates for the reception of healing through faith were issued a white card, which would serve as a type of ticket to gain access to the front of the stage where the anointing took place after the evening's address. To control the numbers and regulate who would be allowed on the platform, Price would only pray for those holding these cards. It was a system that maximized the evangelist's time and circumvented an indiscriminate rush to the stage from those who, lacking faith, would not be healed in any event. Special services were arranged for the healing of children and the elderly.

When the announced healing meeting finally arrived, Victoria found itself amazed at what transpired in its midst. The first person Price prayed for was a man suffering rheumatism, who collapsed onto the platform as the evangelist laid hands upon him. While the man lay on the ground, moaning and shaking his hands, Price explained to the crowd that "the power of God was working in the man," and eventually the man stood up to testify that he felt better. Price also anointed with oil, with many people claiming either minor or major improvements in their condition. To the crowd's excitement, a young boy's dumbness appeared to be cured when he quietly spoke two words.[36]

A series of high profile healings of eminent community members enhanced the public image of the campaign. The elderly Rev. W.J. Knott lay prostrated "under the power" for half an hour, and upon arising he declared that he had been cured of a life-threatening goitre.[37] Even more celebrated was the healing of Rev. J.F. Dimmick's daughter, Ruby, whose spinal difficulty had led to one leg being shorter than the other. A local Methodist minister, Dimmick was sitting with Ruby in the audience when she spontaneously turned to him and cried with joy, "Father, He's come. He's going through me now. Thank God, He has healed me." Both legs were the same length, and Ruby no longer required the use of her steel brace and could run and jump effortlessly. Price anointed her for a hoarseness in her throat, and that too was instantly healed.[38] In a later description of her experience, Ruby explained, "something struck my arm. It went through my shoulder and down my back, all through me. *It just permeated me through and through.*" When she felt a pressure on her spinal column, it snapped back into place. Ruby then recounted that she felt a tugging on her foot, "It was as if someone was pulling it. I looked to see, but saw nobody. But what I did see, was my leg growing into place. Before it was one-and-a-half inches shorter than the other. But it was lengthening until my feet were brought even."[39]

Ruby's physician was none other than Dr Ernest Hall, who was well aware of faith healing both from his earlier experience with the Dowieites and from his own observations of what was happening at the Price campaign. Rev. Dimmick testified at the arena that Hall had pronounced Ruby to be "completely cured," and Ruby ran up the stairs and across the platform to her father as a demonstration of her agility. However, Hall was quoted in the press as offering a more qualified judgment, declaring that Ruby's crippled condition "was not due to organic trouble, but [was] the result of nervous sickness."[40] The debate over the healing of Ruby Dimmick would continue to resonate long after the Price campaign ended in Victoria.

Price also held special meetings for Victoria's Chinese community, using interpreters to communicate his message. Over 800 people packed the New Chinese Theatre, while 200 people were turned away. As in his other meetings, the healings were marked by being "slain in the spirit," collapsing to the floor and trembling, shaking, or moaning. At the end of the campaign, the Chinese community presented Price with an engraved gold medal and a jade pin.[41] As the campaign rolled across western Canada, Price continued this practice of holding special meetings for East Asian communities.

The Victoria campaign was unquestionably the most successful of Price's career thus far, and he even mused to the crowds about possibly moving to the city permanently. However, he first had to complete his other Canadian engagements, including an invitation from the Vancouver Ministerial Association. Even before opening his meetings on the mainland, however, there were indications that Vancouver would not support the evangelist as thoroughly as Victoria. At the Canadian Memorial Church, the liberal Methodist Rev. George O. Fallis told his audience to "go with an open mind," but this advice was prefaced by numerous examples of the "mental condition" serving as a "powerful stimulant to the body."[42]

The hint of criticism towards the campaign certainly did little to hurt attendance. On 6 May, Price attracted 7,000 people to his opening meeting at the hockey arena. When the first healing meeting was announced, the number grew to 8,000. On his final day in Vancouver, Price held a marathon session of three consecutive meetings, ministering to a total of 23,000 people. Over the entire three-week campaign, as many as 250,000 people may have heard the faith healer.[43] The city had seen many evangelists in its day, but none had stirred it like Price.

Faith healing had become a public spectacle, but it was a performance that was shared and shaped by the audience. Despite the controls that Price used to ensure that only those properly prepared would be allowed to seek healing on the stage, even he could not predict exactly how the meetings would proceed. One evening during the Vancouver campaign, Price was about to deliver his address when there was a disturbance on the main floor. A woman was waving her hand above her head and crying out. After telling the ministers on the platform to sing a song, Price left the stage with his jar of anointing oil, and when he returned he explained that a woman's hand was suddenly healed from paralysis. Before he could continue the address, however, more spontaneous cures within the audience broke out, and Price once again went out to anoint them. It became impossible to proceed with the service, so Price simply carried out the healing part of the meeting, bringing up those in the audience with their white cards, and laying hands upon their foreheads. Despite the fact that his own message for the evening was that "No miracle of the healing of the body is equal to the miracle of the regenerating power of the Lord Jesus in the hearts and lives of men," those in attendance were clearly intent on pressing the issue of healing more than conversion.[44]

The problem for Price was that the careful preparation of those interested in seeking healing was becoming impossible in the face of such huge crowds. At one morning preparatory service, 4,000 people showed up. When the evangelist stressed to them the requirements of faith necessary to seek healing, over 1,500 still wished to proceed. Price finally decided to issue cards only for those cases on which physicians had given up hope, stressing that he would try to reach those "cancer, tumor, tuberculosis and similar cases where the patients were suffering great pain."[45] So many people from out of town were travelling to Vancouver to seek healing that Price appealed to anyone from outside points to stay away, since he was already overburdened. The services set aside for children became so packed in numbers that Price was forced to change his style and adopt a "group system" of prayer, rather than spending time with each one individually.[46]

Price freely admitted that not all would be cured instantaneously. Yet almost all fell "under the power" when they were touched or anointed, and sometimes they succumbed without even having this point of contact. Although it was God's power that healed, Price placed great stock in the amount of genuine faith not only in the believer, but in the social space defined by the arena itself. When those in the seats were "filled with faith," the greatest cures were accomplished. The spiritual state of the white card holders was carefully examined and prepared beforehand, but the atmosphere of the revival allowed for a divine expression of tangible power that could be seen working within the trembling bodies of those who collapsed on the platform. Price even measured the amount of faith present by how easily those seeking cures swooned in the faith, and he was not afraid to rebuke his audience for a lack of faith if these manifestations did not result.[47] In the largest healing meetings towards the end of the campaign, Price would line up the afflicted in rows of fifty and anoint them all in a total time of less than five minutes. The rows of people falling at his touch prompted comparisons to machine gun fire.[48]

GENDERING REVIVAL

When lines of the afflicted went "under the power" at Price's touch, only in a few cases did sufferers not swoon. Notably, those who remained standing were often men. Although gender received little comment in Victoria newspapers, the mainland press quickly recognized this aspect of Price's meetings. About thirty women and girls were anointed on the first healing meeting in the Vancouver Arena, all holding white cards to certify that they had attended the preparatory services. As they were led forward one by one, the pianist rendered "monotonously soft music" and the audience shouted "Praise the Lord." All reeled backwards after the laying on of hands, and were lowered to the floor by assistants where the recipient "lay in an emotional ecstacy [sic] praising the Lord and totally oblivious to all else."[49] A week later, the Vancouver Province commented on a similar scene at an arena meeting, where all of the "patients" were women, and "all but one collapsed immediately when treated by the evangelist and his assistant." Their heads were placed on small white pillows, and all recovered after a few minutes "without being interfered with." In case any readers found the scene unseemly, the newspaper added that prior to their healing experience, the women "were required to remove their hats."[50]

It is apparent that despite the transformation of the social space of healing, the practice of divine healing remained deeply gendered. One of Carvell's main roles as Price's assistant was to aid him particularly with women who "were backward about telling their troubles to a preacher."[51] The dominant presence of women was not unique to Price. In 1924 Bosworth published a collection of divine healing sermons entitled Christ the Healer. In the final chapter, which was composed of testimonials, thirteen were given by women; only two were offered by men.[52]

The largest sample of healing narratives directly related to a single revival come from a collection of testimonial cards that Price gathered during a return visit to Vancouver in 1929. Over a hundred of these cards have survived, and they reveal that ninety-two were completed by women testifying to a personal healing, while only seven were written by men.[53] Even as late as 1938, Price was still healing primarily women's bodies. On this occasion, the Winnipeg Tribune commented that with only a few exceptions, "the women who sought help were more excitable than the men. Moaning and shrieking, filling the arena with mournful wailing, they struggled in the throes of their emotional and religious experience, threshing the air with their hands and shouting their praises and pleas to the four corners of the rink."[54] As a bodily experience, falling under the power was carefully defined within a sacred space, despite the public nature of the arena environment. Women's bodies could therefore exhibit tremblings, or "ecstasies," and express emotional outbursts that would have been socially unacceptable in almost any other context.

The gendering of faith healing was not simply a sexual division of those who sought healing, but also related to the types of ailments narrated by men. While some mens' testimonials followed the common patterns discussed in chapter 2, many of them situated their illnesses with reference to physical work or other forms of male activity. Men who wrote to Price complained of afflictions that ranged from falling down a mine shaft to the emotional and physical effects of being "buried alive at Paschendale."[55] One of the more sensational stories of faith healing was that of an American veteran brought to Toronto by Oswald J. Smith in 1921. John Sproul suffered from exposure to mustard gas, and his subsequent recovery at the hands of the Bosworths allowed him to return his disability pension in favour of his original job with a railroad company.[56] Men framed their healing experience as a restoration of productive labour, taking up one's rightful place in the workforce.

The moral vices of a masculine rough culture also figured prominently in narratives written by men. The testimony of A. Oster offers a remarkable contrast with the Victorian testimonials of Carrie Judd and Maggie Scott. Oster, born outside of Toronto in 1873, grew up reading "cheap yellow-backed" novels that filled him with "the supreme desire to be a wild cowboy ... like Buffalo Bill." Most of the four-page narrative relates his exciting – if sin-filled – life, working his way westward and eventually reaching the Klondike during the gold rush. Only one small paragraph discussed suffering from "bronchial asthma," while drunkenness, associations with criminals, and thoughts of suicide formed the rest of the narrative. Saved at Price's campaign in Vancouver, Oster declared that his desire for "liquor, tobacco, shows and gambling" had disappeared. Almost as an afterthought, Oster recounted that his asthma was also healed, allowing him to "work steadily at my old job on the C.P.R. waterfront."[57] Women's testimonials dwelt at length on their inward state, while twentieth-century laymen focused on outward expressions of masculinity, defining the self through bodily actions.

This distinction in how men related to their bodies was noted in other contexts as well. The pentecostal evangelist Elizabeth Sharpe reported that at one revival, "Many happy men testified to the Lord delivering them from the tobacco habit and other sinful habits, cleaning them up as well as healing their wives after years of suffering when past medical aid." At McPherson's 1920 Montreal campaign, young men were observed "emptying out of their pockets cigarette cases and tobacco, getting cleaned up ready to join the mighty army of redeemed soldiers."[58] In both of these examples, men are portrayed as requiring "cleaning" rather than "healing"; the latter activity is undertaken by "their wives." It is the moral nature of men that requires attention, just as it is the physical nature of women that is deemed to be deficient.

SHIPWRECKING THE FAITH

After a week of Price's meetings in Vancouver, the city fell into an uproar when Congregational minister A.E. Cooke, the local chairman of the campaign, resigned his position and completely disassociated himself from the campaign. It was a stunning act, since Cooke was also the president of the Vancouver Ministerial Association, under whose auspices Price had been invited in the first place. In his letter of resignation, Cooke complained that Price was invited to offer "a campaign of evangelism for the salvation of men and women from sin unto righteousness, with the question of physical healing entirely secondary." However, from the beginning Price's meetings had focused on divine healing, which "already threatens to have the most tragic consequences in the physical, mental, and spiritual life of our city." Particularly odious in Cooke's eyes was the "exploitation of human suffering" being carried out in relation to the hopes of hundreds of afflicted children whose expectations were being "cruelly shattered." The campaign threatened to "shipwreck the faith of thousands of sufferers in the days to come." Cooke feared the tragic consequences of "Hundreds of parents ... being wounded to the heart," and ended with a prayer that God might send Vancouver "a mighty baptism of the Spirit of sanctified commonsense."[59]

Cooke's complaint that faith healing was more dominant than expected is difficult to accept. The ministerial association had received full reports on the Price campaign in Victoria, and Vancouver newspapers had diligently carried numerous accounts of healings from across the straits. More instructive is Cooke's allusion to the suffering of children, with its additional cryptic reference that "For reasons known to you all I was more than willing to be convinced on that point, if Dr. Price had any new truth to bring to us." What the other members of the association undoubtedly knew was that Cooke's daughter, Eileen Annie, had contracted "sleeping sickness" when she was twelve and remained paralyzed until her eventual death in 1936.[60] Although he never admitted it publicly, the issue of divine healing was undoubtedly fraught with emotional pain for the city's most recognizable Congregationalist.[61]

The day following the announcement of Cooke's resignation, the *Vancouver Sun* stoked the fire by printing a front-page editorial entitled "Prostituting Religion." Based on correspondence with newspaper sources in Albany, Oregon, the *Sun* reported that no "pathological cures" had taken place there and Price's only success was in raising the local death rate and increasing the business for undertakers. Churches and families were divided against each other, and the paper warned that "This will be his effect on Vancouver unless our ministers use their

Fig. 6.1. Price campaign audience in Edmonton, 9 October 1923. McDermid Studio, Photographer. Flower Pentecostal Heritage Center, P16275

influence to restore their members to sanity." Price's "bootleg brand of religion" threatened the practical work of Vancouver's churches and was nothing less than a "hideous travesty on the divine spirit of Jesus." There was no question that the evangelist was "dangerous to the health and well being of this community. His daily prostitution of religion must not be allowed to go on."[62]

Despite the warnings and continuing controversy, Price did go on, holding successful revivals in Calgary, Brandon, Edmonton, Toronto, Winnipeg, Regina, and numerous other points in Canada, crossing the country many times during the 1920s and 1930s. Professional photographers were hired to document the packed arenas and concert halls, as seen in figures 6.1 and 6.2. The years 1923 and 1924 marked the peak of his career, packing the Edmonton arena with 12,000 spectators, while those outside smashed windows and threw money into the arena to pay for the damage.[63] In Calgary, the healing campaign single-handedly boosted the city's Blue Line street car service into the black for the first time in months.[64]

Price's influence started to wane, however, as his message became more distinctly pentecostal in tone. While the focus on tongues was dismaying to those who wanted to maintain ties to established, mainline churches, it came as practically a relief to pentecostals in Canada, who

Fig. 6.2. Price campaign audience at Toronto's Massey Hall, 1923. James and Son, Photographer. Flower Pentecostal Heritage Center, P16288

had been somewhat hesitant about Price's mainstream appeal. By 1927, however, one attendee at a Price meeting in Regina could report that the evangelist was "out and out for the full pentecostal experience, and preaches it strongly, and the necessity of having it."[65] Price was also having difficulty in keeping the broad support of ministerial associations, since the aesthetics of professional evangelism increasingly became a point of contention between liberals and conservatives fighting theological battles.[66] His visible association with pentecostalism only complicated the situation, since pentecostals found themselves in the awkward position of stridently holding their own anti-modernist views while being shunned by traditional fundamentalists who rejected tongues.[67]

Although the theological tensions were palpable, what drew most Canadians to hear Price was faith healing itself. Given the sheer numbers of those who crammed into local arenas and auditoriums, the practice could hardly be characterized as a marginal activity. The phenomenal campaigns of the faith healers were remarkable enough, but the public nature of the healings also produced strong public reactions. The issue of faith healing resonated in the consciousness of the inhabitants of many cities long after the evangelist had moved on.

MIND OVER MATTER

The letter that E.J. Savage wrote to the *Toronto Evening Telegram* was unequivocal in its conviction that faith healing was not only ineffective as a cure, but also deadly in its operation upon the mind. According to Savage, his wife had attended the Bosworth meetings at Massey Hall in excellent physical condition. There was "No suspicion of the insanity in her family or herself." However, as a result of the revival excitement, she was now "a raving religious maniac with slight hope of life." With no hope from attending specialists, Savage despaired "I have lost half of my life through Bosworth's fanaticism." When the newspaper investigated the incident, Savage reported that a few days following her attendance at Bosworth's meetings, his wife became "violently insane," first "throwing a Bible at me and then tearing off my spectacles and trying to scratch my eyes, that I might 'see the light!'" Savage was particularly incensed that his wife did not seem to recognize him and forbade him to "touch her with my 'earthly intelligence,'" in contrast with a worker from the Bosworth campaign whom she recognized at once, and who not only prayed with her through the night but had visited the house when the husband was absent. The worker advised Savage not to allow doctors to see her.

When the *Evening Telegram* interviewed one of Mrs Savage's physicians, Dr Fletcher, he confirmed a diagnosis of "acute mania" that may have been related to the revival, although he was less certain that it was the only factor to be considered: "Apparently the religious excitement started it, but it may have been caused by some other excitement."[68] When Mrs Savage died a few days later, the death certificate stated the cause of death as "complete exhaustion following acute mental disease of ten days' duration." Although he did not ask for an inquest, Mr Savage's own personal written tribute to his wife's gravestone left no doubt that his feelings towards the faith healers remained intense: "At the Great Day the prophets also shall be judged. Au revoir." The grieving widower would not have been assuaged by Bosworth's insensitive comment that "It is unheard of for one to die after a few days insanity. I have known the worst cases to live for years. I have been told Mrs. Savage dabbled in spiritism. They often become insane."[69]

Savage's conviction that religious excitement had led to his wife's death was not very far removed from the nineteenth-century warnings of the "unhealthy effects" of religious enthusiasm. By the 1920s, however, a more specific discourse on the power of the mind had developed as various psychological theories were popularized. Particularly as a result of World War I and the diagnosis of shell shock, the mind was receiving more attention than ever before. Just one day before it received Savage's letter, the *Telegram* had reflected on how the war experience had brought to light "the close connection between mental feeling and bodily state." Since the post-war age was for many "no less distressing than war," perhaps faith healing in the hands of a preacher "who possesses unusual magnetism" could provide a treatment for the "Shell Shock of Peacetime." The newspaper was convinced that "Certain types of mind respond to revivalistic methods, and where a bodily affliction has in reality a nervous basis, it is a scientific fact that cures can be brought about. What can be done by medical advice can be accomplished also by ministerial exhortation."[70] It was not only the "peacetime" version of shell shock that was susceptible to divine healing. When McPherson campaigned in Montreal, it was reported that several victims of shell shock recovered from deafness and paralysis.[71]

The power of the mind over the body was a discourse that had developed considerably since Daniel Clark's analysis of the faith cure in 1891. In the early months of 1923, Vancouver witnessed a parade of secular and religious speakers eager to discuss how the powers of the mind could be harnessed. From Paris came Professor J. Armand who lectured on "Self-Healing by Suggestion." He was followed a few weeks later by Professor S.J.F. Stranack, a "Mental Physician," who demonstrated "Psychological Vibratory Healing and Mental Suggestion." Not to be surpassed in this new vein was a travelling Baptist minister from Washington, Rev. Dr E.L. Swick, who offered lectures on "Bible Psychology," "Bible Healing," "The Subconscious Mind," and "The Chemistry of Thought." Few could match the feat announced by the Anglican Archbishop of Caledonia, however. Bishop F.M. Du Vernet announced that he had proved that human thought could be transmitted telepathically from one mind to another. Using a pendulum attached to a pencil, he explained that he had transferred a six-letter word from Metlakatla to Prince Rupert, a distance of seven miles, via this "radio mind." His experiments demonstrated that while "our conscious minds tend to individualize us, our subconscious mind tend to unite us. We are not isolated units. We are all members of one vast mental complex. Slowly we are realizing our mental union with the Universal Mind."[72]

One of the most innovative theories on the nature of the faith healing accomplished by Price was offered by N.B. Raymond in a letter to the *Vancouver Sun*. According to Raymond, human bodies emanated waves of electrical energy that could be directed into a measurable force. It was the crowd of people in the arena who, "by their sympathy and religious emotions ... [formed] a powerful electro-magnetic storage battery in Price who by the laying on of hands wills it to the nervless [sic] sick patients." Raymond suggested that if his interpretation was challenged, perhaps Price would allow his hands to be connected to "a galvanometer by means of aluminum plates and an electric cord and watch the results of his emotions on the dial."[73] Another letter writer offered a more direct assessment of Price, asserting that he was a "spirit medium" who "long ago submitted into the power of 'Lucifer.'"[74]

However, the foremost critical assessment of faith healing in the 1920s was the conviction that it was some form of hypnotism. Although once hailed as a miracle cure, hypnotism as a medical therapy had been largely reduced to ridicule in the twentieth century.[75] Nevertheless, popular images of hypnotism remained and often merged with newer concepts of psychotherapy. For Cooke, the swooning and falling under the power could only be a "cataleptic or hypnotic trance," after which the believer heard "the authoritative pronouncement, 'You are Healed!' 'She's got it!' in their ears – a tremendous climax to the whole train of suggestion, exalted religious fervour and ecstatic hope, powerfully calculated to bring about the well-known results of hypnotic suggestion and psycho-therapy."[76] One letter to the *Daily Province* warned that while hypnotism had the power to cure various nervous diseases, it could be dangerous in the hands of public entertainers who did not understand the "delicate organism of the higher brain centres," and wondered if Price's campaign offered examples of "collapse, hysteria, or nerve shock resulting from careless use of hypnotism on sane subjects."[77] Another letter writer suggested to the *Vancouver Daily World* that "what Dr. Price does is to exert a hypnotic influence over the patient, relieving him for the time being of his conscious mind, when he then commands the sub-conscious mind to exert such influence over the body that it is forced to obey, and in so doing it accomplishes temporarily what, under the power of the conscious mind it never would be able and possibly should not attempt to do."[78]

The *Vancouver Sun* even interviewed a local expert on hypnotism, N.B. Maysmith, who had retired from twelve years of entertaining and engaging in "psychological research" and had taught at a Seattle school for mental suggestion. The hypnotist claimed that Price's methods were "executed with such attention to detail" that it was impossible for him to have stumbled upon it by accident. That the evangelist knew he was employing hypnotism was obvious by the fact that his first healings in Vancouver were not in the arena, but at the Chinese meeting. Only someone trained in hypnotic practice would "know that the people of southern countries are very much more susceptible to hypnotic suggestion than those of the northern climates."[79]

Maysmith's comment revealed a discourse of race and gender that associated modern faith healing with mental weakness. One critic of hypnotism dismissed it as little more than a "perversion of nervous force" and "induced hysteria."[80] The *Sun* turned to medical books to discover that hysteria was characterized by "[a]ttacks of ecstacy," and "hyper-suggestibility."[81] The critique of faith healing maintained its gendered overtones; now framed within the context of hypnotism, "susceptibility" replaced the late-Victorian concern with "sentimentalism." One doctor in Vancouver reported that common rationalizations of faith healing included the assertion that Price "only picks out the weak-minded and mostly women."[82] The fundamentalist critic, A.C. Gaebelein, noted that "Women are especially subject to diseases, or supposed diseases, which originate in hysteria. That is why seventy-five per cent. of the supposed cures are performed on women." Gaebelein was convinced that the divine healing campaigns were "a form of mass-hypnotism."[83]

The number and variety of opinions linking faith healing to hypnotism prompted one moderate supporter of Price to observe "The press discussion revealed the remarkable fact that there were so many people in the country who claimed to have made a special study of hypnotism and knew without any shadow of doubt all about what was taking place at the Arena."[84] Rumours spread that the smartly dressed Carvell was the "real power" behind the evangelist, perhaps serving as a spiritual medium or clairvoyant when she touched the believer before leading her to Price. When the evangelist informed the crowd that Carvell had the capacity of "discerning faith" in others when it came to distributing cards for healing, it was quickly interpreted as either a confirmation of her hidden powers or a ploy to selectively choose those who might fall easily under his control.[85] The accusations of hypnotism grew to such an extent that Price was forced to disprove the critics by having other ministers anoint the ill while Carvell remained in the audience instead of assisting him on stage.[86]

One of the most direct attacks on Price from this perspective was launched by Dr D.R. Dunlop during the evangelist's campaign in Calgary. Unlike the relatively low profile maintained by physicians in Victoria and Vancouver, Dunlop became the leading voice opposing Price's work in Calgary, first in a public lecture entitled "Mental Deception in Medicine," and again later in a letter to the *Calgary Herald*. Dunlop explained that when hypnotism opened the subject's mind to suggestion, "his faculty of judgment is completely removed," and the pain of the afflictions cease. However, the physician stressed that "Cures of hypnotism cannot be cures at all ... Pain impressions are temporarily obliterated from the patient's consciousness. The mind only, is acted upon." The dangers of hypnotism were well known, since practitioners work, "for the most part with the brains of unusually hysterical mediums, often imposing upon them impressions which in time may do great damage to health." Dunlop also feared that young people would become "morbidly interested" in the subject and start experimenting with hypnotism for themselves, which could lead to the experimenter acquiring "the mental attitude of his subjects" and becoming "a person of abnormal susceptibility to suggestion."[87]

Dunlop was not alone in his fears that modern youth were prone to such states. The *Calgary Albertan*, quoting from J.J. Walsh's *Cures: The Story of the Cures that Fail* (1923), suggested that "our generation is intensely-hysterical-minded" since "we are bringing up our young folks on suggestion to such an extent that super-suggestibility is almost inevitable, and from that to giving themselves suggestions, which is one form of hypnotism, sometimes labelled 'auto-suggestion.'" It was accordingly the evidence of "greatest excitement, much of it bordering on hysteria," that was the dangerous aspect of Price's campaign, and what made it threatening not only for the individual, but also "for the community at large."[88] The *Vancouver Sun* worried that the "wills of hysterical people have been materially weakened by all this mesmeric hocus-pocus."[89]

Walsh's use of the phrase "auto-suggestion" pointed to the growing fascination not only with the power of the mind through hypnotism, but also with the self therapies and concepts of suggestion popularized by the French pharmacist, Émile Coué (1857–1926). Coué advocated harnessing the power of the unconscious, but instead of relying upon the regular trances of hypnotism, he argued that a continuous mental stimulation of healthful thoughts would filter through the conscious to the unconscious strata of the mind. "If we fill our minds with the thought of the desired end, provided that end is possible, the Unconscious will lead us to it by the easiest, most direct path." Coué's method for filling the mind with healthful thoughts was the repetition of the phrase "Day by day, in every way, I'm getting better and better," twenty times before going to bed and repeated upon rising in the morning.[90] The liberal Methodist, George C. Workman, agreed with some of Coué's principles, but he derided the use of these "silly" formulas, which appealed "chiefly to the emotional and imaginational," as demonstrated by the fact the most of Coué's patients were "neurasthenics and hypochondriacs."[91]

A different tack on Coué was offered by Robert E. Fairbairn in a Ryerson essay that was published just as the Price campaign began touring the west coast. Since the practice of autosuggestion becomes a "deliberate and continued *seeing* of the desired state," Fairbairn found it natural for the Christian to substitute the power of imagination for faith. It is the "quiet, unrestrained holding of the conscious attention upon the idea of positive health [that] is the best, in fact, the only sure way of reaching the subconscious mind that controls our physical economy." However, Fairbairn admits, "the cure is brought about by the power in the organism itself," not through divine intervention. For the enlightened, there was no real conflict between religion and psychological process, but "[i]gnorant people" did not understand this. Therefore the churches should encourage the sick "in the ways they can understand; and by prayer ... to seek healing from God." Fairbairn also advocated the use of "healers," but cautioned that they be properly instructed, "lest the fanaticism they rouse become a greater evil than all the sickness they cure."[92] Fairbairn's suggestion that Christians practice autosuggestion clothed in a deceptive religious language of transcendence mirrored the very accusations hurled at Price by critics of divine healing.

Price's most determined opponent, A.E. Cooke, generally agreed with Fairbairn's assessment on the state of knowledge of the masses, complaining that "99 per cent of our people ... are totally ignorant of the psychological laws which control, not only the individual, but the entire audience under such circumstances." However, instead of employing the traditional categories of transcendence, the real object should be to educate the public that "the laws of body and mind as revealed by modern science are a Divine revelation, and that any attempt to establish a treatment, by whatever name it may be called, in which these laws are openly or tacitly ignored, is contrary to good sense, to sound morals and to genuine religion."[93] Mistaken beliefs that divine cures had taken place were both spiritually and physically dangerous, since faith would be crushed by the inevitable realization that the condition had worsened without proper medical condition. Cooke portrayed piteous scenes of children who "should be in bed under rigid control," but were instead "running around without medical care because they were 'healed' by 'the power of God' at the Arena – positively doomed to painful death by the misguided 'faith' of their parents."

For liberals, the Price campaign was part of a broader problem fostered by fundamentalism's promotion of anti-intellectualism and its suspicions of modern thought. Cooke openly worried that practices such as faith healing only made "the educated and thinking laity ... express their disgust at what they style the degradation of Christianity." If religion did not maintain a supportive association with modern advances in science and thought, it risked losing the "splendid abilities and intelligent faith" of those who should be at the forefront of Christian service.[94] The very public, and popular, display of faith healing within an evangelistic context openly challenged Cooke's assumptions of the role of religion in society, and he was determined to expose divine healing as both a fraud and a danger to society.

PUBLIC DISPLAYS

Cooke was far from alone in his dislike for the style of evangelism employed by the faith healers. By the end of the 1920s, even conservatives were reconsidering the question of professional evangelism and divine healing. Never known as one to mince his words, the thundering fundamentalist Baptist pastor, T.T. Shields, pronounced to loud applause that "these divine-healing campaigns, from the Atlantic to the Pacific, without one solitary exception, are one of the most colossal frauds that were ever foisted on the religious world."[95] Churches of all denominations were suffering from the "plague of religious quacks advocating so-called 'divine-healing.'"[96] Engaging in one of his many public battles, in 1930 Shields turned his sights on Oswald J. Smith, denouncing the "religious jazz" offered by the "tabernacle purveyors of religious stimulants." No longer with the Alliance, Smith had recently taken charge of the Toronto Gospel Tabernacle on Gerrard Street, which was in close proximity to Shields's own Jarvis Street Baptist Church. The war of words only escalated when a visiting American evangelist, one of many invited by Smith to preach, objected to Shields's proclamations and made reference to the "Jarvis Street religious sewer."[97]

Notwithstanding Shields's militant tone, the attack on Smith represented a deeper concern with the aesthetics of modern religion. Both Shields and Smith had opposed the middle-class demeanour of mainstream Protestantism, which emphasized rational expositions and heavy classical music that seemed to overwhelm evangelical concerns of heartfelt penitence and conversion.[98] Smith adapted his revivalistic techniques to appeal to the times, but in so doing he encountered the wrath of Shields, who disliked this new evangelistic style almost as much. Shields labelled Smith a "religious show man" who conducted "emotional orgies" through the sensational preaching of professional evangelists who regularly took the pulpit at his tabernacle.[99] Of these, none was more detestable than the faith healer. Shields complained that "in the twenty years which I have been here, I have seen the Bosworth Brothers' Campaign, Dr. Price's Campaign, and a great many lesser lights. I have seen people go up and be healed over and over again ... I have never been able to understand why these people who talk so lightly about being healed, should need to be anointed every time a divine-healer comes to town."[100]

Like Shields, other fundamentalists were expressing concern over both the theology of divine healing and its performance as a public spectacle. Rowland V. Bingham complained that "Cripples were lifted on their feet and urged and helped to stagger a few steps while people cheered, only to return to their helplessness." The "manipulations" that others endured in the theatre of the faith healer were "entirely foreign to the pictures of the healing of Christ."[101] Newspapers had also noticed that the professional evangelism of the 1920s appeared to be rather removed from the style of Dwight L. Moody or even that of Crossley and Hunter. The old evangelist, "equipped as he was with the ability to exhort and warn the public of the future, does not apparently draw large crowds." Today's modern evangelist "is either a healer or a peculiar kind of prophet." The *Albertan* was puzzled at the change in religious tone and expressed concern that the new evangelists were all "unbelievers in the discoveries of modern science" and "bitterly critical of the doctrine of evolution."[102]

While fundamentalists voiced their displeasure with the style and theology of contemporary faith healing, liberal modernists drew different conclusions from the evangelistic environment of the divine healing campaigns. In 1923 Ernest Thomas, field secretary for the Department of Evangelism and Social Service of the Methodist Church, published an article on the Price campaign in the *Christian Guardian* under the pen name Edward Trelawney. Complaining that the singing was the "usual emotional type with a total absence of ethical content," Thomas observed that it was also "strong in capacity to promote mass emotion. Strongly marked rhythm with the slightest obstruction in the form of ideas, but rich in the more obvious forms of religious suggestion, it greatly aided the process."[103] Cooke was more specific in his characterization of how the singing produced a suggestive state: "Hymn after hymn was sung, of the type calculated to arouse the emotions of the audience to the highest pitch of fervour, and submerge all reflective and critical action of the mind."[104] Dunlop similarly saw an insidious motive behind the trappings and setting of revival meetings, since the "environment must influence the senses" to bring about "the concentration of attention upon a single impression." When the evangelist added "arranged cushions, a man on one side and a woman on the other ready to receive the victim in their arms," it produced a "trance-like environment." After multiple sessions of excitement, the physician suggested that the fatigue made those suffering in body "easy victims for the mystic healer." In the end, the evangelist may not be an active hypnotist, but rather "he has prepared them to unconsciously hypnotise themselves."[105] It was not simply the concept of faith healing, but the manner in which it was practiced that mattered. The public space created by the mass revival was integral to the manifestations and results.

Defenders of the faith healers denounced the ridiculousness of hypnotism as a source for healing, while simultaneously embracing the public setting as the an important element of the modern faith healing experience. Addressing "brother business man," Rev. Thomas J. McCrossan commented, "You don't like Dr. Price's demonstrations and contend he ought only to pray for the sick in private. You add, It [sic] savors too much of a big advertising scheme to get the people to attend. Praise God, I believe that is just why He displays this strange power before a large audience and in some public space." Adding that two other evangelists working with Price had found that "they seldom have anyone fall under the power except when they pray in public," McCrossan concluded that it was "positive proof that *God wants Dr. Price to pray in public for the sick*, and by sending this power He will assure him large congregations."[106] Faith healing as a mass spectacle functioned as both a tool of evangelism and produced an environment blessed by God for the expression of divine power.

McCrossan's reference to "a big advertising scheme" reflected growing fears that urban evangelism had become too comercialized. By the end of the 1920s, even proponents of divine healing were starting to have second thoughts about the sensational nature of the healing campaigns and the role of professional evangelism in general. As the editor of the *Pentecostal Testimony*, R.E. McAlister launched a full assault on the excesses and consumerist ethos of modern revivalism, claiming that some have "tried to imitate Mrs. McPherson by frizzling their hair, dressing in white and getting a photo taken showing their teeth; perhaps standing on tip-toe. What a farce in the name of religion! ... All this loud gush and dress parade and theatrical stuff is a stench in the nostrils of God and we are glad that the pentecostal people in Canada are rising up almost in a body unanimously and expressing their disgust of it."[107]

In many ways, McAlister's position was a longing to return to the original sense of pentecostalism as a close community that truly represented the restored apostolic church. The blurring of lines between secular entertainment and sacred evangelism was paralleled by blurring the lines between the true church and the infidelity that occurred when unsaved mayors were used to open campaigns for publicity purposes, or unsaved musicians were employed for their skill alone. "To conform to this world and be like the world in order to reach the world and accomplish the end of saving their souls is wrong. God does not say, 'Go in amongst them and be like them, and dress like them and act like them in order to win them.'" For McAlister, without a strict boundary between the faithful and the profane, "you enter upon the road to deterioration and no end would ever justify the means."[108]

McAlister was critical of the trends of professional evangelism in general, rather than the specific role of healing within it. However, healing had clearly become implicated through its close association

with the sensational reports of cures during the large campaigns. Six
years following the arrival of the Bosworths in Toronto, Smith re-
evaluated the experience in a far less celebratory light, admitting that
"hundreds sought healing who did not get it" and regretting the
"scores who testified to being restored who were not. False reports without the sanction of the workers were published far and wide."[109] However, Smith was emphatic in maintaining that many were in fact healed,
despite the difficulties encountered in publicizing accurate reports. The
issue of misrepresentation was actually part of a broader problem facing
the professionalized public version of faith healing, and from his experience, Smith concluded that "it is a great mistake to offer healing to the
general public." Modern methods of evangelism were not the solution,
and Smith longed nostalgically for a previous age: "Dr. A.B. Simpson's
practice can hardly be improved on; namely, a quiet afternoon service
specially set apart from instruction and anointing with nothing of a
spectacular aspect. Or, in the case of those too ill to come, a literal sending for the elders. Such a plan, of course, would not attract the crowds,
but on the other hand it would safeguard against a commercialized ministry, the gravest danger that confronts evangelism today."[110] Like
McAlister, Smith was concerned that the consumerism of professional
evangelism had corrupted it and degraded divine healing in the process.
He was also one of the few to accurately perceive how far the practice of
faith healing had travelled since the days of Simpson. The "spectacular"
aspects of healing were a product of the Jazz Age, but uncoupling divine
healing from professional evangelism was no simple task.

It was the onset of the Depression in the 1930s, rather than the success
of its critics, that stalled the expansion of faith healing through professional evangelism in Canada. The large urban campaigns of the 1920s
were simply too expensive to mount in a harsh economic climate. On a
smaller scale, Price continued to tour Canada and the northern states,
and numerous other evangelists, usually pentecostals, would continue to
press the message of divine healing. However, the broad public interest
shown in this activity declined, and it was not until the post-World War
II revivals of faith healing that it would re-emerge with any force.[111] For
a brief moment, however, faith healing had captured the nation's attention on a scale that remains unsurpassed.

In the 1920s, divine healing clearly became incorporated within professional evangelistic campaigns. Pentecostalism had laid the groundwork
for an understanding of healing as a manifestation of divine power, expressed within a prescribed public space defined by a community of believers. Now, in the hands of the evangelists, healing became a full
public spectacle, as bodies were restored before the very eyes of large,

expectant audiences. The style of the music, the spatial arrangements of the arena, the carefully organized workers, and the believers themselves were part of a ritualized performance played out by participants and audience alike. The form of penitent sinners being saved and testifying to their conversion was a familiar one, but the addition of healing infused a tangible divine power into the meetings. Bodies were dabbed with oil, laid upon with hands, and prayed over in the expectation that faith and power would produce spiritual improvements and physical relief. The audience could see God working upon the trembling bodies of women (mostly) and witnessed the afflicted walk without their crutches or read books without their glasses.

Critics read the evangelistic context of the faith healing campaigns in a very different way, associating its spatial elements with the inducement of hypnotic states or the practice of autosuggestion. They also saw divine healing as performance, but for them it was a malicious manipulation of the will exercised upon unsuspecting victims, rather than the divine power of God, that produced the spectacle. Indeed, it was the very reduction of religion to such "degrading" theatrics to which critics objected. Even proponents were starting to fear that the consumerist ethos of professional evangelism was corrupting it.

The competing concerns of theological controversies, popular ideas of the mind, and dissatisfaction with the style of evangelism all attempted to subdue the public practice of faith healing with little success. However, one of the by-products of the urban campaigns was a series of scientific investigations into the cures proclaimed by the faith healers. Faith healing could be disclaimed in the newspapers, but the type of report produced by clerical and medical committees offered much more than offhand assertions that mental healing could be readily explained. The medical gaze understood the body in a very different way than the faith healers. In the end it was not actual theories of hypnotism, but rather differing perceptions of the body that stood at the heart of the debate between proponents and critics of divine healing.

Exposing the Body

Medical science too is full of mysteries, and must be studied like the words of Christ. These two callings – the promulgation of the word of God and the healing of the sick – must not be separated from each other. Since the body is the dwelling place of the soul, the two are connected and the one must open access to the other.

Paracelsus, *Opus Paramirum* (c. 1531)

The professional faith healing evangelists hit the height of their popularity in the early 1920s, and for a time they were the object of analysis, criticism, and apologetics for a variety of commentators. One enterprising Calgary promoter even arranged to bring to the city a play about faith healing, "The Miracle Man," based on the Frank Packard novel, just as the Charles S. Price meetings were drawing to a close. Divine healing was in the air, and even the *Ladies' Home Journal* commented that "Almost any Sunday now in your own church you may hear of divine healing."[1] The *Vancouver Daily World* explained that newspapers would not be concerned with the "religious or evangelistic features" of a revival under normal circumstances; but when it came to the recovery of the sick, then "the matter assumes a public interest far beyond what appears at first sight."[2] Faith healing gained national attention not as a theology, but as a particular therapeutic that had profound implications for the body. From the point of view of the secular press, it was as a bodily process that faith healing summoned a "public interest."

It was in the name of this public interest that prominent community members declared faith healing to be a phenomenon that needed to be "investigated." Illustrious men were recruited to fill the ranks of special committees that balanced clerical and medical interests. Although many such committees were formed, only one resulting report received substantial coverage, namely the investigation into the 1923 Price healing campaign in Vancouver. This report lay claim to the notion of strict, scientific objectivity in its investigation of the Price cures. However, vested interests steered the committee and its results toward conclusions specifically designed to undermine both the practice of divine healing and the credibility of the faith healer himself.

As important as the conclusions of the report on Price's campaign were, the document also revealed the operation of a particular technique of bodily investigation that was at odds with the way proponents of divine healing understood and accessed the body. In rendering its report, the committee employed scientific categories and language that cut the body off from the sacred ground claimed by faith healing. Divine healing relied upon the uniqueness of personal authority to narrate the bodily experience of the divine, but medicine depersonalized the body and discounted non-professional claims to bodily knowledge. This divergence in perceptual approaches to the body was fortified and symbolized by the way in which both the investigative committee and the faith healers employed the technology of photography.

The Price investigative report displaced claims to faith healing by extending a medical ordering of the body, but this construction was far from impervious to resistance or critique. The epistemological grounding of the body in objective science, through a process of exposing and imprinting its discrete elements, was never conceded by proponents of faith healing who could always trump such "human" knowledge with the workings of the divine. The limitations of medicine in accounting for a wider cosmological reality prompted a small but significant group of physicians to adopt faith healing at the expense of their professional medical practice.

In the twentieth century, no physician wrote more about divine healing than Dr Lilian B. Yeomans. Her life and writings offer a unique personal perspective on the distance between medicine and faith healing. Yeomans struggled to come to terms with the entrenched mental structures of her medical training long after she had turned to divine healing. Her reflections on her former profession reveal that medical knowledge was not simply a static representation of the body, but rather a particular approach to seeing and understanding the body. While scientific committees investigated Price's cures, Yeomans used her position as a former physician to promote faith healing, and in the process she offered her own exposures of medical practice.

INVESTIGATING PRICE

When faith healers entered a new city and received massive publicity about their cures, the public was assured that respectable authorities would thoroughly investigate the phenomenon. Ministerial associations and local campaign committees promised that names and addresses would be collected and followed up, and a full report on the benefits of the campaign would be issued. Ministers and physicians would cooperate with other prominent members of the community, such as aldermen and lawyers, to produce an impartial and objective accounting of the results.

Rarely were such laudable goals achieved. Persuading the faith healer in question to cooperate proved to be impossible, and little pressure could be brought to bear once the evangelist had left town. As the evangelist's team usually held all of the recorded names and addresses, committees were left appealing for public help through the press. Since the faith healer did not sanction the investigative process, those who were cured viewed the committees with considerable distrust. Even those who were not convinced of the cures were often wary about probing the subject; if the healer's visit had been accompanied by factional bitterness between modernists and fundamentalists, many in the community simply wanted to forget about the campaign that had caused such dissension, rather than risk re-opening the wounds.

For these reasons, investigative committees found that they could not produce what had been promised. The single most important exception was in Vancouver, where the Vancouver General Ministerial Association (VGMA) established an investigation committee to examine the results of the 1923 Charles Price campaign. For six months after the meetings had ended, the committee diligently gathered evidence and accounts, issuing a final report at the end of December. It was one of the most detailed examinations of faith healing relating to a single revival that was ever produced.[3]

The Vancouver committee was composed of eleven ministers, eight physicians – all described as being members of Christian churches and "specialists in such diseases as were most likely to be subject of investigation" – three university professors, and one lawyer. Of the ministers, the committee included two Anglicans, two Baptists, two Methodists, and two Presbyterians in addition to one Congregationalist, and one representative each from the Salvation Army and the Plymouth Brethren.[4] Although the range was impressive on paper, a closer examination of the committee reveals a network of affiliations that was far from impartial. The sole Congregationalist was none other than A.E. Cooke, one of Price's greatest detractors, and almost all of the ministers in Vancouver who had publicly opposed the faith healer were also members. Cooke was elected to chair the committee, and there is little question that he was a driving force behind the report.[5]

Of the physicians, the most significant was Dr W.B. Burnett, a former president of the Vancouver Medical Association who had served the region for more than twenty years. A close friend of Cooke, the pair had joined forces in publicity efforts against chiropractic just prior to the Price campaign.[6] The third important figure on the committee was H.T.J. Coleman, dean of Arts at the University of British Columbia. Coleman taught the single course in psychology offered in the university's Department of Philosophy. Together, Coleman, Burnett, and Cooke participated in the "Open Forum," a lecture series held at First Congregational Church that was dedicated to the "clarification of thinking along the lines of Religion and Social Progress." Only a few months after the committee submitted its report, Coleman delivered an address to the Ministerial Association on "Modern Developments in Psychology."[7]

Not surprisingly, Price refused to have anything to do with the committee, and most groups faithful to the evangelist were similarly reluctant to submit themselves to investigation. A number of ministers who had supported Price withdrew themselves from the original committee once they saw its composition. The Baptist Ministerial Association of Greater Vancouver passed a resolution refusing to cooperate and protested that too many critics of the campaign were now investigating it.[8] In the face of this opposition, the committee turned to public appeals in the Vancouver papers for people to step forward, and from these submissions a subcommittee chaired by Coleman sorted through 350 cases of those who had been anointed for healing during the campaign.

The introduction to the committee's final report set out the terms of reference and provided a clear indication of where its members stood, declaring that it was "the Committee's own belief that in the healing of the body, the Divine Power is always exercised in conformity with God's own laws."[9] Having asserted that the power of the divine was grounded firmly in natural law, the committee then proceeded to divide all of their cases into two groups, depending on whether the patient was suffering from an "organic" or a "functional" disease. The former was accompanied by "demonstrable structural change in some organs or parts of the body"; the latter consisted of cases where organs showed "no evidence of structural change," but the "patient nevertheless suffers many, or all, the discomforts and manifests the symptoms ordinarily due to organic disease of these organs."[10]

Out of the 350 cases, the committee declared that only five people had benefitted sufficiently to qualify as being "cured." It was emphasized repeatedly, however, that all five of these cases were certainly "functional" in nature, rather than "organic." Thirty-nine people attended by Price had died, and five had gone insane within six months, not including four additional cases of insanity involving family members of those who had sought healing. Thirty-eight people did exhibit some improvement, as a result of an "improved mental and spiritual outlook," while 215 cases offered no improvement.[11]

All five cases where healing had been determined were discussed in varying levels of detail. Short descriptions related the case histories of a stammering young man whose speech was distinctly improved, a young woman who was suffering from "neuralgia pains which she herself diagnosed as neuritis," and a man of a "nervous type" who had an "internal goitre." According to the report, the man never consulted a physician, but he felt a sensation in his throat and was completely healed after "going under the power." It was explained that it was a "typical case of nervous condition" known to physicians as "Globus Hystericus (an hysterical lump in the throat)." One invalided woman had consulted many physicians, who labeled her as suffering from "Hysteria," or some form of "disordered 'nerve complex.'" Her ultimate healing was described as "an excellent illustration of the type of functional nervous disease which is amenable to auto-suggestion, or modern psychotherapeutic treatment, of which there have been countless examples following the war."[12]

The longest description for any single reported cure related to "Case A," a young woman who had what "might properly be called 'acquired club foot,'" marked by a shortening of the leg and curvature of the spine. According to the report, the young woman found it necessary to "draw her leg up" on one side, which made it appear two inches short, although "measurements showed the legs to be of equal length." The patient was reported to have seen specialists who "pronounced her deformity to be of a functional nature," a condition produced by "auto-suggestion." The cure that Price had supposedly provided was the drawing of the foot into a normal position by "will-power"; the hip dropped into its natural place, and the spine straightened itself.[13] It was very obvious that Case A was a direct reference to Ruby Dimmick, who, through newspapers and later testimonials, had become a high profile example of the power of faith healing. Price regularly narrated the particulars of her case to other cities as he traversed the country. The report laid out the details of Case A in such a manner that no one who had followed the west coast campaign could miss identifying her.

In the category of those who had received improvement but were not cured, four examples were outlined. They included cases such as a "maiden lady past middle life" suffering from "anemia" and "catarrhal discharge," who came into "a much richer religious experience" through the Price campaign. It was said that she had "ceased to worry over and rebel against her maidenly state in life and accepted her lot as divinely appointed." This blessing was described as a perfect expression of "the beneficial effect of the law of faith over a functional condition." In another case, a young lady with infantile paralysis had not recovered from an operation the way she should have, and she found walking difficult. It was explained that in these type of cases, the "fullest co-operation" from the patient was required, or the procedure would not achieve its "fullest results." She was anointed, pronounced cured, and could walk much better than before; however the structure of the foot itself had not changed. Therefore, the case offered improved function through the will of the patient, but the young lady was reportedly cognizant that "she is not cured in the sense in which at first she hoped she would be."[14]

As the report made clear, however, the benefits that had been accrued by the campaign were more than outweighed by its dangers. Seventeen cases demonstrated worsening conditions, largely through the neglect of "proper" scientific treatment. The three examples used to discuss these cases all related to the premature removal of braces or casts, allowing the patient to testify on the platform while running or jumping. The ultimate effect, however, had been a deterioration and sometimes permanent damage to the bones and joints in question.

Of the cases that had resulted in fatalities, the neglect of medical treatment was again emphasized as a direct cause of death. One woman died of diabetes and another left an abdominal tumor "too late for effective treatment." A third woman discontinued the radium treatment for her cancer of the tongue; fortunately, the prospect of her death "did not shake her Christian faith," and she became resigned to it "with proper spirit." A fourth girl eventually died from pulmonary tuberculosis, and her physician was convinced that "the extra exertion and excitement" of the campaign "hastened her end."[15]

If faith healing was dangerous for the body, it could also be damaging for the soul. Many cases were reported where failure to achieve healing led to depression. The committee was particularly worried about the large number of blind children "whose hopes were built up to a very high pitch, only to prove vain." This situation had led some of them "to question their belief in the love of God," undoing the faith that had been "built up in their lives." One patient, who the committee admitted may have had a previous "mental obsession," was anointed, but then lapsed into an "unrestrainable state of mental excitement" and died a week later from "the exhaustion of acute mania." It is perhaps not surprising that Cooke would finally highlight the case of a girl who was injured by an automobile accident. Her father professed a conversion, and the child was anointed. However, when no change resulted the father "became violently insane."[16]

The report of the investigating committee did more than simply educate the public as to what had occurred at the Price campaign; it also prescribed a course of action on what should be done about faith healers. Such mental therapeutics were valuable, but only in the hands of qualified physicians. Canadian law had not "as yet taken cognizance of the need for public protection, by confining the use of such measures to properly qualified persons and for medical purposes only."[17] The call for legal action against the faith healers had been heard long before the report was issued. One complainant in Vancouver had protested that

Price's conduct was a "travesty on the word religion," and if it were possible to prove it a fraud it "should not be tolerated for a day longer, and is a case for action by the civic fathers, and the police department."[18] In Calgary, Dr Dunlop maintained that "No person, no matter how well gifted in hypnotism, should be permitted to hypnotise for any purposes whatsoever, excepting under the supervision of a qualified medical practitioner."[19] The state, however, was far more reluctant to prosecute the popular faith healers in the 1920s than it had been in jailing Dowieites at the turn of the century.

In Vancouver, even medical authorities were not eager to engage Price on legal grounds. When a man dying from "pulmonary tuberculosis" visited Price and later died, the attending physician expressed surprise that the patient had been taken to the arena but hesitated in declaring that this excursion had hastened the death. Although the coroner, Dr T.W. Jeffs, spoke to Price about the case, the *Vancouver Sun* discovered that Jeffs was also a supporter of the faith healer, and was himself personally convinced that "If we have faith we will get healing." Price tried to discourage people in a dying condition from attending the meetings, and although he prayed with the man in question, he did not anoint him or make promises of healing. The coroner was satisfied with the evangelist's explanation, and the medical health officer maintained that the law did not allow him to interfere.[20]

Ironically, Price's legal difficulties in Canada came not from the government officials or medical associations, but rather from a "drugless healer," J.J. O'Malley, who tried to take the evangelist to court in Calgary for practicing medicine without a licence. O'Malley had recently been fined on the same charge, and he pursued his action to protest the "abnormally wide terms" of the Alberta Medical Professions Act, rather than out of any particular animosity towards Price. The city's magistrates refused O'Malley's persistent applications, and an appeal to the attorney general was flatly denied.[21] Despite the dire warnings about the dangers of hypnotism, government officials had no intention of intervening. Price certainly never outrightly attacked the practice of medicine. Despite the outbreak of the Spanish flu epidemic only a few years previously, infectious diseases were never a factor in the arena campaigns, and Price did not appear to offer the same threat to public health that Eugene Brooks and the Dowieites had. City officials were far more concerned about the damage that might be caused by the stampeding crowds trying to see Price than by the health issues resulting from faith healing.

All but two members of the committee signed the final report. The dissenters were both Methodists, Rev. R.J. McIntyre and William Savage, who was the only lawyer on the committee. McIntyre was one of Price's strongest ministerial supporters in Vancouver and had taken over as chair of the campaign after Cooke's resignation. Producing their own minority report, McIntyre and Savage pointed out that the 350 cases examined by the committee represented less than 6 per cent of the total number of 6,000 who were anointed. They also argued that the claim that this sample was in any way representative was false because many refused to appear before the committee for "reasons of conscience" and believed their healing had been "of such a sacred nature that it could not be ascertained by mental process." If the sample was truly representative, then the number of deaths could be extrapolated from thirty-nine to the horrifying sum of 668 expected deaths in the Vancouver area. However, government statistics actually showed a decrease in the death rate over the seven months following the campaign when compared with the previous year. According to the minority report, it was more likely that the reported cases of death constituted the total number for the campaign rather than a representative sample.[22]

The minority report agreed with the dichotomy outlined between functional and organic, but balked at the use of the concept of functional diseases as a means to marginalize faith healing, quoting one source that claimed that 75 per cent of those who applied to physicians for aid were suffering from functional diseases. The real issue at stake, however, was the majority report's willingness to agree that organic illness could not be healed "without the use of physical means in accordance with certain laws known to medical science." McIntyre and Savage reasserted that God may and does "heal both functional and organic diseases through other laws than those revealed to medical science, that there are laws without number which make for health of which medical science is as yet ignorant, any one of which God may use in answering prayer and restoring health."[23] In 1889, when the *Toronto Empire* had solicited the city's clergy on their opinion of faith healing, the majority of respondents had expressed their confidence in the ability of God to intervene in natural law, but they had opposed the atonement position that suggested healing could be expected if one had sufficient faith. By 1923, maintaining God's transcendence had become a minority position for Protestant ministers.

Cooke, apparently without informing the rest of the Ministerial Association, released the majority report to two Vancouver newspapers even before it was presented to the Association, with the agreement that its contents would not be published until authorized to do so. It was clear that Cooke wanted to publicize the committee's work as a stand against Price and other faith healers. The *Christian Guardian* reproduced the majority report in full, while it condensed and abridged the minority report. Despite the fact that the association voted not to publish either report, Cooke somehow managed to have the majority report printed in pamphlet form for a wider distribution.[24]

The majority report was intended to serve as the definitive word on what had actually occurred at the Price campaign. An enterprising "Dr. Dorchester" used the release of the Price report to advertise his own system of healing and physical exercise. He even offered testimonials from people such as Mrs Leamon, who "went to the Arena, and thought she was cured, but wasn't. Then she went to the Dorchester Institute, and has never had any return of her trouble since." The committee had proved that "faith without physiological co-operation in the shape of either specific treatment, exercise, diet, etc. or all, if necessary, can never give any but the most temporary results." The advertisement triumphantly proclaimed, "Price Disclosures Prove Again that DORCHESTER is RIGHT."[25] However, the conclusiveness of the report that was appropriated by Dorchester was far from universally shared. Given its tone and underlying assumptions, the document seemed to stir as much as still the religious waters. Rev. A.W. McCleod of North Vancouver's First Baptist Church complained that there "never was *a more gross, more unfair document* ever concocted by an assembly of ecclesiastics, than that incorporated in the majority report!"[26]

BODIES OF KNOWLEDGE

The Price investigation committee's conclusions continued to be debated in many forums, but the distance between critics and proponents of faith healing went deeper than the theological questions of God's role in the universe. The Price majority report revealed a particular way of seeing the body, and in its claim to survey the healings of Price objectively, the report reframed corporeal knowledge in a manner that was antithetical to the bodily perspective maintained by proponents of divine healing.

The committee's procedures demonstrated this epistemological gap from the beginning. In their minority report, McIntyre and Savage complained that the cases under consideration were all gathered "from parties outside the committee," and the committee itself had little opportunity to actually hear personal statements related to individual healings. Instead, "[i]t was taken for granted that many of these persons were incapable of judging accurately as to whether they were healed or not."[27] Far from disputing this claim, Cooke openly agreed with the assessment, asking in a sermon, "How many people are capable of diagnosing their own condition? When you or I take really ill the first thing we need is a trained expert to tell us just what is wrong."[28]

The personal authority that claimed experiential knowledge over one's body was displaced by the dispassionate gaze of medicine. The reports of physicians could be assumed to be objective in presenting the details of a case, but personal claims, even when the original condition was diagnosed by a physician, were insufficient.

The use of personal healing narratives was a well-established tradition for proponents of faith healing, and this remained the basis for establishing claims to cures. Even during the later public campaigns, when healing was observed as a public spectacle, oral testimonials were featured at the beginning of almost every meeting. The validity of these claims was bolstered by the presentation of personal names and addresses, signifying that the healing narrative was the extension of a real person and not simply fabricated. Each person that lay claim to a cure through faith healing offered a unique story of redemption in body and soul. The body was understood through these personal texts, a scripted performance that offered a unique social space for constructing illness, health, and religious devotion. By denying the personal narrative, the investigative committee effectively disembodied the religious voice from its material grounding.

Personal testimony was regarded with suspicion in part because the committee had adopted a psychological perspective that emphasized the power of the subconscious over the conscious expression of will. Many of the diseases under review were seen to be the result of "mental stress and conflict" that had become embedded within the subconscious and were "therefore not recognized by the patient." When such conditions became "too threatening or irksome," relief was obtained through subconscious processes that "develop in them some physical disorder calling for sympathy, consideration and attention which they would not otherwise receive."[29] It came as no surprise that within the context of religious revivals such "psychogenetic" disorders were cured, since in accepting a deeper religious experience, the believer faced their deepest fears or anxieties and restored mental harmony. Revivalism strikes at "the very root of wrong mental attitudes," and when the experience is successful it makes "the physical manifestation of the former attitude incompatible with the new outlook, and the disease has to go." Therefore, not only was personal testimony not trustworthy (since it could not reveal the workings of the subconscious), but the nature of religious experience was psychologized as an expression of mental therapy. Émile Coué was approvingly cited for suggesting that "every idea which enters the conscious mind, if it is accepted by the subconscious, is transformed by it into a reality and forms henceforth a permanent element in our life."[30] According to the committee, those who testified to being cured knew not of what they spoke.

The ability of the committee to construct its object within a medical discourse went beyond simply discounting the claims of personal narratives. The report deliberately projected a scientific demeanour by reducing bodily cures to a series of "cases." Significantly, cases were never personalized or named, but simply given a clinical classification of letters, and anonymity was preserved as professional medical standards dictated. This form of presentation staked a claim to scientific and confidential medical knowledge, yet many of the extended descriptions of the cases offered enough detail to identify the person being discussed. It was believed that if the cases remained truly anonymous, Price would simply continue to make claims that real cures had occurred. Therefore, comments such as, "Case was advertised as a cure and received much publicity as man was well-known in the City," were common. It would be hard to mistake the reference to "Case K," described as a "well-known" Alaskan dog team driver, whose healing had incurred the attention of "members of his fraternal order."[31] There was little reason to include such details other than to ensure that Price was discredited for advertising these cases as proof of divine healing.

This strategy was particularly evident when it came to the inclusion of Ruby Dimmick in the majority report. Case A obviously referred to her public healing, and this inclusion infuriated her father, Rev. J.F. Dimmick. Other than a notice that they were considering her case, no one on the committee had actually interviewed him or Ruby, nor did they even discuss the case with Dr Hall. Since Ruby had been healed in Victoria, she technically should not have even fallen within the scope of the investigation, which was specifically designed to examine "the Results of a Campaign of Healing held in Vancouver, B.C., in May 1923, by Rev. C.S. Price." One physician on the committee had seen her, but only for a fifteen-minute consultation six years previously. When her father took his concerns to the press, the committee responded that they had gotten their information from a physician in Toronto, and it was based largely on a certificate of examination that indicated she was free of "organic disease." However, Dimmick claimed that this examination was done in order for Ruby to gain admittance to the Toronto Orthopedic Hospital. Since they dealt with "deformities," they would not accept patients with infectious diseases. Her examination stated that she was indeed free of disease, but it had nothing to do with the state of her spine or foot. As Dimmick pointed out, "it was the very evidence of these deformities that made my daughter a candidate for the Orthopedic Hospital! Just fancy an orthodox Orthopedic hospital taking in a *case of confirmed hysteria!*"

Dimmick also testified that, despite Hall's earlier reservations, by 1926 the physician had become fully convinced of the miraculous nature of the healing, and even signed a statement for Dimmick after the doctor had interviewed Ruby: "[Dr Hall] had her walk up and down before him. He asked her questions. He sized her up. His eyes filled with tears. He was no longer unable to restrain himself, and he threw his arms about her. 'This is wonderful,' he said."[32] According to Price's defenders, even the very standards of scientific investigation asserted by the report's authors had fallen short. T.J. McCrossan, who claimed to know two members of the committee well, suggested that unlike Hall, the committee's physicians simply refused to accept clear examples of previously diagnosed tuberculosis and cancer being healed, replying instead that the original diagnoses were mistaken.[33]

One other important feature of the report illustrated the extension of medical perceptions of the body. Four of the cases described were accompanied by supporting photographs. Figure 7.1 shows a one-year-old infant with an enlarged leg being held before the camera to demonstrate the continuing presence of the child's affliction, even after being anointed by Price. The picture was cropped at the shoulders, keeping the head out of the frame, and the genitalia was appropriately obscured by a fig-leaf.[34] A second photo, figure 7.2, offers the profile of a six-year-old child with a hump in his back from "tuberculosis of the spine." According to the report, the child was still in the process of recovering from his illness, but as a result of prematurely removing the plaster cast after his anointing by Price, he would likely be afflicted with the hump permanently.[35] As demonstrated in the photograph, the shot is framed with the head cut off and part of the body isolated to emphasize the ailment.

Photography captured the body in its "real" state and was employed to reinforce the objective status of the report.[36] The headlessness of the subjects reflected their status as "cases," and the meanings applied to these bodies were carefully prescribed and directed in both the captions and the text of the report. Photographs provided more than evidence; they invited the viewer to "see" the body from a particular perspective, atomized into discrete parts and divorced from any sense of personal subjectivity. In figure 7.2, diagrammed arrows map the hump upon the body, training the uneducated eye both to see the affliction and to view the body from the "objective" position of a medical professional. Image and text were thus merged in the framing of evidence, producing only one possible medical conclusion.

The two remaining pictures used in the report exposed the body in a very different way. The development of X-rays as a diagnostic tool offered a means to reveal internal structures not visible to the eye without physically dissecting the body.[37] Even before Price's campaign had ended in Vancouver, there were intimations that this technology would

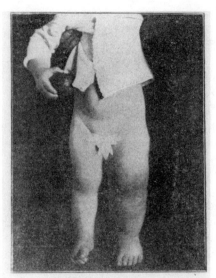

FIGURE 2.—(Case L).
Shows right leg of normal size and left much larger.

Fig. 7.1 "Case L" from *Report on a Faith-Healing Campaign held by Rev. C.S. Price in Vancouver, B.C., May 1923*. Photographer unknown. United Church of Canada, British Columbia Conference Archives

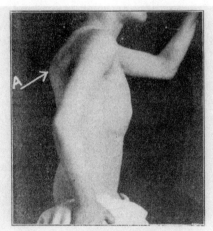

FIGURE 4.—(Case Q).
Tubercular Disease of spine. "A" shows the marked "hump" of the back.

Fig. 7.2. "Case Q" from *Report on a Faith-Healing Campaign held by Rev. C.S. Price in Vancouver, B.C., May 1923*. Photographer unknown. United Church of Canada, British Columbia Conference Archives

be employed to test the cures. The *Vancouver World* reported that while Price was performing a healing service at a Japanese meeting, a Japanese-Canadian physician, Dr Shimo-Takahara, was cataloguing the cases, as many of the patients were known to him. Those who claimed to be cured would be examined and X-rays taken, which would then be "compared with X-ray photographs now in his possession, taken while the patients were under his care." This scientific approach would produce "indisputable evidence" on the effectiveness of faith healing. The penetrating eye of the X-ray was the sole arbiter, as the newspaper made clear: "No attention will be paid to the statements of those treated. Only actual conditions as shown by the several examinations will be used in arriving at a decision."[38] Although not listed as one of the eight physicians originally asked to serve on the committee, Takahara was "called into consultation owing to his professional knowledge of the Oriental cases" and signed the majority report. Whether any of the X-rays used in the report were the ones taken by Takahara is unknown. Certainly the final report did not physically display the before and after scenario suggested by the newspaper.[39]

The two X-ray pictures used in the published version of the report were exposures of the pelvis that illustrated problems with the hip. "Case O" was a child who suffered from "hip-joint disease and curvature of the spine," and who had been removed prematurely from a plaster cast at the Price meetings. Three weeks after his anointing, the child was taken to a hospital and, according to the report, "pus drained from the hip-joint and tubes inserted for drainage. An X-ray was taken at this time, and again four months later, which showed much destruction of the bone at the hip-joint, the joint out of its socket and about 2½ inches shortening of the leg with considerable curvature of the spine." Presumably, it was the second X-ray that was published in the report (figure 7.3), with diagrammed arrows again explaining where the separation of the hip can be observed and comparing the diseased hip socket with the healthy one on the other side.[40]

The second X-ray, figure 7.4, was associated with "Case H," a "young lady" suffering from "congenital dislocation of both hips." Arrows and letters guide the viewer's eye to what should be seen. The commentary on this case was one of the few to offer a limited acknowledgment of the individual's personal testimony within a carefully circumscribed ground. The report noted that several people near the arena stage had heard a snapping of her joints falling into place, then qualified this testimony by stating "Congenital dislocations do not 'snap' into place when reduced, as the socket is undeveloped and the head of the bone does not fit." While admitting that the patient could now walk better than before, this was explained as being a result of

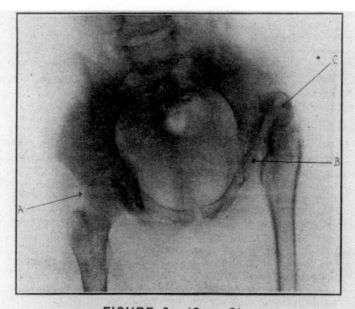

FIGURE 3.—(Case O).
Hip Disease. "A" shows normal hip-joint. "B" shows position of diseased hip socket. "C" shows the much diseased bone out of place. The head of the bone has been completely destroyed.

Fig. 7.3. "Case O" from *Report on a Faith-Healing Campaign held by Rev. C.S. Price in Vancouver, B.C., May 1923.* Photographer unknown. United Church of Canada, British Columbia Conference Archives

"improved muscle function," which ultimately mattered little since an X-ray demonstrated no change in the position or condition of the hip joints.[41] In this example, the committee used the X-ray to expose the body as a betrayal of personal knowledge. The reports of "snapping" are discounted as irrelevant, since it did not fit the established category of the disease in question. That the subject had improved motor function is not doubted, but the qualification of "improved muscle function" marginalized the healing as a functional improvement, rather than a change in organic condition.

While X-rays reinforced medical representations, the general technology of photography remained versatile in its application and was hardly restricted to medicine. Faith healers had also turned to the camera as a means of validating the efficacy of faith healing. Even in the nineteenth century, John Alexander Dowie utilized professional studio

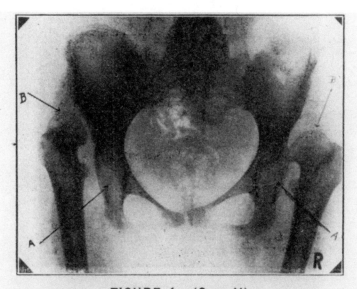

FIGURE 1.—(Case H).
Double Congenital Dislocation Hips. "A" indicates position of hip-sockets. "B" indicates position of heads of hip-
bones which are out of the sockets.

Fig. 7.4. "Case H" from *Report on a Faith-Healing Campaign held by Rev. C.S. Price in Vancouver, B.C., May 1923*. Photographer unknown. United Church of Canada, British Columbia Conference Archives

photographs to great effect in the *Leaves of Healing*. When he asked his audience for proof of the power of divine healing in cases of childbirth, literally hundreds of baby pictures were mailed to Zion and reproduced in the magazine. Both the Bosworths and Price hired professional photographers to capture the packed interiors of their arena meetings as evidence of the massive crowds they could draw. When a man converted by Price in Winnipeg handed him the instruments he had used to inject himself with morphine, the evangelist published a picture of the drug paraphernalia in his *Golden Grain* magazine, and even explained to his audience how the bent spoon, needle, and syringe were operated.[42]

More often, however, photography was employed in conjunction with healing testimonials. Here was modern "proof" of the restored body. Where possible, the healthy subject was placed next to (or holding the instruments of) medicine that formerly caged the body. In the case of young Johnny Patterson, a damaged knee had incapacitated the energetic

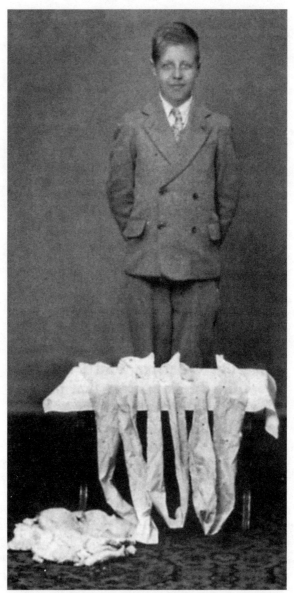

Fig. 7.5. Johnny Patterson. Photographer unknown. *Golden Grain*, October 1929, p. 19. Flower Pentecostal Heritage Center

boy, and a physician informed him that it would be a month to six weeks before being able to return to school. The pain and swelling disappeared after being anointed by Price in Vancouver.[43] Figure 7.5 illustrates how the *Golden Grain* presented photographic evidence in conjunction with the story of his healing. A dapper Johnny stands straight with the unravelled cloth bandages displayed prominently in front of him. The body is presented whole, with the head and face clearly visible. The scientific language of anonymous cases is replaced with a personalized account of God's healing power, manifested in the visual representation of the restored body in triumph over bandages.

Although Patterson's healing was presented in the third person, other stories deliberately related first-person testimonials to photographic evidence of restored health. The narrative of "Sunshine," Edna Perle Lang, recounted the harrowing depths of suffering from a car accident, which led to operations, electrical treatments, and plaster of Paris body casts. One year, a "fifty dollar cage of steel" back brace was her birthday present. Curvature of the spine, the shortening of one leg, and gall bladder difficulties all compounded her pain. Anointed by Price at his campaign stop in Brandon, Manitoba, Lang immediately felt her bones moving into place as she sensed herself "slipping away under the power of God." The power continued to surge through her body all night, and the following morning "Sunshine" could walk straight and without assistance.[44]

The long testimonial of "Sunshine" was accompanied by two photographs. A wedding portrait demonstrated her recent marriage to evangelist Elvin Lang, while a separate image, figure 7.6, shows her restored state of health and the birthday brace. Rather than simply reproducing a picture of the brace alone, the *Golden Grain* presented Lang as cheerfully victorious over her illness by holding forth the dreaded implement, a trophy in the battle to achieve health. The text of her letter to Price surrounds the image, interlinking the personal voice with the photographic subject. The uncomfortable sight of the steel brace, a symbol of the body in bondage, provides a stark contrast with the bright smile of "Sunshine." Although her legs are not visible, Lang is apparently standing without aid, restored physically and spiritually. The photograph serves as visual evidence of a cure through faith and reflects the structural essence of the textual narrative, carrying the viewer from darkness to light, from bondage to freedom, from sickness to health.

The embedded "truth" of photography proved to be malleable in the hands of both critics and proponents of faith healing. In contrast to the headless and nameless body parts presented in the investigative report, Price used the technology of photography to provide evidence of the body and spirit made whole. While the committee disembodied the

The Story of "Sunshine"
OF BRANDON, MAN.

The girl whose life was changed from misery to happiness, from tears to laughter, and who has come to be known as "Sunshine" because of her expression of joy.

Brandon, Man.

Dear Dr. Price:

Yes, Praise the Lord my healing has lasted. I am completely well today and in gratitude to the Lord Jesus Christ, my Saviour and healer, and with the prayer that this testimony might be used for the glory of God, and the healing of others, I tell this story:—

I was in a motor accident, July 29th, 1918, and the windshield struck me in the shoulder, making a terrible bruise, but the doctor who examined

"THE LORD DELIVERED ME FROM THIS"

me did not think there was very much wrong. But from that moment I began to fail in health. My head was drawn to one side, and all the medicine that I took failed to give me relief, and at last, acting on my doctor's advice, I went to the hospital for five weeks treatment. The treatment did not do any good whatever, and by this time

I was a wreck, to such an extent, that my doctor advised me to go to a clinic, where I spent eight days.

After the clinic I was taken to the hospital, where I underwent a major operation. I was in the hospital for five weeks, and then went to my home, later returning to Brandon, Man., where I had five weeks more of electrical treatments. These treatments did not help. After X-ray had been taken, the curvature of the spine was revealed. It was impossible for me to keep my head straight, and so I was placed in a plaster of Paris cast. I could not lie down, and the pain was so terrific I could not stand it, so the cast was taken off, and I was sent to Winnipeg for a steel brace. It was my birthday, and the fifty dollar cage of steel that held my body was my birthday present. What a present! The brace extended from the hips and under my arms, and fastened across the abdomen.

All the time I was taking serum for tubercular hip. This serum continued for a year and a half. I had also taken vaccine for five months. But all the time I was getting worse, to such an extent that I would go into spasms, and morphine and cocaine were given me to bring me out. The spasms would last for hours. Every two weeks I had to take X-ray treatments, and this continued all the winter of 1922. In July, 1922, my tonsils were removed. I was dieting for gall bladder trouble, but I was steadily getting worse.

Then in 1923, I had another major operation and I lay on a bed of suffering in the hospital for five weeks. I was very weak and sickly. I would lay down on hot water bottles; one leg was

Fig. 7.6. Healing testimonial of "Sunshine," holding her back brace. Photographer unknown. *Golden Grain*, September 1926, p. 33. Flower Pentecostal Heritage Center

subjective voice, healing narratives in the *Golden Grain* reasserted the validity of personal experience in determining authentic claims to healing. In their respective approaches to photographic evidence, critics and faith healers reveal their disparate understandings of the self and bodily knowledge. That both sides turned to photography to establish their positions reflects the growing authority of the camera as a documentary witness in the early twentieth century.[45]

When Price returned to Vancouver for his third revival in August 1929, the campaign was specifically designed to counter the effects of the report, which was still circulating six years later. The crowds were not quite as overflowing as in 1923, but they were still large enough to fill the civic auditorium. Two services were specifically set aside for people to testify to their healing from either the 1923 or 1924 campaigns, and hundreds did so in meetings that lasted well into the night. A special issue of the *Golden Grain* was dedicated to printing more than sixty of these testimonials, which were endorsed as "faithful witnesses of the power of Christ to heal in our day" by a coalition of Vancouver ministers.[46] The investigative committee had maintained that no organic cures had been effected from faith healing in Vancouver. In response, Price produced a multitude of healed bodies that testified otherwise. Proponents and critics of faith healing saw the body through very different eyes, and these conceptual modes shaped the way they used evidence to establish their respective claims to truth. It was not simply a matter of which bodies were observed by each side, but how those bodies were perceived.

PHYSICIAN, HEAL THYSELF

The medical profession was far from monolithic in its attitudes towards faith healing. As noted earlier, while some doctors were eager to discredit the practice of faith healing, others were willing to share the platform with Price. A small number of physicians, however, took their engagement with divine healing one step further, giving up their traditional medical practice to adopt faith healing. To transform oneself from physician to faith healer was no small feat, as it involved a complete epistemological reorientation in how one viewed the world, illness, and the body. Dr Mina Ross Brawner starkly contrasted the scientific assumptions of medicine with her new religious understanding of healing:

Oh, if disease is only a matter of germs I am not afraid of germs. I know their names, their habits of life and mode of reproduction. I'll just put on a cap and long white surgical gown, and rubber gloves, and then sail right into the battle

with lance and disinfectants! But when I see that back of those death dealing
germs stands the devil as the first cause I will not undertake to deal with him.
So I take off my gown and rubber gloves, make one heap of all my weapons of
warfare, my years of study and credentials, and carry them all to the foot of the
Cross where I see the bleeding, mangled body of my Lord.[47]

Brawner did not deny the existence of germs, but the religious space of
faith healing allowed her to see beyond (at the "back of") the germs and
perceive their "first cause." Bacteriology was transcended by wider cosmological realities that required more than a microscope to recognize.

Like Brawner, most of the physicians who adopted divine healing appear to have been women. Although the few men who transformed
themselves in this manner were well-known, such as Dr Charles Cullis
in the nineteenth century and Dr Finis E. Yoakum in the twentieth century, from the evidence offered by testimonials, women remained the
dominant voice in this domain as well. For Dr Jane Baker it was the
discovery of her own breast cancer, which "grew very large, and caused
me great pain when I laid on my right side," that led to a spiritual crisis
that turned her to faith healing, and when the healing took place, "it
seemed as if someone had heated irons red hot and thrust them through
my breast."[48] For Dr Elizabeth Keller, a carriage accident left her with
an effusion in the shoulder joint and injury to her nerves, and healing
from her painful illness only came after a group of believers spent the
entire night praying for her.[49] In a fall from a veranda, Dr Florence
Murcutt suffered both internal injuries and a fractured arm, but
anointing and prayer effected a healing that was confirmed by x-rays.[50]
One of the childbirth "nurses" at Yoakum's Pisgah Home, Sister Nelle,
was reportedly a former osteopathic physician.[51]

On the northern side of the border, it was similarly women physicians who adopted divine healing. The first licensed woman officially
to practice medicine in Canada was Dr Jenny Kidd Trout, who was
also instrumental in establishing the Women's Medical College at
Queen's University.[52] By 1891, however, Trout was an invalid, plagued
by "nervous bodily ailments." Interested in pursuing divine healing,
she wrote to John Salmon, and he along with R.J. Zimmerman visited
the physician at her bedside to anoint and pray with her. Her recovery
marked the beginning of her active involvement with the Christian Alliance, serving as a member of the Dominion Auxiliary Branch executive.[53] After moving to California, Trout was described by Carrie Judd
Montgomery as "a retired physician who is greatly used in praying for
the recovery of the sick."[54]

The preeminent woman physician to take up the banner of divine
healing in North America was unquestionably Dr Lilian B. Yeomans.

As noted earlier, Yeomans boasted an impressive medical background as the daughter of two physicians. After conquering her addiction to morphine at Dowie's Zion in 1898, Yeomans returned to Canada determined to give up her medical practice in order to serve as a missionary. This goal proved difficult to obtain, as Yeomans discovered that extricating herself from her professional credentials was no simple matter. In her work as a missionary in northern Manitoba, she found that as the only doctor within five hundred miles, she was continually pressed into service by the Hudson's Bay Company. When epidemics broke out among the aboriginal population, the government required her to take charge of them, and she found herself carrying large quantities of drugs once again.[55] With her adopted child, Tanis, Yeomans returned to Winnipeg, where she appears to have been ordained by a short-lived Holiness Association and apparently served as a preacher for the Holiness Movement Church.[56]

Yeomans relocated to Calgary in 1905, using family connections to secure employment as a stenographer in the postal inspector's office. It was there, in 1907, that she experienced the baptism of the spirit. She became active as an assistant in a small pentcostal mission on Ninth Avenue, where faith healings were reported to have occurred.[57] In 1912 Yeomans started to write articles for Carrie Judd Montgomery's periodical, *Triumphs of Faith*, and when Dr Yoakum held a campaign in Calgary the following year, she testified to her healing.[58] She spent seventeen years in Calgary, working at the mission and carrying out extensive evangelistic work, but her later writings are quite vague on the details surrounding these endeavours. In the early 1920s Yeomans moved to San Francisco. She became an ordained evangelist with the Assemblies of God and made regular appearances at Carrie Judd Montgomery's Home of Peace. Yeomans served as a teacher of divine healing at Glad Tidings Bible School and taught at the Berean Bible School in San Diego before she was invited to take a position at Aimee Semple McPherson's L.I.F.E. Bible Institute (originally the Angelus Temple Training School) in Los Angeles. The author of numerous books, Yeomans was one of North America's leading pentecostal voices promoting divine healing.

Yeomans's affiliation with Angelus Temple did not endear her to some elements within the Assemblies of God. McPherson had also been an ordained evangelist with the Assemblies, but she had returned her ministerial credentials in 1922. As the influence and notoriety of McPherson grew in the 1920s, the local Assemblies district council cast suspicion upon Yeomans's association with the flamboyant evangelist. When Sister Aimee fell ill in 1930, Yeomans attended her at the bedside, an incident which created further friction with the Assemblies.

Yeomans considered resigning, but felt strongly that there was no contradiction in participating in a wide spectrum of activity that included Angelus Temple, Assemblies evangelistic work, and occasional teaching at a fundamentalist bible school.[59] In 1930 she even accompanied Price in leading evangelistic meetings for the North Central District of the Assembles of God.[60]

Long after she had given up medical practice, Yeomans continued to define herself in relation to her professional identity as a physician. Her numerous published works all included the initials "M.D." after her name, and she was not reluctant to use her authority as a physician to promote divine healing. Medicine certainly provided her with an endless stock of metaphors for her evangelistic pursuits; even such technically sophisticated topics as modern germ theory could be used to promote spiritual ends: "Human blood defends the body by actually conquering deadly microbes when they get into the circulation. The soldiers of the blood, tiny white corpuscles, called leucocytes, stand up and fight them to the death. So the blood of the Lamb overcomes all Satan's power of sin, sickness, and death."[61] Like Brawner, it is not the existence or operation of germs that Yeomans rejects, but rather the cosmological reality behind them.

Despite the fact that Yeomans had been healed by the notoriously anti-medicine Dowie, she was not interested in "belittling the wonderful results achieved, and the self-denying devotion displayed, by students of medical science in all ages." Indeed, the "worst thing" Yeomans would suggest about physicians was that "they are men, and not God, and their activities flesh, not spirit." Since God has "deigned to assume charge of the bodies of His people" through the atonement, "no one else is good enough for our Physician."[62] While she refrained from adopting Dowie's denunciations of her former profession, Yeomans nevertheless did offer an implicit critique of medicine, both in her representation of the body and the way knowledge of the body was discerned.

No pentecostal author placed as much attention on the body as Yeomans. Since all of her works tended to emphasize the issue of divine healing, a corporeal presence might not be unexpected; but Yeomans practically bursted with exuberance for the "beautiful body" of God's creation: "Preparing to be a doctor, I had to know every bone, muscle, nerve and blood vessel. The more I studied it the more wonderful it seemed."[63] Her representation of the body echoed, in somewhat more romantic language, the Paleyite argument from design:

Even to this day, though sadly defaced and marred by sin and its results, the human body bears the impress of the divine image and superscription as surely as the coin they handed to Jesus bore that of Caesar. I shall never forget the first time I saw a human brain. I was only a young girl, a medical student, worldly, utterly forgetful of my Creator in the days of my youth, but I can truly say that a feeling akin to holy awe filled me when I beheld it in all its wondrous complexity and beauty. Yes; those pearly gray, glistening convolutions seemed to me the most beautiful things I had ever seen and when I realized that they were the home of thought parts of the organ through which the most intricate processes of reasoning were carried out, the marvel of it well nigh stunned me. I could have fallen on my knees, young heathen though I was, before this mystery, and its Author, the writing and superscription were so evidently divine.[64]

As wonderful as the body itself was, it could not simply be left to function autonomously. The body was still "defaced and marred" by sin, which manifested itself physiologically through afflictions. The material body alone was incomplete, but could be made whole in "divine health." All that was required was "a great, big, faith-inspired, God-given laugh – a laugh that will clear your brain, steady your heart's action, stir up your liver, house clean your entire system, send living lightnings flashing along your nerve trunks, and make the corpuscles dance in your veins and arteries. This laugh is nothing less than God's omnipotence released in your being by faith."[65] In this way the body was "lifted above the plane where Satan can inoculate you with his germs."[66] Yeomans reasserted many of the nineteenth-century constructions of the body made perfect through divine health, while at the same time allowing the pentecostal emphasis on power to "dance" through the body.

The distance between faith healing and conventional medicine was only partly related to competing representations of the body. As the work of the investigating committees demonstrated, proponents and critics disagreed on their respective approaches to the body. Medical practice functioned as a way of seeing, and, as Byron Good suggests, it reflected "a distinctive perspective, an organized set of perceptions and emotional responses that emerge with the emergence of the body as a site of medical knowledge."[67] Yeomans revealed her partial awareness of this medical epistemology in a light-hearted, but illuminating, anecdote about a childhood experience of being examined by a doctor, which entailed sticking out her tongue. As a young girl, Yeomans "could not fathom" how her "tongue told tales on me, for the doctor would take just one, keen, searching glance at the trembling little tongue that was obediently thrust out for his inspection and say: 'This child has been eating trash. Let her have *no* supper; give her a dose, a *full* dose, of castor oil, and put her early to bed.'" The body betrays the self, while the physician held not only the power to diagnose the tell-tale signs upon the tongue, but also prescribed the punishment for transgressions of health. Yeomans goes on to suggest that medical knowledge is not simply a static collection of facts, but is actually a way of perceiving the body. Her own career as a physician illustrated how professional training endowed her with the new authority to pronounce judgment upon the body: "there came a day when I, too, was a doctor able to say, in a commanding voice to the submissive patient trembling before me, with possible castor oil, calomel, rigid dieting, perhaps even fasting, looming darkly in their horizon, with all proper professional dignity, 'Put out your tongue,' and when that day came I knew that a perfectly clean tongue was a sure sign of physical well being, while a dirty, furry, flabby tongue was as surely an evidence of ill health."[68] As a physician, the "commanding voice" and "professional dignity" are ultimately linked with the ability to see what is occurring within the body through an apparatus of knowledge.

The medical authority to exercise power over patients was something that Yeomans was very familiar with, and although her critiques were usually jovial they turned somewhat more serious in relation to a personal bout of pneumonia she suffered in 1923. Attended by her sister, Amy, who had been trained as a registered nurse, Yeomans consented to having a physician examine her, but only because she feared the legal ramifications for Amy should she die. Her commentary on what the doctor would likely do in her case is revealing:

I committed myself to God, for I well knew that while the physician would agree to everything I said, to the effect that I would not take remedies, or allow myself to be removed to an institution – for doctors never disagree with patients who are running high temperatures, and have enfeebled heart action – he would take my poor sister into the next room and very likely frighten her out of her senses, by telling her that I was in a most critical condition and "something," meaning the hospital, "would have to be done immediately."

Yeomans foresaw how a physician would simply look beyond her own wishes and understanding of the body and attempt to place the body within an institutional space for proper treatment and observation.

Because of her professional background, Yeomans could articulate a particular critique of medicine that most proponents of faith healing could not. It was not always easy to separate herself from the medical structure of knowledge that she maintained long after giving up her practice. The encounter with pneumonia produced an inner dialogue between her entrenched medical rationality and her religious belief, when the "enemy" tried to convince her that "'You have pneumonia of the right lung, with some involvement of the left; it is complicated by pleurisy, which causes that intolerable agony when you cough. Look at your blue face! See how motionless your right lung is! Notice your rapid, shallow respiration, feeble pulse and laboring heart.'" The diagnostic signs, which she still recognized as constituting a particular medical truth, had to now be resisted as "lying symptoms."[69] To admit them would have meant defeat, since health was achieved by looking beyond these constructions to the cosmological forces that ultimately determined sickness and health.

Lilian Yeomans occupied a unique position, seeing the world through two sets of eyes. Most proponents of faith healing could not have expressed such an effective response to the medical understanding of the body, nor would they have necessarily understood the full reach of the medical gaze. Nevertheless, Yeomans's experience illustrates the depth of the conceptual reorientation required to cross over from medicine to divine healing. The practice of Protestant faith healing involved far more than simply believing in a miracle; the reclamation of the body as a site for divine operation also involved reconsidering how the body could be known and accessed in an era when medical knowledge appeared to be preeminent.

Medical pronouncements on the reality and nature of faith healing were far from new. However, the public interest raised by the massive healing campaigns of the 1920s prompted a new expression of medical surveillance that went much further than vague pronouncements on the operation of mental powers. The majority report of the Vancouver investigating committee was the most thorough examination ever directed at a single healing campaign, but it also represented a particular coalition of clerical, medical, and educational interests that framed the report in such a manner as to discount automatically the operation of transcendent intervention in natural law. Cooke, Burnett, and Coleman were all committed to furthering social progress, and to adopt the practice of faith healing without grounding it in scientific principles was, in Cooke's words, "a travesty of the Gospel of Christ and a plain reversion to the superstition and religious hysteria of the Dark Ages."[70] The *Vancouver Sun* might have agreed with this sentiment. Towards the end of the Price campaign, the newspaper printed "Six Reasons Why Everybody Should go to Church Regularly." Set below the volatile letters section (dominated by opinions on Price) and in a large box, the *Sun* urged people to find a church because it produced "the best type of human character," which would "build a clean, safe, sane, abiding social order."[71]

The majority report used the appearance of scientific authority and knowledge to discredit faith healing as practiced by Price. However, the debate over the "reality" of the cures was only one part of an underlying epistemic divide in attitudes towards the body. Divine healing relied upon whole bodies to narrate their experience to the glory of God, and these stories constituted an extension of the self. Medicine saw the body through its discrete parts, disconnected from local expressions of knowledge except in particular cases where the disease in question could be relegated to the "functional" realm. These underlying visual perspectives were reinforced by the use of photography and X-rays, which also constructed the body through their own claims to represent reality. The report's representation of the Price campaign proved to be effective, since even American fundamentalists continued to turn to it as a resource for denouncing faith healing well into the 1930s.[72]

A different perspective on the dialogue between medicine and faith healing is provided by the life and writings of Dr Lilian Yeomans. As a trained physician, Yeomans was conscious of her own divided mentality. A professional education pointed her towards one version of material reality while her religious experience and beliefs led her to perceive the body as intimately connected to a broader cosmological realm. To "see through" her ordeal with pneumonia, Yeomans had to step outside of her own diagnostic tendencies and reject the scientific meanings that her "lying symptoms" presented. To trust in faith and prayer for healing represented more than a faint hope for miraculous intervention; it was rather an epistemological statement about the body and its relation to the divine.

Conclusion

Even when we were stricken in body, we did not come to ignoble supplication of the doctors. But although, to speak by the grace of the gods, we possessed the friendship of the best doctors, we took refuge in the [temple] of Asclepius, in the belief that if it was fated for us to be saved, it was better to be saved through his agency, and that if it was not possible, it was time to die.

Aelius Aristides, *Orationes* (c. 147 C.E.)

The contemporary image of the faith healer continues to be informed by a stereotype popularized in Sinclair Lewis's *Elmer Gantry* (1927). Even though faith healing only played a minor role in the novel, the characterization of Gantry as the hustling con artist and amoral evangelist who unscrupulously played upon his audience's hopes and fears is a popular representation that has only been reinforced in the public consciousness by the television evangelist scandals of the late-1980s. Like the ahistorical question of whether faith healing is "real," the faith healer himself is often also taken to be a static construct, typically seen as manipulating the masses for personal gain as long as people remain irrational in their beliefs.

Lewis's portrayal was far from accurate even in the 1920s, let alone a half century before or after. A very different conception of the faith healer emerges in pre-World War I literature, such as Edward Eggleston's *The Faith Doctor* (1891), where divine healing is perceived as the mistaken but sincere devotional practice of a young middle-class woman whose piety has led her astray. The heroine, Phillida, scrupulously disclaims any public recognition for her work, preferring to visit the afflicted quietly at the bedside. After unpleasant encounters with greedy Christian Science practitioners and a close call with a case involving infectious disease, Phillida recognizes the functional limitations of faith and is herself restored to mental and physical health through a somewhat more worldly reconciliation with her estranged lover. Eggleston restores the world to order by marrying the happy couple, allowing medicine and its faithful dedicated practitioners to reign supreme, and banishing Christian Science from the immediate vicinity.[1]

Even more illuminating is William Vaughn Moody's *The Faith Healer* (1909), which opened on Broadway in 1910. Here the faith healer is a curiously hesitant, mystical, and ultimately feminized figure, whose appearance divides a household between the men who refuse to accept such "hocus-pocus" and the women who are more willing to accept the possibility of faith healing. Unlike Eggleston's reduction of divine healing to the familiar category of a functional mental cure, Moody uses his subject to expose the fallacy of the certainty of knowledge. When the head of the household, Matthew Beeler, explains that the "new medical books" have unravelled how faith healing works, his niece retorts, "Do you think, because they give it a name, that they explain it?" Beeler is implacable in his conviction, reiterating that the world only lives on "Hard-boiled sci-en-ti-fic facts!"[2]

This book has explored aspects of divine healing that intersect themes central to all three of these fictional works, from the gender divide of the Beeler household and the exposure of medical materialism, to the class of respectability that Eggleston projects upon his faith healer, whose sincere supplications are heard quietly at the bedside. If Elmer Gantry himself is personally irredeemable, the context of the professional evangelistic campaigns in which he operated does provide an underlying sense of the elements of consumerism and public spectacle that vaulted faith healing into the limelight in the 1920s. And yet, the body itself remains curiously absent from these fictional accounts. From the mystical to the spectacle, it is the issue of belief that occupies these authors, not its embodiment.

The categorization of "religion" as primarily a sphere of intellectual belief inherently marginalizes activities like faith healing, which resolutely embraced the corporeal. In order to understand this phenomenon, historians must come to terms with the body itself as the crossroads between religious practice and social meaning. Scholars also need to be aware of the creativity and imaginary power of religion to shape everyday life experience, or in Robert Orsi's words, to be mindful of "what people *do* with religious practice, what they make with it of themselves and their worlds."[3] This perception of "lived religion" allows us to see faith healing as a dynamic engagement rather than a marginal or delusional belief. In the tension between the personal subjective experience and the wider constructions of medicine, health, and religion, a multitude of cultural meanings were negotiated.

To take the Lord for the body entailed tremendous personal conviction as well as a willingness to enter into a wide range of contested domains. In tracing the history of Protestant faith healing over a half century, three themes emerge as central to understanding how this devotional act engaged the surrounding cultural worlds. First, it is clear that women dominated the practice of faith healing in Canada, and this

phenomenon cannot be understood apart from the gendered constructions surrounding it. Second, the social geography of faith healing was
transformed dramatically between 1880 and 1930. And finally, faith
healing implicitly and explicitly challenged the position of medicine in
society on many different levels.

EMBODYING GENDER

Women were not simply a part of the divine healing movement, their
bodies were the movement. It was primarily women's bodies that were
healed, and it was primarily women who testified to their experience.
Women formed the first informal networks that brought the divine
healing movement to Canada, and they continued to be actively involved over the next half century in almost every facet of the practice
of faith healing.

It could be argued that women's presence simply reflected the general dominance of women in North American religion in this period.
Ann Braude notes that "Women have made the existence of religious
institutions possible by providing audiences for preaching, participants
for rituals, and the material and financial support for physical
structures ... There could be no lone man in the pulpit without the
mass of women who fill the pews."[4] While the strong associations between women and religion certainly played a substantial role in determining women's participation in faith healing, it was not the only
factor at work. The rendering of women as fundamentally religious in
nature conjoined with bodily assumptions that deemed women to be
prone to sickness and ultimately unable to achieve a state of health
based on the universal male norms. Through the subjective experience
of the divine, women could lay claim to strength and to a wholeness of
body that elevated it to a "perfect" state. The gendered constructions
of the body were as important as the gendered constructions of religion
in shaping women's participation in faith healing.

Men were not excluded from the movement, but male participation
generally fell into two categories. By far the greatest majority of male
testimonials to faith healing came from the ranks of the clergy. Considering the religious idiom in which the experience of healing was expressed, this ministerial presence is not unexpected. Men in other
professions tended to dwell on their illness only if the affliction was received while engaging in a masculine activity, such as work accidents or
moral vices. Even after faith healing had moved away from the domestic realm of Victorian piety, men were generally reluctant to seek
anointing and were less likely to fall "under the power" at the evangelist's touch. In an age when the male physical body no longer "contained" the man but rather "*was* the man," the religious space of faith

healing held only a limited appeal as a therapeutic option with its emphasis on the inner subjectivity of religion as the basis for laying claim to health.[5]

Faith healing also appealed to women because its holiness ethos emphasized personal testimonials to healing. Healing narratives were a social space that followed an established pattern, but they were also flexible enough to allow a personal voice to emerge. Testimonials were a personal expression of healing and health that simultaneously spoke to devotional aspects of the subjective experience as well as wider cultural issues. Most proponents of divine healing disclaimed any antagonism towards medicine, but healing narratives offered a different story, portraying encounters with medicine in a manner less than complimentary. This cultural engagement cannot be neatly separated from the personal understanding of one's subjective religious experience. The two were intimately connected. Turning again to Robert Orsi in his study of Catholic women's devotions to the patron saint of hopeless causes: "The devotion inverted the illness meanings available in culture: isolation became connection, hopelessness hope, submission confidence, silence voice. The inverting saint turned the cultural experience of illness inside out."[6] The cultural practice of faith healing offers a unique perspective on the gendered self and illustrates how the larger social forces of medicine and religion were reshaped and negotiated on a personal level.

To suggest that women exercised agency through faith healing is not to remake them into liberal crusaders for women's health, nor would they likely characterize their actions as speaking to anything beyond the devotional purpose at hand. Neither should it be automatically assumed that the decision to adopt faith healing was always beneficial. Faith healing narratives spoke to successes, but failures, if resulting in death, precluded the personal voicing of dissonance. Certainly the death of Annie Harman suggests that in some cases the typical gendered roles were reversed, with her women relatives demanding the presence of a physician in childbirth and the husband refusing. It is difficult to judge whether Annie herself was following her husband's will out of personal conviction, deference, or a combination of both.

THE BODY IN SPACE

By far the most pliable aspect of the cultural practice of faith healing between 1880 and 1930 was the social geography that surrounded the body. In the nineteenth century, the gendered associations of religion and domestic space were aligned to make the bedroom the preferred site for treating the afflicted. This was a physical space that was increasingly privatized in Victorian homes as architectural trends separated bedrooms further away from one another and from other parts of the dwelling.[7] Access was restricted to family members except in cases of illness, when this space could be opened to allow a physician, minister, or close friend to attend.

The social structure of the divine healing movement was built on informal networks of women who visited at the bedside or corresponded by mail. The bedroom became the place for contemplating devotional literature, having testimonials read aloud, and engaging in long prayers. The experience of illness was often framed within the common parameters of Victorian martyrdom, and moral preparation was required to die the "good death." Faith healing both adopted this romantic imagery and subverted it by pronouncing the body healed. Just as the good death could offer a glimpse of the divine at the point of entering a final resting place, faith healing projected attention towards the divine, only it was the joy of bodily strength rather than the peaceful soul that was celebrated.

The institutions of the divine healing movement reflected these social configurations of experience and physical space. Divine healing conventions encouraged faith and offered anointing services, but they were not a place for ecstatic outbursts or miraculous cures. It was an experience that was often brought back to the bedroom, where God's grace could be further contemplated. Faith homes surrounded those seeking healing with familiar elements of Christian domesticity, and they provided matronly guidance to encourage both physiological and spiritual perfection.

A number of developments redefined the social space of healing in the twentieth century. The emergence of pentecostalism transformed the cultural practice of faith healing. Speaking in tongues was a bodily experience that marked one as part of the restored primitive church, and glossolalia as an expression of the spirit was most effective in the presence of other saints. The gatherings to support those seeking the baptism of the spirit could be as intimate as the earlier healing prayer networks, but this new activity took place in mission kitchens, after meetings, and "upper rooms," rather than in the personal private space of the bedroom. The modernization of hospitals and development of new diagnostic techniques correspondingly undercut the position of the bedroom and, by extension, the Victorian faith homes as proper sites for bodily restoration. The communal social space and instantaneous nature of tongues were characteristics transferred to the experience of faith healing despite the maintenance of a traditional theology of the atonement. Instances of gradual healings never disappeared, but noticeably more personal narratives offered healing as a "miracle" and even occasionally merged the baptism of the spirit with a cleansing of the body.

In Canada it was only after World War I that faith healing was constituted as a public spectacle within urban evangelistic campaigns. Various
evangelists had carried forth the message of divine healing long before,
but the actual practice of healing had never been "performed" quite like
it was in the hands of Aimee Semple McPherson, the Bosworth Brothers, and Charles Price. As a tool of evangelism, healing attracted crowds
and publicity on an unprecedented scale. The prospective body was now
systematically guided through preparatory meetings, required to fill out
cards, and lined up in rows to receive the touch of the faith healer. The
space of the arena was where the spirit moved bodies to swoon and
healed afflictions. As a public spectacle, the tendencies of faith healing
to become increasingly instantaneous and "miraculous" were reinforced. Instead of sharing devotional literature and healing testimonials
through the mail, souvenirs and books were sold at the arena door. The
silence that pervaded the bedroom (and the meditative anointing sessions of the early divine healing conventions) was replaced with professional music leaders who kept the audience entertained with song
services and provided soothing background music while the afflicted
were slain in the spirit.

KNOWING THE BODY

Writing to the *Vancouver Sun* in 1923, one "Doubting Thomas" commented that "If half of the reports of what Dr. Price is accomplishing,
in the way of faith healing, is true it is perfectly obvious that we shall
all have to readjust our opinions on the law of medicine as well as carefully review our own position in regard to religion."[8] It was a sentiment that echoed the reflections a half century earlier of William
Dawson LeSueur, who wondered how faith healing could have "any
general efficacy without the science of medicine being completely overturned?"[9] Despite the assurances of most faith healers that they had no
quarrel with the medical profession, the presence of faith healing could
not help but challenge medicine's claim to the body.
     Medicine exercised power within society on many different levels.
Doctors could physically take control of the body, such as when the
Maltby children were removed from their parents. Patent medicines
and drugs regulated the operation of the body and could potentially
control or suspend the will. Public health concerns gave medicine a social role in surveying the landscape in search of dangerous microbes
and watching for the conditions that could produce them. Medical authorities issued death certificates, acted as coroners, served as medical
health officers, and provided expert testimony in court cases.

Unquestionably the most dramatic opposition to these forms of direct medical control over the body was offered by the followers of Dowie in Canada. They routinely refused to report the presence of infectious diseases, as required by law, and actively resisted attempts to treat children even in cases where interventionist techniques were required immediately. Doctors were regarded with hostility and suspicion, attitudes confirmed by the administration and prescription of alcohol as a stimulant. The cosmological world of sin, sickness, and disease demanded an absolute trust in God's ability to heal the body, and any reliance upon human knowledge only hindered this engagement with the divine.

Given the belligerence of the Zionites, it was not entirely unexpected that legal action was taken against them. It is almost more surprising that so few cases actually made it to the courts. Both the state and medical authorities were very reluctant to take on the issue of faith healing, despite the fact that in the wake of Brooks's conviction in Victoria a legal precedent had been clearly established. With a few notable exceptions, even medical opinions on faith healing activities remained relatively muted; the most determined critics of the practice tended to be clergy rather than physicians. Perhaps the medical profession identified with the position of Dr H.O. McDiarmid, who described the predicament physicians faced in Brandon, Mantitoba, during Price's healing campaign in that city:

many of the doctors were asked why we did not do something. Why not denounce him from the hill-tops? Why not examine the cures and publish the findings? [F]or by our silence we were admitting that he possesses some mysterious power that we did not. What was the use when he always could reply that any failure to make a perfect cure rested with the afflicted themselves[?] ... I did proceed to enlighten some women in my office one day and tell them what I thought of such an impostor. I might say I did it only once. The amount of resentment shown by one of them convinced me that many people have all the education they can absorb and it is a mistake to try to pour new wine into an old crock.

McDiarmid's condescension notwithstanding, there is an underlying sense that despite the acknowledged authority of medicine in society and the possible challenge that the faith healers posed, physicians served their own interests best by simply maintaining a policy of "watchful waiting." In this manner, McDiarmid reports, "We did not – as a body at least – make enemies of those who were his faithful followers. We are still here carrying on as before."[10]

In the end it was not the visible forms of power and control that served as the main site of contestation between faith healing and medicine; rather it was in the epistemic realms that the rival priesthoods negotiated their respective claims to health and the body. The ability of medicine to diagnose the body through scientific categories endowed it with its professional authority. Bryan Turner suggests that "The basis of professional knowledge is cognitive rationality whereby the privileged status of the profession is grounded in a scientific discipline."[11] Of course, staking a claim to represent "cognitive rationality" does not necessarily make it so. When physicians were called as medical experts in the Maltby case, the competing theories of the exact cause of death exposed some of the vulnerabilities of this position. The writings of Lilian Yeomans demonstrate another manner in which many of the professional aspects of medicine could be undermined. Yeomans was particularly effective in this vein since, as a proponent of divine healing, she could also speak with the authority of a former physician.

Faith healing was able to supersede the scientific categories of medicine by reconstructing the body as a natural receptacle for the divine. Atonement theology was the means to redeem the body, not only from its carnal state but also from the materialistic categories of medicine. In his analysis of faith healing within the context of debates over the miraculous, Robert Bruce Mullin marginalizes the role of atonement theology, suggesting that the "real issue ... was the reality of supernatural activity in the natural order." It was only the "logic of the faith healing argument" that propelled it towards the rejection of medicine or other material means.[12] However, this supposition overlooks the unique role of the body as the site of religious experience and fails to account for the multitude of expositions on faith healing as part of the natural order, rather than as a transgression of it. A wide variety of fundamentalists and others continued to maintain that God's omnipotence could heal bodies in the modern age, but atonement theology reconstructed the body as a vessel designed to receive such divine infusions. The natural, and healthy, body was one in a state of divine communion, reaching beyond the soul to incorporate one's entire corporeal state. It was this remapping of the body that provided the divine healing movement with its impetus, and it is what facilitated faith healing's circumvention of the medicalized body.

Atonement theology provided an alternative construction of the body, but the encounter between the faith healers and medicine was also one of competing perceptual modes. Medicine saw disease as microbial germs and atomized the body as a series of discrete parts. The reality of disease and the body was therefore only visible through the microscope, the stethoscope, X-rays, or other diagnostic instruments.

Faith healing laid claim to the body through personal knowledge and experience, the same way that other religious experiences, such as conversion and sanctification, could be known and to which they could testify. This individual subjectivity was irrelevant to medical discourse, which preferred to diagnose bodies as anonymous entities. The practice of faith healing looked to the subjective bodily experience as the site for both a divine encounter and a physical manifestation which could be known and felt. It was in the personal religious understanding of the body in "divine health," that faith healing could challenge the epistemological position of medicine.

In Robertson Davies's *The Cunning Man*, the altar rail stands between the rival priesthoods of religion and medicine. A contest of wills pits Dr Jonathan Hullah against Rev. Charlie Iredale. And yet, this boundary proved to be more symbolic than real. The priest saw the sacred body of the venerable Father Hobbes as a holy relic, while the physician immediately tried to diagnose the external symptoms of the dead man as a series of signs that pointed towards a scientific truth. Religious understandings of the body did not end at the door to the church, just as medical ways of knowing the body were not confined to the hospital room. Nowhere were these transgressions more apparent than in the realm of faith healing, which resolutely intersected multiple fields of contested meanings.

To ask what faith healing "really is" betrays the historically specific sites of engagement that the practice of divine healing negotiated with its surrounding cultural worlds. It is where faith healing constructed bodily spaces and epistemologies, and how these constructions related to the subjective experience of religion, that offers a sense of its historical import. To take the "Lord for the Body" positioned the body within a sacred space, but the meanings behind this statement can only be understood in relation to the points of exchange that lay beyond the altar rail.

Notes

INTRODUCTION

1 Davies, *The Cunning Man*, 3–4, 481.
2 A.B. Simpson, *The Discovery of Divine Healing*; D.W. LeLacheur "Divine Healing," *Living Truths* 3 (October 1903): 189–97; Henry Wilson, "Four Foundations of Divine Healing," *Living Truths* 3 (October 1903): 209–12. This historical approach was also very strong in Gordon, *The Ministry of Healing*.
3 Cutten, *Three Thousand Years of Mental Healing*, 8.
4 Kelsey, *Healing and Christianity*; Kydd, *Healing Through the Centuries*.
5 Thomas, *Religion and the Decline of Magic*, 251.
6 For example, Janice Dickin maintains the importance of assessing "what was really going on" in the healing ministry of Aimee Semple McPherson. Many of her speculations on the role of stress, mass hypnotism, and the nature of functional cures, mirror the psychological theories of faith healing critics discussed in chapters 6 and 7. Dickin, "Take Up Thy Bed," 145–8.
7 Feher, "Introduction," 11.
8 Different varieties of the history of the body certainly existed before Foucault, as outlined in Outram, *The Body and the French Revolution*, 6–26. However, as Greg Ostrander notes, "the history of the body – how it became what it became, not biologically, but politically … this history has only begun to be written and it bears the name of Foucault." Ostrander, "Foucault's Disappearing Body," 169–70.
9 Foucault, "Nietzsche, Genealogy, History," 148.
10 Thomas Laqueur worries that such an approach will cause the body to "disappear entirely." His own work counters Feher's definition by examining "the *space* between [the real transcultural body] and its representations." Laqueur, *Making Sex*, 12.
11 Porter, "History of the Body," 208, 215.

12 This is not to suggest that Foucault denied that resistances were possible. After the production of power on a body "there inevitably emerge the responding claims and affirmations, those of one's own body against power, of health against the economic system, of pleasure against the moral norms of sexuality, marriage, decency … Power, after investing itself in the body, finds itself exposed to a counter-attack in that same body." Foucault, *Power/Knowledge*, 56. On the question of resistance and medicine, a brief overview is given in Lupton, "Foucault and the medicalisation critique."

13 Kleinman, *Writing at the Margin*, 97. Italics in original.

14 Good, *Medicine, Rationality, and Experience*, 62.

15 Orsi, "Everyday Miracles," 15.

16 Mullin, *Miracles*, 119. On Catholic faith healing in Canada, see Asselin, *Les Rédemptoristes au Canada*, Boglioni and Lacroix, eds. *Les Pèlerinages au Québec*, and Catta, *le Frère André*. One of the best works outlining popular devotions and healing in the nineteenth century is Kselman, *Miracles and Prophecies*.

CHAPTER ONE

1 Some of the issues surrounding the complex nature of medicalization are discussed in Morgan, "Contested Bodies, Contested Knowledges," which notes that "At its core 'medicalization' refers to the unintentional or intentional expansion of the domain of medical jurisdiction." 85. On medicine and secularization, see Turner, *The Body and Society* and his *Medical Power and Social Knowledge*.

2 Chappell, "The Divine Healing Movement"; Cunningham, "From Holiness to Healing"; Dayton, "The Rise of the Evangelical Healing Movement." Baer's "Perfectly Empowered Bodies" is the best work to date specifically on the movement, but the focus remains on leadership and theology. Mullin's *Miracles* offers an excellent intellectual context, but provides little on medicine, health, or the body.

3 Ostrander, *The Life of Prayer*, 17–22; Turner, "John Tyndall and Victorian Scientific Naturalism."

4 "Prayer and Natural Laws," *Canadian Baptist*, 2 March 1882, p. 4.

5 Mullin, *Miracles*, 16–25; LeMahieu, *The Mind of William Paley*, 175–7.

6 Two key works along this line include Thomas Reid's *Inquiry into the Human Mind on the Principles of Common Sense* (1764) and Dugald Stewart's *The Philosophy of the Active Powers and Moral Powers of Man* (1828). For a broad survey of these issues, see Haakonssen, *Natural Law and Moral Philosophy*.

7 David Bebbington provides a "quadrilateral" definition of evangelicalism that includes conversionism, activism, biblicism, crucicentrism. See Bebbington, *Evangelicalism in Modern Britain*, 1–19.

8 Gauvreau, *The Evangelical Century*, 62–4; Butler, *The Analogy of Religion*, 219. For an extended discussion on this passage, see Penelhum, *Butler*, 178–83.

9 Butler, *The Analogy of Religion*, 55. This aspect of Butler's thought is discussed in Roberts, "Butler and Immortality"; on Butler's use of intuition see Jeffner, "Our Knowledge of Ourselves."

10 Michael Gauvreau argues that Canada, isolated from the urban culture of polite learning, only selectively shared in Scottish enlightenment thought. Instead, Canadian evangelicalism developed an indigenous tradition that stressed Butler and a form of Baconian induction while displacing Paleyite natural theology and even much of Scottish philosophy. Having shifted their concern from the natural world to that of human society, especially through historical studies of humanity's relationship with God, Gauvreau suggests that Canadian evangelicals were better positioned to engage the challenge of Darwin. Gauvreau, *The Evangelical Century*, 15–19, 59–77. Other historians see Paley's natural theology as far more prevalent in Canada. See, for example, McKillop, *A Disciplined Intelligence*, chapter 3; Vaudry, *The Free Church*, 59–62; Berger, *Science, God, and Nature*, chapter 2.

11 Fidelis [Agnes Machar], "Prayer for Daily Bread," *Canadian Monthly and National Review* 7 (1875): 421. On Machar, see Brouwer, "The 'Between-Age' Christianity of Agnes Machar."

12 McKillop, "Preface" in *A Critical Spirit*, ix. On LeSueur's thought see also McKillop, *A Disciplined Intelligence*, 141–69, and Holland, *William Dawson LeSueur*.

13 LeSueur, "Prayer and Modern Thought," *Canadian Monthly and National Review* 8 (1875): 148.

14 Fidelis, "Prayer for Daily Bread," 423–4.

15 LeSueur, "Prayer and Modern Thought," 150–1. Italics in original.

16 Fidelis, "Prayer and Modern Doubt," *Canadian Monthly and National Review* 8 (1875): 229–30.

17 D.H. MacVicar, "Science and Prayer," *Presbyterian Review* 6 (1885): 472–3.

18 See chapters 4 and 7.

19 Crossley, *Practical Talks*, 72.

20 Dieter, *The Holiness Revival*, 18–25.

21 The classic work in this regard is Smith, *Revivalism and Social Reform*.

22 On Palmer see Raser, *Phoebe Palmer* and White, *The Beauty of Holiness*.

23 Raser, *Phoebe Palmer*, 121–2; Van Die, "A March of Victory and Triumph"; Bush, "James Caughey, Phoebe and Walter Palmer," 106–40. Although Canadian Methodism was clearly interlinked with these developments in American (and British) Methodism, measuring the depth of this influence is difficult. Neil Semple claims that while Canadian Methodists did welcome the renewed emphasis on sanctification, they rejected

Palmer's "easy road" to holiness. See Semple, *The Lord's Dominion*, 139. However, Marguerite Van Die notes that theologian Nathanael Burwash was heavily indebted to Palmer when he underwent a series of intense experiences in seeking sanctification, but later in life his autobiography replaced the emotion of his search with a calmer version of gradually improving his spiritual condition. Van Die, *Nathanael Burwash*, 80–1.

24 Bebbington, "The Holiness Movements," 219.

25 Bebbington, *Evangelicalism in Modern Britain*, 151–80; Marsden, *Fundamentalism and American Culture*, 72–80.

26 Sawatsky, "Unholy Contentions." See also Whiteley, "Sailing for the Shore" and Synan, *The Holiness-Pentecostal Tradition*, 22–82.

27 Crossley, *Practical Talks*, 72.

28 Fuller, *Alternative Medicine*, 20.

29 On Graham and Alcott, see Whorton, *Crusaders for Fitness*; Whorton, "Christian Physiology"; Sokolow, *Eros and Modernization*, chapters 5 and 7.

30 Quoted in Whorton, *Crusaders for Fitness*, 60.

31 As quoted in Haley, *The Healthy Body and Victorian Culture*, 17. Italics in original.

32 Miller, "From Edwards to Emerson." Miller later stated that he never intended to suggest a "direct line of intellectual descent" between Edwards and Emerson (p. 184–5), but the lineage runs very deep in American religious historiography. See, for example, Clebsch, *American Religious Thought*.

33 See Lears, "From Salvation to Self-Realization."

34 Notable works include Satter, *Each Mind a Kingdom* and Gottschalk, *The Emergence of Christian Science*. For a Canadian perspective, see Jasen, "Mind, Medicine, and the Christian Science Controversy."

35 Haller, *American Medicine in Transition*, 133. Satter, *Each Mind a Kingdom*, offers an excellent analysis of the New Thought Movement which provides a similar critique of the teleological assumptions of this narrative.

36 Albanese, "Physic and Metaphysic."

37 For an overview of homeopathic practices, see Kaufman, *Homeopathy in America*.

38 Connor, "Minority Medicine," 404.

39 Smith, *Lecture on the History of Medicine*, 36.

40 Through the homeopathic process, "the inert matter of the substance is destroyed, and the active principle is set free." Smith, *Lecture on the History of Medicine*, 34.

41 J.C. Peterson, quoted in Kaufman, *Homeopathy in America*, 114.

42 Nichol, *The Misrepresentations of Homoeopathy*, 132.

43 Connor, "Homeopathy in Victorian Canada," 123.

44 Kaufman, *Homeopathy in America*, 25–6.

45 Whorton, "Christian Physiology," 466.

46 Rosenberg, "The therapeutic revolution." On the shift from "natural" to "normal" see Warner, *The Therapeutic Perspective*, 83–91.

47 Roberts Bartholow, as quoted in Warner, *The Therapeutic Perspective*, 263.

48 See Rogers, "American Homeopathy."

49 As quoted in Gidney and Millar, *Professional Gentlemen*, 366.

50 Gidney and Millar, *Professional Gentlemen*, 339–40, 352–3.

51 Boardman, *Faith Work Under Dr. Cullis*, 14–16; Baer, "Perfectly Empowered Bodies," 50–1; Chappell, "The Divine Healing Movement," 104–43.

52 Boardman, *Faith Work Under Dr. Cullis*, 226.

53 [Cullis], *The Ninth Annual Report*, 44–5.

54 Cullis, *Dorothea Trudel*, 7.

55 On Cullis's influence, see Baer, "Perfectly Empowered Bodies," 50–75; Chappell, "The Divine Healing Movement," chapters 2 and 3

56 Chappell, "The Divine Healing Movement," 32–54.

57 Mullin, *Miracles*, 99.

58 Boardman, *The Great Physician*, 210. Mullin recognizes this distinction but views it as a theological means to reassert the supernatural in the nineteenth century. See Mullin, *Miracles*, 93–101.

59 Carter, *The Atonement*, 17–18.

60 Ibid., 18–19, 35. Italics in original.

61 Warfield, *Miracles*, 159–64.

62 A.B. Simpson, "Divine Healing and Natural Law," *Christian Alliance and Foreign Missionary Weekly* 13 (30 November 1894): 515.

63 See, for example, Dayton, *Theological Roots*.

64 Carter, *The Atonement*, 77–80.

65 Fuller, *Mesmerism and the American Cure of Souls*, 136.

66 Cullis, *Faith Healing*, 11–2. Baer notes that Cullis "hinted at" but never fully developed a position on the atonement. Baer, "Perfectly Empowered Bodies," 67.

67 Carter, *The Atonement*. This was noted by Cunningham, "From Holiness to Healing," 503. On the Willard Tract Repository, see also Chappell, "The Divine Healing Movement," 138–9.

68 Daniels, *Dr. Cullis*, 363. Also quoted in Cunningham, "From Holiness to Healing," 502.

69 Baer, "Perfectly Empowered Bodies," 150; *Historical Dictionary of the Holiness Movement*, s.v. "Carter, R. Kelso."

70 Carter, *"Faith Healing" Reviewed*, 108.

71 "Medical Missions," *Christian Alliance and Missionary Weekly* 8 (13 May 1892): 304–5.

72 Haley, *The Healthy Body*, 21.

73 Turner, *Body and Society*, 216–19.

CHAPTER TWO

1 *Triumphs of Faith* 1 (June 1881): 94.
2 Ibid., 110.
3 "Prayer for Miraculous Healing. No. 1," *Canadian Baptist*, 2 November 1882, p. 1.
4 On Judd, see Albrecht, "Carrie Judd Montgomery," and Carrie Judd, *The Prayer of Faith*.
5 Mallory, ed., *Touching the Hem*, 40, 71; *Triumphs of Faith* 8 (December 1888): 287–8.
6 The number of existing subscribers to the magazine was not revealed. *The Way of Faith* generally emphasized "entire sanctification" more than healing, but divine healing and healing testimonials did receive coverage, including testimonials from Canada. *The Way of Faith* (18 November 1896): 2; Ibid. (2 December 1896): 5; Ibid. (23 December 1896): 1; Ibid. (13 October 1897): 3.
7 Mallory, ed., *Touching the Hem*, back cover.
8 This sampling was based on 82 narratives in the *Triumphs of Faith*, published between 1890 and 1898; 56 (86 per cent) of the 65 gender-identified testimonials were from women, while only 9 (14 per cent) were written by men. In the *Christian Alliance and Foreign Missionary Weekly* between 1894 and 1896, 131 gender-identified first-person testimonials were printed; 108 (82 per cent) were from women while only 23 (18 per cent) were from men. The 1890s offered the most consistent period in which testimonials were featured in distinct sections of both serials, but similar patterns can be seen in the 1880s and well into the twentieth century. Third person testimonials and testimonials where the gender could not be accurately identified were excluded.
9 On Victorian domestic space, see Wright, *Moralism and the Model Home*, 29–32; Ward, *A History of Domestic Space*, 80–8; Adams, *Architecture in the Family Way*. Also useful is Ott, *Fevered Lives*, 80–6.
10 *Triumphs of Faith* 10 (March 1890): 71.
11 *Christian and Missionary Alliance* 28 (31 May 1902): 317.
12 Gainforth, *Experience of Divine Healing*, 20–2, 24.
13 Ibid., 23–4. See also Opp, "Healing Hands," 241.
14 *Triumphs of Faith* 2 (December 1882): 192.
15 *The Word, The Work and the World* 9 (July 1887): 20–1.
16 Daniels, *Dr. Cullis and His Work*, 247–8.
17 Gainforth, *Experience of Divine Healing*, 20–2. On Simpson's conventions in Canada, see chapter 3.
18 *Triumphs of Faith* 3 (March 1883): 71–2.
19 Palmer, *Faith and Its Effects*, 113.
20 Charles Ryder, "The Gospel of Healing," *Triumphs of Faith* 8 (January 1888): 8.

21 *Triumphs of Faith* 11 (June 1891): 117.
22 Ellen Hatch, "How the Lord Healed Me, or, Taking God At His Word," pamphlet, Reynolds Fonds, ATA.
23 Kimmel, *Manhood in America*, 120. See also Kasson, *Houdini, Tarzan and the Perfect Man*, and Rotundo, *American Manhood*.
24 Ott, *Fevered Lives*, 76.
25 See, for example, Simpson, *The Gospel of Healing*.
26 Brereton, *From Sin to Salvation*, 28–9.
27 See Albrecht, "Carrie Judd Montgomery," 107–10.
28 Reynolds, *Footprints*, 133; *Cornwall Freeholder*, 10 February 1893, p. 2.
29 Mrs A.C. Milliken of Nevada City, California, credited a version of Scott's narrative that was published in the *Pacific Herald of Holiness* as being an inspiration for her own healing from a heart condition. See *Christian Alliance and Foreign Missionary Weekly* 14 (June 1895): 382.
30 The following comparison is based on Judd, *The Prayer of Faith*, 9–19, and Scott, *Ten Years*, 76–91. In this latter work, Maggie's brother, Alexander, reproduces a long letter that appears to be the most complete version of her healing. Later in her life, Carrie Judd Montgomery produced a more thorough autobiographical account, *Under His Wings*.
31 Judd, *The Prayer of Faith*, 9–10.
32 Scott, *Ten Years*, 78–9. There is a wide range of historical work outlining the role of "hysteria" and various forms of other diseases related to women's "nerves." See, for example, Smith-Rosenberg, *Disorderly Conduct*, 195–216, and Showalter, *The Female Malady*, chapter 5.
33 Montgomery, *Under His Wings*, 53.
34 Scott, *Ten Years*, 79–80.
35 Mallory, ed., *Touching the Hem*, 11.
36 Poe, "The Philosophy of Composition." For an extended discussion on aspects of Victorian femininity and death, see Bronfen, *Over Her Dead Body*, and Holubetz, "Death-Bed Scenes."
37 Pat Jalland challenges the use of "beautiful death" to describe nineteenth-century deathbed scenes, arguing that an evangelical "good death" provides a better model, but I prefer to see them as complementary and overlapping, rather than competing, concepts. Jalland, *Death in the Victorian Family*, 7–8. Jalland's main target here is Philippe Ariès, *The Hour of our Death* (1981). Canadian scholars have been more accepting of Ariès, see Marshall, "Death Abolished."
38 Montgomery, *Under His Wings*, 53. Italics in original.
39 Judd, *The Prayer of Faith*, 14–16.
40 Scott, *Ten Years*, 89.
41 Barbour, comments in "Forum: Religion and American Autobiographical Writing," 13.
42 *Pentecostal Evangel*, 24 July 1920, p. 11.

43 Lyman et al., *20th Century Family Physician*, 883.

44 Pierce, *The People's Common Sense Medical Adviser*, 737. This popular home remedy book was in its seventy-eighth edition by 1914 and was widely available in Canada, having a publishing office in Bridgeburg, Ontario.

45 Mitchinson, *The Nature of Their Bodies*, 51.

46 Daniel Clark, "Faith Cure," *Knox College Monthly* 11 (February 1890): 200.

47 Carrie Judd Montgomery, "How to Keep in Health," *Pentecostal Evangel*, 23 July 1921, p. 5; Wilson, *The A, B, C, of Divine Health*, 25.

48 Brereton, *From Sin to Salvation*, chapter 3.

49 John Alexander Dowie, "Doctors, Drugs and Devils; or, The Foes of Christ the Healer," *Leaves of Healing* 2 (10 April 1896): 389.

50 Cullis, *Faith Healing*, 25.

51 Boardman, *The Great Physician*, 101.

52 Charles Ryder, "The Gospel of Healing," *Triumphs of Faith* 8 (January 1888): 17.

53 *Triumphs of Faith* 6 (May 1886): 117.

54 *Triumphs of Faith* 7 (April 1887): 91–6.

55 *Christian Alliance and Foreign Missionary Weekly* 16 (21 February 1896): 190.

56 *Triumphs of Faith* 1 (July 1881): 110.

57 *Triumphs of Faith* 11 (July 1891): 154–5.

58 Buckley, *Faith-Healing*, 6.

59 Davis, *Modern Miracles*, 147.

60 "Doctors, Drugs and Devils," *Leaves of Healing* 3 (29 August 1897): 697–8. From a different perspective, Ann Douglas Wood commented on the alleged immorality of physicians in "The Fashionable Diseases." See also Regina Morantz's response, "The Perils of Feminist History."

61 *Leaves of Healing* 4 (29 July 1899): 765–6.

62 Cullis, *Other Faith Cures*, 51–9.

63 *Christian Alliance and Missionary Weekly* 8 (28 January 1892): 75.

64 *Triumphs of Faith* 8 (December 1888): 287.

65 *Triumphs of Faith* 6 (October 1886): 237–40.

66 *The Word, Work and World* 3 (October 1883): 152.

67 This is not to suggest that women were without agency in interacting with medical culture. See for example, Mitchinson, "Agency, Diversity, and Constraints."

68 Boardman, *The Great Physician*, 183.

69 *Triumphs of Faith* 6 (October 1886): 239.

70 *Triumphs of Faith* 1 (November 1881): 175–6.

71 *Triumphs of Faith* 9 (June 1889): 141–3.

72 *Christian Alliance and Foreign Missionary Weekly* 17 (2 October 1896): 318.

73 *Christian Alliance and Foreign Missionary Weekly* 12 (9 March 1894): 275.

74 *Victoria Daily Colonist*, 21 March 1901, p. 6.

75 Pernick, *A Calculus of Suffering*, chapter 3. On the sexual politics that surrounded the issue of chloroform in the nineteenth century, see Poovey, "Scenes of an Indelicate Character."

76 "Doctors, Drugs and Devils," *Leaves of Healing* 3 (28 August 1897): 697–8.

77 *Canadian Alliance and Missionary Weekly* 9 (30 December 1892): 425. On Whittemore's later activities, see Robinson, ed., *Mother Whittemore's Records*.

78 *Globe*, 9 May 1889, p. 5.

79 Mrs Edward [Sarah] Mix, *Faith Cures*, 163.

80 *Leaves of Healing* 4 (26 February 1898): 350. See also Lilian B. Yeomans, "Delivered from the Use of Morphine," *Triumphs of Faith* 41 (September 1921): 199–203; Lilian B. Yeomans, "How I Found Healing," *Triumphs of Faith* 46 (June 1926): 101–5.

81 *Triumphs of Faith* 8 (June 1889): 141; 12 (August 1892): 191.

82 On Victorian domestic religion, see McDannel, *The Christian Home*.

83 *Triumphs of Faith* 9 (June 1889): 142.

84 See Adams, *Architecture in the Family Way*.

85 Montgomery, *Under His Wings*, 78.

86 *Christian Alliance and Foreign Missionary Weekly* 17 (17 July 1896): 63.

87 *Christian Alliance and Missionary Weekly* 4 (14 February 1890): 107.

88 Reynolds, *Footprints*, 189–90; *Peterborough Daily Examiner*, 29 May 1889, p. 4; *Triumphs of Faith* 10 (January 1890): 15–19.

89 R.L. Fletcher, "Bethany Home, Toronto," *Triumphs of Faith* 10 (May 1890): 105.

90 "First Fruits of 'Bethany Home,' Toronto," *Triumphs of Faith* 10 (July 1890): 161.

91 Buckley, *Faith Healing*, 57. Buckley originally made this comment in a *Century* article, which was promptly reprinted by the *Christian Guardian*. See "Faith Healing," *Christian Guardian*, 16 March 1887, p. 161.

92 [Cullis], *The Seventeenth Annual Report*, 33. Also quoted in Chappell, "The Divine Healing Movement," 148. While some instantaneous healings were reported, only rarely were these visible, public manifestations, such as those described in chapters 5 and 6.

93 *Hamilton Daily Spectator*, 6 February 1889, p. 4.

94 *Triumphs of Faith* 12 (April 1892): 95–6.

95 *Hamilton Daily Spectator*, 16 February 1889, p. 4.

96 James Hendrie Lloyd, "Faith Cures," *The Medical Record* (New York), 27 March 1886, p. 350. Also quoted in Baer, "Perfectly Empowered Bodies," 138.

97 *Christian Guardian*, 1 November 1882, p. 345.

CHAPTER THREE

1 As early as 1880 Charles Cullis's written material was circulating in Montreal, and one clergyman interested in divine healing, Rev. Hugh Johnston, went south to give an address at an Old Orchard convention in 1881. See [Cullis], *The Seventeenth Annual Report*, 94–5.
2 *Empire*, 9 May 1889, p. 5 and 7 May 1889, p. 5.
3 Salmon's remarkable life is covered extensively in Reynolds, *Footprints*. See also Reid, "Towards a Fourfold Gospel" and John Salmon, "Testimony," *Triumphs of Faith* 5 (December 1885): 287–8.
4 Exactly who Salmon encountered in London is not known, but W.E. Boardman had taken up residence there to complete his major exposition on faith healing, *The Lord that Healeth Thee* (1881), and by 1882 he had founded Bethshan healing home. Chappell, "The Divine Healing Movement," 201–5.
5 *Peterborough Daily Review*, 30 May 1889, p. 3; *Peterborough Daily Examiner*, 30 May 1889, p. 4; Reynolds, *Footprints*, 73.
6 *The Christian and Missionary Alliance*, 24 March 1900, p. 185; Salmon, "Testimony," *Triumphs of Faith* 5 (December 1885): 287–8.
7 *Evening Telegram*, 25 November 1886, p. 4.
8 Ellen Hatch, "How the Lord Healed Me, or, Taking God At His Word," pamphlet, Reynolds Fonds, ATA. See also *Triumphs of Faith* 7 (November 1887): 263.
9 *Canadian Independent*, 1 September 1886, p. 235.
10 *Canadian Independent*, 15 September 1886, p. 244, 248–9. This submission is included as an appendix in Reynolds, *Footprints*, 483–8.
11 See chapter 4.
12 Boardman, ed., *Record of the International Conference*, 160.
13 On Simpson's early years, see Thompson, *The Life of A. B. Simpson* and Reid, "'Jesus Only.'"
14 Nienkirchen, *A.B. Simpson and the Pentecostal Movement*, 6–12; Thompson, *The Life of A.B. Simpson*, 63–71.
15 Thompson, *The Life of A.B. Simpson*, 72–81.
16 *Christian Alliance*, January 1888, p. 10. On the "fourfold gospel" see Sawin, "The Fourfold Gospel."
17 The incident is discussed in Knowles, "Irreverent and Profane Buffoonery." See also Schuman, *A Bishop and His People*, 152–5; Henry Wilson, "What the Salvation Army has Done for Me," *Triumphs of Faith* 12 (April 1892): 85–7.
18 Wilson and Simpson, *Henry Wilson*, 40; Wilson, *The A, B, C, of Divine Health*, 9–10.
19 Reynolds, *Footprints*, 106–15, 117.
20 *Christian Alliance and Missionary Weekly* 4 (3 January 1890): 11.
21 On Howland's tenure as mayor, see Morton, *Mayor Howland* and Dochuk, "Redeeming the Time," chapter 3.

22 *Dictionary of Canadian Biography*, vol. 12, s.v. "Howland, William Holmes," 453–4; *Globe*, 9 May 1889, p. 5; *Christian Alliance and Missionary Weekly*, 17 and 24 October 1890, p. 243.

23 Sawatsky, "Looking for that Blessed Hope," 124–7; Reynolds, *Footprints*, 161.

24 *Peterborough Daily Examiner*, 29 May 1889, p. 4; *Peterborough Evening Review*, 29 May 1889, p. 3.

25 The exact relationship between Boston and Toronto is not clear. The third edition of Cullis's *Dorothea Trudel* (1872), lists Toronto as an office along with Boston and New York. The most extensive treatment of the depository is in Sawatsky, "Looking for that 'Blessed hope,'" chapter 4. However, Sawatsky appears to have been unaware of the early connection to Cullis.

26 *Books and Notions* 3, no. 4 (November 1886): 74.

27 Reynolds, *Footprints*, 127; *Christian Alliance*, 27 September 1889, p. 130.

28 *Christian Alliance and Missionary Weekly*, 2 October 1891, p. 209.

29 *Mail*, 13 December 1887, p. 4.

30 *Empire*, 9 May 1889, p. 6.

31 Reynolds, *Footprints*, 145–8.

32 The tensions between Fenton and Salmon were long-standing, and doctrinal questions over sinless perfection, as well as a certain amount of jealousy, also played a role in the division. See Fenton, *Letter to Rev. A.B. Simpson*, 6.

33 In the interim, meetings were held in Zimmerman's home. Reynolds, *Footprints*, 151, 182–7.

34 *Christian Alliance and Missionary Weekly* 7 (2 October 1891): 210.

35 *Empire*, 13 December 1893, p. 8.

36 *Toronto Evening News*, 12 December 1893, p. 1.

37 *Empire*, 9 May 1889, p. 6.

38 Buckley, *Faith-Healing*, 46–7.

39 *Empire*, 9 May 1889, p. 6.

40 *Christian Guardian*, 1 November 1882, p. 345.

41 Vance, *The Sinews of the Spirit*; Putney, *Muscular Christianity*. On the Social Gospel and gender, see Fishburn, *The Fatherhood of God* and Dean, "Writing Out of Orthodoxy," 28–37.

42 *Christian Guardian*, 22 November 1882, p. 374.

43 Ibid., 372.

44 *Peterborough Daily Review*, 30 May 1889, p. 3; *Peterborough Daily Examiner*, 30 May 1889, p. 4.

45 *Peterborough Daily Examiner*, 31 May 1889, p. 4.

46 Marvin R. Vincent, "Modern Miracles," *The Presbyterian Review* (New York) 4, no. 15 (July 1883): 496, 500.

47 *Christian Alliance and Missionary Weekly* 4 (3 January 1890): 8; *Triumphs of Faith* 11 (April 1890): 95–6. Carline's own testimony can be found in *Triumphs of Faith* 11 (March 1890): 71–2.

48 *Empire*, 9 October 1889, p. 8.

49 *Empire*, 10 October 1889, p. 8.

50 Taves, *Fits, Trances, & Visions*, 208–12, 226–32.

51 "Faith Cures," *Canada Lancet* 19 (October 1886): 57–8.

52 Daniel Clark, "Faith Cure," *Knox College Monthly* 11 (February 1890): 200–1.

53 Ibid., 198.

54 Ibid., 200.

55 *Christian Guardian*, 1 November 1882, p. 372.

56 See Walker, *Pulling the Devil's Kingdom*, Winston, "The Cathedral of the Open Air," and Marks, *Revivals and Roller Rinks*, chapters 6 and 7.

57 On the Salvation Army in Canada, see Moyles, *The Blood and Fire*. On Coombs and the early formation of the Army in Canada, see Ashley, "The Salvation Army in Toronto."

58 Reynolds, *Footprints*, 105, 124, 171; *War Cry*, 18 August 1888, p. 4–5.

59 *War Cry*, 14 March 1885, p. 2.

60 *War Cry*, 20 June 1885, p. 3.

61 *War Cry*, 23 March 1889, p. 12.

62 *War Cry*, 18 May 1889, p. 8; 6 April 1889, p. 9; 18 August 1888, p. 4. On British reports, see Robinson, "Bodily Compassion," 39–44. Robinson suggests that Boardman's 1885 International Conference on divine healing sparked some of the Army interest in the practice.

63 *War Cry*, 30 March 1889, p. 3.

64 *War Cry*, 3 March 1888, p. 6.

65 *Orders and Regulations*, 685–6.

66 *War Cry*, 9 March 1889, p. 2–3. Italics in original.

67 *Orders and Regulations*, 52–3.

68 *War Cry*, 6 April 1889, p. 13.

69 See Robinson, "Bodily Compassion," 46–9.

70 Ashley, "The Salvation Army in Toronto," 77–97; Moyles, *The Blood and Fire*, 123–33.

71 Reynolds, *Footprints*, 170–3. Philpott's testimony was included in Davis, *Modern Miracles*, but in this account he was only suffering from a sore throat. Six months earlier, Philpott had attended a divine healing meeting of Salmon and Zimmerman's but "was so disgusted at what I then thought was the biggest lot of humbug I had ever heard from religious teachers, that I left the service before it was half over." (Davis, 143–5). See also Philpott's account in *Christian and Missionary Alliance* 24 (19 May 1900): 329.

72 Reynolds, *Footprints*, 170–3, 369–70. On Philpott see also Elliott, "Knowing No Borders."

73 *War Cry*, 23 September 1899, p. 7.

74 *War Cry*, 29 October 1892, p. 12.

75 *War Cry*, 16 March 1889, p. 9.

76 Booth-Clibborn, *For the Word of God*, 34.

77 On Kate's hesitation towards Dowie and divine healing, see Robinson, "Bodily Compassion," 49–50, 52–4.

78 Booth, *Faith Healing*, 9–10, 32, 36, 53–5.

79 Robinson, "Wondrously kind to their Sinners," 7, and "Bodily Compassion," 18.

80 Booth, *In Darkest England*. See also Sandall, *The History of the Salvation Army*.

CHAPTER FOUR

1 The exact order and timing of Lilian Yeomans's search for a cure is difficult to follow. See *Leaves of Healing* 4 (5 February 1898): 295, and "How I Found Healing," *Triumphs of Faith* 46 (June 1926): 101.

2 One source suggests that Augustus was also addicted to chloral hydrate and died as a result of an overdose. See Gardiner, *Out of Zion*, 128.

3 Amelia served as the provincial president of the Dominion Women's Enfranchisement Association, president of the Manitoba Women's Christian Temperance Union, Vice-President of the Dominion WCTU, and was a founder and the first president of the Manitoba Equal Franchise Club. Cleverdon, *The Woman Suffrage Movement*, 49–53; *Dr. Amelia Yeomans*.

4 *Leaves of Healing* 4 (26 February 1898): 350–1.

5 *Leaves of Healing* 4 (22 January 1898): 255. My thanks to Glenn Gohr for calling this baptism to my attention.

6 Dowie published his account in tract form, entitled "The Gospel of Divine Healing and How I Came to Preach It." This was reprinted in Dowie, *The Personal Letters*, 314–16. Italics in original. See also Cook, *Zion City*, chapter 1.

7 Dowie did attract attention when word reached Victoria that the San Francisco *Examiner* was alleging that Dowie was thrown out of one church as a result of its own exposé of the "faith-healing fake." See Dowie and Dowie, *Our Second Year's Harvest*, 4–20. The evangelist was also involved in a strange incident when a man suffering from a "religious form" of "dementia" jumped through a window where Dowie was staying. See *Victoria Daily Times*, 30 August 1889, p. 4.

8 *Leaves of Healing* 3 (28 August 1897): 697; Cook, *Zion City*, 12–14.

9 Cook, *Zion City*, chapter 2.

10 Chappell, "The Divine Healing Movement," 302–4; Dowie and Dowie, *Our Second Year's Harvest*, 175.

11 Dowie, *The Personal Letters*, 314–15.

12 Only after a local minister criticized Dowie did the evangelist receive much interest from the press. *Globe*, 13 December 1890, p. 7; *Empire*, 13 December 1890, p. 6.

13 Quoted in Clark, *Of Toronto the Good*, 173.

14 *Empire*, 23 December 1890, p. 3; *Globe*, 23 December 1890, p. 8. W.J. Fenton reported that it was "the leaders in Mr. Salmon's meeting" who invited Dowie to Toronto. Fenton, *Letter to Rev. A.B. Simpson*, 8.

15 *Peterborough Daily Examiner*, 15 December 1890, p. 4; *Peterborough Daily Review*, 15 December 1890, p. 4.

16 *Peterborough Daily Review*, 16 December 1890, p. 3; 17 December 1890, p. 3.

17 Dowie disclosed that in his career he had laid hands upon 15,000 people so far, and of these, 11,000 had been women who often suffered from "female troubles and internal diseases which could not be spoken of in detail." *Peterborough Daily Review*, 22 December 1890, p. 3; see also *Peterborough Daily Examiner*, 22 December 1890, p. 4.

18 According to later accounts, Dowie left Toronto with a branch association of "hundreds of members," but within a few months "the Apostate Churches made havoc of it." *Leaves of Healing* 6 (24 February 1900): 574.

19 "Religious Unrest in Bruce," *Chesley Enterprise*, 23 February 1899.

20 Ibid.; *Leaves of Healing* 6 (11 November 1899): 83.

21 *Leaves of Healing* 5 (30 May 1899): 565.

22 *Paisley Advocate*, 23 February 1899.

23 *Leaves of Healing* 5 (18 February 1899): 321; 5 (20 May 1899): 566–7; "Religious Unrest in Bruce," *Chesley Enterprise*, 23 February 1899.

24 *Leaves of Healing* 5 (4 March 1899): 350–2.

25 *Leaves of Healing* 5 (11 November 1889): 566.

26 *Paisley Advocate*, 23 February 1899; *Leaves of Healing* 5 (4 March 1899): 350, and 5 (11 November 1889): 567.

27 *Leaves of Healing* 5 (18 February 1899): 307.

28 "Divine Healing," *Paisley Advocate*, 23 February 1899. For a history of Brant township, see Gateman, ed., *The History of the Township of Brant*.

29 *Leaves of Healing* 5 (18 February 1899): 305–10.

30 On McDonald, see *Chesley*, 309–11.

31 *Chesley Enterprise*, 25 May 1899.

32 Brooks and Brooks, *Conflicts in the Narrow Way*, 25.

33 *Leaves of Healing* 6 (28 October 1899): 7, 26; 5 (13 May 1899): 550.

34 Brooks and Brooks, *Conflicts in the Narrow Way*, 25–6, 64–5.

35 On stage and later in his memoirs, Brooks denied being a pro-Boer, but the *Enterprise* claimed that "hundreds of respectable witnesses" had heard him speak his "disloyal speech." *Chesley Enterprise*, 22 February 1900.

36 Threats of riots against the Zionites apparently predated the arrival of Eugene Brooks. According to Sara Brooks an earlier evangelist encountered a similar reaction when he held a baptismal service at the Leggetts' pond, although in the end only "jeers" were thrown by the "mob." Sara Brooks to Gordon Gardiner, 13 September 1938, file 27/7/6, Brooks Fonds, FPHC.

37 *Leaves of Healing* 6 (24 February, 1900): 571–2; 6 (3 March 1900): 595.

38 Brooks and Brooks, *Conflicts in the Narrow Way*, 26; *Leaves of Healing* 6 (3 March 1900): 595.

39 *Victoria Daily Colonist*, 28 November 1900, p. 8.

40 *Victoria Daily Colonist*, 24 November 1900, p. 8.

41 Testimony of R.L. Fraser, p. 56, Rex v. Brooks and Maltby, file 1901/44, Box 88, GR419, ABC.

42 Ivan Maltby to Willie Maltby, file 1901/44, Box 88, GR419; copy in GR429 file 1:1500/01, Box 7, ABC.

43 See Fee and Porter, "Public health"; Rosenberg, "Disease and social order"; Bilson, "Public health."

44 *Victoria Daily Colonist*, 23 November 1900, p. 8; 28 November 1900, p. 8; Inquisition into the death of Claude O. Maltby, pp. 12, 15, 18–19, file 123/00, GR1327, ABC.

45 *Victoria Daily Colonist*, 1 December 1900, p. 5; Reg. vs. Eugene Brooks and Willie W. Maltby, witness deposition of James Wilson, 30 November 1900, p. 13, file 1901/44, Box 88, GR419, ABC.

46 *Victoria Daily Colonist*, 28 November 1900, p. 8; Inquisition into the death of Claude O. Maltby, p. 12, file 123/00, GR1327, ABC.

47 *Victoria Daily Colonist*, 28 November 1900, p. 8.

48 The first count charged both Maltby and Brooks with manslaughter. The second count charged Maltby, as legal custodian, with criminal neglect. The third and fourth counts related to Brooks's contributing to the neglect of the child and for counselling Maltby in his actions. In the fifth count, Maltby was charged with criminal neglect while the sixth and seventh counts held Brooks liable for assisting Maltby in criminal neglect. The eighth charge held Maltby under common law with neglecting to care for or provide the necessities of life for his son. The ninth and tenth counts were laid against Brooks for acting as a principal in this neglect. The final charge jointly accused the two of conspiring to cause the death of Claude Maltby. *Victoria Daily Colonist*, 17 May 1901, p. 5.

49 *Leaves of Healing* 9 (25 May 1901): 146.

50 Testimony of E.C. Hart, p. 4, Rex v. Brooks and Maltby, file 1901/44, Box 88, GR419, ABC.

51 Testimony of Ernest Hall, p. 38, Rex v. Brooks and Maltby, file 1901/44, Box 88, GR419, ABC.

52 *Victoria Daily Colonist*, 24 May 1901, p. 8.

53 This outline of events is drawn from statements and depositions made by Brooks and Rogers. See Inquisition into the death of Cecil Alexander Rogers and Inquisition into the death of Victoria Helen Rogers, file 1902/03, Box 91, GR419, ABC.

54 Testimony of R.L. Fraser, p. 26, Rex v. Eugene Brooks and John Rogers, file 1902/03, Box 91, GR419, ABC.

55 C.A. Rogers Inquisition, file 1902/03, Box 91, GR419, ABC.

56 Four counts were related to each child's death for a total of eight. Section 209 of the Criminal Code related to failing to provide the necessaries of life, while Section 210 referred specifically to the legal responsibilities of a parent in this regard. See *Victoria Daily Times*, 26 September 1901, p. 3.

57 On the final day of the Rogers trial, the *Colonist* reported that Rogers claimed he had not had an opportunity to secure counsel, which the judge denied, declaring that proceedings had been delayed for two days for that purpose. Rogers then clarified that he had not received a reply from Chicago about whether or not to employ an attorney, which the judge dismissed as having little to do with him. Brooks spoke up for Rogers, claiming that the defendant did not have the means and that they had been unable to find Powell. McLean countered that he had dined with Powell only the night before. *Victoria Daily Colonist*, 26 September 1901, p. 5.

58 Testimony of Charles Joseph Fagan, Rex v. John Rogers, file 1902/03, Box 91, GR419, ABC.

59 Hall had stated earlier, "I presume the child died from diptheric poison, it may have died from strangulation the membrane was quite thick." V.H. Rogers Inquisition, file 1902/03, Box 91, GR419, ABC. See also *Victoria Daily Colonist*, 6 September 1901, p. 6. For the exchange between Rogers and Walkem see Testimony of John Rogers, p. 117, Rex v. John Rogers, file 1902/03, Box 91, GR419, ABC.

60 Testimony of Alice Rogers, p. 96, Rex v. John Rogers, file 1902/03, Box 91, GR419, ABC.

61 *Victoria Daily Times*, 26 September 1901, p. 3, 8.

62 *Victoria Daily Colonist*, 26 November 1901, p. 8.

63 Ibid.

64 In a written opinion on the appeal, Walkem pointed to the English precedent of *Reg. v. Senior* (1899), which similarly involved a case whereby a child had died in the custody of a father who also held religious beliefs against the use of medicine. *Victoria Daily Colonist*, 12 January 1902, p. 8. The King v. Brooks, *Canadian Criminal Cases* 5: 372–9. See also Reg. v. Senior, *Cox's Criminal Cases* 19: 219–24.

65 Testimony of Eugene Brooks, p. 37, Rex v. John Rogers, file 1902/03, Box 91, GR419, ABC.

66 Brooks and Brooks, *Conflicts in the Narrow Way*, 42. This "deferral" of sentence may have been simply the time between the original sentence and the appeal, since Sara claims that Brooks was in jail in January 1902, the same month the decision on the appeal was reached.

67 Ibid., 32–3.

68 *Leaves of Healing* 16 (15 April 1905): 817.

69 E. Brooks to M. Harman, 27 April 1904, File Harman 1904, Box 8, RG22-3891, AO.

70 Ibid.; E. Brooks to M. Harman, 5 July 1904, File Harman 1904, Box 8, RG22-3891, AO.

71 See depositions included in File Harman 1904, Box 8, RG22-3891, AO.

72 Deposition of Jane Ann Thompson, 31 August 1904, File Harman 1904, Box 8, RG22-3891, AO.

73 Depositions of Mary Thom, Catharine Thompson, Hewitt Thompson, 31 August 1904, File Harman 1904, Box 8, RG22-3891, AO.

74 Deposition of Marshall Harman, Rex v. Eugene Brooks, File Brooks 1905, Box 8, RG22-3891, AO.

75 Strange, "Wounded Womanhood."

76 Between the two trials, the Harman infant was kept in the care of Zionite brethren in Toronto. The sick child was eventually sent to Zion City and died before Brooks's trial began. E. Brooks to M. Harman, 5 September 1904, File Harman 1904 and Testimony of Marshall Harman, Rex v. Eugene Brooks, p. 27–8, File Brooks 1905, Box 8, RG22-3891, AO.

77 Ibid., p. 24.

78 Rex v. Eugene Brooks, *Ontario Law Reports* 11: 525–9. Brooks wrote in his memoirs that he opposed the use of lawyers in this case, preferring to "trust God alone as my Defense," but church authorities instructed otherwise. Brooks and Brooks, *Conflicts in the Narrow Way*, 36–9.

79 Ibid., 36.

80 On the legal aspects of Christian Science, see Schoepflin, *Christian Science on Trial*, which provides an appendix of court cases that includes Canada. On the Lewis case in particular, see Rex v. Lewis, *Ontario Law Reports* 6: 132–46.

CHAPTER FIVE

1 Glossolalia is generally defined as "the religious phenomenon of making sounds that constitute, or resemble, a language not known to the speaker." For the purposes of this chapter, I have simply allowed that phenomenon defined by pentecostals as "tongues" to stand as such, without a strict differentiation between the expression of sounds and utterances that do not resemble a known language and xenolalia, which is the speaking of an identifiable language that was unknown to the speaker. *New International Dictionary of Pentecostal and Charismatic Movements*, s.v. "glossolalia."

2 *Good Report* 1 (May 1911): 4.

3 See, for example, Dayton, *Theological Roots* and Baer, "Redeemed Bodies," 736–71.

4 *Promise* 1 (May 1907): 1–3.

5 *Promise* 15 (March 1910): 2. Miller, *Canadian Pentecostals*, 44.

6 Goff, *Fields White Unto Harvest*, 57–79; Anderson, *Vision of the Disinherited*, 47–57, 80–7.

7 Blumhofer, "The Christian Catholic Church"; Goff, *Fields White Unto Harvest*, 119–27; Brooks and Brooks, *Conflicts in the Narrow Way*, 68.

8 Martha had been partly raised by her uncle, a Methodist minister, in Kemptville, Ontario, while English-born Harry had spent a significant part of his life in Toronto before leaving for Zion City in 1901. Gardiner, *Radiant Glory*, 18–20, 93, 122. See also Parham, *The Life of Charles F. Parham*, 192–3.

9 Brooks and Brooks, *Conflicts in the Narrow Way*, 40.

10 Rumours about Parham were already starting to spread by the time he reached Toronto, and his reputation was destroyed when he was charged in Texas with sodomy. Parham was never indicted on this charge. See Goff, *Fields White Unto Harvest*, 135–42.

11 Menzies, "The Non-Wesleyan Origins," 91–4; Synan, *The Holiness-Pentecostal Movement*, 147–53

12 Miller, *Canadian Pentecostals*, 107–9. Donald Klan notes that there was great opposition to the Finished Work doctrine in Vancouver's Apostolic Faith Mission, led by the former Hornerite Rev. George S. Paul. See Klan, "Pentecostal Assemblies," 40–51. In general, however, the Finished Work doctrine found a home in northern urban centres where independent pentecostal missions dominated. This was in contrast to the southern states where existing holiness organizations had adopted the pentecostal baptism. Synan, *The Holiness-Pentecostal Movement*, 149–50.

13 A.G. Ward, "How the Pentecostal Experience Came to Canada," MS, PAOC, n.d., 6. See also the account in *Confidence* 2, no. 7 (July 1909): 146–8, 151–2. On King, see Alexander, "Bishop J.H. King."

14 McAlister's relationship to the Holiness Movement Church is provided by Klan, "Pentecostal Assemblies," 24, and Fuller, "The Effect of the Pentecostal Movement," 18. However, a more recent work could not find evidence that McAlister was actually an HMC evangelist. See Fortune, "Ralph Cecil Horner," 203.

15 Reed, "Aspects of the Origins of Oneness Pentecostalism"; Anderson, *Vision of the Disinherited*, 176–82. At issue were the words used in baptism: Matthew 18:19 uses the full trinity, while Acts 2:38 suggests that the apostles simply baptized "in the name of Jesus Christ." Since Acts was the authority for pentecostal gifts, and pentecostals regarded their work as a restoration of the apostolic church, this minor issue over formula held a deep theological significance.

16 Anderson, *Vision of the Disinherited*, 182. See also Blumhofer, *Restoring the Faith*, 127–35.

17 Argue, *A Vision and a Vow*, 23–37; Argue, *Contending for the Faith*, 9–12; Miller, "The Significance of A.H. Argue," 120–1.

18 As early as 1935 Argue dated his healing to 1906, but Simpson only made trips to Winnipeg in 1904, 1905, and 1908. A.H. Argue, "The Prayer of

Faith," *Word and Work* 57 (August 1935): 13; Reynolds, *Footprints*, 36–8. See also A.H. Argue, untitled MS, PAOC, n.d.

19 Miller, "A.H. Argue," 120–8; Argue, *A Vision and a Vow*, 37–42. In addition to eggs and stones, Argue mentions that the police were taking down the names of the faithful, but no indication is given of why they were doing so. See "To the Saints in all Lands," *Apostolic Messenger* 1 (February and March 1908): 2.

20 Miller, "A.H. Argue," 132–5. Argue, *Contending for the Faith*, 83.

21 *Promise* 12 (February 1909): 3.

22 *Promise* 15 (March 1910): 1, 2. Miller, *Canadian Pentecostals*, 105–7, 113.

23 The original formation of the PAOC was hampered by the fact that many western churches directly joined the Assemblies of God. The PAOC itself followed suit in 1920, becoming the Eastern Canadian District Council for the Assemblies. Disputes over the control of missionary funds led both the eastern and western Canadian districts to withdraw and re-form the PAOC in 1922. Miller, *Canadian Pentecostals*, 114–19.

24 Bedford, "A larger Christian life," 220–1, 225–6, 234–235. Nienkirchen, *A.B. Simpson and the Pentecostal Movement*, 74–92.

25 *Christian and Missionary Alliance* 29 (26 October 1907): 55.

26 G.A. Chambers, untitled MS, PAOC, n.d.

27 On this shift in terminology, see Dayton, *Theological Roots*, 87–108.

28 *Living Truths* 6 (September 1906): 513. Cited in Nienkirchen, 89.

29 Reynolds, *Footprints*, 293–4, 350–1; Nienkirchen, *A.B. Simpson and the Pentecostal Movement*, 95–6.

30 Reynolds, *Footprints*, 243.

31 Carter, *"Faith Healing" Reviewed*, 113–14. The issue of medicine and missionaries is covered extensively in Bedford, "A larger Christian life," 322–38.

32 Bingham, *The Bible and the Body*, 66. McKenzie, "Fundamentalism, Christian Unity, and Premillennialism," chapter 1.

33 *Winnipeg Tribune*, 12 October 1907, p. 11. Cited in Reynolds, 337.

34 *The Thirteenth Annual Report of the Christian and Missionary Alliance* (n.p., 1910), 77.

35 Miller, *Canadian Pentecostals*, 71–3.

36 *Holiness Worker* (May 1907): 2.

37 *Promise* 12 (February 1909): 8.

38 Bartleman, *How Pentecost Came*, 117.

39 *Confidence* 2, no. 1 (January 1909): 22–3; 2, no. 7 (July 1909): 146.

40 Reynolds does not mention Fisher in connection with Alliance work after 1901, but he is consistently mentioned in the memoirs of pentecostal pioneers. See G.A. Chambers, untitled MS, and A.G. Ward, "How the Pentecostal Experience Came to Canada," MS, PAOC, n.d., 6.

41 *Confidence* 2, no. 9 (September 1909): 211.

42 Gardiner, *Radiant Glory*, 140.

43 Montgomery, *Under His Wings*, 164–9.

44 Dayton, *Theological Roots*, 174.

45 *Globe*, 6 July 1901, p. 22.

46 Synan, *The Holiness-Pentecostal Tradition*, 108. This is not to suggest that Canada completely lacked radical holiness impulses, but groups such as the Gospel Workers Church, the Canada Holiness Association, and the Holiness Movement Church never exercised the scale of influence of their southern brethren, nor did they accept the atonement position on faith healing. On this tradition, see Whiteley, "Sailing for the Shore."

47 Cited in Gardiner, *Radiant Glory*, 158. See also Blumhofer, "Life on Faith Lines, Part 2."

48 Brooks and Brooks, *Conflicts in the Narrow Way*, 43–4.

49 Cited in Gardiner, *Radiant Glory*, 171. Italics in original.

50 Gardiner, *Radiant Glory*, 214–9. Blumhofer, "Life on Faith Lines, Part 2." Blumhofer notes that dispensationalism was also rejected.

51 On some of the roles of faith homes in this era, see Blumhofer, "Life on Faith Lines: Faith Homes," 10–2, 22.

52 Bedford, "A larger Christian life," 270–1.

53 Rosenberg, "Looking backward." See also Rosenberg, *The Care of Strangers*. For an excellent Canadian example of this process, see Gagan, *A Necessity Among Us*.

54 On the early years of Aimee Semple McPherson and the introduction of pentecostalism into the Ingersoll area, see Blumhofer, *Aimee Semple McPherson*, 23–50, 60–8, 75–9.

55 *Pentecostal Testimony* (Chicago) 1, no. 5 (1 July 1910): 5–6.

56 McPherson, *This Is That*, 255–6. The Mount Forest Revival is detailed most extensively in Easterbrook, "The Victory Mission."

57 Grant Wacker estimates that about one-third of early pentecostal worship services might have been devoted to testimonials. Wacker, *Heaven Below*, 58.

58 Ibid., 38–40. This is not to suggest that glossolalia could not actually occur in private. Lilian Yeomans told her mother that in her private prayers, she was speaking almost completely in tongues. It remained, however, a defining community experience in a manner different than sanctification. See Yeomans, ed., *Pentecostal Letters*, 32–3, 40.

59 *Good Report* (Ottawa) 1 (May 1911): 7.

60 As recorded in Zelma Argue, *A Vision and a Vow*, 41.

61 Wigger, *Taking Heaven*, chapter 5; Walker, *Pulling the Devil's Kingdom*, 88–93. For a Canadian example of Wesleyan holiness enthusiasm, see Greenshields, "Testimonies from a Camp Meeting," 218–31.

62 On Woodworth-Etter, see Warner, *The Woman Evangelist*.

63 *Good Report* (Ottawa) 1 (May 1911): 7.

64 *Promise* 15 (March 1910): 5.

65 George E. Fisher, "'I Will Come and Heal Him', Divine Healing in the Atonement," *The Latter Rain Evangel* (June 1910): 6–7.

66 Ibid., 7.

67 *Pentecostal Testimony* (Chicago) 1, no. 5 (1 July 1910): 6.

68 *Confidence* 8, no. 3 (August 1910): 178.

69 As noted earlier, "pentecostal" language was already part of the lexicon of many holiness and higher-life advocates, a line of continuity repeatedly stressed in modern pentecostal historiography. However, judging from published testimonials related to Canada, this linguistic shift had little impact on the *practice* of faith healing until the actual outbreak of tongues.

70 See, for example, Blumhofer, *Restoring the Faith.*

71 The history of dispensationalism is usually traced to John Nelson Darby (1800–1882), but it was popularised by Cyrus I. Scofield (1843–1921), particularly through the annotated notes of the influential *Scofield Reference Bible* (1909). The following eschatological discussion draws upon Sandeen, *The Roots of Fundamentalism*, 62–80, 222–4, and Weber, *Living in the Shadow*, 16–24, 45–51.

72 Dispensationalists traditionally regarded tongues and apostolic gifts as expressions that ended with passing of the Apostolic Age, a position used to attack pentecostalism. However, pentecostals reoriented the timeline to suggest that the Church Age actually began with the speaking of tongues, and its return in the twentieth century marked the end of the dispensation. See Wacker, "The Functions of Faith," 370.

73 A.H. Argue, "Jesus, the Great Physician," *Triumphs of Faith* 37 (October 1917): 223–5. This article had wide circulation, as it was reprinted in *Triumphs of Faith* 43 (June 1923): 130–2, 142; *Bridal Call* 4, no. 1 (June 1920): 6–7; *Pentecostal Testimony* (January 1921): 3. Argue's argument of the gifts marking both the opening and closing of the dispensation was the classic pentecostal modification of dispensationalism (see n. 72).

74 *Pentecostal Evangel*, 29 October 1921, p. 2.

75 Reprinted in *Christian Evangel*, 9 August 1919, p. 8.

76 *Word and Work* 44 (December 1923): 7.

77 "The Use of Handkerchiefs in the Ministry of Healing," *Pisgah* 1, no. 16 (January 1915): 11.

78 *Word and Work* 41 (April 1920): 32.

79 Griffith, "Female Devotional Practices," 197.

80 *Latter Rain Evangel*, August 1913, p. 22.

81 *Christian Evangel*, 4 October 1919, p. 3.

82 Yeomans, *Resurrection Rays*, 106–9. Lilian introduced the baptism to her mother, Amelia, three weeks later. Yeomans, ed., *Pentecostal Letters*, 9–10, 22–6.

83 Yeomans, *Resurrection Rays*, 66. Yeomans downplayed the issue of gifts in her writings, stressing the traditional continuities of healing as expressed throughout the ages. See Yeomans, *Healing from Heaven*, chapter 10.

84 Wacker, "The Functions of Faith," 357.

CHAPTER SIX

1 *Lethbridge Herald*, 5 June 1920, p. 13. Article was contributed, not written by the *Herald*'s regular correspondent.

2 Ibid., 29 May 1920, p. 7; 31 May 1920, p. 12; 2 June 1920, p. 11.

3 Ibid., 1 June 1920, p. 11.

4 Moore, *Selling God*. On Sunday see Dorsett, *Billy Sunday and the Redemption of Urban America*; McLoughlin, *Billy Sunday Was His Real Name*. For a perceptive examination of Canadian evangelists and their relation to consumer culture, see Kee, "Revivalism."

5 *Bridal Call* 4, no. 8 (January 1921): 12–13.

6 C. Swann, "The Revival Flame in Montreal," *Bridal Call* 4, no. 8 (January 1921): 6.

7 *Star*, 25 June 1920, p. 8.

8 Mews, "The revival of spiritual healing." On Hickson, see Mullin, *Miracles*, 237–49. Unfortunately, very little work has been done on Anglican spiritual healing in Canada.

9 *Word and Work*, October 1923, p. 1; Argue, *What Meaneth This?*, 18–19, 29.

10 *Revival Broadcast* 1 (December 1923): 7, 10.

11 *Lethbridge Herald*, 7 June 1920, p. 14.

12 *Revival Broadcast* 1 (December 1923): 6.

13 Argue, *What Meaneth This?*, 30–6; *Pentecostal Evangel*, 11 December 1920, p. 2–3.

14 *Bridal Call* 4, no. 8 (January 1921): 13.

15 Reynolds, *Rebirth*, 62–3.

16 "Report of the Canadian District 1921/22," *Annual Report of the Christian and Missionary Alliance*, May 1921, 1–2. Cited in Reynolds, *Rebirth*, 54–5.

17 On some of the theological differences, see Reynolds, *Footprints*, 383–96, and Kee, "Revivalism," chapter 3.

18 "B.B." stood for Burton Bell. On the Bosworths, see Perkins, *Joybringer Bosworth*; Blumhofer, *Restoring the Faith*, 135–47; F.F. Bosworth, *Bosworth's Life Story* (Toronto: Alliance Book Room, c.1921), pamphlet, file 3/8/5, FPHC.

19 *Star*, 18 April 1921, p. 22; 22 April 1921, p. 5; 25 April 1921, p. 17.

20 *Globe*, 27 April 1921, morning edition, p. 14. The *Globe* offered much more favourable coverage on the Bosworth campaign than other Toronto papers, since its publisher, William G. Jaffray, was a member of the Cana-

dian district committee of the Christian Alliance and the brother of an Alliance missionary, Rev. Robert A. Jaffray. See Reynolds, *Rebirth*, 50, 58.

21 *Star*, 25 April 1921, p. 17.

22 *Globe*, 23 May 1921, morning edition, p. 11.

23 Reynolds, *Footprints*, 388–97. Smith left the Alliance in 1926, and after travelling between Canada and the United States, he eventually took over the Toronto Gospel Tabernacle, which became the Peoples Church. On Smith see Kee, "Revivalism," chapter 3, and Neely, *Fire in His Bones*.

24 Reynolds, *Rebirth*, 69.

25 *Citizen*, 15 May 1924, p. 14.

26 *Citizen*, 17 May 1924, p. 6.

27 On Catholic pilgrimages in Quebec, see Boglioni et Lacroix, eds., *Les Pèlerinages au Québec*.

28 *Citizen*, 19 May 1924, p. 4, 9; 26 May 1924, p. 19. See also *Ottawa Journal*, 26 May 1924, p. 5.

29 *Citizen*, 26 May 1924, p. 4. The warnings to Catholics appear to have been more effective as only fifty identified themselves by the end of the campaign. *Ottawa Journal*, 24 May 1924, p. 5.

30 *Ottawa Journal*, 27 May 1924, p. 7; *Citizen*, 27 May 1924, p. 18.

31 *Citizen*, 23 May 1924, p. 33.

32 Charles S. Price, "A Personal Testimony," *Triumphs of Faith* 42 (August 1922): 176–80. "The Testimony of Dr C.S. Price," *Bridal Call* 6, no. 5 (October 1922): 11–13; Price, *The Story of My Life*. On McPherson's San Diego campaign, see Blunhofer, 156–64.

33 *Vancouver Daily Province*, 2 May 1923, p. 4; see also Johns, *History of Metropolitan Church*, 176–7, 274–6, and Price, *The Story of My Life*, 42–3.

34 On the Oliver campaign, see Burkinshaw, *Pilgrims in Lotus Land*, chapter 2. The literature on fundamentalism and modernism is voluminous, but in the period before 1925 the most important work is Marsden, *Fundamentalism and American Culture*. The Canadian scene is discussed in Opp, "Culture of the Soul."

35 Burkinshaw, 103; *Victoria Daily Colonist*, 1 May 1923, p. 5. The largest meeting was the final service, which both city newspapers placed at 9,000. The seats were filled within fifteen minutes of the doors opening. The crowd on the outside twice pushed open the doors to try to gain admittance, but were held back. One newspaper estimated that about 1,000 people remained outside at the exits, while 3,000 to 4,000 simply gave up after seeing the size of the crowd surrounding the arena. *Victoria Daily Times*, 30 April 1923, p. 20.

36 *Victoria Daily Colonist*, 14 April 1923, p. 1; *Victoria Daily Times*, 14 April 1923, p. 12.

37 *Victoria Daily Colonist*, 18 April 1923, p. 6; *Victoria Daily Times*, 18 April 1923, p. 5. For Knott's later testimony, see *Golden Grain* 4 (February 1930): 22.

38 *Victoria Daily Colonist*, 21 April 1923, p. 13; *Victoria Daily Times*, 21 April 1923, p. 12.

39 *Golden Grain* (1 November 1926): 25. Italics in original.

40 *Victoria Daily Times*, 23 April 1923, p. 18.

41 Ibid., 25 April 1923, p. 17; *Victoria Daily Colonist*, 25 April 1923, p. 14; 1 May 1923, p. 5.

42 *Vancouver Daily Province*, 7 May 1923, p. 11.

43 Price claimed that the figure of 250,000 came from the owner of the arena, but of course this number would not take into account those who came to more than one meeting. Price, *The Story of My Life*, 44. For the final day tally, see *Vancouver World*, 28 May 1923, p. 8.

44 McCrossan, who was on the platform with Price in Vancouver, related to the assembled crowd that a similar incident had happened in Albany, where fifty-four healings had broken out in the audience. *Vancouver Daily Province*, 11 May 1923, p. 3.

45 Ibid., 15 May 1923, p. 1, 17.

46 *Vancouver World*, 19 May 1923, p. 1.

47 Ibid., 25 May 1923, p. 3.

48 Ibid., 26 May 1923, p. 2.

49 *Vancouver Daily Province*, 10 May 1923, p. 11.

50 Ibid., 17 May 1923, p. 4.

51 *Vancouver World*, 19 May 1923, p. 3.

52 In addition to these fifteen in the Bosworth collection, one testimony was from a young boy. See Bosworth, *Christ the Healer*, 145–80. Similar numbers can be found in Price's book, *Miracles*, which is primarily a collection of personal healing narratives that included twelve accounts by women and only four by men. Of the men Price relied upon, all but one were ordained ministers.

53 Of the remaining cards, seven could not be identified according to sex and two were related to the healing of children. Price Fonds, FPHC. At the 1924 Bosworth meeting in Ottawa, those who sought healing were described as including "old men and young girls, boys and women." In other words, practically everyone except young men. See *Citizen*, 26 April 1924, p. 7.

54 *Winnipeg Tribune*, 11 May 1938, p. 15.

55 *Golden Grain* 4 (December 1929): 11, 22–3.

56 "A Notable Miracle – John Sproul Saved and Instantly Healed," *The Prophet* (Toronto) 1, no. 2 (April 1923): 3–4.

57 A. Oster, "Through the Cariboo to Calvary," *Golden Grain* 4 (November 1929): 25–8.

58 *Word and Work*, April 1920, p. 32; *Bridal Call* 4, no. 8 (January 1921): 14.

59 A.E. Cooke to Members of the Executive Committee in Charge of the Dr Price Evangelistic Campaign, 13 May 1923, Vancouver General Ministerial Association Fonds, VST. Also withdrawing their support were the Anglican Rev. A.H. Sovereign and liberal Baptist Rev. A.S. Lewis.

60 Obituary clipping, biography file, Cooke Fonds, VST; *New Outlook*, 18 November 1936, p. 1058. Eileen was sixteen years old in 1923.

61 Cooke was one of Vancouver's most controversial clerical figures, fighting numerous public battles in the name of progressive social reform. On these activities see Tillotson, "Politics and Moral Principles."

62 "Prostituting Religion," *Vancouver Sun*, 15 May 1923, p. 1.

63 Price, *Story of My Life*, 50–1.

64 It was reported that the line to the arena carried 199,725 passengers, "the majority of which were carried two [*sic*] and from the Price meetings." *Morning Albertan*, 6 October 1923, p. 2.

65 Gordon Atter Diary, 7 September 1927, PAOC. Despite his emphasis on tongues, Price still managed to draw crowds of more than 3,000 to the arena. Ibid., 10 September 1927. Even in 1923, however, there were undercurrents of tongues, and it was reported that at a meeting in Calgary, Price was speaking in Chinese. *Morning Albertan*, 15 September 1923, p. 3.

66 The relationship between evangelism, revivalism, and the modernist-fundamentalist controversies has recently become a point of debate in Canadian historiography. Christie and Gauvreau, *A Full-Orbed Christianity*, argues that social reformers within the church tapped the revivalist tradition to promote a new "social evangelism," and the early support of some social reformers for the Price campaign is cited as evidence of this alliance. However, this interpretation does not account for the subsequent divisions that occurred in Vancouver and elsewhere that clearly followed theological lines. In contrast, Phyllis Airhart and Neil Semple have both noted that the rhetoric and style of post-World War I revivals were largely the domain of conservative evangelicals and fundamentalists, not social reformers. See Airhart, *Serving the Present Age*, 123–41, and Semple, *The Lord's Dominion*, 391.

67 See Wacker, "Travail of a Broken Family," 505–28.

68 *Evening Telegram*, 13 May 1921, p. 21.

69 Ibid., 17 May 1921, p. 10.

70 Ibid., 16 May 1921, p. 16.

71 John Kidman, "The Montreal Revival," *Bridal Call* 4, no. 9 (February 1921): 16. On the Canadian experience of shell shock, see Brown, "Shell Shock."

72 Advertisements for these lectures were listed in the *Vancouver Daily Province*, 6 January 1923, p. 22; 20 January 1923, p. 22; 3 February 1923, p. 24; 17 February 1923, p. 24. On Du Vernet, see *Vancouver Daily Province*, 11 January 1923, p. 1; 27 January 1923, p. 15.

73 *Vancouver Sun*, 21 May 1923, p. 4.

74 Ibid., 16 May 1923, p. 5.

75 On the history of hypnotism, see Gauld, *A History of Hypnotism*.

76 A.E. Cooke, "Divine Healing Campaign in Vancouver," *Presbyterian Witness* (6 September 1923): 6.

77 *Vancouver Daily Province*, 11 May 1923, p. 27.

78 *Vancouver World*, 14 May 1923, p. 4.

79 *Vancouver Sun*, 19 May 1923, p. 5.

80 Walsh, *Cures*, 152–3.

81 *Vancouver Sun*, 18 May 1923, p. 3. The *Sun* received its lesson on hysteria from an "eminent medical man," who was an authority on the subject. He furnished the newspaper with two books on the subject: Archibald Church and Frederick Peterson, *Nervous and Mental Diseases* (1899) and William A. White and Smith Ely Jelliffe, *Modern Treatment of Mental and Hysterical Disease* (1913). Both titles were held in the library of the Vancouver Medical Association prior to June 1923. See "Books and Journals in the Vancouver Medical Association Library," ABCM.

82 *Vancouver Sun*, 14 May 1923, p. 4. This physician, Dr O. De Much, openly supported Price.

83 Gaebelein, *The Healing Question*, 108–9, 111.

84 W.H. Smith, "The Gospel of Redemption and Healing in Vancouver," *Presbyterian Witness* (7 June 1924): 7.

85 *Vancouver Sun*, 18 May 1925, p. 9.

86 *Morning Albertan*, 19 September 1923, p. 2.

87 *Calgary Herald*, 22 September 1923, p. 3. In Vancouver it was intimated that the physicians, while avoiding public controversy, were watching the Price campaigns carefully, and "all state that his methods 'are typical of the hypnotist.'" *Vancouver World* (15 May 1923): 2.

88 *Morning Albertan*, 12 September 1923, p. 4. Walsh's comments on the hysterically minded generation is in Walsh, *Cures*, 157.

89 "Prostituting Religion," *Vancouver Sun*, 15 May 1923, p. 1.

90 Brooks, *The Practice of Autosuggestion*, 66, 78–84. This book was one of the major English introductions of Coué's work and was often quoted by critics of faith healing.

91 Workman, *Divine Healing*, 28.

92 Fairbairn, *Faith Healing*, 19–20.

93 A.E. Cooke, "What Attitude Should the Church take toward 'Faith Healing?'" 28, 50, unpublished manuscript, 1926, Cooke Fonds, VST.

94 Cooke, "Divine Healing Campaign in Vancouver," 7–8.

95 "The Plague of Religious Quackery," *Gospel Witness*, 2 October 1930, p. 10. On Shields, see Russell, *Voices of American Fundamentalism*, and Tarr, *Shields of Canada*.

96 "An Example of a 'Religious Spree,'" *Gospel Witness*, 25 September 1930, p. 4.

97 Ibid.; "Religious Sprees," *Gospel Witness*, 26 June 1930, p. 1–3. Smith's tabernacle underwent many name changes and was known as both Metropolitan Tabernacle and Cosmopolitan Tabernacle before finally being named the Peoples Church in 1933. See Kee, "Revivalism," chapter 3.

98 Both Shields and Smith ran into difficulties with their choirs on this issue early in their careers. See Opp, "Culture of the Soul," 52–66.

99 T.T. Shields to B.A. Witten, 21 November 1931, JSBA.

100 "The Plague of Religious Quackery," *Gospel Witness*, 2 October 1930, p. 9. Shields had no problem in believing that God could heal through the intervention of natural law, but like Bingham he rejected atonement theology, denying that anyone could expect to receive bodily restoration. See "Is the So-Called Divine Healing a Fact or Fancy? What Saith the Scripture?" *Gospel Witness*, 2 October 1924, p. 1–11.

101 *Evangelical Christian*, July 1921, p. 200, newspaper clipping, Reynolds Fonds, ATA. The most forceful attack on faith healing from the fundamentalist perspective is Warfield, *Counterfeit Miracles*.

102 *Morning Albertan*, 3 October 1923, p. 4.

103 *Christian Guardian*, 20 June 1923, p. 4.

104 Cooke, "Divine Healing Campaign in Vancouver," 6.

105 *Calgary Herald*, 22 September 1923, p. 3.

106 Thomas J. McCrossan, "The Healing Mininstry of Dr. Price," *Golden Grain* 2 (November 1927): 22. Italics in original.

107 *Pentecostal Testimony*, October 1929, p. 12.

108 *Pentecostal Testimony*, November 1929, p. 5.

109 Smith, *The Great Physician*, 112.

110 Smith, *The Great Physician*, 110.

111 See Harrell, *All Things Are Possible*.

CHAPTER SEVEN

1 Mabel Potter Daggett, "Are There Modern Miracles?" *Ladies' Home Journal* 40 (June 1923): 20.

2 *Vancouver Daily World*, 16 May 1923, p. 4.

3 The release of the Vancouver report may have pre-empted the work of investigative committees in other cities, which might explain why no other significant reports were produced. However, many different committees were struck to examine Price's cures.

4 "Report on a Faith Healing Campaign held by C.S. Price in Vancouver, B.C., May 1923," 4, pamphlet, A.E. Cooke Fonds, VST. The report was widely reprinted, but this pamphlet version with its inclusion of photographs, was the most complete one. The official name of the report presented to the Ministerial Association was "Report of a Clerical, Medical and Educational Committee of Enquiry Into the Results of a Campaign of Healing held in Vancouver, B.C., in May 1923, by Rev. C.S. Price."

5 Some of the other members included A.H. Sovereign, A.S. Lewis and G.O. Fallis. The committee selection was criticized even within the ministerial association. The Presbyterian minister J.R. Robertson protested that the

investigation committee "is largely composed by those who previously and publicly announced their decision and proclaimed their opposition with reference to the matter to be investigated. This is specially true of the Chairman of the Committee, and I believe wisdom would have suggested that he should not have been on that Committee." J.R. Robertson to G.H. Hamilton, 21 July 1923, File 3, Box 1, Vancouver General Ministerial Association (VGMA) Fonds, VST.

6 In 1922 the British Columbia Medical Association (BCMA) had 5,000 copies of an address Cooke had given on chiropractic printed and distributed to the medical community, MLAS, and service clubs. Burnett was the head of the publicity and educational committee at the time, and he advocated this type of publicity campaign to "answer to the propaganda of the 'irregular cults.'" BCMA Minutes, 23 August 1922, annual meeting, and 20 October 1922, executive meeting, ABCM.

7 Description of the "Open Forum" is taken from the pamphlet, A.E. Cooke, "Evolution and Religion," A.E. Cooke Fonds. See also VGMA minutes, 7 April 1924, VGMA Fonds, VST.

8 Baptist Ministerial Association to G.H. Hamilton, 13 June 1923, File 3, Box 1, VGMA Fonds, VST.

9 "Report on a Faith healing Campaign," 2.

10 Ibid., 6.

11 Ibid., 5.

12 Ibid., 7–8.

13 Ibid., 7.

14 Ibid., 8.

15 Ibid., 13.

16 Ibid., 14.

17 Ibid., 16.

18 *Vancouver Daily World*, 14 May 1923, p. 4.

19 *Calgary Herald*, 22 September 1923, p. 3.

20 *Vancouver Sun*, 19 May 1923, p. 4.

21 O'Malley and his lawyer, J.O. Campbell, were refused in Police Court because in the magistrate's opinion the action "was being taken for the furtherance of law and order only." However, instead of trying to adopt formal mandamus proceedings to have the issue clarified, Campbell approached every magistrate and justice of the peace in the city and finally got the signature he required for a hearing. The sitting magistrate, however, promptly threw out the charges and rebuked Campbell for his abuse of procedure. *Morning Albertan*, 13 September 1923, p. 2; 14 September 1923, p. 2; 15 September 1923, p. 3.

22 Price Investigation Committee Minority Report, p. 2, VGMA Fonds, VST.

23 Ibid., 4–5.

24 VGMA Minutes, special meeting, 12 December 1923, VGMA Fonds, VST.

25 *Vancouver Sun*, 30 December 1923, p. 7.

26 *Golden Grain* 1 (November 1926): 25. Italics in original.

27 Price Investigation Committee Minority Report, p. 3–4, VGMA Fonds, VST.

28 Cooke, "What Attitude Should the Church Take Towards 'Faith Healing?'", MS, 1926, p. 38, A.E. Cooke Fonds, VST.

29 "Report on a Faith Healing Campaign," 15.

30 Ibid., 16.

31 Ibid., 9.

32 *Golden Grain* 1 (November 1926): 17, 20. Italics in original.

33 "A Statement given by Dr. Thos. J. McCrossan," *Golden Grain* 7 (July 1932): 30–1.

34 "Report on a Faith Healing Campaign," 10.

35 Ibid., 12.

36 This approach to photography has been informed by Sontag, *On Photography*, and Lalvani, *Photography, Vision, and the Production of Modern Bodies*.

37 On the development of X-rays, see Kevles, *Naked to the Bone*.

38 *Vancouver World*, 28 May 1923, p. 9.

39 According to one newspaper, Price suggested that he was having X-rays taken of people both before and after he had prayed for them. *Vancouver Sun*, 18 May 1923, p. 9.

40 "Report on a Faith Healing Campaign," 11–12.

41 Ibid., 8–9.

42 *Golden Grain* 15 (August 1940): 23–4.

43 *Golden Grain* 4 (October 1929): 19.

44 *Golden Grain* 1 (September 1926): 33–4

45 Tagg, *The Burden of Representation*; Trachentenberg, *Reading American Photographs*. For a Canadian example of religious uses of social documentary photography, see Opp, "Re-imaging the Moral Order."

46 *Golden Grain* 4 (December 1929): 5–34.

47 Mina Ross Brawner, "Jesus Destroys the Works of the Devil," *Triumphs of Faith* 46 (February 1926): 55–6.

48 Jane M. Baker, "Is Cancer Curable," *Christian Alliance and Missionary Weekly* 9 (23 September 1892): 201–2.

49 Elizabeth Keller, "An Experience," *Triumphs of Faith* 30 (June 1910): 129.

50 *Triumphs of Faith* 42 (May 1922): 117–18.

51 *Pisgah* 1, no. 15 (April 1914): 11.

52 For the medical history of Trout, see Hacker, *The Indomitable Lady Doctors*, 38–52, and Strong-Boag, "Canada's Women Doctors," 109–29.

53 Reynolds, *Footprints*, 160; *Christian Alliance and Missionary Weekly* (24 May 1902): 307.

54 "Service for the Master," *Triumphs of Faith* 32 (November 1912): 252.

55 Lilian B. Yeomans, "Delivered from the Use of Morphine," *Triumphs of Faith* 41 (September 1921): 202–3.

56 Application for Ordination Certificate, file 31/6/4, Lilian B. Yeomans Fonds, FPHC.
57 *Confidence* 4, no. 5 (May 1911): 111.
58 *Pisgah* 1 (August 1913): 4. Yoakum visited Calgary in 1911 and 1913. See *Morning Albertan*, 2 June 1911, p. 1; 8 June 1911, p. 7; 9 June 1911, p. 1; 28 May 1923, p. 8.
59 Blumhofer, *Aimee Semple McPherson*, 255–6. A number of letters attest to the strained relationship between Yeomans and certain elements within the Assemblies of God. See particularly Lilian B. Yeomans to J.R. Evans, 15 September 1930, and J.R. Evans to Lilian B. Yeomans, 18 September 1930, file 31/6/4, Lilian Yeomans Fonds, FPHC. She was ultimately successful in maintaining her credentials until her death in 1942.
60 "Resolution of Appeciation," 1930, file 31/6/4, Lilian B. Yeomans Fonds, FPHC.
61 Yeomans, *Balm of Gilead*, 26.
62 Yeomans, *Resurrection Rays*, 36–7.
63 Yeomans, *The Royal Road*, 4, 7.
64 Yeomans, *Healing from Heaven*, 24.
65 Yeomans, *Resurrection Rays*, 98.
66 Yeomans, *Divine Healing Diamonds*, 64.
67 Good, *Medicine, Rationality, and Experience*, 72.
68 Yeomans, *Resurrection Rays*, 51–2. Italics in original.
69 Lilian B. Yeomans, "He Brought Me Through," *Triumphs of Faith* 43 (March 1923): 54–7.
70 Cooke, "What Attitude Should the Church Take Towards 'Faith Healing?'", MS, 1926, p. 37, A.E. Cooke Fonds, VST.
71 *Vancouver Sun*, 20 May 1923, p. 6.
72 Biederwolf, *Whipping-Post Theology*. Biederwolf, a Baptist fundamentalist, declared that "No more intelligent, careful, and unbiased investigation could possibly be made than that of the Committee established for the purpose of making a study of the results which were supposed to attend the campaign of Charles S. Price in Vancouver, B.C. The report has been printed and given wide circulation." (p. 91)

CONCLUSION

1 Eggleston, *The Faith Doctor*.
2 Moody, *The Faith Healer*, 127. See also Mullin, *Miracles and the Modern Religious Imagination*, 208–10, 219–20.
3 Orsi, "Everyday Miracles," 7. Italics in original.
4 Ann Braude, comments in "Forum: Female Experience." See also Braude, "Women's History Is American Religious History."
5 Kimmel, *Manhood in America*, 127.

6 Orsi, *Thank You, St. Jude,* 183.
7 Ward, *A History of Domestic Space,* 80–8.
8 *Vancouver Sun,* 16 May 1923, p. 5.
9 William D. LeSueur, "Prayer and Modern Thought," *Canadian Monthly and National Review* 8 (1875): 151.
10 H.O. McDiarmid, "Community Psychosis," *Canadian Medical Association Journal* 14 (1924): 508.
11 Turner, *Medical Power,* 135.
12 Mullin suggests that the inclusion of healing in the atonement was simply a means to assert one type of miraculous power without being called upon to imitate Christ's feats, such as walking on water. Mullin, *Miracles,* 95, 99–100.

Bibliography

ARCHIVAL COLLECTIONS

ARCHIVES OF BRITISH COLUMBIA, VICTORIA, BRITISH COLUMBIA (ABC)
Government Record Series GR419, GR429, GR1327

ARCHIVES OF THE BRITISH COLUMBIA MEDICAL ASSOCIATION,
VANCOUVER, BRITISH COLUMBIA (ABCM)
Minutes and Records of British Columbia Medical Association
Minutes and Records of Vancouver Medical Association

ARCHIVES OF ONTARIO, TORONTO, ONTARIO (AO)
Government Record Series RG-22-3891, RG-8-1-1

ARCHIBALD-THOMSON ARCHIVES, ALLIANCE UNIVERSITY COLLEGE,
CALGARY, ALBERTA (ATA)
Lindsay Reynolds Fonds

BILLY GRAHAM ARCHIVES, WHEATON, ILLINOIS (BGA)
Aimee Semple McPherson Fonds
F.F. Bosworth Fonds
Oswald J. Smith Fonds

FLOWER PENTECOSTAL HERITAGE CENTER, SPRINGFIELD, MISSOURI
(FPHC)
F. F. Bosworth Fonds
Brooks Fonds
Charles Price Fonds
Dr. Lilian Yeomans Fonds
Dr. Amelia Yeomans Fonds
Amy Yeomans Fonds

JARVIS STREET BAPTIST CHURCH ARCHIVES, TORONTO, ONTARIO (JSBA)
Correspondence Files

PENTECOSTAL ASSEMBLIES OF CANADA ARCHIVES, MISSISSAUGA,
ONTARIO (PAOC)
Gordon Atter Diary
W.E. McAlister taped interview
Biographical Files

UNITED CHURCH OF CANADA, BRITISH COLUMBIA CONFERENCE
ARCHIVES, VANCOUVER SCHOOL OF THEOLOGY, VANCOUVER, BRITISH
COLUMBIA (VST)
A. E. Cooke Fonds
Vancouver General Ministerial Association Fonds
First Congregational Church Fonds
Hugh Dobson Fonds

PRINTED WORKS

Adams, Annmarie. *Architecture in the Family Way: Doctors, Houses, and
Women, 1870–1900.* Montreal and Kingston: McGill-Queen's University
Press, 1996.
Aikens, Alden Warren. "Christian Perfection in Central Canadian Methodism
1828–1884." Ph.D. diss., McGill University, 1987.
Airhart, Phyllis. *Serving the Present Age: Revivalism, Progressivism, and the
Methodist Tradition in Canada.* Kingston and Montreal: McGill-Queen's
University Press, 1992.
Albanese, Catherine. "The Poetics of Healing: Root Metaphors and Rituals in
Nineteenth-Century America." *Soundings* 63, no. 4 (winter 1980): 381–406.
– "Physic and Metaphysic in Nineteenth-Century America: Medical Sectarians
and Religious Healing." *Church History* 55 (1986): 489–502.
– *Nature Religion in America: From the Algonkian Indians to the New Age.*
Chicago: University of Chicago Press, 1990.
– "Body Politic and Body Perfect: Religion, Politics, and Thompsonian Medi-
cine in Nineteenth-Century America." In *New Dimensions in American Reli-
gious History*, edited by Jay P. Dolan and James P. Wind. Grand Rapids, MI:
Eerdmans, 1993.
Albrecht, Daniel E. "Carrie Judd Montgomery: Pioneering Contributor to
Three Religious Movements." *PNEUMA: The Journal of the Society for Pen-
tecostal Studies* 8 (fall 1986): 101–19.
Alexander, David A. "Bishop J.H. King and the Emergence of Holiness Pentecostalism." *PNEUMA: The Journal of the Society for Pentecostal Studies* 8
(fall 1986): 159–83.

Anderson, Robert Mapes. *Vision of the Disinherited: The Making of American Pentecostalism*. New York: Oxford University Press, 1979.

Argue, Zelma. *What Meaneth This?* n.p., 1923.

– *Contending for the Faith*. Winnipeg: Messenger of God Publishing House, 1928.

– *Garments of Strength*. Springfield, MO: Gospel Publishing House, 1935.

– "This Is My Dad." *TEAM* 3, no. 3 (1956): 3–6.

– *A Vision and a Vow or The Vision and Vow of a Canadian Maiden: The Story of My Mother's Life*. Springfield, MO: Gospel Publishing House, n.d.

Ariès, Phillipe. *The Hour of Our Death*. 2nd ed. Translated from the French by Helen Weaver. New York: Knopf, 1981.

Armstrong, David. "Bodies of Knowledge/Knowledge of Bodies." In *Reassessing Foucault: Power, Medicine and the Body*, edited by Colin Jones and Roy Porter. New York: Routledge, 1994.

Ashley, Stephen M. "The Salvation Army in Toronto, 1882–1896." Master's Thesis, University of Guelph, 1969.

Asselin, Jean-Pierre. *Les Rédemptoristes au Canada: Implantation à Sainte-Anne-de-Beaupré, 1878–1911*. Montréal: Bellarmin, 1981.

Atter, Gordon F. *The Third Force*. 3rd ed. Peterborough, ON: College Press, 1970.

Baker, Elizabeth V. *Chronicles of a Faith Life*. 1926. Reprint, New York: Garland, 1984.

Bainbridge, Harriette S. *Life for Soul and Body*. New York: Christian and Missionary Alliance Publishing Co., 1906.

Baer, Jonathan R. "Redeemed Bodies: The Functions of Divine Healing in Incipient Pentecostalism." *Church History* 70 (December 2001): 736–71.

– "Perfectly Empowered Bodies: Divine Healing in Modernizing America." Ph.D. diss., Yale University, 2002.

Barbour, John D., comments in "Forum: Religion and American Autobiographical Writing." *Religion and American Culture* 9 (winter 1999): 8–13.

Bartleman, Frank. *How Pentecost Came to Los Angeles*. 2nd ed. 1925. Reprinted as *Witness to Pentecost: The Life of Frank Bartleman*. New York: Garland, 1985.

Bebbington, David W. *Evangelicalism in Modern Britain*. London: Routledge, 1992.

– "The Holiness Movements in British and Canadian Methodism in the Late Nineteenth Century." *Proceedings of the Wesley Historical Society* 50 (October 1996): 203–28

Bedford, William Boyd, Jr. "'A Larger Christian Life': A.B. Simpson and the early years of the Christian and Missionary Alliance." Ph.D. diss., University of Virginia, 1992.

Bendroth, Margaret. "The Search for 'Women's Role' in American Evangelicalism, 1930–1980." In *Evangelicalism and Modern America*, edited by George Marsden. Grand Rapids, MI: Eerdmans, 1984.

– *Fundamentalism and Gender, 1875 to the Present*. New Haven: Yale University Press, 1993.

Berger, Carl. *Science, God and Nature in Victorian Canada*. Toronto: University of Toronto Press, 1983.

Biederwolf, William Edward. *Whipping-Post Theology, or Did Jesus Atone for Disease?* Grand Rapids, MI: Eerdmans, 1934.

Bilson, Geoffrey. "Public Health and the Medical Profession in Nineteenth-Century Canada." In *Disease, Medicine, and Empire: Perspectives on Western Medicine and the Experience of European Expansion*, edited by Roy MacLeod and Milton Lewis. London: Routledge, 1988.

Bingham, Rowland V. *The Bible and the Body, or, Healing in the Scriptures*. 2nd ed. Toronto: Evangelical Publishers, 1924.

Blumhofer, Edith L. "The Christian Catholic Apostolic Church and the Apostolic Faith: A Study in the 1906 Pentecostal Revival." In *Charismatic Experiences in History*, edited by Cecil M. Robeck. Peabody, MA: Hendrickson, 1985.

– "A Confused Legacy: Reflections of Evangelical Attitudes Toward Ministering Women in the Past Century." *Fides et Historia* 22 (1990): 49–61.

– "Life on Faith Lines: Faith Homes and Early Pentecostal Values." *Assemblies of God Heritage* (summer 1990): 10–12, 22.

– "Life on Faith Lines, Part 2: Zion Faith Homes." *Assemblies of God Heritage* (fall 1990): 5–7, 21–2.

– *Aimee Semple McPherson: Everybody's Sister*. Grand Rapids, MI: Eerdmans, 1993.

– *Restoring the Faith: The Assemblies of God, Pentecostalism and American Culture*. Urbana and Chicago: University of Illinois Press, 1993.

Boardman, W.E. *Faith Work Under Dr. Cullis, in Boston*. Boston: Willard Tract Repository, 1874.

– *The Great Physician (Jehovah Rophi)*. Boston: Willard Tract Repository, 1881.

– , ed. *Record of the International Conference on Divine Healing and True Holiness*. London: J. Snow and Bethshan, 1885.

Boglioni, Pierre, and Benoit Lacroix, eds. *Les Pèlerinages au Québec*. Québec: Les Presses de L'Université Laval, 1981.

Booth, William. *In Darkest England and the Way Out*. London: International Headquarters of the Salvation Army, 1890.

– *Faith-Healing. A Memorandum*. London: International Headquarters of the Salvation Army, 1902.

Booth-Clibborn, Arthur. *For the Word of God and the Testimony of Jesus*. London: Arthur Booth-Clibborn, 1902.

Bosworth, F.F. *Christ the Healer*. Miami Beach: F.F. Bosworth, 1924.

Braude, Ann. "The Perils of Passivity: Women's Leadership in Spiritualism and Christian Science." In *Women's Leadership in Marginal Religions*, edited by Catherine Wessinger. Urbana and Chicago: University of Illinois, 1993.

- Comments in "Forum: Female Experience in American Religion." *Religion and American Culture* 5 (winter 1995): 1–21.

Brereton, Virginia Lieson. *From Sin to Salvation: Stories of Women's Conversion, 1800 to the Present*. Bloomington and Indianapolis: Indiana University Press, 1991.

Brooks, C. Harry. *The Practice of Autosuggestion by the Method of Emile Coué*. Rev. ed. New York: Dodd, Mead and Company, 1922.

Brooks, Eugene, and Sara M. Brooks. *Conflicts in the Narrow Way*. Zion, IL: by the authors, 1944.

Brouwer, Ruth Compton. "The 'Between-Age' Christianity of Agnes Machar." *Canadian Historical Review* 55, no. 3 (1984): 347–70.

Brown, Tom. "Shell Shock and the Canadian Expeditionary Force, 1914–1918: Canadian Psychiatry in the Great War." In *Health, Disease, and Medicine: Essays in Canadian History*, edited by Charles G. Roland. Toronto: Hannah Institute, 1982.

Buckley, J.M. *Faith-Healing, Christian Science and Kindred Phenomena*. New York: Century Co., 1892.

Burkinshaw, Robert K. "Pentecostalism and Fundamentalism in British Columbia: 1921–1927." *Fides et Historia* 24 (winter/spring 1992): 68–80.

- *Pilgrims in Lotus Land: Conservative Protestantism in British Columbia, 1917–1981*. Montreal and Kingston: McGill-Queen's University Press, 1995.

Bush, Peter George. "James Caughey, Phoebe and Walter Palmer and the Methodist Revival Experience in Canada West, 1850–1858." Master's thesis, Queen's University, 1985.

Butler, Joseph. *The Analogy of Religion, Natural and Revealed, to the Constitution and Course of Nature*. Edited by B.F. Tefft. Cincinnati: L. Swormstedt and J.H. Power, 1851.

Burton, Robert. *The Anatomy of Melancholy*. 3 Vols. 1621. Reprint, London: J.M. Dent and Sons, 1932.

Bynum, W.F. *Science and the Practice of Medicine in the Nineteenth Century*. Cambridge: Cambridge University Press, 1994.

Carter, R. Kelso. *The Atonement for Sin and Sickness; or, A Full Salvation for Soul and Body*. Boston: Willard Tract Repository, 1884.

- *"Faith Healing" Reviewed after Twenty Years*. Boston: The Christian Witness Company, 1897.

Cayleff, Susan E. *Wash and Be Healed: The Water-Cure Movement and Women's Health*. Philadelphia: Temple University Press, 1987.

Chappell, Paul G. "The Divine Healing Movement in America." Ph.D. diss., Drew University, 1983.

Chesley ... Past & Present. Chesley: Chesley Centennial Committee, 1980.

Christie, Nancy, and Michael Gauvreau. *A Full-Orbed Christianity: The Protestant Churches and Social Welfare in Canada, 1900–1940*. Montreal and Kingston: McGill-Queen's University Press, 1996.

Clark, C.S. *Of Toronto the Good*. Montreal: The Toronto Publishing Company, 1898.

Clark, Daniel. *Mental Diseases*. Toronto: William Briggs, 1895.

Clebsch, William A. *American Religious Thought: A History*. Chicago: University of Chicago Press, 1973.

Cleverdon, Catherine. *The Woman Suffrage Movement in Canada*. 2nd ed. Toronto: University of Toronto Press, 1974.

Connor, J.T.H. "Minority Medicine in Ontario, 1795–1903: A Study of Medical Pluralism and Its Decline." Ph.D. diss., University of Waterloo, 1989.

– "Homeopathy in Victorian Canada and Its Twentieth-Century Resurgence: Professional, Cultural and Therapeutic Perspectives." In *Culture, Knowledge, and Healing: Historical Perspectives of Homeopathic Medicine in Europe and North America*, edited by Robert Jütte, et al. Sheffield: European Association for the History of Medicine and Health Publications, 1998.

Cook, Philip L. *Zion City, Illinois: Twentieth-Century Utopia*. Syracuse: Syracuse University Press, 1996.

Crossley, H.T. *Practical Talks on Important Themes*. Toronto: William Briggs, 1895.

Csordas, Thomas J. *The Sacred Self: A Cultural Phenomenology of Charismatic Healing*. Berkeley: University of California Press, 1994.

Cullis, Charles. *Dorothea Trudel; or, The Prayer of Faith*. Boston: Willard Tract Repository, 1872.

[Cullis, Charles] *The Ninth Annual Report of the Consumptives' Home, and Other Institutions connected with a Work of Faith*. Boston: Willard Tract Repository, 1873.

[Cullis, Charles] *The Tenth Annual Report of the Consumptives' Home, and Other Institutions connected with a Work of Faith*. Boston: Willard Tract Repository, 1874.

– *Faith Healing*. Boston: Willard Tract Repository, 1879.

[Cullis, Charles] *The Seventeenth Annual Report of the Consumptives' Home, and Other Institutions connected with a Work of Faith*. Boston: Willard Tract Repository, 1881.

– *Other Faith Cures; or, Answers to Prayer in the Healing of the Sick*. Boston: Willard Tract Repository, 1885.

Cunningham, Raymond J. "From Holiness to Healing: The Faith Cure in America 1872–1892." *Church History*, 43 (December 1972): 499–513.

Cutten, George Barton. *The Psychological Phenomena of Christianity*. New York: Charles Scribner's Sons, 1908.

– *Three Thousand Years of Mental Healing*. New York: Charles Scribner's Sons, 1911.

– *Speaking With Tongues: Historically and Psychologically Considered*. New Haven: Yale University Press, 1927.

Daggett, Mabel Potter. "Are There Modern Miracles?" *Ladies' Home Journal* 40 (June 1923): 20, 165–71.

Daniels, W.H. *Dr. Cullis and His Work*. Boston: Willard Tract Repository, 1885.

Davies, Robertson. *The Cunning Man*. Toronto: McClelland and Stewart, 1994.

Davis, H.T. *Modern Miracles*. Cincinnati: M.W. Knapp, 1901.

Dayton, Donald W. "The Rise of the Evangelical Healing Movement in Nineteenth Century America." *PNEUMA: The Journal of the Society for Pentecostal Studies* 4, 1 (spring 1982): 1–18.

– *The Theological Roots of Pentecostalism*. Peabody, MA: Hendrickson, 1987.

– "The Limits of Evangelicalism: The Pentecostal Tradition." In *Variety of American Evangelicalism*, edited by Donald W. Dayton and Robert K. Johnston. Downers Grove, Il: Intervarsity Press, 1991.

Dean, Joanna. "Writing Out of Orthodoxy: Lily Dougall, Anglican Modernist, 1858–1923." Ph.D. diss., Carleton University, 1999.

Dickin, Janice. "'Take Up Thy Bed and Walk': Aimee Semple McPherson and Faith-Healing." *Canadian Bulletin of Medical History / Bulletin canadien d'histoire de la médecine* 17 (2000): 137–53.

Dieter, Melvin Easterday. *The Holiness Revival of the Nineteenth Century*. Metuchen, NJ: Scarecrow Press, 1980.

Dochuk, Darren T. "Redeeming the Time: Conservative Evangelical Thought and Social Reform." Master's thesis, Queen's University, 1998.

Dorsett, Lyle W. *Billy Sunday and the Redemption of Urban America*. Grand Rapids, MI: Eerdmans, 1991.

Dowie, John Alexander. *The Personal Letters of John Alexander Dowie*. Edited by Edna Sheldrake. Zion City, Il: Wilbur Glenn Voliva, 1912.

Dowie, John Alexander, and Jane Dowie. *American First-Fruits*. San Francisco: Leaves of Healing, 1890.

– *Our Second Year's Harvest*. Chicago: International Divine Healing Association, 1891.

Dr. Amelia Yeomans. Winnipeg: Manitoba Culture, Heritage, and Recreation, 1985.

Drinka, George Frederick. *The Birth of Neurosis: Myth, Malady, and the Victorians*. New York: Simon and Schuster, 1984.

Easterbrook, Ian. "The Victory Mission Mount Forest: The Summer of 1915." *Wellington County History* 9 (1996): 17–32.

Elliott, David R. "Knowing No Borders: Canadian Contributions to American Fundamentalism." In *Amazing Grace: Evangelicalism in Australia, Britain, Canada, and the United States*, edited by George A. Rawlyk and Mark A. Noll. Montreal and Kingston: McGill-Queen's University Press, 1994.

Eggleston, Edward. *The Faith Healer*. 1891. Reprint, Ridgewood, NJ: Gregg Press, 1968.

Fairbairn, Robert E. *Faith Healing*. Toronto: The Ryerson Press, 1923.

Fee, Elizabeth, and Dorothy Porter. "Public health, preventive Medicine and Professionalization: England and America in the Nineteenth Century." In *Medicine in Society: Historical Essays*, edited by Andrew Wear. Cambridge: Cambridge University Press, 1992.

Feher, Michel. "Introduction." In *Fragments for a History of the Human Body: Part I*. Edited by Michel Feher. New York: Zone, 1987.

Fenton, W.J. *Letter to Rev. A.B. Simpson, Replying to His Strictures on the "Promotion of Companies."* Toronto: n.p., 1902.

Fishburn, Janet Forsyth. *The Fatherhood of God and the Victorian Family: The Social Gospel in America*. Philadelphia: Fortress Press, 1981.

Fortune, Clifford Roy. "Ralph Cecil Horner: Product of the Ottawa Valley." Master's thesis, Carleton University, 1999.

Foucault, Michel. *The Birth of the Clinic: An Archaeology of Medical Perception*. Translated from the French by A.M.S. Smith, 1973. Reprinted, London: Routledge, 1990.

– "Nietzsche, Genealogy, History." In *Language, Counter-memory, Practice: Selected Essays and Interviews*, edited by Donald Bouchard. Ithaca: Cornell University Press, 1977.

– *Power/Knowledge: Selected Interviews and Other Writings, 1972–1977*. Edited by Colin Gordon. New York: Pantheon Books, 1980.

– *The History of Sexuality. Vol I: An Introduction*. Translated from the French by Robert Hurley, 1978. Reprint, New York: Vintage Books, 1980.

Fuller, Clare. "The Effect of the Pentecostal Movement on Canadian Methodist and Holiness Churches 1906–1930." Unpublished research paper. On file at the Pentecostal Assemblies of Canada Archives.

Fuller, Robert C. *Mesmerism and the American Cure of Souls*. Philadelphia: University of Pennsylvania Press, 1982.

– *Americans and the Unconscious*. Oxford: Oxford University Press, 1986.

– *Alternative Medicine and American Religious Life*. Oxford: Oxford University Press, 1989.

Gaebelein, Arno Clemens. *The Healing Question*. New York: Our Hope, 1925.

Gainforth, Mary E. *Experience of Divine Healing and Salvation*. Salem, OR: F.P. Kyle, 1911. Canadian Institute for Historical Microreproductions (CIHM) No. 80830.

Gagan, David. *'A Necessity Among Us': The Owen Sound General and Marine Hospital 1891–1985*. Toronto: University of Toronto Press, 1990.

Gardiner, Gordon P. "Unquestionably The Apostle of Divine Healing in His Day." *Bread of Life* 6 (March 1957): 3–15.

– *Radiant Glory: The Life of Martha Wing Robinson*. Brooklyn: Bread of Life, 1962.

– *Out of Zion into All the World*. Shippensburg, PA: Companion Press, 1990.

Gateman, Laura M., ed. *History of the Township of Brant, 1854–1979*. Elmwood, ON: Brant Township Historical Society, 1979.

Gauld, Alan. *A History of Hypnotism*. Cambridge: Cambridge University Press, 1992.

Gauvreau, Michael. *The Evangelical Century: College and Creed in English Canada from the Great Revival to the Great Depression*. Montreal and Kingston: McGill-Queen's University Press, 1991.

Gidney, R.D., and W.P.J. Millar. *Professional Gentlemen: The Professions in Nineteenth Century Ontario*. Toronto: University of Toronto Press, 1994.

Goff, James R. *Fields White Unto Harvest: Charles F. Parham and the Missionary Origins of Pentecostalism*. Fayetteville: University of Arkansas Press, 1988.

Good, Byron J. *Medicine, Rationality, and Experience: An Anthropological Perspective*. Cambridge: Cambridge University Press, 1994.

Gordon, A.J. *The Ministry of Healing*. Boston: H. Gannett, 1882.

Gottschalk, Stephen, *The Emergence of Christian Science in American Religious Life*. Berkeley: University of California Press, 1973.

Greenshields, Malcolm. "Testimonies from a Camp Meeting," *North American Religion* 2 (1993): 218–31.

Griffith, R. Marie. "Female Devotional Practices in American Pentecostalism." In *Women and Twentieth-Century Protestantism*, edited by Margaret Bendroth and Virginia Brereton. Urbana and Chicago: University of Illinois Press, 2002.

Haakonssen, Knud. *Natural Law and Moral Philosophy: From Grotius to the Scottish Enlightenment*. Cambridge: Cambridge University Press, 1996.

Haller, John S. Jr. *American Medicine in Transition, 1840–1910*. Urbana: University of Illinois Press, 1981.

Harrell, David Edwin Jr. *All Things Are Possible: The Healing and Charismatic Revivals in Modern America*. Bloomington: Indiana University Press, 1975.

Haley, Bruce. *The Healthy Body and Victorian Culture*. Cambridge: Harvard University Press, 1978.

Harlan, Rolvix. *John Alexander Dowie and the Christian Catholic Apostolic Church in Zion*. Evansville, WI: R.M. Antes, 1906.

Historical Dictionary of the Holiness Movement. Edited by William C. Kostlevy. Lanham, MD: Scarecrow Press, 2001.

Holland, Clifford G. *William Dawson LeSueur, A Canadian Man of Letters: The Sage of Ottawa*. San Francisco: Mellen Research University Press, 1993.

Holubetz, Margarete. "Death-Bed Scenes in Victorian Fiction," *English Studies* 67 (1986): 14–34.

Jalland, Pat. *Death in the Victorian Family*. Oxford: Oxford University Press, 1996.

Jasen, Patricia. "Mind, Medicine, and the Christian Science Controversy in Canada, 1888–1910." *Journal of Canadian Studies* 32, 4 (winter 1998): 5–22.

– "Maternalism and the Homeopathic Mission in Late-Victorian Montreal."
   *Canadian Bulletin of Medical History / Bulletin canadien d'histoire de la mé-
   decine* 16 (1999): 293–315.
Jeffner, Anders. "Our Knowledge of Ourselves." In *Joseph Butler's Moral and
   Religious Thought*, edited by Christopher Cunliffe. Oxford: Clarendon
   Press, 1992.
Johns, Mrs. Thomas H. *History of Metropolitan Church, Victoria, BC.* MS, de-
   posited at Vancouver School of Theology, United Church of Canada Ar-
   chives, British Columbia Conference.
Jones, Charles Edwin. *A Guide to the Study of the Pentecostal Movement.*
   Metuchen, NJ: Scarecrow Press, Inc., 1984.
Joyce, James. *Ulysses.* 1922. Reprint, London: Bodley Head, 1960.
Judd, Carrie. *The Prayer of Faith.* Chicago: Fleming H. Revell, 1880.
Kasson, John. *Houdini, Tarzan and the Perfect Man: The White Male Body
   and the Challenge of Modernity in America.* New York: Hill & Wang, 2001.
Kaufman, Martin. *Homeopathy in America: the Rise and Fall of a Medical
   Heresy.* Baltimore: Johns Hopkins, 1971.
Kee, Kevin. "'The Heavenly Railroad': An Introduction to Crossley-Hunter
   Revivalism." In *Aspects of the Canadian Evangelical Experience*, edited by
   George A. Rawlyk. Montreal and Kingston: McGill-Queen's University
   Press, 1997.
– "Revivalism: The Marketing of Protestant Religion in English-Speaking
   Canada, with Particular Reference to Southern Ontario, 1884–1957." Ph.D.
   diss., Queen's University, 1999.
Kelsey, Morton T. *Healing and Christianity.* London: SCM Press, 1973.
Kevles, Bettyann Holtzmann. *Naked to the Bone: Medical Imaging in the
   Twentieth Century.* Reading, MA: Addison-Wesley, 1997.
Kimmel, Michael. *Manhood in America: A Cultural History.* New York: Free
   Press, 1996.
Klan, Donald Thomas. "Pentecostal Assemblies of Canada Church Growth in
   British Columbia from Origins Until 1953." Master of Christian Studies, Re-
   gent College, 1979.
Kleinman, Arthur. *Writing at the Margin: Discourse between Anthropology
   and Medicine.* Berkeley: University of California Press, 1995.
Knowles, Norman. "Irreverent and Profane Buffoonery: The Salvation Army
   and St. George's Anglican Cathedral, Kingston." In *St. George's Cathedral,
   Two Hundred Years of Community*, edited by Donald Swainson. Kingston:
   Quarry Press, 1991.
Kostlevy, William. *Holiness Manuscripts: A Guide to Sources Documenting the
   Wesleyan Holiness Movement in the United States and Canada.* Metuchen,
   NJ: Scarecrow Press, 1994.
Kselman, Thomas A. *Miracles and Prophecies in Nineteenth Century France.*
   New Brunswick: Rutgers University Press, 1983.

Kulbeck, Gloria G. *What God Hath Wrought: A History of the Pentecostal Assemblies of Canada*. Toronto: The Pentecostal Assemblies of Canada, 1958.

Kydd, Ronald. "Canadian Pentecostalism and the Evangelical Impulse." In *Aspects of the Canadian Evangelical Experience*, edited by George A. Rawlyk. Montreal and Kingston: McGill-Queen's University Press, 1997.

– *Healing Through the Centuries: Models for Understanding*. Peabody, MA: Hendrickson, 1998.

Lalvani, Suren. *Photography, Vision, and the Production of Modern Bodies*. Albany: State University of New York Press, 1996.

Laqueur, Thomas. *Making Sex: Body and Gender from the Greeks to Freud*. Cambridge: Harvard University Press, 1990.

Lears, T.J. Jackson. "From Salvation to Self-Realization: Advertising and the Therapeutic Roots of the Consumer Culture, 1880–1930." In *Culture of Consumption: Critical Essays in American History, 1880–1930*, edited by Richard Wightman Fox and T.J. Jackson Lears. New York: Pantheon, 1983.

LeMahieu, D.L. *The Mind of William Paley: A Philosopher and His Age*. Lincoln: University of Nebraska Press, 1976.

Lupton, Deborah. "Foucault and the Medicalisation Critique." In *Foucault: Health and Medicine*, edited by Alan Petersen and Robin Bunton. London: Routledge, 1997.

Lyman, Henry M. et al. *20th Century Family Physician*. Chicago: Charles C. Thompson Co., 1917.

Mallory, E.F., ed. *Touching the Hem: A Record of Faith Healing*. Montreal: F.E. Grafton, 1884. CIHM No. 64647.

Marks, Lynne E. *Revivals and Roller Rinks: Religion, Leisure, and Identity in Late-Nineteenth-Century Small-Town Ontario*. Toronto: University of Toronto Press, 1996.

Marsden, George M. *Fundamentalism and American Culture: The Shaping of Twentieth-Century Evangelicalism, 1870–1925*. Oxford: Oxford University Press, 1980.

Marshall, David B. *Secularizing the Faith: Canadian Protestant Clergy and the Crisis of Belief, 1850–1940*. Toronto: University of Toronto Press, 1992.

– "'Death Abolished': Changing Attitudes to Death and the Afterlife in Nineteenth-Century Canadian Protestantism." In *Age of Transition: Readings in Canadian Social History, 1800–1900*, edited by Norman Knowles. Toronto: Harcourt Brace, 1998.

McAlister, R.E. *God's Sovereignty in Healing*. Toronto: Full Gospel Publishing House, nd.

McCrossan, Thomas J. *Bodily Healing and the Atonement*. Seattle: T.J. McCrossan, 1930.

McDannel, Colleen. *The Christian Home in Victorian America, 1840–1900*. Bloomington: Indiana University Press, 1986.

McGinnis, Janice Dickin. "Aimee Semple McPherson: Fantasizing the Fanta-
sizer? Telling the Tale of a Tale-Teller." In *Boswell's Children*, edited by R.B.
Fleming. Toronto: Dundurn Press, 1992.

McLoughlin, William G. *Billy Sunday Was His Real Name*. Chicago: University of Chicago Press, 1955.

– "Aimee Semple McPherson: 'Your Sister in the King's Glad Service.'" *Journal of Popular Culture* 1, 3 (winter 1967): 193–217.

– *Revivals, Awakenings, and Reform*. Chicago: University of Chicago Press,
1978.

McKenzie, Brian Alexander. "Fundamentalism, Christian Unity, and Premillennialism in the Thought of Rowland Victor Bingham (1872–1942): A Study
of Anti-Modernism in Canada." Ph.D. diss., Toronto School of Theology,
1985.

McKillop, A.B. *A Disciplined Intelligence: Critical Inquiry and Canadian
Thought in the Victorian Era*. Montreal and Kingston: McGill-Queen's University Press, 1979.

–, ed. *A Critical Spirit: The Thought of William Dawson LeSueur*. Toronto:
McClelland and Stewart, 1977.

McPherson, Aimee Semple. *This Is That: Personal Experiences, Sermons and
Writings*. Los Angeles: Bridal Call Publishing, 1919.

Menzies, William W. "The Non-Wesleyan Origins of the Pentecostal Movement." In *Aspects of Pentecostal-Charismatic Origins*, edited by Vinson
Synan. Plainfield, NJ: Logos, 1975.

Mews, Stuart. "The Revival of Spiritual Healing in the Church of England
1920–26." In *The Church and Healing*, edited by W.J. Sheils. Oxford: Basil
Blackwell, 1982.

Meyer, Donald. *The Positive Thinkers: A Study of the American Quest for
Health, Wealth and Personal Power from Mary Baker Eddy to Norman Vincent Peale*. New York: Doubleday, 1965.

Miller, Perry. *Errand into the Wilderness*. Cambridge: Harvard University
Press, 1956.

Miller, Thomas William. "The Canadian 'Azusa': The Hebden Mission in Toronto." *PNEUMA: The Journal of the Society for Pentecostal Studies* 8 (spring
1986): 5–29.

– "The Significance of A.H. Argue for Pentecostal Historiography." *PNEUMA:
The Journal of the Society for Pentecostal Studies* 8 (fall 1986): 120–58.

– *Canadian Pentecostals: A History of The Pentecostal Assemblies of Canada*.
Mississauga: Full Gospel Publishing House, 1994.

Mitchinson, Wendy. "Causes of Disease in Women: The Case of Late 19th Century English Canada." In *Health, Disease and Medicine: Essays in Canadian
History*, edited by Charles G. Roland. Toronto: Hannah Institute, 1982.

– *The Nature of Their Bodies: Women and Their Doctors in Victorian Canada*. Toronto: University of Toronto Press, 1991.

- "'It's Not Society That's the Problem, It's Women's Bodies: A Historical View of Medical Treatment of Women." In *Intersections: Women on Law, Medicine and Technology*, edited by Kerry Petersen. Aldershot, England: Ashgate, 1997.
- "Agency, Diversity, and Constraints: Women and Their Physicians, Canada, 1850–1950." In *The Politics of Women's Health: Exploring Agency and Autonomy*, edited by Susan Sherwin. Philadelphia: Temple University Press, 1998.

Mix, Mrs. Edward [Sarah]. *Faith Cures and Answers to Prayers*. Springfield, MA: Springfield Printing Co., 1882.

Montgomery, Carrie Judd. *"Under His Wings," the Story of My Life*. Oakland: Office of Triumphs of Faith, 1936.

Moody, William Vaughn. *The Faith Healer*. Boston and New York: Houghton Mifflin, 1909.

Moore, R. Laurence. *Selling God: American Religion in the Marketplace of Culture*. Oxford: Oxford University Press, 1994.

Morantz, Regina Markell. "Making Women Modern: Middle Class Women and Health Reform in 19th Century America." *Journal of Social History* 10, 4 (June 1977): 490–507.

- "The Perils of Feminist History." In *Women and Health in America*, edited by Judith Walzer Leavitt. Madison: University of Wisconsin Press, 1984.

Morantz-Sanchez, Regina Markell. *Sympathy and Science: Women Physicians in American Medicine*. Oxford: Oxford University Press, 1985.

Morgan, Kathryn Pauly. "Contested Bodies, Contested Knowledges: Women, Health, and the Politics of Medicalization." In *The Politics of Women's Health: Exploring Agency and Autonomy*, edited by Susan Sherwin. Philadelphia: Temple University Press, 1998.

Morton, Desmond. *Mayor Howland: The Citizens' Candidate*. Toronto: Hakkert, 1973.

Moyles, R.G. *The Blood and Fire in Canada: A History of the Salvation Army in the Dominion 1882–1976*. Toronto: Peter Martin Associates Ltd., 1977.

Mullin, Robert Bruce. *Miracles and the Modern Religious Imagination*. New Haven: Yale University Press, 1996.

Murray, Andrew. *Divine Healing*. New York: Christian and Missionary Alliance Publishing Co., 1900.

Mussio, Louise. "The Origins and Nature of the Holiness Movement Church: A Study in Religious Populism." *Journal of the Canadian Historical Association* 7 (1996): 81–104.

Neely, Lois. *Fire in His Bones: The Official Biography of Oswald J. Smith*. Wheaton, IL: Tyndale House, 1982.

New International Dictionary of Pentecostal and Charismatic Movements. Revised and Expanded Ed. Edited by Stanley M. Burgess and Eduard M. Van der Maas. Grand Rapids, MI: Zondervan, 2002.

Nichol, Thomas. *The Misrepresentations of Homoeopathy.* Montreal: W. Drysdale & Co., 1888. [CIHM No. 39195]

Nicklaus, Robert L. et al. *All for Jesus: God at Work in the Christian and Missionary Alliance Over One Hundred Years.* Camp Hill, PA: Christian Publications Inc., 1986.

Nienkirchen, Charles W. *A.B. Simpson and the Pentecostal Movement: A Study in Continuity, Crisis, and Change.* Peabody, MA: Hendrickson, 1993.

Opp, James. "'Culture of the Soul': Fundamentalism and Evangelism in Canada, 1921–1940." Master's thesis, University of Calgary, 1994.

– "Healing Hands, Healthy Bodies: Protestant Women and Faith Healing in Canada and the United States, 1880–1930." In *Women and Twentieth-Century Protestantism*, edited by Margaret Bendroth and Virginia Brereton. Urbana: University of Illinois Press, 2002.

– "Re-imaging the Moral Order of Urban Space: Religion and Photography in Winnipeg, 1900–1920." *Journal of the Canadian Historical Association* 13 (2002): 73–93.

– "The Word and the Flesh: Religion, Medicine, and Protestant Faith Healing Narratives in North America, 1880–1910." *Social History / histoire sociale* 36, no. 71 (May 2003): 205–24.

Ostrander, Greg. "Foucault's Disappearing Body." In *Body Invaders: Panic Sex in America*, edited by Arthur Kroker and Marilouise Kroker. Montreal: New World Perspectives, 1987.

Ostrander, Rick. "The Life of Prayer in a World of Science: Protestants, Prayer, and American Culture, 1870–1930." Ph.D. diss., University of Notre Dame, 1996.

– *The Life of Prayer in a World of Science: Protestants, Prayer, and American Culture, 1870–1930.* Oxford: Oxford University Press, 2000.

Orders and Regulations for Field Officers of the Salvation Army. London: Headquarters of the Salvation Army, 1891.

Orsi, Robert. Comments in "Forum: The Decade Ahead in Scholarship." *Religion and American Culture* 3 (winter 1993): 1–8.

– *Thank You, St. Jude: Women's Devotion to the Patron Saint of Hopeless Causes.* New Haven: Yale University Press, 1996.

– "Everyday Miracles: The Study of Lived Religion." In *Lived Religion in America: Toward a History of Practice*, edited by David D. Hall. Princeton: Princeton University Press, 1997.

Ott, Katherine. *Fevered Lives: Tuberculosis in American Culture since 1870.* Cambridge: Harvard University Press, 1996.

Outram, Dorinda. *The Body and the French Revolution: Sex, Class and Political Culture.* New Haven: Yale University Press, 1989.

Palmer, Phoebe. *Faith and Its Effects, or, Fragments from My Portfolio.* 22nd ed., 3rd Canadian ed. Toronto: G.R. Sanderson, 1856. CIHM No. 64159.

– *The Way of Holiness.* 52nd ed. 1867. Reprinted as *The Devotional Writings of Phoebe Palmer.* New York: Garland, 1985.

– *The Life and Letters of Mrs. Phoebe Palmer,* edited by Richard Wheatley. 1881. Reprint, New York: Garland, 1984.

Paracelsus. *Selected Writings.* Edited by Jolande Jacobi. Translated by Norbert Guterman. 1951. Reprint, Princeton: Princeton University Press, 1973.

Parham, Sarah E. *The Life of Charles F. Parham: Founder of the Apostolic Faith Movement.* 1930. Reprint, New York: Garland, 1985.

Penelhum, Terence. *Butler.* London: Routledge and Kegan Paul, 1985.

Perkins, Eunice M. *Joybringer Bosworth: His Life Story.* Dayton: John J. Scruby, 1921.

Pernick, Martin S. *A Calculus of Suffering: Pain, Professionalism and Anesthesia in Nineteenth-Century America.* New York: Columbia University Press, 1985.

Pierce, R.V. *The People's Common Sense Medical Adviser.* 78th ed. Buffalo: World's Dispensary Medical Association, 1914.

Poe, Edgar Allan. "The Philosophy of Composition." In *The Works of Edgar Allan Poe.* Vol. 1. New York: Funk and Wagnalls, 1904.

Porter, Roy. "History of the Body." In *New Perspectives on Historical Writing,* edited by Peter Burke. University Park, PA: Pennsylvania State University Press, 1992.

Poovey, Mary. "'Scenes of an Indelicate Character': The Medical 'Treatment' of Victorian Women." In *The Making of the Modern Body: Sexuality and Society in the Nineteenth Century,* edited by Catherine Gallagher and Thomas Laqueur. Berkeley: University of California Press, 1987.

Price, Charles S. *Miracles, Being an Account of Miraculous Healings in the Charles S. Price Evangelistic Campaigns.* Seattle: Charles S. Price Publishing Co., 1930.

– *The Story of My Life.* Pasadena: Charles S. Price Publishing Co., 1935.

Putney, Clifford. *Muscular Christianity: Manhood and Sports in Protestant America, 1880–1920.* Cambridge: Harvard University Press, 2001.

Raser, Harold. *Phoebe Palmer: Her Life and Thought.* Lewiston, NY and Queenston, ON: Edwin Mellen Press, 1987.

Reed, David. "Aspects of the Origins of Oneness Pentecostalism." In *Aspects of Pentecostal-Charismatic Origins,* edited by Vinson Synan. Plainfield, NJ: Logos, 1975.

Reid, Darrel R. "'Jesus Only': The Early Life and Presbyterian Ministry of Albert Benjamin Simpson, 1843–1881." Ph.D. diss., Queen's University, 1994.

– "Towards a Fourfold Gospel: A.B. Simpson, John Salmon, and the Christian and Missionary Alliance in Canada." In *Aspects of the Canadian Evangelical Experience,* edited by George A. Rawlyk. Montreal and Kingston: McGill-Queen's University Press, 1997.

Reynolds, Lindsay. *Footprints: The Beginnings of the Christian and Missionary Alliance in Canada.* Toronto: Christian and Missionary Alliance in Canada, 1981.

– *Rebirth: The Redevelopment of the Christian and Missionary Alliance in Canada*. Willowdale, ON: Christian and Missionary Alliance in Canada, 1992.

Roberts, John H. *Darwinism and the Divine in America: Protestant Intellectuals and Organic Evolution, 1859–1900*. Madison: University of Wisconsin Press, 1988.

Roberts, T.A. "Butler and Immortality." In *Joseph Butler's Moral and Religious Thought*, edited by Christopher Cunliffe. Oxford: Clarendon Press, 1992.

Robinson, Barbara. "'Wondrously Kind to Their Sinners, but Very Severe on Their Saints': The Salvation Army and the Rhetoric of Health, 1880–1900." Paper presented at the Canadian Historical Association, University of Ottawa, 30 May 1998.

– "'Bodily Compassion': Values and Identity Formation in the Salvation Army, 1880–1900." Ph.D. diss., University of Ottawa, 1999.

Robinson, F.A., ed. *Mother Whittemore's Records of Modern Miracles*. Toronto: Missions of Biblical Education, 1937.

Rogers, Naomi. "American Homeopathy Confronts Scientific Medicine." In *Culture, Knowledge, and Healing: Historical Perspectives of Homeopathic Medicine in Europe and North America*, edited by Robert Jütte, et al. Sheffield: European Association for the History of Medicine and Health Publications, 1998.

Rosenberg, Charles E. *The Care of Strangers: The Rise of America's Hospital System*. New York: Basic Books, 1987.

– "Disease and Social Order in America: Perceptions and Expectations." In *Explaining Epidemics and Other Studies in the History of Medicine*, edited by Charles E. Rosenberg. Cambridge: Cambridge University Press, 1992.

– "The Therapeutic Revolution: Medicine, Meaning and Social Change in Nineteenth-Century America." In *Explaining Epidemics and Other Studies in the History of Medicine*, edited by Charles E. Rosenberg. Cambridge: Cambridge University Press, 1992.

– "Looking Backward, Thinking Forward: The Roots of Hospital Crisis." In *Explaining Epidemics and Other Studies in the History of Medicine*, edited by Charles E. Rosenberg. Cambridge: Cambridge University Press, 1992.

Rosenberg, Charles E., and Carroll S. Rosenberg. "Pietism and the Origins of the American Public Health Movement: A Note on John H. Griscom and Robert M. Hartley." *Journal of the History of Medicine and Allied Sciences* 23 (January 1968): 16–35.

Rosenkrantz, Barbara Gutmann. "Cart before Horse: Theory, Practice and Professional Image in American Public Health, 1870–1920." *Journal of the History of Medicine* (January 1974): 55–73.

Rotundo, E. Anthony. *American Manhood: Transformations in Masculinity from the Revolution to the Modern Era*. New York: Basic Books, 1993.

Russell, C. Allyn. *Voices of American Fundamentalism: Seven Biographical Studies*. Philadelphia: Westminster Press, 1976.

Salmon, John. *A Work of Faith and Labor of Love*. Toronto: n.p., 1903.

Sandall, Robert. *The History of the Salvation Army, 1883–1953, Social Reform and Welfare Work*. Vol. 3. London: Nelson, 1955.

Sandeen, Ernest R. *The Roots of Fundamentalism: British and American Millenarianism, 1800–1930*. Chicago: University of Chicago Press, 1970.

Satter, Beryl. *Each Mind a Kingdom: American Women, Sexual Purity, and the New Thought Movement, 1875–1920*. Berkeley: University of California Press, 1999.

Sawatsky, Ronald. "Unholy Contentions about Holiness: the Canada Holiness Association and the Methodist Church." *Papers of the Canadian Society of Church History 1982*.

– "William Stephen Rainsford (1858–1933): The Story of a Varied Life." *Canadian Society of Church History Papers* (1984): 1–25.

– "'Looking for That Blessed Hope': The Roots of Fundamentalism in Canada, 1878–1914." Ph.D. diss., University of Toronto, 1985.

Sawin, John. "The Fourfold Gospel." In *The Birth of a Vision*, edited by David F. Hartzfeld and Charles Nienkirchen. Regina: His Dominion, 1986.

Schoepflin, Rennie B. *Christian Science on Trial: Religious Healing in America*. Baltimore: Johns Hopkins University Press, 2003.

Schuman, Donald M. *A Bishop and His People: John Travers Lewis and the Anglican Diocese of Ontario, 1862–1902*. Kingston: Anglican Church of Canada, Ontario Synod, 1991.

Scott, Alexander Hugh. *Ten Years in My First Charge*. Toronto: Hart and Company, 1891.

Semple, Neil. *The Lord's Dominion: The History of Canadian Methodism*. Montreal and Kingston: McGill-Queen's University Press, 1996.

Shorter, Edward. *A History of Women's Bodies*. New York: Basic Books, 1982.

– *Bedside Manners: The Troubled History of Doctors and Patients*. New York: Simon and Schuster, 1985.

– *From Paralysis to Fatigue: A History of Psychosomatic Illness in the Modern Era*. New York: Free Press, 1992.

Showalter, Elaine. *The Female Malady: Women, Madness, and English Culture, 1830–1980*. New York: Pantheon, 1985.

Simpson, A.B. *Friday Meeting Talks, or Divine Prescriptions for the Sick and Suffering*. New York: Christian Alliance Publishing Co., 1899.

– *The Discovery of Divine Healing*. New York: Christian Alliance Publishing Co., 1903.

– *The Gospel of Healing*. Rev. ed. Harrisburg, PA: Christian Publications, 1915.

– *The Lord for the Body; with Questions and Answers on Divine Healing*. New York: Christian Alliance Publishing Co., 1925.

Sizer, Sandra S. "New Spirit, New Flesh: The Poetics of Nineteenth-Century Mind-Cures." *Soundings* 63, no. 4 (winter 1980): 407–22.

Sklar, Kathryn Kish. "All Hail to Pure Cold Water!" In *Women and Health in America*, edited by Judith Walzer Leavit. Madison: University of Wisconsin Press, 1984.

Smith, Oswald J. *The Great Physician*. New York: Christian Alliance Publishing Co., 1927.

Smith, Timothy L. *Revivalism and Social Reform*. Baltimore: Johns Hopkins University Press, 1980.

Smith, R.J. *Lecture on the History of Medicine and the Science of Homeopathy*. Toronto: Blackburn City Steam Press, 1857. CIHM No. 22632.

Smith-Rosenberg, Carroll. *Disorderly Conduct: Visions of Gender in Victorian America*. New York: Alfred A. Knopf, 1985.

Sokolow, James A. *Eros and Modernization: Sylvester Graham, Health Reform, and the Origins of Victorian Sexuality in America*. Rutherford: Fairleigh Dickinson University Press, 1983.

Sontag, Susan. *On Photography*. New York: Dell Publishing, 1977.

Spiher, H.H. *The World's Physician, Christ the Lord, or, Five-Hundred Testimonials of Divine Healing in Answer to Prayer through the Ages*. n.p., 1895.

Stackhouse, John G., Jr. *Canadian Evangelicalism in the Twentieth Century*. Toronto: University of Toronto Press, 1993.

Stanton, Robert L. *Gospel Parallelisms: Illustrated in the Healing of Body and Soul*. Buffalo: Office of Triumphs of Faith, 1883.

Stoesz, Samuel J. "The Doctrine of Sanctification in the Thought of A.B. Simpson." In *The Birth of a Vision*, edited by David F. Hartzfeld and Charles Nienkirchen. Regina: His Dominion, 1986.

Strange, Carolyn. "Wounded Womanhood and Dead Men: Chivalry and the Trials of Clara Ford and Carrie Davies." In *Gender Conflicts: New Essays in Women's History*, edited by Franca Iacovetta and Mariana Valverde. Toronto: University of Toronto Press, 1992.

Strong-Boag, Veronica. "Canada's Women Doctors: Feminism Constrained." In *A Not Unreasonable Claim: Women and Reform in Canada, 1880s–1920s*, edited by Linda Kealey. Toronto: Women's Press, 1979.

Synan, Vinson. *Holiness-Pentecostal Movement in the United States*. Grand Rapids, MI: Eerdmans, 1971.

Tagg, John. *The Burden of Representation: Essays of Photographies and Histories*. Basingstoke: Macmillan, 1998.

Tambiah, Stanley Jeyaraja. *Magic, Science, Religion, and the Scope of Rationality*. Cambridge: Cambridge University Press, 1990.

Tarr, Leslie K. *Shields of Canada*. Toronto: The Gospel Press, 1967.

Taves, Ann. *The Household of Faith: Roman Catholic Devotions in Mid-Nineteenth-Century America*. Notre Dame: University of Notre Dame Press, 1996.

– *Fits, Trances, & Visions: Experiencing Religion and Explaining Experience from Wesley to James*. Princeton: Princeton University Press, 1999.

Taylor, Malcolm. "A Historical Perspective on the Doctrine of Divine Heal-ing." *EPTA Bulletin: Journal of the European Pentecostal Theological Asso-ciation* 14 (1995): 54–84.

Thomas, Keith. *Religion and the Decline of Magic*. Rev. ed. Harmondsworth: Penguin, 1973.

Thompson, A.E. *The Life of A.B. Simpson*. New York: The Christian Alliance Publishing Co., 1920.

Tillotson, Shirley. "Politics and Moral Principles: Reverend A. E. Cooke and the Social Gospel, Vancouver, 1913–1924." Unpublished research paper, de-posited at Vancouver School of Theology, United Church of Canada, British Columbia Conference Archives.

Torrey, R.A. *Divine Healing. Does God Perform Miracles Today?* Grand Rap-ids: Baker Book House, 1924.

Trachtenberg, Alan. *Reading American Photographs: Images as History, Mathew Brady to Walker Evans*. New York: Hill and Wang, 1989.

Turner, Bryan S. *The Body and Society: Explorations in Social Theory*. Oxford: Basil Blackwell, 1984.

– *Medical Power and Social Knowledge*. London: Sage, 1987.

– , ed. *Regulating Bodies: Essays in Medical Sociology*. London: Routledge, 1992.

Turner, Frank Miller. *Between Science and Religion: The Reaction to Scientific Naturalism in Late Victorian England*. New Haven: Yale University Press, 1974.

– "John Tyndall and Victorian Scientific Naturalism." In *John Tyndall, Essays on a Natural Philosopher*, edited by W.H. Brock. Dublin: Royal Dublin Soci-ety, 1981.

Van Die, Marguerite. *An Evangelical Mind*. Montreal and Kingston: McGill-Queen's University Press, 1989.

– "A March of Victory and Triumph in Praise of 'The Beauty of Holiness': La-ity and the Evangelical Impulse in Canadian Methodism, 1800–1884." In *Aspects of the Canadian Evangelical Experience*, edited by George A. Raw-lyk. Montreal and Kingston: McGill-Queen's University Press, 1997.

Vance, Norman. *The Sinews of the Spirit: The Idea of Christian Manliness in Victorian Literature and Religious Thought*. Cambridge: Cambridge Univer-sity Press, 1985.

Vaudry, Richard W. *The Free Church in Victorian Canada, 1844–1861*. Water-loo: Wilfred Laurier University Press, 1989.

Wacker, Grant. "The Functions of Faith in Primitive Pentecostalism." *Harvard Theological Review* 77, nos. 3–4 (1984): 353–75.

– "The Holy Spirit and the Spirit of the Age in American Protestantism, 1880–1910." *Journal of American History* 72, no. 1 (June 1985): 45–62.

– "Marching to Zion: Religion in a Modern Utopian Community." *Church History* 54 (1985): 496–511.

- "Travail of a Broken Family: Evangelical Responses to Pentecostalism in America, 1906–1916." *Journal of Ecclesiastical History* 47, no. 3 (July 1996): 505–28.
- *Heaven Below: Early Pentecostals and American Culture.* Cambridge: Harvard University Press, 2001.

Waggett, J. MacPhail. *Mental, Divine and Faith Healings.* Boston: Richard G. Badger, 1919.

Walker, Mary. "Between Fiction and Madness: The Relationship of Women to the Supernatural in Late Victorian Britain." In *That Gentle Strength: Historical Perspectives on Women in Christianity,* edited by Lynda L. Coon, *et al.* Charlottesville: University Press of Virginia, 1990.

Walker, Pamela, J. *Pulling the Devil's Kingdom Down: The Salvation Army in Victorian Britain.* Berkeley: University of California Press, 2001.
- "A Chaste and Fervid Eloquence: Catherine Booth and the Ministry of Women in the Salvation Army." In *Women Preachers and Prophets through Two Millennia of Christianity,* edited by Beverly Mayne Kienzle and Pamela J. Walker. Berkeley: University of California Press, 1998.

Walsh, James J. *Cures: The Story of Cures That Fail.* New York: D. Appleton and Company, 1923.

Ward, Peter. *A History of Domestic Space: Privacy and the Canadian Home.* Vancouver: UBC Press, 1999.

Warfield, Benjamin B. *Miracles: Yesterday and Today.* Grand Rapids: Eerdmans, 1965. Reprint of *Counterfeit Miracles.* New York: Scribner's, 1918.

Warner, John Harley. *The Therapeutic Perspective: Medical Practice, Knowledge, and Identity in America, 1820–1885.* Cambridge: Harvard University Press, 1986.

Warner, Wayne. *The Woman Evangelist.* Metuchen, NJ: Scarecrow Press, 1986.

Weber, Timothy P. *Living in the Shadow of the Second Coming: American Premillennialism, 1875–1925.* Oxford: Oxford University Press, 1979.

Westfall, William. *Two Worlds: The Protestant Culture of Nineteenth-Century Ontario.* Montreal and Kingston: McGill-Queen's University Press, 1989.

White, Charles Edward. *The Beauty of Holiness: Phoebe Palmer as Theologian, Revivalist, Feminist, and Humanitarian.* Grand Rapids: Francis Asbury Press, 1986.

Whiteley, Marilyn Färdig. "Sailing for the Shore: The Canadian Holiness Tradition." In *Aspects of the Canadian Evangelical Experience,* edited by George A. Rawlyk. Montreal and Kingston: McGill-Queen's University Press, 1997.

Whorton, James C. *Crusaders for Fitness: The History of American Health Reformers.* Princeton: Princeton University Press, 1982.
- "'Christian Physiology': William Alcott's Prescription for the Millennium." *Bulletin of the History of Medicine* 49 (1975): 466–81.

Wigger, John H. *Taking Heaven by Storm: Methodism and the Rise of Popular Christianity in America*. Oxford: Oxford University Press, 1998.

Wilson, Henry. *The A, B, C, of Divine Health*. New York: Alliance Press Co., 1908.

Wilson, Madèle, and A. B. Simpson. *Henry Wilson, One of God's Best*. New York: Alliance Press Company, 1908.

Wind, James P. "Religion and the Great American Argument about Health." In *New Dimensions in American Religious History*, edited by Jay P. Dolan and James P. Wind. Grand Rapids, MI: Eerdmans, 1993.

Wood, Ann Douglas. "'The Fashionable Diseases': Women's Complaints and Their Treatment in Nineteenth-Century America." In *Women and Health in America*, edited by Judith Walzer Leavitt. Madison: University of Wisconsin, 1984.

Workman, George Coulson. *Divine Healing or True Science vs. Christian Science and Faith-Cure*. Toronto: Ryerson Press, 1923.

Wright, Gwendolyn. *Moralism and the Model Home*. Chicago: University of Chicago Press, 1980.

Yeomans, Amelia, ed. *Pentecostal Letters*. Columbia, SC: J.M. Pike, c. 1908.

Yeomans, Lilian B. *Healing from Heaven*. Springfield, MO: Gospel Publishing House, 1926.

– *Resurrection Rays*. Springfield, MO: Gospel Publishing House, 1930.

– *Divine Healing Diamonds*. Springfield, MO: Gospel Publishing House, 1933.

– *Balm of Gilead*. Springfield, MO: Gospel Publishing House, 1936.

– *The Royal Road to Healthville*. Springfield, MO: Gospel Publishing House, 1938.

– *The Hiding Place*. Springfield, MO: Gospel Publishing House, n.d.

Index

Page numbers in italics refer to illustrations

abolition movements, 20, 22

Adventism, 66

Albany, Ore., campaigns in, 155, 162

Albright, Mrs A.F., 61

Alcott, William, 22, 31

altar theology, 20, 42, 55

American Physiological Society, 22

anaesthesia, 55–6

Anglicanism, 150

anointing with oil, 28, 40–1, 145, 153; gendering of, 205; pentecostalism and, 142; professional evangelism and, 156–7; social geography of, 58, 60–1, 141, 159, 174, 207

antitoxins, 107–9, 112

Apostolic Church of Pentecost in Canada, 127

Argue, Andrew Harvey, 126, 139–40, 143, 150

Argue, Eva, 136

Argue Evangelistic Party, 150–1

Aristides, Aelius, 203

Armand, J., 166

Assemblies of God, 125, 127, 139, 197

Associated Gospel Churches of Canada, 86

atonement theology, 9–10, 29–33, 89, 183, 210; Anglicanism and, 150; Dowieites and, 103; holiness groups and, 130; pentecostalism and, 129, 136–7, 139, 144–5, 151, 207; Salvation Army and, 84–5, 88

Austin, Eli, 83

autosuggestion, 169–70, 175, 180, 185. *See also* hypnotism and hypnotic effects

Azusa Street Mission (Los Angeles), 124–5

Baker, Jane, 196

baptism of the spirit, 121, 124–5, 128, 130, 137, 140–1, 145, 151–2

Baptist Ministerial Association of Greater Vancouver, 179

Barbour, John, 47

Bartleman, Frank, 130

Beard, George M., 80

bedsides/bedrooms, 37, 39–41, 58, 122, 133, 206–7

Bethany Chapel (Toronto), 73, 129

Bethany Home (Toronto), 59–60, 133

Bethany Tabernacle (Toronto), 72–3

Beulah Park, Ohio, 127

Bingham, Rowland V., 129, 171–2

Blumhardt, Johann C., 5, 29

Boardman, W.E., 21, 29, 32, 51, 67–8, 222n4

Bodaly, Alice, 51–2

Boddy, A.A., 125, 138

body, the, 6–9, 13–14, 204; as battleground for good and evil, 93–4, 143–4; control over, 8–9, 55–7, 208; medicalization of, 9, 14, 34, 177, 184–95, 199–201, 210–11; mind-body separation, 16, 19, 27, 31, 165–70; perfectionism and, 19–22, 31, 33, 48–9, 89, 199; public health regulation and, 105, 208; as site to engage the divine, 9, 29, 31, 33, 49, 80, 137, 177, 201, 210–11

Boer War, 102

Booth, Catherine, 82, 84, 86

Booth, Herbert, 86

Booth, Kate, 88

Booth, William, 82, 84, 88

Booth-Clibborn, Arthur, 88
Bosworth brothers (B.B.
   and F.F.), 147, 151–4,
   160–1, 165, 174, 191,
   208, 236n53
Bowles, C.T., 154
Brampton, Ont., 69, 71
Brandon, Man., 193, 209
Braude, Ann, 205
Brawner, Mina Ross, 195–6
Brereton, Virginia, 43–4,
   50
Briggs, S.R., 71
British Medical Associa-
   tion, 5
Brooks, Eugene, 101–3,
   119–20, 124, 132, 182;
   Harman family case and,
   115–18; Maltby family
   case and, 105–10; Rogers
   family case and, 110–11
Brooks, Sara Leggett, 99–
   102, 114–15, 132
Browne, Sir Thomas, 14
Bruce County, Ont., 96–103
Bryson, Mrs (Montreal), 68
Buckley, James M., 52, 60,
   75–6, 80
Burnett, W.B., 178, 201
Burton, Robert, 3
Burwash, Nathanael,
   216n23
Butler, Joseph, 16, 19

C., Miss (Hamilton), 36
Calgary, Alta., 163, 168–9,
   176, 197, 237n65
Calgary Albertan, 169
Calvinism, 20
Campbell, J.O., 240n21
Canada Lancet, 80
Canadian Baptist, 15, 37
Canadian Independent, 67,
   92
Canadian Monthly and Na-
   tional Review, 17
Carline, Sarah, 40, 78
Carter, R. Kelso, 29–32,
   129
Carvell, Edith, 156, 160,
   168

Catholicism, 10, 15, 154,
   206
Caughey, James, 20–1
Caven, William, 72, 75
Champé, Charles, 57, 94,
   98, 95, 98
Chesley, Ont., 99, 102
Chesley Enterprise, 96–7,
   99, 101–2
Chesley Methodist Church,
   97, 99
Chinese communities, 158,
   167
chiropractic, 24, 178,
   240n6
Christian Alliance and Foreign Missionary Weekly,
   39
Christian Alliance and Missionary Weekly, 71-3
Christian and Missionary
   Alliance, 11, 33, 64–5,
   89–90; anointing/laying
   on of hands and, 145;
   conventions of, 60–1,
   69–71, 73, 77, 127–8,
   141; Dowie's campaign
   sponsored by, 95; faith
   homes and, 59, 133;
   founding of, 67–70;
   fourfold gospel of, 64,
   68, 75, 128–9, 139, 151;
   pentecostalism and, 90,
   122, 127–30, 145; pro-
   fessional evangelism and,
   151–4; respectability
   and, 11, 70–4, 90, 130–
   1, 136; Salvation Army
   and, 82–3, 86–7, 89
Christian Catholic Apos-
   tolic Church, 97, 124
Christian Catholic Church,
   94, 96–7, 101, 107, 115
Christian Guardian, 21, 62,
   75–7, 172, 183–4
Christian Science, 23, 59,
   72, 74, 91, 119–20
Christian Workers Mis-
   sions, 86
Christie, Nancy, 237n66
Christie, William, 71

Clark, Daniel, 48–9, 81–2
clergy: authority of, 27, 41;
   as critics/supporters of
   faith healing, 72, 74–8,
   80, 90, 154, 179, 183,
   205, 209; healing narratives and, 39, 43
Coleman, H.T.J., 178–9,
   201
Common Sense philoso-
   phy, 16
congregationalism, 66, 128
Connor, J.T.H., 25
Constantinides, Dr (Tor-
   onto), 79
conventions. See faith healing conventions
conversion experience, 16,
   20–1, 42, 125, 159, 211
conversion narratives, 43–
   4, 50
Cooke, A.E., 162, 167,
   170, 172, 178, 183–4,
   201
Cookman, John, 69
Coombs, Thomas B., 82–3,
   86
Coué, Émile, 169–70, 185
court cases. See legal actions
Covernton, T.S., 79–80
Crossley, H.T., 19, 22, 31,
   102, 172
Cullis, Charles, 27–9, 31–2,
   196; conventions/camp
   meetings of, 60–1, 68,
   222n1; Faith Cures, 38–
   9; on physicians, 51; visits by Canadians to, 41,
   64, 83
Cunning Man, The
   (Davies), 3, 211
Currie, John, 67
Cutten, George Barton, 4–6

Darwinism, 16, 19, 27, 78,
   172
Davie, John, 109
Davies, Robertson, 3, 211
Davis, G.H., 96
Dayton, Donald, 131

Dayton, Ohio, 48
deathbed "peace." *See*
  "good death"
Derby, Leonard, 153–4
Dewart, E.H., 77
Dickin, Janice, 213n6
dietary rules, 22, 84, 97–9
Dimmick, J.F., 157, 186
Dimmick, Ruby, 157, 180,
  186–7
diptheria, 103–5, 107–10,
  112–13
disease, 11, 14, 23, 26–7;
  categorization of, 179,
  183; Dowie's view of,
  93–4; evangelicalism
  and, 28; gendering of,
  43, 48–50, 168, 205;
  mental cures and, 4–5,
  75, 79–82, 165–6; psy-
  chologizing of, 80–2,
  165–70, 175, 180, 185;
  public health and, 11, 92,
  104–6, 114, 119, 182,
  208; Salvation Army on,
  85, 88
dispensationalism, 138–9,
  152. *See also* premillennialism
Dobson, C.J., 99–100
domestic space. *See* social
  geography
Dominion Auxiliary Branch
  (Christian Alliance), 69–
  70. *See also* Christian
  and Missionary Alliance
Dominion Corps. *See* Salvation Army
Dorchester, Dr, 184
Dorland, John T., Jr., 68
Dowell, Captain (Salvation
  Army), 87
Dowie, John Alexander, 11,
  67; anointing/laying on
  of hands and, 145;
  Booth-Clibborns and,
  88; campaigns/mission-
  ary tours of, 93, 95–6;
  controversial stance of,
  32–3, 89, 93–5, 103,
  119–20; dietary rules of,

97–9; on drugs, 56; pho-
  tography, use of, by,
  190–1; physicians, criticism of, by, 51–3, 56,
  94–5; Turner-Fiddis case
  and, 99; visits by Canadians to, 91–2, 96–7, 101
Dowieites, 11, 92, 119,
  132, 182, 209. *See also*
  Zionites
Drake, Justice, 113–14
Drake, Lucy, 28
drugs and remedies: anti-
  toxins, 107–9, 112; control of the body and, 55–
  8, 208; missionaries and,
  128–9; morphine, 56–7;
  rejection of, 54–5, 78,
  84–6, 105, 119
Dr Williams' Pink Pills for
  Pale People, 55
Duncan, Mrs, 51
Dunlop, D.R., 168–9, 172,
  182
Durham, William, 125,
  132, 134–5, 138
Du Vernet, F.M., 166

East Asian communities,
  158, 167
East End Mission (Tor-
  onto), 122–3, 126
Edmonton, Alta., 163
Edward, prince of Wales
  (later Edward VII), 15,
  17
Edwards, Mrs (Wood-
  stock, Ont.), 42
Eggleston, Edward, 64, 203
E.H.P., Miss, 54
Elmer Gantry (Lewis), 146,
  203
Elsey, Mrs Alfred, 143–4
Emory, Jennie, 61
evangelicalism, 16, 28, 90,
  155
Evangelical Missionary Alliance. *See* Missionary
  Alliance
evangelism, professional,
  146–55; Anglicanism

and, 150; Christian Alli-
  ance and, 151–4; criti-
  cisms of, 164–75;
  investigations of, 12,
  176–95, 201–2; pente-
  costalism and, 11, 149–
  51, 163–4, 173; social
  geography of, 11, 147–9,
  159, 172–5, 208. *See also*
  campaigns in specific lo-
  cations
evolutionary theory, 16, 19,
  27, 78, 172

Fagan, C.J., 107–8, 112
Fair, George Armour, 101–
  2
Fairbairn, Robert E., 169–
  70
Faith Doctor (Eggleston),
  64, 203
Faith Healer, The (Moody),
  35, 204
faith healing conventions,
  31, 207. *See also specific*
  locations
faith homes, 31–2, 58–60,
  132–3, 145, 207
Fallis, George O., 158
Feher, Michel, 6
Fenton, W.J., 41, 68–9, 72–
  3, 128
Fiddis family, 97–9, 101
"Fidelis" (Agnes Maule
  Machar), 17
Finished Work doctrine,
  125, 132, 137
fire baptism, 21, 123. *See*
  also baptism of the spirit
Fisher, George E., 82–3, 86,
  130, 137
Fletcher, Rebecca, 59–60,
  73
Foucault, Michel, 6–7, 14
fourfold gospel, 64, 68, 75,
  128–9, 139, 151. *See also*
  premillennialism; sanctification
Fraser, R.L., 104, 107–8,
  110–12
Fuller, Robert C., 22, 31

fundamentalism, 23, 155–6, 164, 170, 171–2

Gaebelein, A.C., 168
Gainforth, Mary, 40–1
Gauvreau, Michael, 16, 215n10, 237n66
gender: disease/health and, 43, 48–50, 76, 205; healing and, 11, 62–3, 75–6, 159–61, 168, 196, 204–6; religion and, 49, 58, 76, 205. *See also* men; women
germ theory, 92, 104–5, 119, 198
Gidney, R.D., 27
"gifts" of the spirit, 138, 141, 145, 166–7
Globe, 131
glossolalia. *See* speaking in tongues
Goff, F.D., 130
Golden Grain, 191, 193, 195
Good, Byron, 8, 199
"good death," 28, 45–6, 207
Gooderham, William, 71, 73–4
Gordon, A.J., 29, 32
Gordon, Mattie, 77–8
gospel of health. *See* health reform movement
Gospel Workers' Church, 130
Grafton, F.E., 39
Graham, Sylvester, 22, 31
Griffith, R. Marie, 143
Griffiths, Miss (Toronto), 59, 73

Hahnemann, Samuel, 24–5
Haley, Bruce, 33
Hall, Ernest, 107–9, 157, 186–7
Hall, Frank, 111–12
Hall, John B., 74
Hamilton, Ont., 21, 60–1, 69–70
Hamilton Daily Spectator, 60–1

Hammerton, Clara, 121–2
handkerchiefs, 140–3, 145
Hanscombe, S.A., 53
Hardman, Nellie, 85–6
Harman family case, 115–18, 206
Harper, Rev. Dr (Brampton), 75
Hart, E.C., 106–8, 110
Hatch, Ellen, 42–3, 67, 69
Hay, Colonel (Salvation Army), 87
healing narratives, 37–50, 160–1, 185; drugs, rejection of, in, 54–8, 105; medicine in, 53–4, 206; of men, 43, 161; photography in, 191, 193, 195, 202; physicians in, 50–4; structure of, 50; of women, 8, 10–11, 39, 41, 43–54, 57–8, 62, 160, 206
health, 14, 33; dietary rules and, 22, 84, 97–9; gendering of, 43, 48–50, 76, 205. *See also* perfectionism
health reform movement, 22, 27, 31, 33, 49, 56
Hebden, Ellen and James, 122–4, 126, 130, 136
Hepworth, George H., 62–3, 75–7, 82
Hickson, James Moore, 150
holiness movement, 21–2, 25, 28–9, 32–3
Holiness Movement Church, 130
Holy Ghost baptism. *See* baptism of the spirit
"Home of Peace" (Beulah Heights, Calif.), 44
homeopathy, 22, 24–5, 27, 33, 74, 108
Hooker, Le Roy, 72
hospitals, 59–60, 122, 133–4, 207
Houlgrave, Henrietta, 52
Howland, Laura, 56, 70

Howland, William, 70–1, 73–4, 87
Hunter, J. E., 102, 172
Huntsville, Ont., 143
hydropathy, 22, 24, 84–5
hypnotism and hypnotic effects, 148, 166–70, 172, 175, 182. *See also* mesmerism
hysteria, 48, 80, 168–9, 180

Inskip, John, 29
International Divine Healing Association, 93–6
International Divine Healing Convention (1885), 92
Irwin, B.H., 39
Ivison, J.A., 41, 76–7

Jaffray, William G., 234n20
Jalland, Pat, 219n37
Jane Eyre (Brontë), 45
Jeffs, T.W., 182
Jesus Only controversy, 125–7
Johnston, Hugh, 75, 222n1
Jones, Owen, 107, 109
Joyce, James, 91
Judd, Carrie. *See* Montgomery, Carrie Judd

Kaufman, Martin, 25
Keller, Elizabeth, 196
Kelsey, Morton T., 5
Kemp, Rose, 78–80
Kennedy, Aimee. *See* McPherson, Aimee Semple
Keswick holiness, 21, 152
King, Joseph H., 125
Kingsley, Charles, 76
Kleinman, Arthur, 8
Knott, W.J., 157
Knox College (Toronto), 68, 72
Kydd, Ronald, 5

Ladies' Home Journal, 176
Lancet, 27
Lang, Edna Perle, 193–4, 194

Lankford, Sarah, 20
Laqueur, Thomas, 213n10
Laurence, Margaret, 121
laying on of hands, 138–40, 142, 145
Lears, T.J. Jackson, 23
Leaves of Healing, 53, 94, 99–102, 191
legal actions, 11, 92, 105–6, 119–20, 181–2, 209; Harman family, 115–18, 206; Maltby family, 103–10, 119, 210; Rogers family, 110–11; Turner-Fiddis case, 96–9, 101
Leggett, Lydia. *See* Mitchell, Lydia Leggett
Leggett, Sara. *See* Brooks, Sara Leggett
Le Messurier, Mrs (Stratford), 35–6
LeSueur, William Dawson, 17–19, 30, 92, 208
Lethbridge, Alta., 146–8
Lethbridge Herald, 146, 148
Lewis, James Henry, 120
Lewis, Sinclair, 146, 203
London, Ont., 134–5
Luke (gospel writer), 51

McAlister, R.E., 125, 127, 136, 151, 173
McCleod, A.W., 184
McCrossan, T.J., 155, 173, 187
McDannell, Colleen, 58
McDiarmid, H.O., 209
McDonald, William, 101–2
Macdonnell, D.J., 75
Machar, Agnes Maule, 17–18
McIntyre, R.J., 182–4
Mack, Mary, 56
McKelvey, Mary, 55
MacKenzie, Alexander Innes, 68
McLean, H.A., 107–9, 111–13
McPherson, Aimee Semple, 48, 134–5, 146–51, 155, 161, 166, 197, 208

McPherson, Harold, 134
MacVicar, D.H., 18–19
Malcolm Gathering, 101–2
Mallory, E.D., 39, 41
Maltby family case, 103–10, 119, 210
Manitoba, 129
Massey Hall (Toronto), 152–3, 165, 164
Masury, Mrs (Ridgeway), 55, 58
Maysmith, N.B., 167
medical education, 27
medicalization, 9, 14, 34, 177, 184–95, 199–201, 210–11
medicine, 25–7, 34, 205, 208–11; the body as viewed in, 9, 177, 184–95, 199–201, 210–11; in healing narratives, 53–4, 206; rejection of, 77–8, 114, 119, 181. *See also* disease; drugs and remedies; physicians
men: body and health as perceived by, 43, 48, 76, 205–6; as critics/investigators of faith healing, 40–1, 62, 76; healing narratives of, 43, 161. *See also* clergy
mental cures, 4–5, 75, 79–82, 165–6. *See also* hypnotism and hypnotic effects
Merrell, Mrs, 55
Mesmer, Franz Anton, 23
mesmerism, 30, 80. *See also* hypnotism and hypnotic effects
Methodism, 20–1, 136, 215n23
Metropolitan Methodist Church (Victoria), 155–6
Millar, W.P.J., 27
Miller, Perry, 23
Milligan, C.M., 75
mind-body separation, 16, 19, 27, 31, 165–70
mind cure movements, 12, 22–5, 72

miracles, 10, 15–17, 29–30, 75, 80, 137–8, 207–8
missionaries, 33, 128–9
Missionary Alliance, 11, 33, 68, 90. *See also* Christian and Missionary Alliance
Mitchell, George, 124
Mitchell, Lydia Leggett, 100–1, 124
Mitchinson, Wendy, 48
Mix, Sarah, 46, 56
modernism, 6, 155–6, 170
Moffatt, F.M., 141
Montgomery, Carrie Judd, 32, 35–6, 49–50; Christian Alliance and, 69; faith homes of, 32, 44, 58–9; pentecostalism and, 131; *The Prayer of Faith*, 36, 38–9, 44–6, 50, 66; *Triumphs of Faith*, 35, 39, 42, 139, 144, 197; visits by Canadians to, 41, 58, 64
Montreal, Que., 38–9, 71–2, 149–51, 161, 166
Moody, Dwight L., 172
Moody, William Vaughn, 35, 204
Moore, Laurence, 149
Mormonism, 96–7
morphine, 56–7
Mottashed, Mrs L.J., 35–6
Mount Forest, Ont., 135
Mullin, Robert Bruce, 29, 210
Murcutt, Florence, 196
Murray, George A., 130
"muscular Christianity," 76
mysticism, 62–3, 76, 80

natural laws, 16–18, 24–5, 29–30, 80, 137, 179
natural theology, 15–16, 33, 215n10
nervous diseases, 48, 75, 80, 157, 166, 168–9, 179–80, 185
networks, informal, 10–11, 37, 40–1, 63, 207

New Age philosophies, 23
"New Calvinists," 20
New Glasgow, N.S., 38
New Thought Movement, 23
North American Journal of Homeopathy, 25
North Avenue Mission (Chicago, Ill.), 125

Old Orchard, Maine, 31, 60–1, 68
Oliver, French, 156
O'Malley, J.J., 182
Oneness controversy, 125–7
Orders and Regulations (Salvation Army), 84–5
Orsi, Robert, 8, 204, 206
Osburn, Libbie, 51
Oster, A., 161
Ott, Katherine, 43
Ottawa, Ont., 151, 153–4, 236n53
Ottawa Citizen, 153–4
Ozman, Agnes, 123

pain and painkillers, 55–6
Paley, William, 15–16, 33, 198–9, 215n10
Palmer, Phoebe, 20–1, 25, 42, 55
Palmer, Walter, 21, 25
Paracelsus, 176
Parham, Charles F., 123–4, 128
Parkdale Tabernacle Church (Toronto), 151–2
Patterson, Johnny, 191–3, 192
Payne, Captain, 84–5
Peale, Norman Vincent, 23
Pentecostal Assemblies of Canada (PAOC), 127
Pentecostal Assemblies of the World, 125
pentecostalism, 11, 30, 121–7, 134–45, 207; atonement theology and, 129, 136–7, 139, 144–5, 151, 207; camp meetings and, 125, 130; Christian Alli-

ance and, 90, 122, 127–30, 145; faith homes and, 132–3; "gifts" of the spirit and, 138, 141, 145; handkerchiefs in, 140–3, 145; professional evangelism and, 11, 149–51, 163–4, 173; "respectability" and, 130–2; social geography of, 122, 135–6, 142, 145, 207; speaking in tongues and, 11, 121–4, 130, 135–6, 138–40, 145, 152, 207. *See also campaigns in specific locations*
Pentecostal Testimony, 173
People's Common Sense Medical Adviser, The, 48
perfectionism, 19–22, 31, 33, 48–9, 89, 199
Peterborough, Ont., 68–9, 77, 95–6
phenomenology, 7–8
Philpott, P.W., 86–7
photography, 163, 177, 187, 190–1, 193, 195, 202
physicians: as critics/supporters of faith healing, 78–82, 90, 153–4, 177, 195–202; faith healers' views of, 51–3, 56, 77, 94–5; in healing narratives, 50–4; public health regulation and, 106, 114, 208; role of, 26–7, 34, 41, 52, 79, 119; women, 196
Pink Pills for Pale People, Dr Williams', 55
Piper, Lydia, 125
Piper, William, 125
Pisgah Home (Los Angeles), 142
Poe, Edgar Allan, 45
Porter, Roy, 7
positive thinking philosophies, 23, 169, 185
Powell, George, 107–9, 111
prayer debates, 10, 15–19, 25, 30, 33, 75
Prayer of Faith, The (Judd), 36, 38–9, 44–6, 50, 66

premillennialism, 68, 86, 88, 139, 155. *See also* dispensationalism
Presbyterianism, 154
Presbyterian Review, 18
Price, Charles S., 147, 155–60, 208; campaigns of, 12, 155–8, 160, 162–4, 168–9, 174, 176, 193, 195, 209, 237n65; hypnotism, charges of, against, 166–70, 238n87; investigation of, 12, 176–95, 201–2; pentecostalism and, 163–4; photography, use of, by, 163, 191
progressivism, 78
public health, regulation of, 11, 92, 104–6, 114, 119, 182, 208

quinine, 128–9
Quinlan, Maimie, 54

Rader, Paul, 151, 153
Randall, Herbert, 135–6
Raymond, N.B., 166–7
Rees, David, 86
Regina, Sask., 164
Reynolds, Lindsay, 69, 128
Robertson, J.R., 239n5
Robinson, Barbara, 89
Robinson, Harry, 124
Robinson, Martha Wing, 124, 130, 131–2
Rodeheaver, Homer, 148
Roffe, Alfred W., 86–7, 151–2
Rogers, Elias, 70–1
Rogers family case, 110–11
Rose, Elizabeth, 53
Roseburg, Ore., 155
Rosenberg, Charles, 26
Rossetti, Dante Gabriel, 45
Ryder, Charles, 51, 67, 69–70

S. Mrs, 85
Salmon, John: Christian Alliance and, 66–70, 72–4; Dowie and, 92, 95;

pentecostalism and, 127–8, 130, 145; on physicians/medical science, 77; Salvation Army and, 83, 86–7; Trout and, 196
Salvation Army, 10, 65, 82–90, 136
sanctification, 20–2, 42–8, 89, 94, 123–5, 135, 137, 144, 211
Sandford, Frank W., 123
Savage, E.J., 165
Savage, William, 182–4
Scanlon, Matilda, 53–4
Schmitz, Mary, 52–3
Scott, Maggie, 44–7, 58, 69, 118
Semple, Aimee Kennedy. See McPherson, Aimee Semple
Semple, Neil, 215n23
Semple, Robert, 134
Senft, Mrs, 55
Sharpe, Elizabeth, 135, 143, 161
shell shock, 165–6
Shields, T.T., 171
Shimo-Takahara, Dr (Vancouver), 189
Siddall, Elizabeth, 45
Simpson, A.B., 32; Christian Alliance and, 64, 67–8, 73, 151; The Discovery of Divine Healing, 4; dispensationalism and, 139; on divine healing and natural law, 30; faith healing conventions of, 61, 66, 68–9, 73, 129; faith homes and, 133; on medical science, 61–2; pentecostalism and, 127–8; visits by Canadians to, 41, 61, 64
Sipes, Mabel, 137–8
Sipprell, W.J., 155
"slain in the spirit" experiences, 138, 158–60, 167, 205
Small, Frank, 127
Smith, May, 87

Smith, Oswald J., 151–3, 161, 171, 174
social geography, 11, 13, 58–62, 89, 205–8; of anointing with oil, 58, 60–1, 141, 159, 174, 207; of the bedside/bedroom, 37, 39–41, 58, 122, 133, 206–7; of Catholic healing sites, 10, 154; of hospitals, 59–60, 122, 133–4, 207; of pentecostalism, 122, 135–6, 142, 145, 207; of professional evangelism, 11, 147–9, 159, 172–5, 208
social gospel, 155–6
social reform movements, 20, 22, 89
speaking in tongues, 11, 121–4, 130, 135–6, 138–40, 145, 152, 207
Spencer, Herbert, 22
Spiher, H.H., 38
spirit baptism. See baptism of the spirit
Sproul, John, 161
Stanton, R.L., 32
Stephens, Mrs R.M.T., 151
Stockmayer, Otto, 29
Stouffville, Ont., 125, 130
Stranack, S.J.F., 166
Strange, Carolyn, 117
Sudan Interior Mission, 129
Sunday, Billy, 148–9
"Sunshine," 193, 194
Swedenborg, Emanuel, 23
Swick, E.L., 166
Synan, Vinson, 132

Taves, Ann, 80
temperance movements, 20, 22, 92
testimonials, public, 42–8, 135. See also healing narratives
theosophy, 23
therapeutic revolution. See medicine
Thomas, Ernest, 172
Thomas, Keith, 5–6

Thomas, Rev. Dr, 75–6
Thorburn, Dr (Toronto), 79–80
tongues. See speaking in tongues
Toronto, Ont.: campaigns in, 95, 124, 150, 152–3, 165, 174; faith healing conventions in, 65–7, 69–71; faith homes in, 59–60; pentecostalism in, 130; Zionites in, 115. See also Christian and Missionary Alliance
Toronto Divine Healing Association, 95
Toronto Empire, 65, 72, 74–5, 77, 79, 183
Toronto Evening Telegram, 165–6
Toronto Mail, 72
Toronto Mission Union, 70–1
Toronto News, 74
Toronto Star, 140–2, 150, 152–4
Toronto Willard Tract Depository, 71
Treadgold, Manton, 71
Trelawney, Edward, 172
Trinity Pentecostal Assembly (Toronto), 140–2
Triumphs of Faith, 35, 39, 42, 139, 144, 197
Trout, Jenny Kidd, 196
Troy, N.Y., 59
Trudel, Dorothea, 28–9, 66
Tucker, Major, 83
Turner, Bryan, 34, 210
Turner, James, 96–9, 101
20th Century Family Physician, The, 48
Tyndall, John, 15, 17, 19

urban evangelism. See evangelism, professional

Vancouver, B.C.: campaigns in, 12, 156, 158–60, 162–3, 176–95, 201–2,

238n87; Christian Catholic Church in, 101–2; "mind over body" lectures in, 166

Vancouver Daily World, 167, 176

Vancouver Province, 160, 167

Vancouver Sun, 162, 166–9, 182, 201, 208

Vancouver World, 189

Van Die, Marguerite, 216n23

Victoria, B.C., 93, 102, 155–8

Victoria, queen of England, 15

vitalism, 14, 23, 27

Voliva, Wilbur Glenn, 120, 124

Wacker, Grant, 135, 145

Walkem, Justice (Victoria), 111–14

Walsh, J.J., 169

War Cry, 83, 85–6, 87

Ward, A.G., 125

Warfield, B.B., 30

Way of Faith, The, 38–9

Welch, Ella, 53

Wesley, John, 20

Wesleyan holiness, 21, 132, 136

Wesleyan Methodist Book Room, 21

Whittemore, Emma, 56

Willard Tract Repository, 28, 31, 71

Williams, Earl, 150

Wilson, Charles, 71

Wilson, Henry B., 49, 68–9, 127

Wilson, James, 107

Winnipeg, Man., 39, 126, 129, 130, 150–1, 160

Wolseley Hall (Toronto), 69, 73, 124, 132

women: as bedside guardians, 39–41, 207; body and health as perceived by, 48–9, 205; control over the bodies of, 8–9, 55–7; conversion narratives and, 43–4; healing narratives of, 8, 10–11, 39, 41, 43–54, 57–8, 62, 160, 206; informal networks of, 10–11, 37, 40–1, 63, 207; as physicians, 196

Woodworth-Etter, Maria, 136

Workman, George C., 169

Wortman, William, 134

Wright, Adam, 79–80

Wycliffe College (Toronto), 70

Wyllie, Rev. Dr, 154

X-ray photography, 187, 189–90, 202

Yates, J.S., 107

Yeomans, Amelia LeSueur, 91–2, 233n82

Yeomans, Augustus, 91

Yeomans, Lilian, 12, 177, 196–202, 210; addiction and cure of, 57, 91–2; pentecostalism and, 144, 197, 199, 232n58

Yoakum, F.E., 142–3, 196–7

Yorkville Congregational Church, 66–7

Zimmerman, R.J., 72–3, 82–4, 86–7, 95, 196

Zinkan, Miss (Southampton), 97

Zion City, Ill., 115, 120, 124, 133

Zion Faith Homes, 133, 152

Zion Home, 91–2

Zionites, 96–7, 99, 101–3, 115, 124, 209. *See also* Dowieites

Zion Tabernacle (Toronto), 115